Cistercian Studies Series: Number Eighty–Four

GOAD AND NAIL

CISTERCIAN STUDIES SERIES: NUMBER EIGHTY-FOUR

GOAD AND NAIL

Studies in Medieval Cistercian History, X

Edited by E. Rozanne Elder

Cistercian Publications
Kalamazoo, Michigan

1985

t/03/+

Available in Britain and Europe through

A. R. Mowbray & Co Ltd
St Thomas House Becket Street
Oxford   OX 1 1SJ

Available elsewhere from the Publisher

Cistercian Publications Inc
W.M.U. Station
Kalamazoo, Michigan 49008

These articles were originally presented as papers at the Cistercian Studies Conferences of 1983 and 1984, held in conjunction with the International Congress on Medieval Studies, Western Michigan University.

The work of Cistercian Publications is made possible in part by support from Western Michigan University.

Composition and cover design by Linda K. Judy
Printed in the United States of America

Table of Contents

Preface

One of the European participants in the 1983
Cistercian Studies Conference sponsored by the Institute
of Cistercian Studies of Western Michigan University
remarked, ruefully, that too little contact exists between
English and German-speaking scholars investigating
the Cistercian phenomenon of the Middle Ages. The
enthusiasm of conversations between North American
and continental scholars at that conference, and at
the next demonstrated that this lack of communication
has nothing whatever to do with lack of common interest,
and that the insights yielded by methodologies developed
in the various language areas support, strengthen,
and sometimes challenge one another.

The present volume, the tenth in the sub-series
Studies in Medieval Cistercian History, contains papers
given at the 1983 and 1984 conferences by American,
Australian, Austrian, Danish, German, Hungarian,
and Swiss scholars. They manifest not only the geographical spread of Cistercian studies but also the rich
diversity of research in progress. The one area not
included is art history. This is not because the discipline is not well-represented at Kalamazoo, but because
those papers appear in a special sub-series, Studies
in Cistercian Art and Architecture, under the editorship
of Meredith Parsons Lillich of Syracuse University.

We are grateful to Professor Brian McGuire of
Copenhagen for allowing us to include a paper he
presented at the 1982 Kalamazoo Conference, and to
the Rev'd Bede K. Lackner, O.Cist., of the University
of Texas-Arlington, for editing and preparing for
publication a paper of his late confrère, Odo Egres,
O.Cist.

We are also—as always—grateful to the staff
of the Medieval Institute of Western Michigan University
for including the Cistercian Studies Conference on
the program of their International Congress on Medieval
Studies, and for their cooperation and efficiency in
making physical arrangements, for providing transporta-
tion and audio-visual equipment at all the requisite
times, and for their unflagging cheerfulness in the
midst of some two thousand visiting medievalists.

E.R.E.

BERNARD THE OBSERVER

Michael Casey, OCSO

Two images taken from the *First Life* of Bernard of Clairvaux seem to have captured the public imagination. The first is his total inattention to his immediate physical surroundings. The second is the fact of his being so constantly nauseated during the choral offices that a container had to be sunk into the ground beside his place.[1] In this paper I shall concentrate on the first wing of the diptych.

The principal passage concerning Bernard's dissociation from his immediate environment occurs in the context of a description of the fervour of Bernard's noviciate, the extreme mortification which he practised and the assertion that all his energies were directed toward God.

> When he was a novice he spared himself in nothing. He was eager to mortify, in every way, not only the lusts of the flesh which arise through the bodily senses, but also the senses themselves. As he began to experience the more frequent and intense illumination of the inner sense through love, he restricted the bodily senses to what was needed for the outward living of human life, fearful of their impact on the inner sense.
>
> Such constant practice led to habit–formation which, in turn, became natural. He was entirely absorbed in the spirit, his whole hope was directed to God and all his memory was occupied in spiritual concentration or reflection. As a result he saw without seeing and heard without hearing. He savoured nothing of what he tasted and was scarcely aware of any bodily sensation.
>
> It is a fact that he spent a whole year in the novices' room and on leaving it was ignorant of whether its ceiling was vaulted. Likewise, for a long period, he had often gone in and out of the church building, yet he thought that there was only one window up the front whereas, in fact, there were three.
>
> In this way, having mortified his sense of curiosity, he was not aware of such things. If it happened that he did see something,

> then his mind was, as they say, otherwise
> engaged, and he failed to notice anything.
> For it is a fact that without mindfulness
> the one who senses perceives nothing.[2]

The story is repeated by the *Second Life*[3] and embodied
in the account of Vacandard and his tributaries.[4]
In this way it has become a regular part of a Bernardine
biography. The question to which we must now address
outselves concerns how historically feasible this pious
tradition is.

The Historical Validity of the First Life

Recent studies by Adriaan Bredero have been
helpful in initiating an *Ideologiekritik* in this matter.[5]
Notwithstanding the strong claim that a contemporary
account has to substantiate veracity, it has to be
asserted that the *First Life,* begun by William without
Bernard's knowledge,[6] has as its objective something
more than the communication of factual details. It
is a hagiography: an interpretation of the life of
a saint with a view to edifying its readers.[7] Its
genre is closer to spirituality than to history. And,
of course, there is always the possibility that the
author may exploit the theme of personal sanctity
in order to legitimate or propagate the values of a
particular movement or to sustain a polemic against
some particular position.

The statement of Bernard's indifference to his
surroundings needs to be read with an understanding
of the spiritual values which it aims to foster. Bernard
is simply presented as a model of the manner of life
which William had so recently recommended to the
novices of Mont–Dieu.

> The eye is an outstanding bodily organ.
> Would that it were able to see itself as it
> sees other things! It is, however, given
> to the inner eye to be able to do this unless,
> following the example of the outer eye, it
> neglects itself to become involved with foreign
> objects. In such a case, no matter how much
> it so desires, it will not have the strength
> to return to itself. Give yourself rather to
> attending to yourself; there you will find
> plenty of scope for your diligence. Shut out
> ––even from your outer eyes––the things you
> usually see, and from your inner eyes the
> objects of your love.[8]

Thus, in William's view, all the monastic means are ordered so that 'the bodily senses are not permitted to wander abroad',[9] so that the novice may return to himself, *redire ad seipsum.*

Another way of describing this vigilance over the external senses is to employ the phrase which Gregory the Great used of St Benedict, *habitavit secum:* he lived with himself, an expression which meant not only a solitary life, but a withdrawn life within community—a life subtracted from mundane involvement and open to the presence of God.[10] The expression is used later in the *Golden Epistle,*[11] and it is also to qualify Bernard's attitude during his schooldays at Châtillon.[12] We find an echo of this in the context of a description of Bernard's total involvement with spiritual affairs and his reluctance to give himself to temporalities: *Libere secum habitans et deambulans in latitudine cordis sui, et ibidem exhibens Christo...coenaculum grande stratum.* 'He freely lived with himself and strolled around the broad avenues of his heart so that he might be able to show Christ, a large supper-room already prepared. And he used to advise others to do the same'.[13]

But, as William recognised, 'when one is with God one is never less alone than when alone'.[14] Hence, as our text about Bernard the novice makes clear, William wishes to be understood as referring less to abstraction *per se* than to the inattention which is consequent upon intense inner involvement with something else. All Bernard's awareness was directed toward God; there was nothing left for external realities. He was unmindful of such things, as William states explicitly, because his *memoria* was otherwise engaged. In other words, Bernard practised the *memoria Dei.*[15]

William seems unable to decide whether this state of recollection is the result of heroic effort on Bernard's part or merely an effect of his natural disposition. On the one hand it is adduced as the outcome of a programme of leaving aside the body,[16] and curbing its lusts through fasts and vigils, and perhaps of extreme and even bizarre attempts to escape distraction, such as filling his ears with flax to keep out the idle chatter of visitors.[17] On the other hand it is presented as the continuation of behaviour dating from his boyhood,[18] and according perfectly with his own nature. *Natura quoque in eo non dissentiebat a gratia.*[19] He had a natural aptitude for contemplating spiritual or divine realities and had little lust for what would work against the spirit. *Curiositatis enim sensu mortificato, nil huiusmodi sentiebat.*[20]

Furthermore, one might doubt whether William

is distinguishing with sufficient clarity between abstraction or interiority and spirituality. Despite the widely-accepted trichotomy of body—soul—spirit, it seems that William jumps too quickly to the conclusion that what is not sensual must be divine. The assertion of Bernard's precocious prayerfulness may amount to no more than a lingering belief that, as a young man, he appeared rather withdrawn from the real world. Certainly he does not seem, in his early days as a monk, to have participated in the ordinary work of the community—he wasn't used to it, he lacked the skill and he was often overcome by weakness.[21] The delicate state of his health must, likewise, have set him apart from his confrères.

In so far as William's description of the novice saint represents any objective data, perhaps it need be understood as no more than an account of an inexperienced young introvert, suddenly plunged into a situation which seemed to give unlimited legitimation to a programme of dissociation from material reality. No wonder his health deteriorated! The fact that the neurotic cycle was eventually broken through the intervention of authority made it possible for subsequent biographers to view these ill-advised beginnings as presages of a sanctity which was yet to come. But it could have been otherwise.

Bernard's lack of concern for ceilings and windows was only a part of a general lack of interest in the world of objects. Pruned of its harmful extremism, it would remain a lifelong personality trait. He is said to have spent a whole day journeying by the Lake of Geneva completely oblivious to it. No wonder *mirati sunt universi*.[22] This is not to say that he remained locked within himself; he responded to people —especially to those who responded to him—he was stimulated by issues, he involved himself in projects and campaigns and embraced with enthusiasm facts and objects which accorded with his basic view of reality. But he remained unsympathetic to those who derived their interests from the external world, he would never quite renounce his scathing denunciation of *curiositas* in the tract on humility,[23] and those who manifested a *cupiditas* for the acquisition of outward objects he regarded as quite beyond the pale.[24] The aesthetics he promoted were largely a matter of achieving such solid harmony that the outward world did not intrude on inner processes, but stilled the senses rather than stimulated them.[25] This is why he favoured nature over artifice or preciosity.[26] Put in its simplest form, Bernard was an introvert and William relays this fact by interpreting it in the most pious light possible.[27]

Bernard and the Outer World

    This, at least, is a conclusion which may be drawn if one regards the *First Life* as having any degree of historical or factual validity. The question which must now be asked concerns whether such a finding is confirmed or countered by the evidence of Bernard's own writings.

    The first thing that has to be said about Bernard's approach to the external world is that it was dominated by his moral purposes. He sought in nature not so much a source but a confirmation of his message. When he writes to Henry Murdac that the trees and the stones have something to teach, he is not thinking of botany, geology or natural history.[28] He means that in the unobtrusive world of nature, one is able to make contact with inner springs of information. At the most, nature can serve as a mirror which makes visible what is within.[29]

    Secondly, it were wrong to think that Bernard's attitude to the natural universe was untypical of his times. One has to wait for the thirteenth century for the emergence of a genuine naturalist such as the Emperor Frederick II (1194–1250) or the acceptance of a more inductive or empirical approach in such matters, instanced for example in Aristotle's *De partibus animalium.* Most of Bernard's contemporaries were reliant for their information about the animal kingdom on the same sources as the bestiaries, Pliny the Elder's *Natural History,* Isidore's *Etymologies* and various other literary and popular accounts of varying factual value. One must interpret Bernard's approach as reflecting not only his own attitudes but also as an effect of the times in which he lived.

    Thirdly, references to the material world seem to become more frequent with the passage of time, especially as Bernard's preferred genre swung away from the treatise in the direction of the sermon. Furthermore, the density of material images increases as time goes on. In the *Sermons on the Song of Songs,* for instance, there is a dividing line which can be drawn around 1138–1139, after which such references are more numerous. The patristic texts on which Bernard modelled his sermons abounded in images drawn from common experience and the world around, and it is not surprising that Bernard has followed this example. The question that we shall have to ask concerns whether such uses flow from an observation of the world around

him or from the mere repetition of patristic and scriptural precedents.

Mirum opus naturae![30] Bernard appreciates the
material world as coming from the Creator's hand
and, as yet, not fully deformed by human malice.
He peppers his words with allusions to the world around
him, to mountains and valleys,[31] to different kinds
of thunder,[32] to the times of day and the seasons
of the year,[33] to the sun and the moon and the heavenly
bodies.[34] He knows the world of plants and mentions
gardens,[35] and flowers[36] and seeds.[37] He speaks a
lot about trees,[38] willows, and olives,[39] figs,[40] cy-
press,[41] and balsam derived therefrom.[42] And the
image of vine and vineyard figures often.[43]

And what can be said about the Bernardine bestiary?
He knows of ants,[44] asps,[45] asses,[46] basilisks.[47]
birds,[48] bees,[49] bulls,[50] camels.[51] cats,[52] centaurs.[53]
colewort,[54] deer.[55] dogs,[56] doves,[57] dragons,[58] eagles.[59]
flies,[60] foxes,[61] frogs,[62] goats.[63] grasshoppers,[64]
harpies,[65] hawks,[66] hens,[67] horses,[68] lions,[69] locusts.[70]
mice,[71] monkeys,[72] oxen,[73] pigs,[74] rams.[75] sheep.[76]
snakes,[77] swallows,[78] tigers,[79] turtle-doves,[80] wolves[81]
and worms,[82] and probably many more besides.

Among all these references, however, not only
is there no information for the naturalist, but there
is scarcely enough evidence to sustain the contention
that Bernard was not blind. Not only does he mingle
mythological and factual, but he spends as much time
on exotic foreign species as he does on examples that
would have been close at hand. We can be reasonably
sure that of the inventory given above, Bernard would
have personally had the opportunity to observe only
about half of the animals listed. On the other hand,
nearly all of them are well documented in the Scriptures
and in the commentaries of the Fathers. Information
about the existence, appearance and behaviour of
animals specific to twelfth century France is exceeding
sparse.

Is Bernard any better observer of human behaviour
and affairs? Certainly his treatise *In Praise of the
New Knighthood* would lead us to think that he was
not.[83] Here we have an entirely imaginary travelogue
of the Holy Land, based on Scripture and not on hard
facts. The guidance given by Bernard to the fighting
men was, likewise, a compound of moral exhortation
and pious fantasy. Despite easy generalisations about
Bernard's 'military sense', it is clear that he knew
relatively little about the conduct of actual warfare-
-a fact subsequently confirmed by the unforeseen degenera-
tion in the armies of the Second Crusade.[84] In his
Parables,[85] we find warfare invested with a fairy-

tale quality, not based on observation but entirely shaped by the rhythms of spiritual warfare, which was his primary focus. Admittedly, he does scatter neologisms and military terms throughout his writing, but in at least one case, he clearly does not understand the meaning of the word he is using.[86]

His interventions in the great affairs of the Church can scarcely be regarded as the outcome of his patiently and objectively sifting data. He assayed most issues with subjective standards: whatever was reform-oriented, non-innovative and pro-spiritual was liable to win his instant and total advocacy. Those who gave evidence of being pliable to Bernard's vehement convictions were, *a priori*, likely to win his support. Lovable as he certainly was, I don't think that Bernard could be regarded as being a reasonable man, in the sense that Peter the Venerable was. Understanding and kind and interesting, he manifestly was, but scarcely a model of detached and disinterested rationality. The philosophy he expounded was not consensual, but a brilliant and intuitive restatement of a common tradition. The leadership he exercised was not based on jurisdiction or consultation, but on the personal qualities which made many willing to follow him.

Nor can it be said that we can gain much information concerning Bernard's method of dealing with practical situations from his published letters since these always have to be read on the understanding that his direct reactions and instructions were often conveyed orally. The letters were more like a permanent record of the moment in so far as it concerned his relationship with the respondent, than either detailed directives or even a summary of practical steps to be taken. As far as I know, a methodology for dealing with the Bernardine *corpus epistolarum* is yet to be formulated.

His descriptions of monkish behaviour in *The Steps of Humility and Pride* are often alleged as evidence that Bernard was a keen-eyed observer of what was going on around him. Yet, there are similar passages also in the *Sermons on the Song of Songs* which are clearly inserted for the sole purpose of adding credibility to the fictional scenario of an abbot preaching to his monks in chapter. Destined for universal distribution, they would scarcely be pen-portraits of local deviants. Both series of texts can best be understood in the context of the tirades *Against Excesses* in the *Apologia*. They are all examples of irony.[87] They concern values rather than facts. Just as the *First Life* exaggerates virtues in order to teach a discipline of life which leads to holiness, so such ironic texts exaggerate vices and aberrations to demonstrate not only what unmonastic beliefs and values are inherent in certain concrete modes of behaviour, but also to hint that the path downwards is steep and once followed quickly leads to substantial decline. No doubt, isolated instances could be found to suggest that the situation was occasionally similar to what Bernard was describing. But the point is that even when Bernard is relating factual impressions, such as those of the church at Cluny, and, perhaps, the retinues attending certain prelates, he is still talking about values, not about material observations. What he sees is gauged against personal standards and exploited for the purpose of making a statement concerning those standards. It is not a question of descriptive writing nor of an objective analysis of data. No wonder the black monks were so incensed; Bernard was quite impervious to any understanding of the reasons behind the practices at issue. That there was irregularity is attested by Peter the Venerable's *Statutes*; Bernard proclaimed it and rejected it, but I don't think that his diatribes can be understood as an objective description of what was taking place, notwithstanding the fact that, according to the rules of the genre, he claims to have been an eyewitness.[88]

Bernard knew that the outside world existed and he had a great deal of information about it, but he was not greatly interested in it nor was he passive before it. When he referred to it, it was more often on the basis of intuitive prejudgements than on sensate impressions. The music he heard was within; the vision which inflamed his imagination was above.

Conclusion

On the basis of the few skerricks of information which it has been possible to assemble, is it feasible to give an answer to the question concerning the historical likelihood of William's statements about Bernard's habitual abstraction?

Firstly; if inwardness be distinguished from the permanent recollection of one far advanced in holiness, then there is no problem about asserting that a beginner was somewhat withdrawn from the sensate world. This means rejecting William's pious interpretations in favour of a more developmental model of holiness. On the other hand, it does mean accepting that the stories do represent a residual trace if not of Bernard's actual behaviour, at least of his character. To that extent, the assertion is historical.

Secondly; that Bernard was temperamentally inclined

toward introversion and intuition is in no way contradict-
ed or even qualified by references to the real world
in his writings. One might suspect that such an approach
would be legitimated and reinforced by the spiritual
discipline of Cîteaux. On the other hand, his pastoral
and ecclesial involvements may well have brought
him out of himself to be less introspective, but would
not have changed his basic stance before reality.

Thirdly; the position advanced may be checked
by comparing Bernard's writing with other comparable
works. Thus is can be said that the *realia* in Bernard's
sermons are less real than in those of Augustine or
Casarius of Arles.[89] He manifests nothing of the empiri-
cism of many of the contemporary tracts *de anima*,[90]
and the wide-ranging interests of Bernardus Silvestris'
Cosmographia cannot be attributed to his namesake
from Clairvaux.[91] Even the fictional scenes created
by Chrétien de Troyes are often more vivid and realistic
than Bernard's purported descriptions of reality.[92]
While aware that the age in which Bernard lived was
certainly less impassioned about 'scientific objectivity'
than our own,[93] it remains true that the exactitude
Bernard demanded was uncommonly concerned with
inward criteria.

Finally, even in his teaching on the senses there
is a certain emphasis evident. Bernard is inclined
to slip away from describing the external senses toward
giving an account, on traditional lines, of the spiritual
senses. Even when he does stay on the external level,
it is surely interesting that he gives disproportionate
emphasis to the sense of smell, the least 'rational',
the most holistic and the most instinctive of the senses
which, nevertheless, does not have the capacity to
enslave the whole personal resources of its possessor,
at most it triggers a momentary response—scarcely
a sensual way of life.[94]

I, for one, am ready to believe that Bernard
did not know that the noviciate was vaulted and didn't
care how many windows were in the front of the church.

Tarrawarra Abbey
Australia

NOTES

1. *Vita Prima* 1.8.39; PL 185:250b.
2. *Vita Prima* 1.4.20; PL 185:238–239. There is an
    earlier and simpler version of the key section
    given in Recension A: ...*cum exiens inde ignoraret
    adhuc UTRUM DESUPER CELATA ESSET domus ipsa;
    Multo tempore frequentaverat intrans et exiens
    domum ecclesi(a)e, cum in eius capite () unam
    tantum fenestram arbitraretur.* Recension B has
    an *haberet domus ipsa testitudinem quam solemus
    dicere celaturam* in explanation of the word *celata*,
    and adds a phrase informing those unfamiliar
    with the church at Cîteaux, that there were,
    in fact, three windows, *ubi tres erant.* Cf. Bredero,
    'Etudes', pp. 33–34 (reference in note 5).
3. *Vita Secunda* 4.16; PL 185:479ab. This version
    reads *saepe* instead of *spe* and modifies the phrasing
    of the rest of one passage. *Saepe tota in Deum
    directa intentione, seu in meditatione spirituali
    tota occupat memoria.* The final sentence is less
    absolute than William would have allowed: *Sine
    memoria quippe sensus sentientis MINUS EFFICAX
    est.*
4. See, for example, Elphège Vacandard, *Vie de
    S. Bernard, abbé de Clairvaux* (2 vols) (Paris:
    J, Gabalda, 1927); vol. 1; pp. 47–48. Watkin
    Williams, *Saint Bernard of Clairvaux,* Historical
    Series LXIX (Manchester University Press, 1935)
    p. 14. Anselme Dimier, *Saint Bernard: Pêcheur
    de Dieu* (Paris: Letouzey and Ané, 1953) pp.
    20–21. Commission d'histoire de l'Ordre de Cîteaux
    (ed.), *Saint Bernard de Clairvaux* (Paris: Alsatia,
    1953) p. 41.
5. Cf. Adriaan H. Bredero, '"Etudes" sur la "Vita
    Prima" de S. Bernard', ASOC 17 (1961) p. 3–72,
    215–260; ASOC 18 (1962) pp. 3–59. 'St Bernard
    and the Historians' and 'The Canonization of
    Bernard of Clairvaux' in M. Basil Pennington
    (ed.), *Saint Bernard of Clairvaux: Studies Commemor-
    ating the Eighth Centenary of his Canonization,*
    CS 28 (Kalamazoo: Cistercian Publications, 1977)
    pp. 27–62, 63–100. 'San Bernardo di Chiaravalle:
    correlazione tra fenomeno cultico e storico', in
    *Studi su San Bernardo nell' octavo centenario
    della canonizzazione,* Biblitheca Cisterciensis
    6 (Rome: Editiones Cistercienses, 1975) pp. 23–
    48. 'The Conflicting Interpretations of the Relevance
    of Bernard of Clairvaux to the History of his
    Own Time', *CN* 31 (1980) pp. 53–81. Jean Leclercq,

in his chapter 'Le premier biographe de S. Bernard', makes much use of Bredero's work: *Nouveau visage de Bernard de Clairvaux: Approches psychohistoriques* (Paris: Cerf, 1976) pp. 11–34. See also Richard M. Peterson, 'Anthropology and Sanctity in the *Vita Prima Bernardi I*', in E. Rozanne Elder (ed.), *Noble Piety and Reformed Monasticism,* CS 65 (Kalamazoo: Cistercian Publications, 1981) pp. 40–51.

6. *Praefatio* to the *Vita Prima*; PL 185:226c.
7. Cf. Jean Leclercq, *The Love of Learning and the Desire for God: A Study of Monastic Culture,* 2 (London: SPCK, 1978) pp. 177–206. I do not, at this time, wish to discuss whether the *First Life* was composed with an eye to utilisation in the process of canonisation. Bredero has adequately covered the ground.
8. *Ep. Aur.* 104; SCh 223:226.
9. *Ep. Aur.* 105; SCh 223:227.
10. Gregory the Great, Dial 2.3.5; SCh 260:142: *solus in superni Spectatoris oculis habitavit secum,* 'he lived with himself alone under the eyes of the heavenly Watcher'. Bernard also used the expression in Div 30.1; SBOp 6a:216.10: *...dummodo sit secum habitans in corde suo et assistens Dominatori universae terrae.* Cf. Jacques Winandy, 'Habitavit secum', *COCR* 25 (1963) pp. 343–354.
11. *Ep. Aur.* 145; SCh 223:258.
12. *Vita Prima* 1.1.3; PL 185:228b.
13. *Vita Prima* 3.1.2: PL 185:304d. The statement is repeated in *Vita Secunda* 14.40; PL 185:492c.
14. *Cum quo enim Deus est, numquam minus est solus quam cum solus est:* Ep Aur 30; SCh 223:168. Cf. Aelred of Rievaulx, *Inst Incl* 5; SCh 76:55 and the whole classical and patristic tradition behind this expression.
15. Cf. M. Casey, 'Mindfulness of God in the Monastic Tradition', *CSt* 17 (1982) pp. 111–126.
16. Bernard as abbot is quoted as saying to new recruits, 'If you are hastening to interior reality in this place, then leave the bodies which you have brought from the world outside, and permit only your spirits to enter. For the flesh profits nothing'. *Vita Prima* 1.4.20; PL 185:238b.
17. *Vita Prima* 1.4.21–22; PL 185:239. In Par 3.2; SBOp 6b:274–275, Bernard recognises the danger of the excessive use of these means by the inexperienced, especially when they are coupled with enthusiasm. Far from quenching lust, they lead to further buffeting by fornication and gluttony. The incident of the stuffing of the ears is given

only in the *Vita Quarta* 2.1; PL 185:540b.

18. *Vita Prima* 1.1.3; PL 185:228b. A later section would have us conclude that Bernard's resolution to remain master of his eyes must have faltered during adolescence. Cf. *Vita Prima* 1.3.6; PL 185:230c.

19. *Vita Prima* 1.4.21; PL 185:239a. Later in the same paragraph William lists three factors in Bernard's goodness: the prevenient grace of God, the gifts of nature and the habit of discipline.

20. *Vita Prima* 1.4.20; PL 185:238a.

21. *Vita Prima* 1.4.23; PL 185:240b. Notwithstanding this picture, William describes Bernard as *communis vitae seu conversationis ferventissimus aemulator* and notes that although often excluded from the common work he found useful employment in ancillary or menial tasks.

22. *Vita Prima* 3.2.4; PL 185:306a.

23. Hum 28–30; SBOp 3:38–40 and *passim*.

24. Cf. QH 11.3; SBOp 4:450, 2–29. The pursuit of appearances seemed to Bernard an even greater futility.

25. Cf. Apo 28–30; SBOp 3:104–107 and the numerous studies which these sections have inspired. Under Bernard's prompting, such bareness became the hallmark of the Cistercian reform. William enunciates the principles in the *Golden Epistle*. 'When our outer circumstances correspond and accord with what is within and follow the likeness of the mind and express, in their own way, our good resolution, then they confer a not inconsiderable benefit. In some cases a poorer style of living inhibits concupiscence, in others it arouses the conscience to a greater love of poverty. In any case the soul should be concerned with inner realities and so prepared to let external things be rough and neglected. In this way it is made known that the soul which lives in a particular house really abides somewhere else. They demonstrate that their whole concern is otherwise engaged in holy things. The one who values external things little shows that the inner realities have been conformed with a good conscience'. *Ep. Aur.* 153–154; SCh 223:264. There is a basis for this position in RB 52, which demands a certain bareness of the place of prayer as a means of promoting inward undistractedness.

26. Cf. Apo 20; SBOp 3:97, 22–25. SC 25:7; SBOp 1:167. 6–10. SC 41:1; SBOp 2:28.14–17.

27. I am using the term 'introvert' with some diffidence. Some of the relevant sections of Jung's presentation

of the introvert may clarify the sense in which I am using the term. Translations are taken from Sir Herbert Read *et. al.* (eds.), *The Collected Works of C. G. Jung,* vol. 6: *Psychological Types,* (London: Routledge and Kegan Paul, 1977). References are to section and page. 'The introvert is distinguished from the extravert by the fact that he does not, like the latter, orient himself by the object and by objective behaviour, but by subjective factors....The introvert interposes a subjective view between the perception of the object and his own action, which prevents the action from assuming a character that fits the objective situation'. (#620; p. 373.) 'Although the introverted consciousness is naturally aware of external conditions, it selects the subjective determinants as the decisive ones'. (#621; pp. 373-374.) 'The predominance of the subjective factor in consciousness, naturally involves a devaluation of the object....The typical form his neurosis takes is psychasthenia, a malady characterised on the one hand by extreme sensitivity, and on the other by a great proneness to exhaustion and chronic fatigue'. (#626; pp. 378-379.) 'Whether introverted thinking is concerned with concrete or abstract objects, always at the decisive points, it is oriented by subjective data. It does not lead from concrete experience back again to the object, but always to the subjective content....Facts are collected as evidence for a theory, never for their own sake'. (#628; p. 380.) The extent to which Bernard conforms to Jung's stereotype is, of course, a matter for endless discussion. Not to be left out of consideration is what Bernard, in the course of a lifetime, made of his natural endowment. Also, it should be pointed out that probably the alienation factor in introversion was probably less pronounced in the monastic world of the twelfth century than it is in contemporary Western technocracy.

A useful exercise in understanding the *First Life* is to compare it with Bernard's *Vita Sancti Malachiae,* a similar combination of hearsay, spirituality, advocacy, *pietas* and pious fantasy.

28. Ep 106.2; SBOp 7:266, 24-267, 1. Cf. *Vita Prima* 1.4.23; PL 185:240cd.

29. Cf. M. Casey, 'Cardiomimesis', *Tjurunga* 20 (1980) pp. 114-122. The idea is that both nature and reading are of value less for the ideas which they pour into the mind from without than for their ability to release the contents of the heart

so that these may be perceived. Such activities
which mirror inner realities are said to 'mimic'
the heart.

30.   Ep 72.2; SBOp 7.176.21.
31.   SC 54:6; SBOp 2:106.11–21. The text concerns the
overflowing of the heavenly river onto earth.
On mountains, cf. Div 33.2; SBOp 6a:222–223,
an explanation of Ps 23:3.
32.   Sent 2.98; SBOp 6b:43.9.
33.   There is a consideration of the dawn based on
Song 6.9 and applied to monks in Div 91.3; SBOp
6a:343.1–8. The seasons are differentiated, for
instance, in SC 58:6; SBOp 2:130–131 and throughout
that sermon. Cf. Ben 6; SBOp 5:5–6.
34.   Cf. Div 91.3–4; SBOp 6a:343–344. SC 27:8; SBOp
1:187, 14–23. The sky is the soul with the intellect
as sun and faith as the moon with the virtues
as stars. It is sometimes very difficult to determine
whether Bernard is speaking about heaven or
the sky.
35.   For instance, SC 23:4; SBOp 1:140–141.
36.   SC 47:3; SBOp 2:63.8–24 distinguishes between
flowers grown in a garden and wildflowers. SC
51 comments on the text from Song 2:5: *Fulcite
me floribus, stipate me malis.* Jesus is compared
to the flower of the field and the lilies of the
valley in SC 58.8; SBOp 2:132, 15–133, 4. In
Ann 3.7; SBOp 5:39.22–23, Bernard notes three
pleasurable things about flowers: their beauty,
their fragrance and their hope of future fruit.
It should be noted that, as will be later remarked,
Bernard seems especially conscious of odours.
Furthermore one of the three qualities is non-
sensate. Bernard occasionally speaks of hyssop
in terms of its humble purgative qualities, SC
45.2; SBOp 2:50.13–14.
37.   Seeds are usually referred to in the context of
various scriptural presentations, for instance,
Sent 2.46; SBOp 6b:35, 3–5. Ep 135; SBOp 7:331,
4–5. Ep 146.1; SBOp 7:348, 11–13. Ep 384; SBOp
8:351, 2–4.
38.   Bernard is particularly interested in the fruitfulness
of trees. Ben 4–6; SBOp 5:3–6. Ep 240.1–3; SBOp
8:123–124. He makes the observation that a healthy
tree often dies when transplanted: Ep 273.2; SBOp
8:184.8–9. He prefaces his remarks with *vidimus,*
although the point of the allegory is not concealed.
39.   Sent 3.87; SBOp 6b:127.9 contrasts the sterility
of willows with the fecundity of olives.
40.   Thus SC 60; SBOp 2:142–145 comments on Song
2:13: *Ficus protulit grossos suos.*

41. SC 46.3; SBOp 2:57, 8–25, discusses cedars and cypresses as woods.
42. Balsam is discussed in SC 44.2; SBOp 2:45, 15–25. Myrrh, another resinous product is treated in SC 43.1; SBOp 2:41–42. Both passages are triggered by the text of the Song of Songs.
43. Ep 141.2; SBOp 7:339, 4–10. SC 30.2–3; SBOp 1:211, 1–20, and SC 30.8; SBOp 1:215, 5–18; these bear upon the text of Song 1:5: *Posuerunt me custodem in vineis. Vineam meam non custodivi.* SC 44.2–3; SBOp 2:45–46. Commenting on Song 1:13, *Botrus Cypri dilectus meus mihi in vineis Engaddi,* Bernard remarks that the wine of Cyprus is plentiful and of good quality. SC 60.6; SBOp 2:145, 4–26 and *passim* in that sermon with regard to Song 2:13, *Vineae florentes odorem dederunt.* SC 63–64; SBOp 2:161–171 discuss the text *Capite nobis vulpes parvulas, quae demoliuntur vineas; name vinea nostra floruit* (Song 2:15).
44. Ep 288.1; SBOp 8:203, 15–16 to his uncle Andrew of Montbard in 1153. He compares human labour to ants sweating under foolish and unprofitable tasks.
45. QH 13.3; SBOp 4:465, 25–26 etc. QH 14.6; SBOp 4:472, 16–19. Both texts refer to Ps 90:13.
46. QH 7.3; SBOp 4:414, 10–26. Palm 2.5; SBOp 5:49, 5–16. Neither description is particularly flattering. Ep 72.2; SBOp 7:176, 24 discusses the animal in connection with the idea of mechanical advantage: a cart is an added burden, yet it makes the pulling easier. Bernard then goes on to exploit the moral possibilities of the theme.
47. QH 13.3–4; SBOp 4:465–466. QH 14.7; SBOp 4:473, 1–14. Both texts refer to Ps 90:13.
48. Bernard often mentions birds including the *rara avis* of SC 45.3; SBOp 2:51.12 and elsewhere. He speaks about the vulnerability of unfledged nestlings in a defective letter to Burchard of Worms, Ep 500; SBOp 8:458, 2–3. The suitability of the design of birds' wings is noted in Ep 72.2; SBOp 7:176, 19–20. They are compared to the yoke of Christ's discipline which elevates the soul in Ep 385.3; SBOp 8:353, 2–6.
49. Adv 2.3; SBOp 4:172, 15–20; Bernard notes that two things are associated with bees, honey, and the sting. He then offers a Christological expansion of the theme.
50. Sent 3.10; SBOp 6b:70, 17–18. The background here is the OT sacrificial system; other texts refer to the bulls of Bashan.
51. JB 6; SBOp 5:180, 5–6. In speaking of the fact

that John is garbed in camel-hair, Bernard expresses the wish that the camel had lost its hump instead of its hair. In a lyric prayer for the intercession of the Virgin Mary, Bernard, basing himself on Gen 24:14 asks that the camels also be watered: O Asspt 15; SBOp 5:274, 18. There is an obvious play on *catelli*, as in Mt 15:27, and *camelli;* see note 56.

52. Ep 2.2; SBOp 7:14, 4: 'The hungry mouse does not dare come out of its hole when the cat is around'.

53. Apo 29; SBOp 3:106, 16. This and some of the other references below come from Bernard's denunciation of grotesques painted on cloister walls.

54. Sent 3.86; SBOp 6b:124, 14–24. Bernard has found himself obliged to search for the meaning of the various terms used in Joel 1:4. He gives his verdict that, *secundum quosdam,* the *eruca* is a *vermis olerii.*

55. Deers and fawns are mentioned in SC 52 (on Song 2:7, *Adjuro vos, filiae Ierusalem, per capreas cervosque camporum...*), SC 55 (on Song 2:9, *Similis est dilectus meus capreae hinnuloque cervorum).* See also note 63. There are many texts which revolve around the opening of Ps 41, *Quemadmodum desiderat cervus ad fontes aquarum...*

56. The *catelli* of Mt 15:27 are old favourites, as in O Asspt 15; SBOp 5:274, 18 and Sept 1.3; SBOp 4:347, 5. Bernard draws from popular lore, *ut vulgo aiunt,* the image of a dog defending a manger in Ep 311.1; SBOp 8:240, 15–16. Another cherished canine similitude is that of Prov 26:11, the dog returning to its vomit, e.g. Ep 2.9; SBOp 7:20, 7–8. This frequently comes to the fore when there is question of somebody deserting monastic life.

57. SC 45.4–5; SBOp 2:52, 4–27, based on Song 1:14, *Oculi tui columbarum.* SC 61.2; SBOp 2:148, 22–149, 19, on Song 2:14, *Columba mea in foraminibus petrae....*In Ep 339; SBOp 8:279, we have one of the many citations of Mt 10:16 about the simplicity of doves. The mildness of the dove is compared to that of the lamb in Epi 1.7; SBOp 4:298, 21–299, 3: *Quod agnus in animalibus, hoc columba in avibus est.*

58. QH 13.5; SBOp 4:466, 28–467, 26: 'Woe to us because of the dragon! It is a huge beast whose fiery breath brings harm to anything it touches, not only to the beasts of the earth, but also to the birds of heaven'. QH 14.6; SBOp 4:472, 16–27: *insidiantis suadibilem sibilum animadvertite draconis.*

By this stage its breath is not only fiery but poisonous. In Ep 332 the *rugitum Petri Leonis* is paralleled with the *sibilos Petri Draconis;* SBOp 8:271, 16. In Ep 189.2; SBOp 8:13, 15–16, there is something similar: *Leonem evasimus, sed incidimus in draconem.* Higher in the same paragraph he speaks of the *Leonina rabies.*

59. Eagles are usually described in terms of Deut 32:11 and other texts. Cf. Sent 2.47; SBOp 6b:35, 7 and Sent 2.19; SBOp 6b:47, 1–4.

60. Occasionally described in terms of Eccles 10:1; for instance, Sent 1.30; SBOp 6b:17, 10.

61. Foxes figure prominently in SC 63–65, where Bernard is commenting on Song 2:15: *Capite nobis vulpes parvulas.* Cf. Ep 242.1; SBOp 8:128, 15–16 and Ep 189.5; SBOp 8:16, 4.

62. Ep 48.3; SBOp 7:139, 18–19. Cf. Apo 1; SBOp 3:82, 11. The reference is to Jerome Ep 17.2; CSEL 64:71.

63. *Haedi* typify curiosity and defective self-knowledge in Hum 28; SBOp 3:38, 9–13. The theme is resumed in SC 35.2, SBOp 1:249–250. Furthermore they have an unpleasant odour: Sent 3.10; SBOp 6b: 71, 3. She-goats, *capreae* are discussed in SC 52, SC 55 and SC 73, as has already been remarked in note 55. Notwithstanding the fact that *capreae* was used as a synonym for the smell of armpits, Bernard understands it in SC 52.6; SBOp 2:93, 26–27 to refer to the saints who have left aside their bodies to become like the angels.

64. Sent 3.86; SBOp 6b:124, 14–24. See note 54.

65. This is how I translated *semihomines* in Apo 29; SBOp 3:106, 17 for CF 1, p. 66. It is, perhaps, a little too specific.

66. Ep 2.2; SBOp 7:14, 3–4; the dove fearfully hides itself at the sight of a hawk.

67. The hen and her chicks are referred to in the context of Mt 23:37, for instance, in Sent 2.47; SBOp 6b:35, 6–7.

68. References to horses are often biblical allusions, often with more interest in the chariot or carriage than in the horse pulling it. For a discussion of equine symbolism with a listing of some of the relevant texts cf. J. Leclercq, 'L'art de la composition dans les sermons de S. Bernard', *Recueil 3*, pp. 150–158. Bernard is not in favour of prelates being ostentatious in their choice of horses or caparisons. Apo 27; SBOp 3:103–104, Csi 4.6; SBOp 3:453, 17, where there is question of the papal white horse, and Ep 78.3; SBOp 7:203, 10–11, regarding Suger. SC 39 comments

on Song 1:8: *Equitatui meo in curribus Pharaonis assimilavi te, amica mea.*

69. QH 13.6; SBOp 4:468, 1–14. QH 14.8–10; SBOp 4:474. See note 58. Apo 29; SBOp 3:106, 16 describes lions as wild, *ferus.*

70. JB 6; SBOp 5:180, 4 describes locusts as *reptilia.* Cf. Sent 3.86; SBOp 6b: 124, 14–24 and note 54 above.

71. Ep 2.2; SBOp 7:14, 4. Cf. note 52 above.

72. Apo 29; SBOp 3:106, 16 describes monkeys as 'unclean'. Csi 2.14; SBOp 3:422, 1–2: 'A foolish king sitting on his throne is a monkey on the roof'.

73. The injunction of Deut 25:4 repeated in 1 Cor 9:13 recurs, for instance, in Ep 397.2; SBOp 8:374, 22–23. Calves are mentioned in Ep 2.2; SBOp 7:13, 23–25.

74. In Ep 279; SBOp 8:191, Bernard writes to Count Henry about the theft of pigs from the Abbot of Châtillon. But generally pigs are associated with filth, Ep 111.2; SBOp 7:284, 14–15 and SC 24.6; SBOp 1:158, 3–4: *...haerere luto, tamquam unam de suibus, amplexarique stercora.* The pearls before swine theme also occurs, for instance, in Ep 203; SBOp 8:63, 1–4, based on Mt 7:6. Boars are mentioned in Ep 141.2; SBOp 7:339, 9.

75. Sent 3.10; SBOp 6b:70, 19–20 describes how a ram withdraws somewhat to collect his strength so that he may attack his adversary more fiercely.

76. The images of the flock and the shepherd, of wolves in sheep's clothing and of lambs abound in Bernard's writings, but mostly they seem to have a conventional, scriptural background. Cf. SC 33 on Song 1:6: *Indica mihi, quem diligit anima mea, ubi pascas...* SC 53.5–6; SBOp 2:98–99.

77. In Ep 242.1, Bernard advises that it is not safe to sleep near snakes; SBOp 8:128, 18–19. There is a reference to *serpens vetustissimus* in Ep 124.3; SBOp 7:307, 6 and to the prudence of Serpents, as in Mt 10:16, in Ep 339; SBOp 8:279, 8–9.

78. Div 3.4–5; SBOp 6a:89. The song of the swallow, is contrasted with the moans of the dove, signifying both the singing of the psalms in the Church and the yearning of private prayers. *Potest et per garrulam aviculam cantus simul psallentium in Ecclesia...designari.*

79. Apo 29; SBOp 3:106, 17: *Quid maculosae tigrides?*

80. Turtle–doves are very positively viewed by Bernard.

SC 59; SBOp 2:135–141 reflects on the text of Cant 2:12, *Vox turturis audita est in terra nostra,* and shows great appreciation for the bird's virtues. SC 40; SBOp 2:24–28 revolves around Song 1:9: *Pulchrae sunt genae tuae sicut turturis.* The image occurs regularly, for instance, in Ep 273.1; SBOp 8:183, 8, usually in a complimentary vein.

81. Wolves are described as *rapaces* Apo 1; SBOp 3:82, 15 and Ep 242.1; SBOp 8:125, 8. The usual idea is that drawn from Mt 7:15 of wolves under sheep's clothing. Thus, Ep 248.2; SBOp 8:142, 22–23 and Ep 285.2; SBOp 8:201, 7–8. Invariably, the wolf is viewed within the context of a flock of sheep and its effect on them. Thus Ep 2.2; SBOp 7: 14, 3. Cf. Csi 4.6; SBOp 3:453, 11–13.

82. Csi 5.25; SBOp 3:488, 15–19 based on Mk 9:43 etc. A similar evocation is found in SC 16.7; SBOp 1:93, 28 with an application to conscience in Conv 7; SBOp 4:78–79, where the text of Is 66:24 is quoted. *Pulices mordaces, immo tineae demolientes* are referred to in Apo 1; SBOp 3:82, 15–16. Cf Csi 4.7; SBOp 3:454, 4 for scorpiones.

83. I note that the genre of the treatise is given as *sermo exhortationis* (Tpl prol.; SBOp 3:213, 7) and I think this is accurate. At the same time I think the *Praise of the New Knighthood* is a good example of how Bernard is able to write at length about realities with which he only appears to be familiar, drawing mainly on his own scripturally-inspired imagination. It is also interesting to note his confidence that monastic experience is universally transferable, and that what is good for the monk serves the ultimate advantage of persons in a completely different situation. Is this an early expression of Raimundo Panikkar's notion of 'the monk as a universal archetype'? Cf. *Blessed Simplicity* (New York: Seabury Press, 1982).

84. Cf. Capitaine H. Charrier, 'Le sens militaire chez saint Bernard', in *Saint Bernard et son temps,* vol. 1, (Dijon, 1928) pp. 68–74. Regarding the Second Crusade, I am merely suggesting that Bernard may have given insufficient thought to the military difficulties of the campaign and too much to its moral and spiritual aspects.

85. Beginning with the first issue of 1983, *Cistercian Studies* quarterly has begun printing translations and introductions to the *Parables.*

86. In Par 2.6; SBOp 6b:271, 22, the messenger named 'Prayer' passes through the enemy's siege lines

to seek help. Bernard uses the word *cuneus* (literal‐
ly, 'a wedge') which was not a siege position
but a formation for attack. There is evidence,
however, that the word was often used loosely
to mean a crowd or throng.

87. Cf. J. Leclercq, *Nouveau Visage*, pp. 61–86.
88. Cf. J. Leclercq, Introduction, CF 1: pp. 3–30;
     for the *attestatio rei visae* see p. 13.
89. Thus M. Mueller writes in an introduction to
     the sermons of Caesarius in *Fathers of the Church*
     31; pp. xvii–xviii: 'Most of his sermons were
     written for the average Christian, and they are
     remarkable for their numerous similes drawn from
     nature and the common daily life of their time'.
90. Cf. Bernard McGinn (ed.) *Three Treatises on Man:
     A Cistercian Anthropology*, CF 24 (Kalamazoo:
     Cistercian Publications, 1977). Id., *The Golden
     Chain: A Study in the Theological Anthropology
     of Isaac of Stella*, CS 15, (Washington: Cistercian
     Publications, 1972). Aelred of Rievaulx, *On the
     Soul*, CF 22 (Kalamazoo: Cistercian Publications,
     1981).
91. Cf. Peter Dronke (ed.), *Bernardus Silvestris:
     Cosmographia* (Leiden: E. J. Brill, 1978).
92. Cf. Norris J. Lacy, *The Craft of Chrétien de Troyes:
     An Essay on Narrative Art*, (Leiden: E. J. Brill,
     1980) pp. 11–23.
93. Cf. Wolfram von den Steinem, *Der Kosmos des
     Mittelalters: Von Karl dem Grossen zu Bernhard
     von Clairvaux*, 2 (Munich: Francke Verlag, 1967);
     note especially pp. 92–96.
94. One only has to recall the frequency with which
     Bernard speaks of fragrances and good odours
     and unguents or perfumes, on the one hand, and
     of his excremental imagery on the other. Thus
     in SC 74.5; SBOp 2:242–243 in a survey of the
     senses, smell is given a double statement. On
     the aroma of new bread cf. Ep 106.2; SBOp 7:266,
     18–19. On swamp odours, cf. SC 33.6; SBOp 1:237,
     21–25—a startling parenthesis in a lyric passage.
     On the malodorous quality of worldly involvement,
     cf. SC 24.6; SBOp 1:157–159. In a more agricultural
     vein, see Div 80.2; SBOp 6b:321, 4.

CHRIST OUR MOTHER:
AELRED'S ICONOGRAPHY FOR CONTEMPLATIVE UNION

Marsha L. Dutton

The soul's consuming hunger for union with Christ governs Aelred of Rievaulx's single treatise on the contemplative life, *A Rule of Life for a Recluse*, addressed to an anchoress and directing her toward a life of purity and devotion. Unlike other works of the genre, however, *A Rule* contains more than guidance for her quotidian life and devotional practice; it promises her the direct, unmediated knowledge of God in this life, not just in the next. While Aelred, like the Fathers who preceded him, always presents such mystical knowledge as available only at God's initiative and through his gift, he repeatedly encourages the contemplative to play an active role in obtaining that gift, to hasten to Christ's embrace, to 'entice him to love and bestow gifts'.[1] In the course of the work Aelred guides her along the steps of preparation, invites her to her bridegroom's chamber, and brings her, like Mary of Bethany, to drink 'from the fountain of divine love'.[2] Through meditation on the humanity of Christ she comes finally to full spiritual union with him as her spouse, her mother, and her Lord.

The received text of *A Rule* contains two largely discrete portions linked by a common audience and subject matter. The first is a short manual for the daily life of the anchoress, 454 lines in C. H. Talbot's edition; the second is a treatise of spiritual direction in 1100 lines.[3] The disjunction between the two parts is largely responsible for readers' failure to recognize the strong contemplative concern of the larger portion; because the two-part work is not itself unified or centrally contemplative, the contemplative core of the second portion has not been generally recognized.[4]

Only two scholars have discussed the contemplative content of the work, and both have failed to note just how many contemplative elements it contains and how they combine to define the journey toward mystical union. Talbot's most pointed statement of the work's mystical qualities appears in the introduction to his edition:

> The Rule is...a warm and enthusiastic exhortation to the practice of the highest form of religious asceticism and contemplation. The recluse should [be]...a contemplative like

Mary, sitting at the feet of Christ, listening
to his words and gazing upon his blessed
countenance....She must rest like Saint John
on the bosom of Christ and become a partaker
of his secrets....In this way, the renuntiation
of all human company and consolation will
not condemn her to absolute solitude but
will ensure her the enjoyment of God's ineffable
presence.5

Teresa Ann Doyle speaks of the work primarily
as a conventional quasi-monastic rule: 'The first
section treats of outward observance which should
regulate the life of a recluse; the second portion
is devoted more exclusively to the development of
the interior spirit of prayer and mortification'.6 Only
once does she note mystical significance within the
work, this in reference to the Last Supper passage
also cited by Talbot: 'Ailred comes to the last supper
and dwells devoutly on the scene where St John rests
his head on the breast of Christ. The incident represents
the fulfillment of the mystic's quest, the meeting of
human and divine love in sweet embrace'. Like Talbot,
Doyle notes but fails to develop this perception of
the contemplative center of the work; she continues
immediately: 'Ailred encourages his sister to meditate
in the manner he has illustrated and by this means
to grow in the love of Christ'.7 The statement is accurate
but incomplete; both the meditation and the love of
Christ are intended by Aelred to culminate in 'the
meeting...in sweet embrace', in mystical union.
   Other writers too have treated *A Rule* as an introduction to the devotional life, or even perhaps as a
first step toward true contemplation, but no more
than that. In his important study of Aelred's writings
Aelred Squire summarizes the work: 'Fundamentally,
Aelred's work too is an ascetic letter on the preservation
of virginity, which incorporates a Benedictine timetable
and dietary, together with some glowing advice on
how to meditate'. Elsewhere he notes that 'there can
be little doubt that the unsophisticated would find
Aelred the easiest and plainest guide to the practical
question of how to begin to pray'. Squire does acknowledge Christ's appearance in the work as the bridegroom
to the soul, the defining element of *Brautmystik* in
contemplative literature, but he perceives it here
rather as a spur to asceticism than a mystical promise:
'The recluse's purpose is to please God in body and
soul in the perfect Christian life. Her virginity is
to be preserved in view of a true espousal with Christ'.8
Mary Felicitas Madigan also comments that 'Aelred

regarded meditation on the humanity of Christ as preparatory purification for higher contemplation'.[9] The same conclusion has been expressed most deliberately and forcefully by John Sommerfeldt. In his recent study of *A Rule* he states:

> Aelred, I am forced to conclude, simply does not mention the possibility of the contemplative experience to his sister, the recluse. The route laid out in the *Rule* passes from meditation to Beatific Vision, with no foretaste of that Vision in contemplation.[10]

In fact, however, the second part of *A Rule* is a unified contemplative work; in it Aelred guides the contemplative toward union with God in this life, then depicts the beatitude she will enjoy in the next. While his concern is primarily with the mystical joys available now, he indicates that these anticipate those to come. The pathway toward temporal union is centrally defined in three passages where Jesus is visually portrayed as mother; a number of associated images and propositional passages reinforce the promise to the contemplative that she may come to full knowledge of God in her life.

Aelred's direction for contemplation, the second portion of *A Rule*, has itself been generally understood as divided in two parts, each of which contains three smaller sections. The first part, according to this view, presents Aelred's teaching on the virtues of chastity, humility, and charity, while the second contains three meditations on the past, the present, and the future. The first of these meditations invites imaginative participation with Christ in his humanity, the second contains Aelred's confessional recollection of his own sinful youth and of God's insistent grace, and the third depicts a conventional Last Judgment.

This two-part understanding of the structure, however, is not in fact correct; for Aelred explicitly incorporates the three meditations into his discussion of charity, 'the end and border of the spiritual garment'.[11] The three speak separately and together of the contemplative's experience of God's love in this life and the next:

> There are two elements in the love of God, interior dispositions and the performance of works. The latter consists in the practice of the virtues, the former in the sweetness tasted by the spirit....So, if that sweet love of Jesus is to grow in your affections,

> you need a threefold meditation, on the past,
> the present, and the future.[12]

Thus the three meditations emerge naturally from within the section on charity rather than standing apart from it.

Aelred's teaching on the three virtues presents the ascetic stage of the contemplative life, the preliminary step of purification and purgation on the mystical journey. Subsequently the first two meditations, those concerning the temporal life, both present both meditation and contemplation, and the third presents beatitude in life to come, the eternal experience of that which in this life is only temporary.

The structure of the treatise does not, then, exactly mirror the contemplative's spiritual progress. Although the maternal scenes themselves depict the journey from purification to union simply and schematically, the structural units of the treatise exemplify Aelred's understanding that the contemplative life is neither so simple nor so straightforward. Precisely because 'in this wretched life nothing is stable, nothing eternal, and man never remains in the same state',[13] the contemplative never lingers long in union with her Lord in Aelred's work. Hence within the two meditations on this life's experience Aelred insists on a movement from the active search for union to its achievement, then once again to its loss and a renewal of the search. The language in which he speaks of contemplative experience in this life recurs in the third meditation, however, showing both that true contemplative experience, however transitory, is available in this life and that it is a foretaste of that to come in and last through all eternity.

Jesus appears as spouse and as mother in passages throughout the teaching on the virtues and the first meditation. Of the three maternal passages the first stands at the center of preparation for the contemplative journey, within the discussion of humility, and the other two come in the meditation on the past. Aelred supplements the metaphorical promise of mystical union contained in the maternal passages and disallows any denial of literal significance to that promise when he twice speaks plainly of the purpose of the contemplative life, first stating the anchoress' goal, then recording her experience of it. The first of these statements comes immediately after the first of the three maternal passages, as a transition between the discussions of humility and charity, moving the anchoress from preparation for the life of true charity into the living of it. The second comes toward the end of the

second meditation, summing up the contemplative experience in this life. During the stage of preparation,
then, Aelred first metaphorically invites the anchoress
to travel forward toward the love and knowledge of
Christ and then plainly states that the goal of that
journey is contemplative union. Within the meditation
on the past he guides her careful steps to that union,
schematically displaying her gradual progress on
the way, and in the meditation on the present he
records her experience as part of her personal history
and as a token of what she may expect in life to
come.

The theme of Christ's motherhood is introduced
subtly when Aelred speaks of Christ the bridegroom
in the words of Ecclesiasticus 24:27: 'His spirit is
sweeter than honey and his inheritance above the
honeycomb'.[14] The biblical passage itself, however,
defines a mother, not a spouse. Wisdom there introduces
herself: 'I am the mother of fair love and of fear
and of knowledge and of holy hope' (24:24-25).[15]
Aelred uses this passage to delight the anchoress
with the charms of her lover and bridegroom but
depends at the same time on its biblical context within
the words of a maternal child of God. This merging
of the spouse and the mother prefigures a thematic
interweaving throughout the treatise of the two kinds
of mystical knowledge and union available to the
contemplative, the familiar *Brautmystik* and what may
be termed *Muttermystik*.

The first of the three central passages of maternal
imagery appears within the exhortation to humility.
Aelred says to the anchoress:

> It should suffice you to have on your altar
> a figure of the Savior hanging on the cross.
> That should represent to you his Passion
> which you are to imitate, invite you to the
> clasp of his embracing arms in which you
> should take delight, and pour out for you
> from his naked breasts the milk of sweetness
> by which you may be comforted.[16]

While Christ has already been identified implicitly
as both bridegroom and mother, this passage is far
more explicit. The anchoress is asked now to ready
herself for the spiritual journey, no longer merely
in virtuous cleanliness but now in active pursuit
of the goal. She is invited to imitate Christ her Lord's
passion, to delight in Christ her Bridegroom's embrace,
and to take comfort in Christ her Mother's milk.

The milk here receives its definition from the

sweetness that throughout the text epitomizes both
the purity of the anchoress and the unity of Christ's
nature. The chastity of the contemplative draws her
bridegroom to her; it 'breathes out its fragrance even
in heaven and leads the king to desire [her] beauty,
him who is the Lord [her] God'.[17] At the same time
sweetness is Christ's nature. At his conception Mary
is 'inebriated with sweetness...when [she] felt in
mind and womb the presence of majesty',[18] in anticipation of his marriage with the contemplative his spirit
is said to be 'sweeter than honey and his inheritance
above the honeycomb', and at his death the contemplative
is exhorted to 'eat the honeycomb with your honey'.[19]
He is throughout the work associated with sweetness
and with honey; in this scene the sweetness is intrinsic
to his definition in oneness, his identity as God and
man, as infant, spouse, mother, and Lord.[20] The anchoress
and Christ are fitting mates, and the sign of that
fact is the sweetness of the milk here offered to her.

That sweetness, especially in its resonance with
the earlier definitions of Christ through sweetness
and honey, also introduces the eucharistic theme that
underlies the maternal imagery of the treatise. Aelred
suggests throughout that there are many paths to
God, that the mystical one by no means winds alone,
even for the contemplative. All Christians may come
to union with Christ through the Eucharist, and indeed
the union of the contemplative with him through his
motherhood and spousehood is itself presented by Aelred
as essentially eucharistic. The vocabulary of contemplation in *A Rule* centers in words of eating and drinking:
its characteristic verbs are *bibo, comedo, inebrio,*
and *nutrio,* its nouns *mel, favus, dulcedo, vinum,*
lac, and *fons.* Aelred explicitly establishes this vocabulary as intrinsic to the contemplative's search for
God when he says that the first of the 'two elements
in the love of God' is 'the sweetness tasted by the
spirit'.

Moreover, the three central passages through
which the contemplative advances to union with God
are all eucharistic in language and in imagery. In
this first of the three she is still a beginner, young
in contemplation; the sweetness of the milk may be
understood to allude to the first communion of the
young in faith, the newly baptized, and especially
to the early Church's practice of offering mingled
milk and honey to new communicants before they first
received the chalice. Hippolytus in his third-century
Apostolic Tradition explains this rite:

And then the offering is immediately brought

by the deacons to the bishop, and by thanks-
giving he shall make the bread into an image
of the body of Christ, and the cup of wine
mixed with water according to the likeness
of the blood, which is shed for all who believe
in him. And milk and honey mixed together
for the fulfilment of the promise to the fathers,
which spoke of a land flowing with milk
and honey; namely, Christ's flesh which
he gave, by which they who believe are
nourished like babes, he making sweet the
bitter things of the heart by the gentleness
of his word. And the water into an offering
in a token of the laver, in order that the
inner part of man, which is a living soul,
may receive the same as the body. The bishop
shall explain the reason of all these things
to those who partake....And the recipients
shall taste of each three times.[21]

The crucifix is only a representation, an object,
in the first scene of maternal invitation, and while
it invites the anchoress to consider its significance
for her, she is not yet expected to respond imaginatively. It is static, frozen in time, a memorial of past
events. Further, Aelred does not at this point encourage
her to linger in thought or prayer at the crucifix;
he adds instruction on adorning the altar instead:

If you like, in order to bring home to you
the excellence of virginity, a picture of
the Virgin Mother and one of the Virgin
Disciple may stand on either side of the
Cross, so that you may consider how pleasing
to Christ is the virginity of both sexes.[22]

These figures are to commend chastity to her and
to lead her to think about it; their purpose is entirely
deliberative. She is now to recognize those who stand
at Christ's side as representatives of the defining
virtue of her life; they demand nothing of her in
return.
    Immediately after this passage, however, Aelred
plainly expounds the goal of her asceticism and purification:

Let these things serve to increase your charity,
not to provide empty show. From all of them
you must ascend to unity, for only one thing
is necessary. That is the one thing, the
unity which is found only in the One, by

> the One, with the One with whom there is
> no variation, no shadow of change. The
> man who unites himself with him becomes
> one spirit with him, passing into that unity
> which is always the same and whose years
> do not come to an end. This union is charity,
> as it were the edge and the border of the
> spiritual vesture.[23]

Her purification is not self-sufficient, her virtue not
its own reward; rather are they a necessary stage
on the way to spiritual unity.

The other two passages in which Christ appears
as mother are both within the meditation on the past,
that extended life of Christ in which the contemplative
is repeatedly urged to participate imaginatively in
each event. Now she has moved beyond purification
and preparation—packing her bags for the journey,
as it were—and is on the road.

Some five years before writing *A Rule* Aelred
had expressed in *Jesus at the Age of Twelve* his understanding of the significance of Christ's human life
for the spiritual traveler: 'Thus his bodily progress
is our spiritual progress, and what we are told he
did at each stage of his life is reproduced in us
spiritually according to the various degrees of progress'.[24] In *A Rule*, however, Aelred asks not that
the anchoress imitate Christ, but that she meet him
within his human life. She is asked not to walk in
his footsteps, but to embrace his crib, wash his feet,
pray beside him, bear up his bloody limbs. She is
to be his friend and his disciple, and she imitates
those who in his human life were mother, friend,
and disciple to him. Her place in Paradise is earned
not by imitating him but by ministering to him, and
so too she may experience in this life foretastes of
that eternal joy.

The contemplative's changed status in this meditation
is marked in the second maternal scene, at the Last
Supper:

> Why do you hasten to leave? Delay a little.
> Do you not see? Who is that, I ask, who
> is reclining on his breast and bends back
> his head to lay it in his bosom? Happy is
> he, whoever he may be. O, I see: his name
> is John. O John, tell us what sweetness,
> what grace and tenderness, what light and
> devotion you are imbibing from that fountain.
> There indeed all the treasures of wisdom
> and knowledge, the fountain of mercy, the

abode of loving kindness, the honeycomb of eternal sweetness....Exult now, virgin, draw near and do not delay to claim for yourself some portion of this sweetness. If you are not capable of greater things, leave John to inebriate himself with the wine of joy in the knowledge of the divinity, while you, running to the breasts of the humanity, press out milk by which you may be nourished.[25]

In this passage the anchoress, by Aelred's guidance now advanced to the stage of meditation on Christ in his humanity, has become an active, assertive participant in the Last Supper itself. She is to go forward, to claim for herself the sweetness of Christ's embrace, to run to the breasts and press out their milk. In the Latin all the verbs of which she is subject are active except *nutriaris;* the nourishment of the milk remains in the gift of God. In the previous maternal passage the crucifix was chief actor, the subject of all active verbs, while the anchoress was the subject of only passive constructions.[26] Even the first verb of that passage, a verb of direction, was not an active imperative, but an impersonal construction with dative, *sufficiat tibi.*

The milk in the second maternal passage has taken on different significance as it flows from the breasts of Christ's humanity, and it receives additional definition as it is complemented by Christ's divinity. Aelred here supports his iconographic contemplative theology with an orthodox speculative theology, a Pauline insistence that one comes to God, even on contemplative paths, only through the Son, the Incarnate Lord, who in his humanity manifests the Godhead, but that knowledge of Jesus only in that humanity is insufficient: one must pass beyond it.

The sweetness is still present, but no longer only through the milk, and it is now explicitly available to the one who knows the living Christ while before it was only offered by the naked breasts of the crucified one. In the first maternal passage the sweetness of spirit, but now that the milk is to be redefined as representing only one portion of that spirit, Christ's human nature, the sweetness must be understood as no longer that of the milk alone. The no-longer beginning contemplative is still not ready to know Christ in his divinity, but she has become able at least to recognize the preserve of that divinity, which completes his humanity while remaining separate from it. Sweetness characterizes Christ in both his human and his divine natures, but when she knew him only in his humanity

she could associate the sweetness only with that humanity. The sweetness, his intrinsic oneness, remains
undivided, the indivisible issue of the fountain of
his nature and his love. Meanwhile the contemplative
can as yet receive only 'some portion' of 'this honeycomb
of eternal sweetness', as she can receive only the
milk, a partial emanation of his spirit, while John,
who receives the divinity with the humanity, imbibes
sweetness 'from that fountain'. Aelred insists again
on the oneness and indivisibility of Christ at the
same moment that he first speaks of Christ's dual
nature, just as he earlier defined Christ in his sweetness
as one when enunciating his triple way of being known
by the anchoress.

The contemplative has taken an important step
forward on her path to union, but she is still only
halfway there. She is nourished by the gift of Christ's
humanity, known in milk, but she is not yet able
fully to know Christ in both flesh and spirit, in both
humanity and divinity. That ability, possessed already
by John, is represented by wine as well as milk,
by inebriation as well as nourishment. John here lies
upon Christ's bosom, receiving the wine and inebriated
by it; his knowing of Christ is poured into him, not
expressed by him. He knows God fully rather than
in part.

In fact Aelred qualifies his direction to the contemplative at this point, not altogether sure how quickly
she has traveled or how far progressed. He begins
his exhortation to her in this passage with 'if you
are not capable of greater things'; presumably if
she has taken the journey at a single bound she may
already join John at the breast, to drink not only
milk but wine with him. The rapidity with which a
contemplative may come to full knowledge of Christ
is, as Aelred shows elsewhere, variable and unpredictable.

Surprisingly, Aelred does not here mention the
feast, the other disciples, or the words in which on
this occasion in the Gospel narrative Jesus instituted
the Eucharist. The bread and wine are not explicitly
present; the disciples and their Lord do not eat and
drink together. Contemplative metaphor replaces sacramental and liturgical narrative; John at the table
of the Last Supper partakes of Christ's body and
blood as he reclines against him and receives the
'wine of gladness in the knowledge of the divinity'.
The spiritual transformation of Christ's flesh takes
place in the receiving of it by him who loves and
experiences Christ in his humanity and through it
approaches his divinity. No physical symbol for the

body is necessary for one who can reach the body itself, and the anchoress, new traveler that she is, is like John in her ability to drink from that body. The Eucharist needs no words of institution here; its true celebration appears in John's inebriation through the wine of joy.

The third maternal passage accomplishes the journey to union, through the same vocabulary and a crucifix already familiar in its implications from the first such passage. Now that crucifix upon the altar has become the cross with the dying Christ upon it, now the small figures of John and Mary are come to life, weeping together at the foot of the cross:

> But you, virgin, who can feel more confidence with the Virgin's Son than the women who stand at a distance, draw near to the Cross with the Virgin Mother and the virgin disciple, and look at close quarters upon that face in all its pallor....Then one of the soldiers opened his side with a lance and there came forth blood and water. Hasten, linger not, eat the honeycomb with your honey, drink your wine with your milk. The blood is changed into wine to inebriate you, the water into milk to nourish you. From the rock streams have flowed for you, wounds have been made in his limbs, holes in the walls of his body, in which, like a dove, you may hide while you kiss them one by one. Your lips, stained with his blood, will become like a scarlet ribbon and your word sweet.27

Here the anchoress has come to full knowledge of God through Christ. She knows him still through the milk of his humanity, but now the wine of his divinity is also available to her. She can now go beyond Mary and John, after first briefly standing and weeping with them, to receive the sweetness of Christ's body—the honeycomb with the honey—and the mingled milk and wine, humanity and divinity, no longer distinguished or distinguishable for her. The milk no longer flows from his two breasts, but as a fountain from his opened side, just as in the previous passage John received the wine while 'imbibing from that fountain'. The sweetness is now fully present for the anchoress at last, no longer associated merely with Christ's humanity or reserved for John.

At the culmination of this scene the contemplative actually enters Christ, becomes one with him by entering the hole in the wall of his body. There she dwells.

In the perfection of contemplation the anchoress has moved beyond the partial knowledge of Christ as the God who nourishes as a mother nurses her child to full knowledge of the God who bears his lover within him as a mother bears her unborn child. Here union occurs at last, total knowing imaged forth in physical terms. The contemplative at rest within the womb of her mother Christ is enfolded in an embrace even closer than the sexual union with her bridegroom for which she has so long prepared.

At the same time, this is a sexual union as well: the contemplative in entering the body of the crucified Christ becomes indeed flesh of his flesh. The bridal union so long anticipated here takes place; the marriage has begun. While the anchoress has all along been understood as a fitting bride for Christ through their mutual sweetness, at the moment of union she has come to resemble him even more closely: as she kisses his wounds her lips take on the color of his blood and her word becomes newly sweet.

The biblical texture of the passage reinforces the blended maternal and spousal themes defining the contemplative's union with Christ. As the verse from Ecclesiasticus earlier introduced Christ explicitly as bridegroom and implicitly as mother, so here the text's narrative level, especially through its resonance with earlier maternal passages, presents Christ as a mother while the language of the Song of Songs, of which this passage is a pastiche, language inherently erotic rather than maternal, recalls his identity as bridegroom. In both cases Aelred transforms a biblical metaphor so as to allow the passage to show Christ both as mother and as lover-spouse.[28] At the same time he alerts readers familiar with the mystical uses and interpretation of the Song of Songs in medieval contemplative writing to his central idea throughout the work, the love of and longing for union with God.

One version of *A Rule,* a late fourteenth-century English translation found in the Bodleian Vernon manuscript, concludes its scene of maternal and spousal union at the Passion with birth of living offspring, so binding the two metaphors even more explicitly together than do any of the extant Latin manuscripts: 'And just as in a dovecote holes are made in the walls to wash the doves in, so in the wall of Christ's flesh are made nests all hot with blood that you should hide in and bring forth spiritual birds'.[29] Here the wound in the side becomes a physiologically recognizable womb, and the sexual union produces living issue.[30]

In defiance of normal physiology, the final maternal

passage presents Christ, who appeared earlier as
a nursing mother, now as a gestating one, though
milk is normally produced only upon the birth of
a child.[31] The inversion of the expected temporal
and physiological sequence here is part of Aelred's
treatment of time throughout the three meditations
and, more specifically, in the three maternal scenes.
The first of the scenes remembers past events; the
second and third move forward in the narrative context,
but the anchoress has had to move imaginatively back-
ward in real time to participate in the present reality
of the event represented in the first scene and recalled
there as long past. Aelred insists on the beginning
and the end as identical rather than distinguishable
in language and imagery and in the confusing presentation of time. Time past and time present merge in
this scene of unity, the return from alienation and
separation.[32]

The two central metaphors through which Aelred
has guided the contemplative to union with Christ
also cease to be distinct and achieve unity in this
passage. Just as physically the water and blood,
symbolically the milk and wine, theologically the
humanity and divinity, and temporally the past and
present merge in the Passion, so do the two humanly-
conceived relationships through which the contemplative
has been aided to love and to know her Lord. As
the early definition of Christ presented him as both
mother and spouse, and as the anchoress' altar invited
her to come to him as both mother and spouse, so
here finally this union must be understood as that
of the contemplative with Christ in all the ways she
has come to know and love him. In his Passion he
is no longer merely mother or merely spouse, but
Lord, and his motherhood and spousehood are partial
but essential understandings of that lordship. Just
as Aelred insists that one cannot know God in his
divinity except by knowing him first in his humanity,
but that knowledge is itself incomplete, so too he
insists that while a contemplative may approach union
with God envisaged as mother or spouse, finally the
mother and the spouse must be subsumed in the crucified
Lord. No partial understanding is sufficient. With
Paul, Aelred brings the contemplative finally 'to know
nothing...but Jesus Christ and him crucified'.

Still another instance of unity from diversity
occurs in the scene at the culmination of the Passion,
when the contemplative is for the second time in the
treatise portrayed as a dove. In the discussion of
chastity the anchoress was directed to look into Scripture, which flows 'from the clear fountain of wisdom',

Christ, for warning of the devil's approach.33 Having
previously found Christ's protection and her safety
in the written word, now in the meditation on the
past, while meditating on his humanity, she is able
to find protection in his Incarnation and his Passion,
by taking refuge in his wounded side. Here animal
and maternal images merge, as do spousal and maternal
ones.

In both animal and maternal images for union
the contemplative first knows Christ from a distance,
through a memorial of past events, and then comes
to him in his living flesh. At the same time in both
cases the first, static image is presented in the lively
language of liquid flowing from its fount, Christ:
to the dove-anchoress streams of water promise safety,
and to the anchoress at the altar naked breasts offer
milk of sweetness. In the Passion scene, however,
the two figures become one--the dove merges with
the enclosed worshipper and the promised safety and
sweet milk are both attained and surpassed in present
union with Christ.

For Aelred the preparation for the contemplative
journey is essentially passive, demanding that the
traveler consider God's saving action in history, the
giving of the Law and of his Son. The would-be contemplative must begin the journey by looking on, thinking
about, understanding. Once she has begun the search,
however, she becomes more like God, her passivity
turns into action. The journey may be swift--taken
in one beat of the wings--or slower, achieved in daily
footsteps among Jesus' followers. Finally the speed
is unimportant and unpredictable; the goal is available
and equally attainable to all, and the means of travel
or the time it takes does not matter. One may begin
by reading Scripture or by praying before the crucifix;
one may come suddenly to union, without struggle,
without meditation, soaring above the plodders, or
one may walk with them laboriously toward the dwelling
place.

Aelred links his three maternal scenes through
common language and imagery. The first and third
are essentially the same, the first comes to life in
the third, and the shared eucharistic language of
the second and third creates a narrative continuity
between them. What has changed in the course of
the three scenes is the anchoress' relationship with
her Lord. She has moved from invitation through active
participation to total union, from ascetic preparation
through active pursuit to infused contemplation, the
stages of the contemplative journey in this life. Where
at first she was invited by his breasts, then was

able herself to press the milk from them, finally she
enters his very flesh. She has ceased to be a passive
observer and become active in union.

The contemplative's progress is described and
enabled through incarnational and eucharistic language,
so that finally she receives union with Christ precisely
through the elements of the Eucharist, through eating
his body—the honeycomb—and drinking his blood,
the wine. The transformation undergone by the blood
and water that issue from Christ's side is an inversion
of the transformation in the Mass, a necessary and
perhaps heuristic inversion for the anchoress' benefit.
It is clear, in any case, that in the scenes of the
Last Supper and Crucifixion the contemplative comes
to know Christ through his body and blood. Caroline
Walker Bynum says in *Jesus As Mother:* 'Maternal
imagery is part of a new sense of God, which stresses
his creative power, his love, and his presence in
the physical body of Christ and in the flesh and
blood of the eucharist'.[34]

The three incrementally developed maternal passages
conclude with the scene of mystical union presented
as the physical interpenetration of Christ and a woman.
Aelred's iconography for the contemplative journey
is complete. But this last step has in fact taken place
once before in the work, at the conception of Jesus
himself, early in the first meditation and so between
the first two passages in which Christ appears as
mother. That passage, however, is absolutely non-
visual.[35] Aelred speaks first to his anchoress, then
to Mary herself, and finally again to the anchoress:

> Wonder at the Lord who fills earth and heaven
> being enclosed within the womb of a maiden,
> whom the Father sanctified, the Son fecundated,
> and the Holy spirit overshadowed. O sweet
> Lady, with what sweetness you were inebriated,
> with what a fire of love you were enflamed,
> when you felt in your mind and in your
> womb the presence of majesty, when he took
> flesh to himself from your flesh and fashioned
> for himself from your members members in
> which all the fullness of the Godhead might
> dwell in bodily form. All this was on your
> account, virgin, in order that you might
> diligently contemplate the Virgin whom you
> have resolved to imitate and the Virgin's
> Son to whom you are betrothed.[36]

This union is mental and physical, and Mary, in
this case the one whose womb is being entered, is
inebriated by the sweetness of the union while herself

being, like the contemplative whom Aelred addresses,
defined in terms of chastity and sweetness. Immediately
the contemplative is reminded both that she is to
imitate Mary and that she is betrothed to Mary's
son. The maternal and the spousal could hardly be
more explicitly linked. In fact, Mary apparently not
only conceives Christ within her as a son but knows
him also in some sense as lover; Aelred insists on
both relationships in his language of conception: 'the
womb of a maiden, whom...the Son fecundated'.37
        Christ is conceived in wholeness, in humanity
and divinity, and Mary, though no contemplative,
receives infused grace and union. Where Aelred's
contemplative audience receives different tastes at
different times--now milk of sweetness, later milk
of humanity, then wine of divinity mixed with milk
of humanity and honey with the honeycomb--and is
nourished by the milk and inebriated by the wine,
Mary is inebriated by the sweetness, all at once,
non-incrementally, with no stages to traverse. She
knows God in his own unity at the moment of her
union with him. The Annunciation scene is then in
some sense a lyric, ecstatic prefiguring of the highly
visual scene at the cross; in both cases Christ and
a virgin woman come together in spousal and maternal
union.
        The theological basis for Aelred's combination
of the spousal and the maternal union of a woman
with Christ appears in Augustine's *On Holy Virginity:*
Mary "is mother, indeed, in the spirit, not of our
Head, who is our Savior himself, of whom she was
rather born spiritually, since all who believe in him
(among whom she, too, is included) are rightly called
children of the bridegroom'.38
        The passage containing the conception of Jesus
not only adds theological definition to the union at
the Crucifixion, but, occurring at an early stage
of the contemplative's meditative movement toward
union, it clarifies her goal. It gives her in Mary
a model to imitate and to follow, and it promises
a specific reward. Aelred provides two such models
and two such rewards for the anchoress; both appear
at each of the three essential stages of her life, preparation, meditation, and union. On her altar the images
of John and Mary draw her to consider the excellence
of chastity; in her meditation she considers first the
Annunciation--and is told to 'contemplate the Virgin
whom you have resolved to imitate'--and then the
Last Supper, where she observes John's joy in the
knowledge of Christ's divinity. Finally, when she
is ready for contemplative union, John and Mary are

together again, at the foot of the cross, showing her the way.

Having followed, observed, and learned from these two models, having imitated both in virginity, assisted Mary in caring for the infant, drunk beside John at Christ's breast, and finally watched and wept in their company, she is now able herself to go forward to union with Christ. She has not advanced beyond them—chronologically they have preceded her in union—but she is no longer in need of their showing her the way, guiding her steps. She has become one with them, a contemplative bride and child of Christ in her own right. Not only does Aelred guide the anchoress toward her goal through these two models, but he indicates to non-contemplative readers her position on the pathway through comparison with the two who knew Jesus most intimately.

Two passages that stand on either side of the Passion in the first meditation, passages verbally though not visually almost identical, insist on a theologically correct understanding of the Christ elsewhere known as mother. These two passages echo the imagery and language of the three maternal passages, but the echoes are inversions; Jesus is twice known again in his humanity, but for the moment only in his humanity. In these passages Aelred insists that contemplative progress is not possible unless Christ's humanity is properly understod, that his carefully shaped maternal images can only serve as steps on the contemplative way if they are de-allegorized and understood to be only metaphors for the Christ who is man *and* God.

In the first of these two scenes Jesus prays in the Garden of Gethsemane, and Aelred addresses him, saying, 'Your compassion for me makes you show yourself human to the extent that you seem almost to be no longer aware that you are God. You pray prostrate on your face and your sweat has become like drops of blood running down onto the ground'. At once Aelred turns his direction to the watching anchoress, saying, 'Why are you standing there? Run up, consume those sweet drops and lick the dust from his feet'.39 Once again liquid comes from Christ, but it is not now life-giving, like the Scriptural streams of water or the flowing milk and wine. As will be true so soon at the Passion, blood and water are mingled, or rather in fact confused, but they are only blood and water, and they neither nourish nor inebriate. The drops of sweat, naturally salt, are become sweet as they come from the body of Jesus, but the dust insists that he is mortal.

The second of the scenes comes after the Crucifixion,

as Christ is being carried to the tomb, now defeated, broken, and dead. Aelred again implores the contemplative to assist the human Christ, to bear up the feet or arms, 'or at least gather up the drops of precious blood as they fall one by one and lick the dust from his feet'.[40]

In these two scenes the anchoress is led not to milk and wine but to dust and blood and sweat. Dust here replaces milk as a symbol of Christ's humanity, even to the point that it is the dust that the anchoress is twice instructed to lick up rather than the transformed blood and water of the maternal scenes. The dust is not transformed into anything, nor is the blood, precious for its own sake; the sweat may be misunderstood or misidentified—and in its identification with blood, it of course becomes blood for the reader—but it is not in itself changed into something life-giving.

The echoing and inversion of maternal imagery in these scenes serves primarily to draw a theological contrast between these and the truly maternal ones. Christ here does not represent God's motherhood; he is in neither of these scenes active, offering himself to the contemplative and nourishing her. Rather, she must support him, wiping the sweat from his face, watching while he prays, bearing up his limbs. Here the inviting, embracing, nourishing Christ is turned away from the contemplative, and in the withdrawal of her now-expected food she must seize whatever she can from him. The very absence of the mother God calls attention to her earlier presence, and the impotent humanity of Jesus in these scenes emphasizes his majesty, his wholeness as God and man in the other three.

The near-identity of these scenes allows Aelred through them to make not two separate statements, but rather one emphatic one, and their position on either side of the Passion scene allows him more fully to articulate his incarnational understanding of the Christ whom the contemplative knows as mother. The two passages insist on the ineluctable humanity of Christ, 'to the extent that [he is] God', but they stand on either side of that moment of unity in which the contemplative finally knows Christ fully, in humanity and divinity, as spouse, mother, and Lord. At last she has come to know the God who bears and nourishes her children in a full human nature. But if her children do not understand that her nature is divine as well as human, they cannot know her. Only when the water and blood become milk and wine, only when grace transforms the physical outflowing of Jesus into the sacramental elements of the Eucharist, does the union

between the contemplative and God become possible.
If Christ is man only, he cannot nourish, cannot
inebriate, cannot give life; a man, however loving
and however loved, is only a man, finally doomed
to lie bloody, dusty, dead. If the anchoress knows
Christ only as a man, she has failed to know him
at all. These passages, then, continue Aelred's insistence
on a Pauline understanding of Christ's dual nature:
grace comes through the incarnate God—through God
incarnate.

At the same time that Aelred insists on theological
orthodoxy in the contemplative's understanding of
her journey, he also demands care and intelligence
in her reading of his direction for it. He reminds
her in these two passages on either side of the Passion
that if she fails to understand, to de-allegorize, his
iconography for spiritual progress, to understand
the images, the blood and water, wine and milk,
in their reality, as figurative rather than literal
in significance, she will also fail to reach the promised
union. In this concern he follows Augustine, who says
in *On Christian Doctrine:*

> Nor can anything more appropriately be called
> the death of the soul than that condition
> in which the thing which distinguishes us
> from beasts, which is the understanding,
> is subjected to the flesh in the pursuit of
> the letter. He who follows the letter takes
> figurative expressions as though they were
> literal and does not refer the things signified
> to anything else'.41

The union once achieved, however briefly, during
the meditation on the past, the anchoress leaves behind
her imaginative meditation on the life of Christ and
turns her attention to the second meditation, that
on the present. In it she reads Aelred's joyful recounting
of the spiritual benefits she has repeatedly received
in her life:

> But now consider those gifts of God's goodness
> which are known only to you. With how glad
> a face Christ comes to meet one who renounces
> the world, with what delights he feeds her
> in her hunger, what riches of his compassion
> he shows her, what affections he arouses
> in her, with what a cup of charity he inebriates
> her. For if he did not leave his runaway
> and rebellious slave [Aelred himself], called
> solely in his mercy, without the experience

of spiritual consolations, what sweetness
shall I not believe he bestowed on a virgin....How
often he came to your side to bring you
loving consolation when you were dried up
by fear, how often he infused himself into
your inmost being when you were on fire
with love, how often he shed upon you the
light of spiritual understanding when you
were singing psalms or reading, how often
he carried you away with a certain unspeakable
longing for himself when you were at prayer,
how often he lifted up your mind from the
things of earth and introduced it into the
delights of heaven and the joys of Paradise.[42]

In essentially the same language as that of the
maternal passages but now plainly and unequivocally
rather than visually and metaphorically Aelred reminds
the contemplative of the mystical joy she has received
from her Bridegroom Christ, from her Mother Christ,
from her Lord Christ. She is now able to understand
rationally and intellectually what she has previously
experienced with her heart and body through imaginative
meditation. As she was fed with the honeycomb of
Christ's body, nourished by the milk of his humanity,
and inebriated by the wine of his divinity, so now
she recalls the delights, the cup of charity and its
inebriation, the spiritual consolations and their sweetness.

Further, her experience in this life truly prepares
her for that in the next. Aelred makes it clear that
the gladness of Christ's face in meeting her here
is merely an anticipation of the same gladness, enhanced
by its familiarity, in Paradise. The third meditation,
that on the life to come, recalls these joys. First
Aelred urges the anchoress to anticipate her place
at the Last Judgment: 'Now turn your eyes to the
right and look at those among whom he will place
you by glorifying you....Jesus' face shines upon them,
not terrible but lovable, not bitter but sweet, not
frightening but attractive'.[43] Finally, completing
his promises to the contemplative with that greatest
joy of this life and the next, that vision most to
be sought and longed for, he says again:

What is there further for us to seek? To
be sure, what surpasses all these things,
that is the sight, the knowledge and the
love of the Creator....That lovable face,
so longed for, upon whom the angels yearn
to gaze, will be seen. Who can say anything
of its beauty, of its light, of its sweetness?

> The Father will be seen in the Son, the Son
> in the Father, the Holy Spirit in both. He
> will be seen not as a confused reflection
> in a mirror, but face to face.[44]

This knowledge and love, this sight of God's face, awaits the contemplative in the life to come, Aelred assures her, but she is not left waiting until that time, for she has seen its beauty, known its sweetness in her life.

Aelred has insisted throughout his work that the contemplative can come to union with God, can receive the infusion of grace in this life, can be introduced into the delights of heaven while yet alive. In the three maternal passages he has guided her along the journey to attain these delights, depicting Christ as a loving, nurturing, and inebriating mother and at the same time as an embracing lover and spouse and so aiding the anchoress to come finally to unmediated knowledge of God, to spiritual union. But in case the reader has remained throughout unable to understand or to believe the promise contained in his metaphor, he spells out in the second meditation in simple, lyrical language the message and truth contained in the maternal passages. Finally in the third meditation he presents the glory that waits in the next life, glory familiar already to the contemplative who has followed the path laid out for her.

Aelred embodies his profoundly incarnational understanding of mystical progress and union in the language of metaphor and image rather than in that of abstraction and speculation; through images of the flesh he insists on knowledge of an incarnate God as the goal of the contemplative life. So he leads his readers along the journey to God: Bridegroom, Mother, Lord.

The University of Michigan

NOTES

It is with real gratitude that I acknowledge my indebtedness in this paper to several friends and students. Many have discussed the ideas and position here developed with me, but I owe special thanks to four in particular, Macklin Smith, Michael P. O'Connor, Judith Avery, and Stephen Rawson. In a variety of important ways they have contributed to my understanding

of *A Rule,* to the shaping of my argument here contained,
and even to the language in which I present that
argument.

1. Inst incl 14; CCCM 1:650; CF 2:63. I cite page
    numbers in the CF translation of both Inst incl
    and Jesu, but in some cases part or all of the
    translation given is my own.
2. Inst incl 29; CCCM 1:662; CF 2:79.
3. 'The "De Institutis Inclusarum" of Aelred of Rie-
    vaulx', *ASOC* 7 (1951) 12–217; reprinted in CCCM
    1:636–82.
4. See my discussion (published under the name
    Dutton-Stuckey) of the questions surrounding the
    structure of the received text of *A Rule* in 'Getting
    Things the Wrong Way Round: Composition and
    Transposition in Aelred of Rievaulx's *De institutione
    inclusarum'*, CS 68:90–101.
5. Pp. 173–74.
6. Doyle, 'Aelred of Rievaulx' Rule for a Recluse',
    in *The Benedictine Review* 6 (1951) 33.
7. Doyle, pp. 36–37.
8. *Aelred of Rievaulx: A Study* (London: SPCK, 1969;
    Kalamazoo, 1981) 120, 124, 127–28.
9. *The Passio Domini Theme in the Works of Richard
    Rolle* (Salzburg: Institut für englische Sprache
    und Literatur, The University of Salzburg, 1978)
    40.
10. 'The Vocabulary of Contemplation in Aelred of
    Rievaulx' *On Jesus at the Age of Twelve, A Rule
    of Life for a Recluse, and On Spiritual Friendship'*,
    CS 9:75.
11. Inst incl 26; CCCM 1:659; CF 2:74.
12. Inst incl 29; CCCM 1:662; CF 2:79. The division
    into three parts of the CF translation of *A Rule*
    has probably contributed to the conventional misunder-
    standing of the relationship between the three
    virtues (titled 'The Inner Life' in the translation)
    and the three meditations.
13. Inst incl 31; CCCM 1:673; CF 2:92.
14. Inst incl 14; CCCM 1:650; CF 2:63.
15. The introduction of Christ through the words of
    Wisdom should not be taken to mean that he is
    to be understood as equivalent to her; she is
    only a portion of his total definition. Finally
    all partial perceptions of Christ's nature find
    completion and fulfillment in the crucified Lord,
    and this Old Testament type is only a type. The
    eucharistic language unifying the various under-
    standings of Christ in the treatise is at work
    here. Wisdom's words in Ecclesiasticus continue:

'My memory is unto everlasting generations. They
that eat me shall yet hunger, and they that drink
me shall yet thirst' (24:28-29). Cf. Christ's own
words in John 4:13-14.

16.   Inst incl 26; CCCM 1:658; CF 2:73.
17.   Inst incl 14; CCCM 1:650; CF 2:63.
18.   Inst incl 29; CCCM 1:663; CF 2:80.
19.   Inst incl 31; CCCM 1:671; CF 2:90.
20.   This idea also appears in Jesu: '...his words,
      sweet as honey' (Jesu 5; CCCM 1:253; CF 2:6).
      In *A Rule* the contemplative participates in this
      sweetness when her words become sweet in kissing
      Christ's wounds.
21.   *Apostolic Tradition* 21; trans. Burton Scott Easton,
      The Apostolic Tradition of Hippolytus (Cambridge:
      Cambridge University Press, 1934; reprint ed.
      1962) 48-49. See also Tertullian, *De corona militis*
      3 (PL 2:99).
22.   Inst incl 26; CCCM 1:658-59; CF 2:73.
23.   Inst incl 26; CCCM 1:659; CF 2:74.
24.   Jesu 11; CCCM 1:258; CF 2:15.
25.   Inst incl 31; CCCM 1:668; CF 2:87.
26.   The verbs of which she is subject in the first
      passage are *imiteris*, *delecteris*, and *consoleris*,
      only the second of which is truly passive, as
      both *imitor* and *consolor* are deponents.
27.   Inst incl 31; CCCM 1:671; CF 2:90-91.
28.   Caroline Walker Bynum (*Jesus as Mother: Studies
      in the Spirituality of the High Middle Ages* [Berke-
      ley: University of California Press, 1982]) suggests
      that this combined presence of two kinds of feminine
      imagery for mystical union is unusual, saying:
      '*Brautmystik...*, the use of maternal names for
      God, and devotion to the Virgin did not occur
      together in medieval texts; the presence of some
      kinds of feminine imagery seems to have inhibited
      the presence of other kinds' (p. 141). While this
      perception may be simply an error on her part,
      it is equally possible that this treatise is in
      fact unique, that Aelred's curious and almost
      inadvertent shifts from an explicitly female audience
      to an undefined male audience and back again
      may explain the presence of both *Brautmystik*
      and *Muttermystik* in the text. Bynum argues that
      the latter form is typically male in origin and
      significance: 'Given the twelfth-century partiality
      for metaphors drawn from human relationships,
      religious males had a problem. For if the God
      with whom they wished to unite was spoken of
      in male language, it was hard to use the metaphor
      of a sexual union with a male God....We...have

many examples of monks describing themselves
or their souls as brides of Christ—that is, as
female. But another solution...was of course to
see God as female parent, with whom union could
be quite physical (in the womb or at the breast).
We should not ignore the possibility that in such
writings males could express as males certain
sexual desires: play at the breasts and entry
into a female body' (pp. 161–62). Certainly in
A Rule the union involves the contemplative's
entering Christ rather than he her; he is physiologically female in the Passion scene.

29. Stuckey, Marsha Dutton, ed., 'An Edition of Two
Middle English Translations of Aelred's *De institutione inclusarum'* (Ph.D. dissertation, University
of Michigan, 1981) 160.

30. Bynum says of cistercian use of maternal imagery:
'...where birth and the womb are dominant metaphors, the mother is described as one who conceives
and carries the child in her womb, not as one
who ejects the child into the world, suffering
pain and possibly death in order to give life.
Conceiving and giving birth, like suckling, are
thus images primarily of return to, union with,
or dependence upon God....Moreover, other physiological images, such as...Aelred's reference to
hiding inside Christ, express not merely the compassion or love that God offers man but also the
closest possible binding of self to God....Thus
the most frequent meaning of mother-Jesus to twelfth-
century Cistercians is compassion, nurturing,
and union' (p. 150).

31. For Bernard the relationship between childbearing
and milk is equally obscure, apparently; in sermon
9 of the Sermons on the Song of Songs the bridal
kiss results immediately in conception, and the
sign of that fact is the production of milk: 'For
so great is the potency of that holy kiss, that
no sooner has the bride received it than she
conceives and her breasts grow rounded with
the fruitfulness of conception, bearing witness,
as it were, with this milky abundance' (SC 9:7;
CF 4:58).

32. Aelred treats time similarly in the three meditations.
The meditation on the past describes 'what happened
long ago' but relies on present tense verbs,
both imperative and indicative, and demands
that the present-day contemplative involve herself
in those past events; the meditation on the present
discusses the life of the author himself, but it
emphasizes his past and God's mercy toward him

in that past and in the future through the use of past and future verbs. The meditation on the future resolves the temporal paradox, for in it the past and the future become one in God's eternal present. See Stuckey, pp. 56–58.

33. Inst incl 20; CCCM 1:654; CF 2:68.
34. P. 135. Bynum also comments at some length on the intersection of the Eucharist and the desire for mystical union in the lives of women mystics of the thirteenth century, for whom the union was not so much understood in the language of the Eucharist, but achieved through its celebration. See pp. 257–58.
35. Perhaps because the scale implied in the first quoted sentence makes any visualization impossible. It is worth noting that in the course of the three maternal passages the anchoress grows small in relationship to Christ, an inversion of that physical phenomenon at which Aelred marvels here.
36. Inst incl 29; CCCM 1:663; CF 2:80.
37. In *Jesu* Aelred briefly raises the idea of imitating Mary as the mother of Christ, but without a corresponding spousal significance, and the central idea there is essentially that mentioned above, that of growing spiritually in imitation of Christ: 'For just as the Lord Jesus Christ is born and conceived in us, so he grows and is nourished in us, until we all come to perfect manhood, that maturity which is proportioned to the complete growth of Christ' (Jesu 4; CCCM 1:252; CF 2:8).
38. Chap. 6 (PL 40:399); trans. John McQuade, 'Holy Virginity', in *The Fathers of the Church*, Fathers of the Church, 27 (New York: 1955) 149.
39. Inst incl 31; CCCM 1:669; CF 2:88. The verb translated as *consume* in the first of these passages is *adlambe*, a verb commonly used in reference to the action of flame or water in licking against and so washing or eating away at its object. The sense of *consume*, then, is accurate here, but it should not be understood as equivalent to taking into oneself for nourishment.
40. Inst incl 31; CCCM 1:672; CF 2:91.
41. 3:9; trans. D. W. Robertson, Jr. (Indianapolis: Liberal Arts Press, 1958) 84.
42. Inst incl 32; CCCM 1:676; CF 2:96.
43. Inst incl 33; CCCM 1:679; CF 2:99.
44. Inst incl 33; CCCM 1:680–81; CF 2:101.

ABBOT STEPHEN LEXINGTON AND HIS EFFORTS FOR REFORM
OF THE CISTERCIAN ORDER IN THE THIRTEENTH CENTURY

Werner Rösener

A survey of the scholarly publications of the last ten years in the area of monastic research demonstrates the amazing fact that interest in the Cistercian Order has become unusually strong. Of European investigations, one should mention especially the Berlin research project, 'Zisterzienser',[1] the large cistercian exhibit at Aachen in 1980,[2] and the international cistercian congress held in 1981 in Flaran in southern France.[3] As for American research on the Cistercians, special mention should be given to the excellent studies and publications of the 'Institute of Cistercian Studies'.[4] If one examines these several investigations critically, he will see that many of them are one-sidedly specialized and run parallel to each other without cross-reference. The interdependence of various areas of cistercian history is lost sight of, and the total picture of medieval Cistercianism is not sufficiently considered. Research on economic history and the history of spirituality seem to me to make this particularly obvious. On the one side there are investigations into the structure and development of the cistercian economy which take other areas --religious motivations, spiritual elements, the general life within monasteries--too little into consideration. Some scholars speak enthusiastically of the economic productivity of the Cistercians and point to their great success in colonization of the land, but do not inquire into the motivations and contributing factors of this economic activity. On the other hand, students of cistercian spirituality and biographers of great cistercian personalities have often conducted their investigations without glancing at the economic and social aspects of the movement. Great mystics and theologians such as Bernard of Clairvaux, William of St Thierry and Aelred of Rievaulx are presented to us as ethereal beings who had completely withdrawn from the necessities of everyday life and seemed to nourish themselves more on heavenly manna than on daily bread.

The question may be raised whether the research outlined here reflects a particular stage in the development of historical scholarship or instead expresses an essential opposition between spirituality[5] and economics[6] within the Cistercian Order. Were the spirituality and the economic activity of the Cistercians really as disconnected in the High Middle Ages as many publications make them seem? How should the interdependence of these two facets of cistercian life be understood, and what place did the *spiritualia* and *temporalia* hold in overall cistercian life? An attempt to answer some of these questions will be made using the example of the important cistercian abbot, Stephen Lexington, and his various efforts at spiritual, organizational, and economic reform of the Order in the first half of the thirteenth century.

Stephen Lexington[7] was born in Nottinghamshire in 1190, and came from a respected family. His brother John was Henry III's keeper of the seal. Of his brothers, Robert was a royal judge, and Henry, Bishop of Lincoln. Stephen himself was destined for a clerical career and studied in Paris and Oxford under Edmund of Abingdon, with whom he remained in close contact. In 1215 King John offered Stephen a lucrative position as canon, but in 1221 he and seven associates unexpectedly joined Quarr Abbey on the Isle of Wight as cistercian monks. Not long thereafter, Stephen was named abbot of Stanley, a daughter house of Quarr in the diocese of Salisbury. In that position, he received from the 1227 general chapter the difficult task of carrying out a general visitation of Irish cistercian monasteries. The letters which have been preserved, show that Stephen proceeded with great energy to raise monastic discipline and improve the economic conditions of the Irish monasteries.[8] His appointment as abbot of the Norman monastery of Savigny in 1229 marked out for him an area of activity at an important place, and he exercised a great influence on Savigny and its numerous dependencies in France and England until his election in 1243 as abbot of Clairvaux. It is this period of his efforts at reform which are contained in the 'Economic Ordinance for the Monastery of Savigny' and other writings, which form the basis of the present investigation.

The monastery of Savigny had been founded in 1112. It was the mother house of a large congregation which in 1147 joined the Cistercian Order and was placed directly under the abbey of Clairvaux.[9] This particular form of membership in the Cistercian Order, different from that of the other monasteries of the Order, led Savigny and its affiliates to maintain an exceptional position within the Order for a long time. It was a relationship which did not accord with the organizational and economic rules of the Order. The general chapter permitted the abbey of Savigny for a time to retain churches, tithes, and feudal rents, which the statutes of 1134 had forbidden all cistercian

monasteries.[10] Within its congregation, Savigny retained
extraordinary rights of visitation and privileges designed
to insure the control of monastery discipline.[11] In
the ensuing decades, Savigny gradually approximated
the general practices of the Cistercian Order, although
this process was never completed. The rather casual
observance of the Order's rules within the congregation
of Savigny apparently contributed to the less than
normally strict observance of cistercian economic principles and to the establishment of a realistic policy
of accommodation.[12] The special status of Savigny was
underlined by a letter which the Abbot of Clairvaux
wrote to the Bishop of Avranche in 1170:[13] when it
joined the Cistercian Order, the monastery of Savigny
was allowed several departures from the practices
and principles of the Order and given permission
to maintain churches as sources of income. Because
of its location in an infertile territory, the abbey
of Savigny could not do without its income from the
possession of churches.

When Stephen Lexington was called to Savigny
in 1229, there was clearly a need to reform the monastery
and its dependencies. By his Irish visitation, Stephen
had demonstrated such great zeal for the maintenance
of the early discipline of the Order, so good an organizational ability, and so clear an insight into the economic
problems of monasteries that he was considered especially
well-suited to the task of reforming Savigny. He published an 'Ordinance for the Conduct of the Economy'
(*Conductus domus sapienter staurate*) of the abbey,[14]
in 1230, the early phase of his activities at Savigny,
and as soon as he had informed himself in detail
about life in the monastery and its economic conditions.
What are the contents of this 'Economic Ordinance'
and how did it affect the Cistercian Order?

The introduction and the last sentence deal with
the origin of the Economic Ordinance, which was understood as an *ordinatio* for the correct management of
the monastery.[15] The abbot, the council, and the
senior members of the community approved them once
they obtained a picture of the overall situation of
the abbey. The ordinance was above all to provide
the managers of the monastery's economy with a means
for carrying out economic direction (*pro providentia
cellerariorum*).[16] A great deal of space is taken up
with planning, administrating, and controlling monastic
offices. Every year a written report on the general
situation of the monastery was to be presented, in
which all income and expenditures were to be noted,
together with an overview of the losses and gains
of the monastic economy.[17] Twice a year, in spring

and fall, the monastery's stores of food, raw materials, and other goods were to be examined.[18] The consumption of grain and bread was to be carefully monitored and the supply apportioned in weekly rations. The allocation of beer, wine, and pittances was carefully controlled by officials assigned to the task. Several chapters describe the administration of monastic offices and their execution by these officials (*officiales*). A list of strict rules was drawn up for the officials, such as prior, cellerer, and bursar, who came from among the monks, as also for the grange masters who were drawn from the lay-brothers. All officials were strictly controlled and had to present written accounts at regular intervals. Special importance was attached to the bursars, who supervised all the income and expenditures of the monastery and to whom all other officials were immediately to submit income of any kind.[19]

After the detailed rules for the administration of offices and the form of the written accounts, regulations for self-sufficiency and tenancy occupy a great deal of space in the Economic Ordinance. The grange masters, who supervised agricultural work and the monastery's herds and workers were to present accounts four times a year about the management of their farms.[20] In addition, a complete report on the total condition of the granges was expected at the end of each year. This provided an insight into the gains and losses and viability of the different economic areas. At least twice a week grange masters were to inspect the entire farm complex, including the workshops, and were required at any time to give an accounting to the monastery officials who visited the granges. There are also detailed notes on the tenurial economy and on land given out to tenants. Leased land was divided into several rental districts (*balliviae reddituum*), headed by receivers of rents (*ballivi*).[21] In order to make their task easier, lists of holdings and rents (*rotuli*) were to be drawn up in duplicate. In them the amount and the date the peasants' dues and services were given in detail.[22] Twice a year the monks checked all the abbey's rented lands and at an assembly of tenants asked all the peasants about the size of their tenancies and the amount of their obligations.[23]

On the whole, one is impressed by the extraordinary rationality and comprehension of the cistercian economic planning which these Economic Ordinances evince. Abbot Stephen Lexington had without doubt a realistic eye and a clear technical understanding of economic problems and he composed excellent economic ordinances for a cistercian monastery. The competencies of the monastic offices *(officia)* were clearly defined, the officials were obliged to render a strict accounting of all their activities, and had to answer regularly to all levels of monastic control. Surprising is the high level in literacy that was demanded for keeping the account books, making the accounting reports and document registers. In this agrarian economy we recognize a balanced coordination between the self-sufficiency of the granges and the tenant economy on the monastery land leased out. The self-sufficiency of the monastic farms continued to have a central importance for the total management of the abbey, but the system of rents played an ever more important role, as the many regulations on the collection of rents show. Accordingly, the monastic economy of Savigny only partially fulfilled the cistercian demand for self-sufficiency. It is evident that Savigny realistically adapted its monastic economy in the first half of the thirteenth century to the economic conditions of its environment, as can be observed at many other cistercian monasteries of the time.[24]

The initiatives of Abbot Stephen in reforming his abbey did not concern only the monastic economy. Along with his concern for the economic practices of the monastery, his directives clearly state his goals for strengthening monastic discipline and ensuring the internal tranquility of the monastery. In some places in the directives his efforts for the renovation of monastery discipline emerge clearly. Exact rules regarding the monks' food were given, the enjoyment of wine and pittances was limited, the trustworthiness of the monks and lay-brothers was consistently expected, and from the wage laborers exemplary conduct was demanded.[25] In the section on the visitation of granges, the goal was the promotion of the grange economy and the spiritual welfare of the lay-brothers.[26]

This concern for both the spiritual and economic reform of cistercian monasteries appears also clearly in Stephen of Lexington's efforts at the reform of monasteries dependent on Savigny; of these the visitation reports give extensive information.[27] In 1231 Abbot Stephen devoted himself to the reform of the deeply debt-ridden monastery of Longvillers. In order to reduce its indebtedness, he stopped all new building projects, limited the number of monks and ordered the community to economize, the bursars to run the finances more carefully, and everyone to keep accounts in writing. More than the Economic Ordinances for Savigny, the visitation statutes for Longvilliers[28] deal with the reform of the spiritual life. The regulations of the Order on clothing, food, and monastic daily life were brought to the monks' attention, the rules of enclosure and silence were expressly renewed, and the early regulations of the Order on architectural simplicity restated. The visitation of the granges was designed, on the one hand, to increase productivity and self-sufficiency and, on the other, to provide for the spiritual welfare of the lay-brothers.29 In his reform of Longvillers and other dependent monasteries of Savigny, Stephen Lexington gave clear directions for improving monastic discipline and the spiritual life and for promoting the economic well-being of the monasteries.

Once called to the office of abbot of the powerful abbey of Clairvaux in 1243, Stephen Lexington could fight still more effectively for his monastic ideals and for the spiritual, organizational and economic reform of the Cistercian Order. His chief concern became the spiritual renewal of the Order through increased scholarly study, for he saw the insufficient theological scholarly education of Cistercians as the chief deficiency of the Order in relationship to the new mendicant orders. In a letter to the abbot of Pontigny, who was concerned with the needs of the Order and especially with inadequate education Stephen pointed out that any concern with the economic well-being of the Order was pointless if spiritual zeal, *fervor spiritualium*, did not go along with it.30 In his position as abbot of Clairvaux, Stephen Lexington turned to the pope and asked permission to found a cistercian college at Paris.31 Almost as soon as the Pope's permission arrived, Stephen laid the foundation stone for a house of study, the later St Bernard's College. Although a conservative group of abbots was able a few years later to delay the study project, Stephen had already laid a permanent foundation for a stronger cistercian access to learning. By his activities he not only contributed to the economic renewal of the monasteries but also won a lasting reputation as the spiritual renewer of the Order. Spirituality and economy were not unconnected in his life. His efforts were for *spiritualia* as well as *temporalia*, both of which he understood as necessary parts of the cistercian way of life.

In conclusion, we would like to come back to the question of the relationship of spirituality and economy in cistercian studies. The founding fathers of Cîteaux wanted to go back without compromise to the ancient regulations of the *Regula Benedicti* and lead a life removed from the cares of the world in poverty and simplicity. The manual work of the monks and the establishment of self-sufficient granges were to serve the purpose of guaranteeing independence

from   the   world   and   to   give   the   monks   the   economic
means   of   realizing   their   spiritual   goals.   Although
work   with   their   own   hands   held   an   important   place
among   the   Cistercians   as   a   means   of   asceticism   and
charitable   activity—it   held   no   value   in   itself.[32] Manual
labor   and   prayer   are   two   different   ways   of   discharging
the   *servitium   dominicum,*   the   services   which   the   monk
daily   offered   to   God.[33]   Economic   activities   and   the
care   of   worldly   goods   remained   subordinate   to   the
chief   goal   of   cistercian   life,   the   acquisition   of   evangelical   perfection.[34]

Max-Planck-Institut   für   Geschichte
Göttingen

NOTES

1.   *Zisterzienser-Studien* I–IV (Berlin, 1975–1979).
2.   Kaspar   Elm,   (ed.),   *Die   Zisterzienser: Ordensleben
     zwischen   Ideal   und   Wirklichkeit.*   Schriften   des
     Rheinischen Museumsamtes 10 (Bonn, 1980).
3.   *L'économie   cistercienne   du   Moyen   Age   aux   Temps
     Modernes: Troisiémes   Journées   internationales
     d'histoire 16–18* Sept. 1981 (Auch, 1983).
4.   See   Cistercian   Publications   and   the   Institute   of
     the Cistercian Studies in Kalamazoo, Michigan.
5.   M.   B.   Pennington   (ed.),   *The   Cistercian   Spirit.*
     Cistercian   Studies   Series   3   (Spencer–Shannon,
     1970);   L.   Bouyer,   J.   Leclercq,   F.   Vandenbroucke,
     La   spiritualité   du   moyen   âge   (Paris,   1961);   J.
     Leclercq,   'Die   Spiritualität   der   Zisterzienser',
     in   *Die   Zisterzienser*   (Bonn,   1980)   149–156;   W.
     Rösener,   'Spiritualität   und   Okonomie   im   Spannungs-
     feld   der   zisterziensischen   Lebensform',   *Cîteaux*
     34 (1983) 245–274.
6.   R.   A.   Donkin,   *The   Cistercians: Studies   in   the
     Geography   of   Medieval   England   and   Wales.*   Studies
     and   Texts   38   (Toronto,   1978);   Ch.   Higounet,   'Le
     premier   siècle   de   l'économie   rurale   cistercienne'
     in   *Istituzioni   monastiche   e   istutuzioni   canonicali
     in   Occidente   1123–1215:   Atti   della   settima   Settimana
     internazionale   di   studi   medioevali   Mendola   1977*
     (Milan,   1980)   345–368;   W.   Ribbe,   'Die   Wirtschaftstätig-
     keit   der   Zisterzienser   im   Mittelalter: Agrarwirt-
     schaft'   in   *Die   Zisterzienser...*   (Bonn,   1980)   203–
     216;   W.   Rösener,   'Zur   Wirtschaftstätigkeit   der
     Zisterzienser   im   Hochmittelalter',   *Zeitschrift   für
     Agrargeschichte   und   Agrarsoziologie*   30   (1982)

117–148.

7. Stephen de Lexinton (or Lessington): *The Dictionary of National Biography* 11 (Oxford, 1950) 1083; *New Catholic Encyclopedia* 8 (New York, 1967) 690; L. J. Lekai, *The Cistercians: Ideals and Reality* (Kent, 1977) 79–82; B. Griesser (ed.), 'Registrum epistolarum Stephani de Lexinton abbatis de Stanlegia et de Savigniaco', *Analecta S:O:C:* 2 (1946) 1–118 and 8 (1952) 182–378.

8. Griesser, 'Registrum' (1946) 12–116. Translated by Barry O'Dwyer, *Letters from Ireland, 1228–1229.* Cistercian Fathers Series 28 (1982).

9. L. Guilloreau, 'Les fondations anglaises et de l'abbaye de Savigny', *Revue Mabillon* 5 (1909) 290–335; J. Buhot, 'L'abbaye normande de Savigny, chef d'ordre et fille de Cîteaux', *Le Moyen Age* 46 (1936) 1–16, 104–121, 178–190, 249–272; M. Suydam, 'Origins of the Savigniac Order', *Revue Bénédictine* 86 (1976) 94–108; G. W. Day, 'Juhel III of Mayenne and the Lay Attitude Toward Savigny in the Age of Philipp Augustus', *Analecta S:O:C.* 36 (1980) 103–128; B. D. Hill, *English Cistercian Monasteries and Their Patrons in the Twelfth Century* (Urbana, Illinois, 1968) 82–85; F. R. Swietek and T. M. Deneen, 'The Episcopal Exemption of Savigny, 1112–1184', *Church History* 52 (1983) 285–298.

10. J.-M. Canivez, *Statuta Capitulorum Generalium Ordinis Cisterciensis* (Louvain, 1933–1941) I: 14 (cap. 9).

11. Griesser, 'Registrum' (1952) 189.

12. L. J. Lekai, 'Ideals and Reality in Early Cistercian Life and Legislation', *Cistercian Ideals and Reality*, CS 60, ed. J. R. Sommerfeldt (Kalamazoo, 1978) 9.

13. Griesser, 'Registrum' (1952) 189: 'Cum Savigneienses in nostri ordinis societatem transire decreverunt, dispensatione in hac parte habita ecclesias et earum beneficia permissi sunt habere. Durum namque visum est loci cognita infeconditate ab huiusmodi eos prohibere beneficiis. Si quis ergo de perceptione talium beneficiorum adversus eos obloquitur, noverit sinceritas vestra huius ordinis patres misericorditer hoc eis indulsisse'.

14. Griesser, 'Registrum' (1952) 224–232; in a German translation: B. Griesser, 'Die Wirtschaftsordnung des Abtes Stephan Lexinton für das Kloster Savigny (1230)', *Cistercienser-Chronik* 58 (1951) 13–28.

15. Griesser, 'Registrum' (1952) 232: 'vnde tam pro pace fratrum quam utilitate domus dictam ordinationem fecimus annotari, ut omnibus fratribus ad consilium uocatis liquidius pateat, quomodo

regi debeat domus Dei'.

16. Ibid., Griesser, 225.

17. Ibid., 229 (cap. 39): 'Item semel post festum omnium sanctarum animarum coram abbate et consilio domus audiatur status totalis abbatie tam in receptis quam expensis nec non et omnium grangiarum et aliarum domorum et inquiratur, quantum a singulis emolumentum abbatie prouenerit et quis fructus ex earum retentione contingat'.

18. Ibid., 227 (cap. 15).

19. Ibid., 225 (cap. 4/5).

20. Ibid., 229 (cap. 30/31).

21. Ibid., 232 (cap. 49).

22. Ibid., 232 (cap. 50).

23. Ibid., 232 (cap. 49).

24. W. Rösener, *Reichsabtei Salem. Verfassungs- und Wirtschaftsgeschichte des Zisterzienserklosters von der Gründung bis zur Mitte des 14. Jahrhunderts.* Vorträge und Forschungen Sonderband 13 (Sigmaringen, 1974) 118–123; E. Krausen, *Die Klöster des Zisterzienserordens in Bayern* (München, 1953) 15; Higounet, 'Le premier siècle', 363–365; W. Rösener, 'Grangienwirtschaft und Grundbesitzorganisation südwestdeutscher Zisterzienserklöster vom 12. bis 14. Jh.', *Die Zisterzienser...* (Bonn, 1982) 140–141.

25. Griesser, *Registrum* (1952), 228 (cap. 29).

26. Ibid., 231 (cap. 46): 'Prouideant etiam, quod ita temperate ac sobrie se habeant vniuersi, ne eorum adventus plus ad animarum quam culparum lesionem et substancie domus dissipacionem quam ad fructum alium cedat temporalem uel spiritualem'.

27. Ibid., 191–257.

28. Ibid., 191–194.

29. Ibid., 194 (cap. 32): 'Item prior, supprior, magister conuersorum et cellerarii unanimiter et sollicite inuigilent circa informacionem et disciplinam conuersorum'.

30. 'Registrum' (1946), 117: 'Pater in Christo karissime, ipsa tempora periculosa, que iam instant, nos ammonent de uigilancia et sollicitudine pro statu ordinis maxime in spiritualibus. Nam cum effectus sine causa sua stare non possit, frustra mittemus ad curias prelatorum et principum pro obseruatione bonorum temporalium vel libertatum, cum collationis et tuitionis temporalium ipsorum fructus et feruor spritualium hucusque extiterit et adhuc causa sola existat atque precipua'.

31. L. J. Lekai, 'Studien, Studiensystem und Lehrtätigkeit der Zisterzienser', *Die Zisterzienser...* (Bonn, 1980) 165–170; C. H. Lawrence, 'Stephen of Lexington

and Cistercian University Studies in the 13th Century', *The Journal of Ecclesiastical History* 11 (1960) 164–179; P. Dautrey, 'Croissance et adaption chez les Cisterciens au treizième siècle. Les débuts du Collège des Bernardins de Paris', *Analecta S.O.C.* 32 (1978) 122–211.

32. D. Kurze, 'Die Bedeutung der Arbeit im zisterziensischen Denken', *Die Zisterzienser...* (Bonn, 1980) 179–202.

33. *Benedicti Regula* 11; ed. Ph. Schmitz (Maredsous, 1962); 'Constituenda est ergo nobis Dominici scola servitii: in qua institutione nihil asperum, nihil grave nos constituturos speramus'.

34. Ibid. 73; p. 205: 'Ceterum ad perfectionem conversationis qui festinat, sunt doctrinae sanctorum Patrum quarum observatio perducat hominem ad celsitudinem perfectionis'.

THE STANDARD OF LIVING
IN GERMAN AND AUSTRIAN CISTERCIAN MONASTERIES
OF THE LATE MIDDLE AGES

Gerhard Jaritz

This paper represents part of a research project now under progress at the *Institut für mittelalterliche Realienkunde Österreichs*. This institute of the Austrian Academy of Sciences concentrates its work on the investigation and interpretation of medieval daily life and material culture.[1] Research on the daily life and material culture of medieval monastic communities particularly is based on written sources:[2]

1) rules, customaries, paragraphs of visitation-protocols, statutes of General Chapters;

2) economical sources, especially account-books and inventories;

3) contemporary descriptions of monastic life, legal documents, anniversary-lists, lists of donations.

The scope of the sources relevant to our research therefore is a wide one.

The attention which daily life in medieval German cistercian monasteries has received in historical research should be mentioned, especially that given by a recent article (1980) by Reinhard Schneider under the title 'Lebensverhältnisse bei den Zisterziensern im Spämittelalter'. It deals with the way of life in Cistercian communities of the late Middle Ages with particular concentration on monasteries in Hesse. In addition to this, various 'histories' of individual monasteries offer more or less detailed descriptions or remarks on the way of life in these communities. Finally a number of monographs on special aspects of daily life can be found in the early numbers of the *Zisterzienser-Chronik* and the *Studien und Mitteilungen aus dem Benediktiner-Orden*.[3]

The overview we would like to give cannot be based on single examples from random monasteries, but should present certain general patterns and developments perceived in German and Austrian cistercian men's communities of the fourteenth and fifteenth centuries—with special attention given to food and food-consumption, to dress and to aspects of housing.[4]

Daily life in a monastic community is determined by rules. They manifest in a very clear way the attitude of the Order to the material culture of the monasteries' inhabitants. If we look at the different kinds of rules and regulations, we see that the material aspects of life fill a considerable space. This means that for communities like the early Cistercians, who tended to disapprove of the material aspects of life, the rules governing these details were—or probably must have been—quite extensive and detailed. This thesis has been demonstrated for high medieval monasticism in a very clear and impressive way by Gerd Zimmermann in his book *Ordensleben und Lebensstandard*.[5]

One of man's principal material needs is food. Not surprisingly then, the statutes concerning food and food-consumption are quite extensive.[6] To these we can add notes in account-books, inventories and legal documents—all of which contain information of certain aspects of monastic nutrition.[7] From them we can posit some remarks on general trends and developments in German and Austrian cistercian monasteries:

If we look at late medieval cistercian documents, we find food frequently mentioned in connection with the allowance of pittances.[8] This 'extra food' may be used as a very significant example in reconstructing and discussing the standard of living within the communities. Particularly from the end of the twelfth century onwards, we find such allowances of, for example, extra white bread, wine, or fish in increasing numbers.[9] Their popularity may be seen in lists of pittances which have come down to us. The Lower-Austrian abbey of Zwettl, e.g., had ninety-eight days each year when such extra food was served to the monks, according to a list dating to the fourteenth century.[10] A study done for the Lower-Austrian abbey of Heiligenkreuz demonstrates that in the first half of the fifteenth century no fewer than 201-207 days of the year saw extra food.[11] Similar examples could be given for the communities of Buch, Himmerod, Eberbach, Marienstatt, Raitenhaslach, and others.[12] They show clearly that the original restrictions on food had changed. This is also proven by several of the modifications of the rules made by the General Chapter.[13] This development culminated between the second half of the fourteenth and the first half of the fifteenth century. But it also ended in the fifteenth century, when the need for this extra food or, better, this kind of allowance of extra food, decreased and completely vanished. There were no more days when extra food was viewed as a special allowance.[14] The ordinary everyday food which was being served, had changed in such a way that pittances were no longer considered 'treats'. The Styrian abbey of Rein shows this quite clearly. In 1390 sixty-one servings of extra-food are mentioned. Sixty years later, a land-register of 1450 states only twenty-six allowances still being served.[15]

A similar situation developed concerning the general variety of food, which, particularly in the fifteenth century received major attention in cistercian communities. In the thirteenth and fourteenth centuries the pittances had increased the variety of food consumed. White bread, wine and fish improved nutrition and were seen as special things by the communities that normally ate brown bread and vegetables. Fish especially offered a lot more variety—not only through the different methods of preparing it, but also because of the many species which were available. We sometimes see the allowances of pittances—especially rather late ones —include regulations about greater variety. In 1439, for example, a pittance was given to the monks of Altenberg northeast of Cologne: for first course herring, stockfish and a fish called *ertzen*, for second course peppered carp fried in oil; for third course fried carp and salmon. Each monk was also to get good white bread and a large portion of wine.[16]

The desire or need for variety should also be seen in connection with 'foreign' food. This means that abbeys far removed from sea could get sea fish, particularly herring, but plaice and stockfish as well. Account-books over a long chronological period show a variety of different fish bought by the communities. In the Styrian abbey of Rein, already mentioned, nine different species of fish can be proved to have been bought in over the seventeen years—for which fifteenth-century account-books survive.[17] Other monasteries show similar trends: Eberbach, Heilsbronn, Salem or Pforta.[18] But we should emphasize that in comparison to Benedictines or Austin Canons of the same period the cistercian desire for variety, at least of fish, seems less pronounced. The account-books of the Benedictines of Göttweig in Lower Austria contain the names of thirty-five species of fish purchased between 1460 and 1500.[19]

Because 'foreign' food functions as a criterion of the standard of living in the late Middle Ages, it is necessary to deal with other imported food and its consumption in monasteries. Above all one group, regularly listed in account-books and inventories in a section called lenten fare (*quadragesimalia* or in German *fastenspeis*) must be mentioned.[20] These lists contain almost only imported foodstuffs—spices, olive oil, rice, figs, sugar, almonds, raisins. They were all expensive, they were all considered as means to demonstrate material wealth in the secular world. There they were especially used for preparing meals when important guests came, when township meetings

were held or feasts celebrated. We certainly cannot
prove in detail the degree to which these *quadragesimalia*
were served regularly to the communities.[21] The existence
of different kitchens within the monasteries (the abbot's
kitchen; the community's kitchen; the infirmary's
kitchen; the kitchen for the monastery's familiars)
must be taken into consideration.[22] That such lenten
fare was served and that during the fourteenth and
the fifteenth centuries the amount and variety purchased
by cistercian communities increased, we may generally
assume.[23] We may also assume that, as in the secular
world, the time of fasting was often more expensive
for the monastic community than other times of the
year.[24]

The question of meat-consumption in cistercian
abbeys has already been dealt with in historical research.[25] That the fourteenth and fifteenth centuries
brought about the decisive change from an abstinent
to a meat diet, can be clearly proved. What we would
like to emphasize is that meat-consumption shows once
more an 'improvement' in the standard of living—
from a secular point of view. Often the abbots were
first allowed to consume meat, particularly when they
were the guests of high secular authorities or when
these authorities were their guests. That the communities
were also permitted meat on certain days is demonstrated,
for example, by documents from Hohenfurt in Southern
Bohemia (1398 and 1453), from Marienstatt near Cologne
(1412 and 1476) or from Dargun and Doberan in Mecklen-
burg (1432).[26]

An increased need for material goods in cistercian
communities during the late Middle Ages is also shown
by many other individual notices. They all hint that
monks were approaching the way of life and standard
of living of the secular world, a secular world which
must be seen as that of those classes of population
who joined the cistercian communities: nobility, mainly
until the second half of the thirteenth century, and
townsmen, particularly from the fourteenth century
onwards.[27] This may be illustrated by two examples
concerning food. At the abbey of Hude in Northern
Germany the community complained in 1306 about the
scandalous quality of beer being served to them.
In agreement with the abbots of Altenberg and Marienthal
the abbot of Hude decided to change the method of
brewing by using certain income of the abbey to buy
oats and barley.[28] In 1382 permission was given to
the Lower Austrian abbey of Lilienfeld to build a
winter-refectory to prevent the freezing of food and
drink.[29]

Another category of objects which allows us to

judge the monks' standard of living is tableware
and its use. An inventory of the Austrian monastery
of Neukloster dated 1446 shows the general use of
pewterware in the refectory.[30] A comparison with the
secular world provides an interesting insight. The
wills of townsmen, which survive in large numbers
from fifteenth-century Austria, show that for the average
citizen the use of pewterware was not necessarily
a matter of course, but something extraordinary.[31]
Thus we may assume that a community, recruited in
the main from towns, used material objects characteristic of a higher standard of life than the monks
had been used to in the world.

In connection with this example we can give another
concerning the utensils of the abbot's table, mentioned
very often in inventories or account-books. There
we find--again particularly in the fifteenth century
--show-pieces of the secular gold- and silversmith's
art, certainly comparable with objects used among
the nobility.[32] Again the increased openness of cistercian
abbeys to the secular world must be seen as a reason
for this. Serving noble guests simply demanded the
use of spectacular tableware--silver and gilt beakers,
ostrich-eggs in valuable settings, gilt spoons--in
the same way as dining with nobility made it necessary
for cistercian abbots to eat meat. This social obligation
could not--even in the long run--be changed or prevented
by the authority of the General Chapter. The statutes
published in 1250 and 1290 against the use of silver
or gilt tableware had no effect in the fourteenth and
fifteenth centuries.[33]

Another item of monastic material culture is clothing.
On that the rule seems to have been stricter and the
possibilities of changes smaller. We could of course
talk about extremes: dancing monks wearing silken
secular garments or women's clothing, of which we
have an example from the Carniolian abbey of Sittich
(Sticna) at the beginning of the sixteenth century.[34]
But this certainly is not our purpose. If we want
to investigate developments in the late Middle Ages
which can be taken as changes or improvements in
the standard of living, we must posit two chief criteria:
　　　--the number of clothes, or different clothes,
　　　　permitted to and used by the monks;
　　　--the cloth used for the monks' habits.
The increase of the number of monks' clothes during
the late Middle Ages can be demonstrated by some
normative sources and inventories of the German and
Austrian area.[35] More significant for our topic seems
to be the use of different cloth used for making the
monks' habits. In this connection we again find a

phenomenon which we already mentioned in connection with food: the desire to use cloth of higher than usual quality, which was often cloth from well-known and/or far distant textile-producing centres. That meant, for example, for Austria the purchase of cloth from Bohemia or the German cloth-producing centres; that meant for Germany purchases from the country's well-known textile-centres, often situated far from the monasteries, and sometimes, though rather seldom, importation from Flanders.[36] It must be stressed, though, that especially in the fifteenth century the designation of cloth by a place of production did not necessarily mean that it really originated from there. Cloth from Ypern could doubtlessly have been produced somewhere else by weavers taking over the method or the wool used for cloth-production in Ypern.[37] But still it meant something extraordinary. We find that such special or 'foreign' cloth was particularly bought for the abbot's clothing. And again it is not only love of the expensive or 'foreign' object, but also a wish for variety which is manifested in this situation. But we must also emphasize that, at least in the fifteenth-century, Benedictine and Augustinian communities indicated more of these 'desires'. Their account-books show a larger variety of cloth purchased and a greater incidence of 'foreign' cloth.[38]

The use of furs, originally prohibited, could often be legitimate in the cold areas on one hand; on the other hand, it also allowed monks to imitate the wealthy, who used special furs, in the extreme, of course, ermine.[39]

Housing and the standard of living can sometimes be reconstructed by investigating late medieval cistercian abbeys *in situ*. Written sources offer less information. If we look at the situation in the secular world, we find that in the decoration of rooms motives of convenience and comfort were of decisive importance to builders —especially considerations of warmth and light in the rooms.[40] We see similar trends in cistercian communities. The installation of more than one heated room in the monasteries can be proved not only by modified statutes,[41] but also by notes in account-books referring to the building of tiled stoves.[42] Light was provided, especially in the fifteenth century, by the installation of bull's eye glass-windows, particularly in rooms that were used for official purposes.[43]

One thing which played a similarly important role in the secular world was the use of bed-clothes. Again we see an extensive change from the original constitutions to a modified late medieval situation.[44] Silken bedlinen for abbots or certainly for important

62   *Gerhard Jaritz*

guests of the monasteries were obviously no exception.[45]
Let me conclude. The evidence which we have
presented shows that the material culture and thus
also the standard of living in late medieval cistercian
monasteries of Austria and Germany were very much
influenced by developments in the secular world.[46]
Especially in the fifteenth century the food and some
aspects of clothing and housing in cistercian abbeys
prove that the way of life there was sometimes similar
to that of the nobility or of wealthy townsmen. So,
for average fifteenth century men (mainly townsmen),
joining the cistercian monastic community would often
have meant no decline in their accustomed standard
of living. On the contrary, it may be assumed that
it allowed an improvement. The fourteenth century
seems to have been the period in which this situation
began to occur. At one time--until about the end
of the thirteenth century, when mainly members of
the nobility joined monasteries--the situation appears
to have been the other way round. Then the standard
of living seems to have been higher in the secular
world than in the monastery. Just think of the above
mentioned 'treats' of extra food like white bread,
fish and wine, which were certainly no particular
treat for the nobility. We may also say that the original
cistercian zeal for a poor life had generally diminished,
particularly during the fourteenth century. From this
time onwards necessities included no longer only basic
needs like enough to eat or to wear, but goods of
a kind denoting prosperity and sometimes even 'luxury'.
Comparisons with other orders--which have been made
for the Austrian area with Benedictines, Austin Canons
and Carthusians--have shown that in the fifteenth
century the standard of living in Benedictine and
Augustinian communities was--from a secular point
of view--still higher than in Cistercian.[47] On the
other hand--and of course depending on the rules
--the standard of living in Carthusian houses was
lower.[48]
The degree to which the standard of living in
cistercian monasteries itself could become a model
for 'imitations' by the secular world, is a problem
not yet solved. That imitation was not merely a 'one-
way-road' from the secular world to the monastery
is obvious. A more detailed investigation of the contacts
between seculars and Cistercians and their effect on
material culture and way of life will therefore be
one of the objects of research in the future.

Institut für mittelalterliche Realienkunde Österreichs
Krems/D.

NOTES

1. See Helmut Hundsbichler, 'Approaches to the Daily Life in the Middle Ages. Methods and Aims of the "Institut für mittelalterliche Realienkunde Österreichs"', *Medium Aevum Quotidianum-Newsletter* 1 (Krems, 1982) 19–25.

2. For a more detailed discussion of the relevant sources, see Ernest Persoons, 'Klösterliches Leben und Sachkultur im Spätmittelalter', *Veröffentlichungen des Instituts für mittelalterliche Realienkunde Österreichs* 6, Sitzungsberichte der Österreichischen Akademie der Wissenschaften, phil.-hist. Klasse, 433, 200–218; Gerhard Jaritz, 'Zur Sachkultur österreichischer Klöster des Spätmittelalters', *Klösterliche Sachkultur des Spätmittelalters*, Veröffentlichungen des Instituts für mittelalterliche Realienkunde Österreichs 3 = Sitzungsberichte der Osterreichischen Akademie der Wissenschaften phil.-hist. Klasse 367 (Vienna, 1980) 147–150.

3. For the article by Reinhard Schneider, see *Klösterliche Sachkultur des Spätmittelalters* (see note 2) 43–71. See also Louis J. Lekai, *The Cistercians. Ideals and Reality* (1977) 364–377. Other articles and treatises will be mentioned below in connection with the discussed aspects.

4. For general remarks on daily life and material culture in medieval monasteries, see, e.g., Harry Kühnel, 'Beiträge der Orden zur materiellen Kultur des Mittelalters und weltliche Einflüsse auf die klösterliche Sachkultur', *Klösterliche Sachkultur des Spätmittelalters*, 9–29. See also Léo Moulin, *La vie quotidienne des religieux au Moyen Age Xe-XVe siècle* (Paris, 1978).

5. Gerd Zimmermann, 'Ordensleben und Lebensstandard. Die cura corporis in den Ordensvorschriften des abendländischen Hochmittelalters', Beiträge zur Geschichte des Alten Mönchtums und des Benediktinerordens 32 (Münster/Westfalen, 1973). See also Louis Gougaud, 'Anciennes coutumes claustrales', *Moines et monastères* 8 (Saint Martin de Ligugé, 1930). For some general remarks on legislation and life in the early Cistercian Order, see Louis J. Lekai, 'Ideals and Reality in Early Cistercian Life and Legislation', *Cistercian Ideals and Reality*, CS 60 (Kalamazoo, 1978) 4–29; Bede K. Lackner, 'Early Cistercian Life as Described in the *Ecclesiastica officia*', ibid., 62–79.

6. See, e.g., Zimmermann, *Ordensleben und Lebensstandard*, 37–87 and 243–340; Ludwig Dolberg, 'Die Cistercienser beim Mahle. Servitien und Pitan-

tien', *Studien und Mittheilungen aus dem Bene-
dictiner- und dem Cistercienser-Orden* 17 (1896)
609–629; Johannes Jaeger, *Klosterleben im Mittelalter.
Ein Kulturbild aus der Glanzperiode des Cistercien-
serordens* (Würzburg, 1903) 30–34.

7. Cf. Hektor Ammann, 'Untersuchungen zur Wirtschaftsgeschichte des Oberrheinraumes II. Das Kloster
Salem in der Wirtschaft des ausgehenden Mittelalters', *Zeitschrift für die Geschichte des Oberrheins*
110 (1962) 374–387; Gerhard Jaritz, 'Die Reiner
Rechnungsbücher (1395–1477) als Quelle zur klösterlichen Sachkultur des Spätmittelalters', *Die Funktion
der schriftlichen Quelle in der Sachkulturforschung*,
Veröffentlichungen des Instituts für mittelalterliche
Realienkunde Österreichs 1 = Sitzungsberichte
der Österreichischen Akademie der Wissenschaften,
phil.-hist. Klasse 304/4 (Vienna, 1976) 174–220.
See also below.

8. See Dolberg, 'Die Cistercienser beim Mahle', 609–
615 and 624–627; Georg Lanz, 'Servitien und Anniversarien der Cistercienser-Abtei Heiligenkreuz',
*Studien und Mittheilungen aus dem Benedictiner-
und dem Cistercienser-Orden* 19 (1898) 200–204;
Schneider, 'Lebensverhältnisse bei den Zisterziensern', 54–56.

9. Cf. Gerhard Jaritz, 'Seelenheil und Sachkultur.
Gedanken zur Beziehung Mensch–Objekt im späten
Mittelalter', *Europäische Sachkultur des Mittelalters*
Veröffentlichungen des Instituts für mittelalterliche
Realienkunde Österreichs 4 = Sitzungsberichte
der Österreichischen Akademie der Wissenschaften,
phil.-hist. Klasse 374 (Vienna, 1980) 74–75.

10. Johann v. Frast, 'Urkunden und geschichtliche
Notizen, die sich in den Handschriften des Stiftes
Zwettl finden', *Archiv für Kunde österreichischer
Geschichtsquellen* 2 (1849; reprint 1964) 371–376;
Gerhard Jaritz, 'Zur Sachkultur österreichischer
Klöster', 154.

11. Hermann Watzl, 'Über Pitanzen und Reichnisse
für den Konvent des Klosters Heiligenkreuz 1431',
Analecta Cisterciensia 34 (1978) 40–147, esp. 49.
For Heiligenkreuz, see also Lanz, 'Servitien und
Anniversarien', *Studien und Mittheilungen aus
dem Benedictiner-und dem Cistercienser-Orden*
19 (1898) 389–394, 562–569; 20 (1899) 36–51, 246–
265.

12. Franz Winter, *Die Zisterzienser des nordöstlichen
Deutschlands* 3 (Gotha, 1871; reprint Aalen, 1966)
110–111 (Buch); Ambrosius Schneider, *Die Cistercienserabtei Himmerod im Spätmittelalter* (Himmerod,
1954) 156–157; Schneider, 'Lebensverhältnisse

bei den Zisterziensern', 55–56 (Eberbach, Marienstatt); Edgar Krausen, 'Die Wirtschaftsgeschichte der ehemaligen Cistercienserabtei Raitenhaslach bis zum Ausgang des Mittelalters', *Südostbayerische Heimatstudien* 13 (Hirschenhausen, 1937) 69 and 121. On the other hand, e.g., in the abbey of Salem such an accumulation of pittances does not seem to have existed (Werner Rösener, 'Reichsabtei Salem. Verfassungs- und Wirtschaftsgeschichte des Zisterzienserklosters von der Gründung bis zur Mitte des 14. Jahrhunderts', *Vorträge und Forschungen* Sonderband 13 [Sigmaringen, 1974] 157).

13. See Dolberg, 'Die Cistercienser beim Mahle', 624–629.
14. Cf. Hanns Koren, *Die Spende* (Graz, Vienna, Cologne, 1954) 37–41.
15. Norbert Müller, 'Seelgerätstiftungen beim Stift Rein', (Diss., Graz, 1976) 98.
16. 1439 July 25: Hans Mosler, ed., 'Urkundenbuch der Abtei Altenberg 2; in *Urkundenbücher der geistlichen Stiftungen des Niederrheins* III/2 (Düsseldorf, 1955) 147, n. 126).
17. Jaritz, 'Die Reiner Rechnungsbücher', 182–185.
18. Gabriele Schnorrenberger, *Wirtschaftsverwaltung des Klosters Eberbach im Rheingau 1431–1631* (Mainz, 1976) 87–88; Alfred Heidacher, *Die Entstehungs- und Wirtschaftsgeschichte des Klosters Heilsbronn bis zum Ende des 15. Jahrhunderts* (Bonn, 1955) 118–119 and 146; Ammann, 'Untersuchungen zur Wirtschaftsgeschichte des Oberrheinraumes', 386–387 (Salem); Robert Pahncke, *Schulpforte: Geschichte des Zisterzienserklosters Pforte* (Leipzig, 1956) 123.
19. Jaritz, 'Zur Sachkultur österreichischer Klöster', 152.
20. Ibid., 153–154.
21. For the purchase of such goods by cistercian monasteries, see, e.g., Franz Bastian, 'Das älteste Aldersbacher Rechnungsbuch und die Verwendung klösterlicher Zollfreiheiten im bürgerlichen Handel', *Staat und Volkstum* (Diessen, 1933) 23–24; Heidacher, *Die Entstehungs-und Wirtschaftsgeschichte des Klosters Heilsbronn*, 146; Ammann, 'Untersuchungen zur Wirtschaftsgeschichte des Oberrheinraumes', 387 (Salem); Schnorrenberger, *Wirtschaftsverwaltung des Klosters Eberbach*, 89–90; Jaritz, 'Die Reiner Rechnungsbücher', 192–193, 198–206; the Zwettl archives, ms. 270; an account-book of abbot Wolfgang 1495–1510, foll. 9r, 24v, 41r, 72r, 76r, 78v, etc.
22. For the kitchens in the monasteries, see Ludwig

Dolberg, 'Die Kirchen und Klöster der Cistercienser
nach den Angaben des "liber usuum" des Ordens',
*Studien und Mittheilungen aus dem Benedictiner-
und dem Cistercienser-Orden* 12 (1891) 51; Jaritz,
'Die Reiner Rechnungsbücher', 209–211.

23. Cf., e.g., the statute of the General Chapter
of 1357, which generally condemned excesses in
monastic nutrition (certainly including pittances,
lenten fare, etc.): Josephus-Maria Canivez, *Statuta
Capitulorum Generalium Ordinis Cisterciensis* III
(1935) 533, n. 1357,4.

24. Cf. the statutes of the General Chapter of 1486
for Eberbach, Heisterbach, Marienstatt and Eusser-
thal, making certain concessions regarding the
consumption of meat because of the high price
of fish and other lenten fare: Canivez, *Statuta*
V:552, nn. 1486, 74–77. For an example of the
aristocratic secular world, see Helmut Hundsbichler-
Gerhard Jaritz-Elisabeth Vavra, 'Tradition? Stagnation? Innovation? –Die Rolle des Adels für die
spätmittelalterliche Sachkultur', *Adelige Sachkultur
des Spätmittelalters,* Veröffentlichungen des Instituts
für mittelalterliche Realienkunde Österreichs 5
= Sitzungsberichte der österreichischen Akademie
der Wissenschaften, phil.-hist. Klasse 400, 65–
66.

25. See Gregor Müller, 'Der Fleischgenuss im Orden',
Cistercienser-Chronik 18 (1906) 25–30, 58–61, 125–
128, 183–187, 212–221, 247–252, 278–283, 367–370;
Klaus Schreiner, 'Zisterziensiches Mönchtum und
soziale Umwelt. Wirtschaftlicher und sozialer Struk-
turwandel in hoch- und spätmittelalterlichen Zister-
zienserkonventen', in Caspar Elm, ed., *Die Zisterzienser. Ordensleben zwischen Ideal und Wirklichkeit,
Ergänzungsband* (Cologne, 1982) 106–109.

26. Hohenfurt: 1398 December 4, Rome (Mathias Prangerl,
ed., 'Urkundenbuch des Cistercienserstiftes B.
Mariae V. zu Hohenfurt in Böhmen', *Fontes rerum
Austriacarum* 2/XXIII [Vienna, 1865] 219–220,
n.CLXXXVII); 1453 September 6, Wilhering (*Ibid.*
280, n.CCXXV). Marienstatt: Schneider, 'Lebensverhältnisse bein den Zisterziensern', 54, n.66. Dargun
and Doberan: 1432 April 21, Rome (Gerhard Schlegel,
'Das Zisterzienserkloster Dargun 1172–1552', *Studien
zur katholischen Bistums- und Klostergeschichte*
22 [Leipzig, 1980] 70, n.37). A concession for
a resigned abbot to eat meat because of his senility
(*senio confractus*) is known from the monastery
of Hude: 1412 June 11, Rome (Gustav Rüthning,
'Urkundenbuch der Grafschaft Oldenburg. Klöster
und Kollegiatkirchen', *Oldenburgisches Urkundenbuch*

[Oldenburg, 1928] p. 214, n. 519). The *Landbuch* of the cistercian abbey of Zinna (1470) clearly shows that meat was served; it contains interesting remarks concerning the monastic officers responsible for meals with or without meat: Wolfgang Ribbe-Johannes Schultze, edd., 'Das Landbuch des Klosters Zinna', *Zisterzienser-Studien* II (Berlin, 1976) 168 and 172. That a meal without meat in a cistercian monastery could nevertheless be delicious is shown by a description of bishop Siegfried of Speyer concerning his visit to Maulbronn in 1456 (Karl Klunzinger, *Urkundliche Geschichte der vormaligen Cisterzienser-Abtei Maulbronn* [Stuttgart, 1834] 110–111).

27. See, e.g., Schreiner, 'Zisterziensisches Mönchtum und soziales Umfeld', 100–102; Gerhard Jaritz, 'Die Konventualen der Zisterzen Rein, Sittich und Neuberg im Mittelalter', *Cîteaux: Commentarii Cistercienses* 29 (1978) 60–92 and 268–303.

28. Rüthning, 'Urkundenbuch der Grafschaft Oldenburg', p. 151, n. 345 (1306 April 30, Hude).

29. Gerhard Winner, 'Die Urkunden des Zisterzienserstiftes Lilienfeld', *Fontes rerum Austriacarum* 2/81 (Vienna, 1974) p. 333, n. 888 (1382 February 26, Vienna).

30. Inventory of Neukloster/Wiener Neustadt (Lower Austria) of 1446 April 19, two years after the foundation of the monastery (Neukloster archives, Wiener Neustadt, ms. K 363, fol. 93r): 'Item in refectorio pro conventu habentur cantari parvi et magni 27, item in cellario cantari magni 4, scutelle pro refectorio stanneae 50, item scutelle magne 12, item mediocres 10, disci stanneae 12'. See also, e.g., Zwettl archives, ms. 270, foll. 16v, 31v, 33v, 36r, etc. For the German monastery of Altenberg, see Mosler, 'Urkundenbuch der Abtei Altenberg 2', 317–318 (1499–1502).

31. See Gerhard Jaritz, 'Österreichische Bürgertestamente als Quelle zur Erforschung städtischer Lebensformen des Spämittelalters', *Jahrbuch für Geschichte des Feudalismus* 8 (1984), in press. For Germany, see Max Hasse, 'Neues Hausgerät, neue Häuser, neue Kleider-Eine Betrachtung der städtischen Kultur im 13. und 14. Jahrhundert sowie ein Katalog der metallenen Hausgeräte', *Zeitschrift für Archäologie des Mittelalters* 7 (1979) 33 and 39.

32. Some examples of cistercian inventories in which such secular show-pieces are mentioned: Neukloster (1446; see note 30), fol. 92v; Zwettl (1451 June 20, archive of Zwettl, ms. 95, fol. 135v); Heiligen-

kreuz (1470 July 2 and 1516 May 21; see Hermann
Watzl, 'Die zwei ältesten Inventare der Cisterce
Heiligenkreuz von 1470 und 1516', *Jahrbuch für
Landeskunde von Niederösterreich*, NF 36 [1964]
269–279); Lilienfeld (1497 May 16; see Winner,
'Die Urkunden des Stiftes Lilienfeld', pp. 451–
452, n. 1243). See also Jaritz, 'Zur Sachkultur
österreichischer Klöster', 158.
Precious tableware is also mentioned in late
medieval donations to cistercian monasteries or
purchases by the abbot or a member of the community; see, e.g., Jaritz, 'Seelenheil und Sachkultur',
71–73; Georg Muck, *Geschichte von Kloster Heilsbronn*
1 (Nördlingen, 1879) 169, 183, 210–211, 241–242;
Edgar Krausen, 'Die Zisterzienserabtei Raitenhaslach', *Germania Sacra* 11/1, (Berlin–New York,
1977) 282 (1447 January 20); Michael Frey, ed.,
*Urkundenbuch des Klosters Otterberg in der Rhein-
pfalz* (Mainz, 1845) pp. 365–366, n. 416 (1329
March 27); archive of Zwettl, ms. 270, foll. 32v
(1497), 44r and 44v (1498), 69v (1501), etc.
    For such objects ordered or bought by abbots
and used as presents for secular and ecclesiastical
authorities, see, e.g., N. Muffat, 'Historische
Notizen aus einem Rechnungsbuche des Klosters
Aldersbach', *Quellen zur bayerischen und deutschen
Geschichte* I (Munich, 1856) 458.
33. Canivez, *Statuta* II: p. 347, n. 1250, 6; III:
     p. 246, n. 1290, 4. See also Schneider, 'Lebensver-
     hältnisse bei den Zisterziensern', 48.
34. Archive of Rein (Styria), Lat. A 9, 6, foll. 4r–
     4v (1522 May 18, Sittich); see Jaritz, 'Zur Sachkul-
     tur österreichischer Klöster', 159–160.
35. For the kind and number of clothes given to novices
     and monks of a cistercian monastery in the late
     Middle Ages, see, e.g., Schneider, 'Lebensverhält-
     nisse bei den Zisterziensern', 58–60. See also
     the regulations of the abbey of Altenberg of 1499–
     1502 ('Eynen novicien zo cleyden'; 'Eynen zo
     der profess zo cleyden'): Mosler, 'Urkundenbuch
     der Abtei Altenberg 2', 317. For a comparison
     with the rules of early Cistercians and other
     monastic communities of the High Middle Ages,
     see Zimmermann, *Ordensleben und Lebensstandard*,
     88–117 and 341–403; see also Ludwig Dolberg,
     'Die Tracht der Cistercienser nach dem liber usuum
     und den Statuten', *Studien und Mittheilungen
     aus dem Benedictiner- und dem Cistercienser-Orden*
     14 (1893) 359–367 and 530–538; Jaeger, *Klosterleben*,
     36–39. Concerning the 'luxury' of clothes condemned
     by the General Chapter and visitation-protocols,

36. see, e.g., J. B. Kaiser, 'Das Visitationsprotokoll des Klosters Werschweiler vom Jahre 1473', *Cistercienser-Chronik* 27 (1915) 260; Schneider, 'Lebensverhältnisse bei Zisterziensern', 57-59.

36. See, e.g., Jaritz, 'Die Reiner Rechnungsbücher', 222-227; Muck, *Geschichte von Kloster Heilsbronn* 1, 597; Heidacher, *Die Entstehungs- und Wirtschaftsgeschichte des Klosters Heilsbronn*, 129; Ammann, 'Untersuchungen zur Wirtschaftsgeschichte des Oberrheinraumes', 383-385 and 400-404; Bastian, 'Das älteste Aldersbacher Rechnungsbuch', 26-27; Schnorrenberger, *Wirtschaftsverwaltung des Klosters Eberbach*, 92.

37. See Hektor Ammann, 'Deutschland und die Tuchindustrie Nordwesteuropas im Mittelalter', *Die Stadt des Mittelalters* 3, Wege der Forschung 245 (Darmstadt, 1973) 132.

38. For Austrian examples, see Jaritz, 'Zur Sachkultur in österreichischen Klöstern', 159. For the cistercian situation concerning 'foreign' goods, see the general remarks by Ammann, 'Untersuchungen zur Wirtschaftsgeschichte des Oberrheinraumes', 397-398.

39. See, e.g., Schneider, 'Lebensverhältnisse bei den Zisterziensern', 58-59; Jaritz, 'Die Reiner Rechnungsbücher, 233-237; Zwettl archives, ms. 270, foll. 11v, 18r, 27v, 30r, etc.; Rein archives, Lat. A 9, 6, fol. 4r (1522 May 18, Sittich).

40. For the situation in the secular world, see, e.g., Harry Kühnel, 'Ziele der Erforschung der Sachkultur des Mittelalters', *Rotterdam Papers* 4 (1982) 119-123. For the comfort in a cistercian *domus abbatis*, see, e.g., Schnorrenberger, *Wirtschaftsverwaltung des Klosters Eberbach*, 24-25 (1501).

41. For the heating of cistercian monasteries, see, e.g., Dolberg, 'Die Kirchen und Klöster', 50; Jaeger, *Klosterleben im Mittelalter*, 40. See also particularly a statute of the General Chapter of 1442: 'Abbati monasterii de Caritate praecipitur districtissime, quatinus caminos et ostia camerarum quae sunt in dormitorio monasterii de Balerna, quantocius poterit accedendo ad praefatum monasterium, omnino destruat et extirpet,...' (Canivez, *Statuta* 4: p. 527, n. 1442, 527).

42. See Jaritz, 'Die Reiner Rechnungsbücher', 168-169; Zwettl archives, ms. 270, foll. 63v, 64v, 69r, 76v, 77r, etc.

43. Jaritz, 'Die Reiner Rechnungsbücher', 164; Zwettl archives, ms. 270, foll. 29r, 29v, 30r, 30v, 32r, 32v, etc.

44. For the use of bed-clothes in the Cistercian
Order, see Dolberg, 'Die Kirchen und Klöster',
47-48; Mosler, 'Urkundenbuch der Abtei Altenberg',
317-318 (regulations 1499-1502).

45. See, e.g., Schneider, 'Lebensverhältnisse bei
den Zisterziensern', 50; Jaritz, 'Die Reiner Rechnungsbücher', 240-241.

46. Cf. the regulations for the administration of-
---partly very secular--donations to the monastery
of Walkenried given by the abbot (1376 September
17): '...omne genus pannorum nobilium coloratorum
et intextorum, sericum, bissum, purpuram, etc.
Item culcitras, cussinos ornatos, pelles omnigenas,
fibulas, aurum, argentum, ceram, sepum et quicquid
datur pro missis....omne pannum lineum et vesti-
menta qualiacunque, qualitercunque colorata,
jopulas, equos et annonam cujuslibet generis
et quicquid datur ad structuram....lineum pannum
non coloratum, cussinos simplices, lectos cujuslibet
conditionis et sacrofagos'. ('Die Urkunden des
Stiftes Walkenried 2', *Urkundenbuch des historischen
Vereins für Niedersachsen* III|1, Hannover, 1855.
p. 302, n. 160).

47. For some examples, see Jaritz, 'Zur Sachkultur
österreichischer Klöster', 147-168; idem, 'Zur
Alltagskultur im spätmittelalterlichen St. Peter',
Festschrift St Peter zu Salzburg 582-1982, Studien
und Mitteilungen zur Geschichte des Benediktiner-
Ordens und seiner Zweige 93 (1982) 548-569.
See also Laurenz Strebl, 'Zu Schreibung, Sprache
und Kulturleben in Klosterneuburger Rechnungsbüchern' (Diss. Vienna, 1956); Floridus Röhrig,
'Das kunstgeschichtliche Material aus den Klosterneuburger Rechnungsbüchern des 14. und 15. Jahrhunderts', *Jahrbuch des Stiftes Klosterneuburg*,
NF 6 (1966) 137-178.

48. For Austria, see Gerhard Jaritz, 'Zu Alltagsleben
und Sachkultur in niederösterreichischen Kartausen
des Spätmittelalters', *Die Kartäuser in Österreich*
3, Analecta Cartusiana 83 (Salzburg, 1981) 21-
33.

GRADATION: RHETORIC AND SUBSTANCE
IN SAINT BERNARD

Robert M. Dresser

No small part of Bernard of Clairvaux's formative influence in Christian spirituality is due to his rhetorical powers. Certainly his legendary attractiveness and his capacity for persuasion depended upon his skill with words. Still, that in itself would have been no guarantee that his efforts would produce any enduring advance in the science of devotion. Yet the fact is that even today we are able to recognize a transforming potential in Bernard's ability to take commonplace observations and turn them into profound, fresh insights. That synthesis of elegant expression and authentic invention is abundantly present in his treatises, perhaps more there than elsewhere in his writings. My purpose is to examine some of these treatises to demonstrate how this is so.

Three of the treatises immediately illustrate the point: first, the earliest of Bernard's published works, *De gradibus humilitatis et superbiae (The Steps of Humility and Pride)*;[1] then a slightly later and more sophisticated work, *De diligendo Deo (On Loving God)*;[2] and, finally, a work of Bernard's authorial maturity, *De consideratione ad Eugenium Papam (On consideration: To Pope Eugene)*.[3] These will form the basis for this study.

Among the artifices of composition which distinguish these texts, one figure of thought is particularly generative of new perceptions of truth, viz., 'gradation'.[4] Sometimes this is called 'climax' or—in Latin —*scala*, both meaning a ladder. It means, simply, presenting related ideas in ascending order of importance. It is common both to profane and to ecclesiastical writing, but seldom has its effectiveness been realized as fully as in Saint Bernard's work.

The first of the works, *De gradibus humilitatis,* is concerned with ethical and ascetical questions. It is cast in two parts: a theoretical and a practical. In anticipation of finding an even more striking example in the initial part, we turn first to the latter portion. Here, Bernard names twelve steps of pride and shows how each in turn becomes more insidious. The sequence occupies chapters ten through twenty-one of the treatise. The elements of the gradation are sufficiently self-explanatory to be listed by title:

1. *Curiositas*	vain inquisitiveness
2. *Levitas animi*	frivolity
3. *Inepta laetitia*	foolish mirth
4. *Jactantia*	boastfulness
5. *Singularitas*	singularity
6. *Arrogantia*	conceit
7. *Praesumptio*	audacity
8. *Defensio peccatorum*	excusing sins
9. *Simulata confessio*	hypocritical confession
10. *Rebellio*	defiance
11. *Libertas peccandi*	freedom to sin
12. *Consuetudo peccandi*	habitual sinning[5]

At first glance, this list seems to be simply a random catalogue. If we classify the twelve steps into successive triplets, however, we see that they constitute an incremental progression, that is, from acting the nuisance to self-service and thence to hard-heartedness and ultimate mutiny. The scale begins with veniality and leads to consummate errancy—even though the individual sins, considered separately, are seemingly unremarkable.[6]

Since no sane person intentionally sets out to excel in evil, it is clear that the gradation is intended ironically. It assumes the form of climax, but its content is just the opposite; it is a *metacosmesis* or descending gradation. The intended message is given rhetorical force by its playful expression; the reader cannot help but acknowledge the gravity of what is being said (as familiar as the sentiments may be) because of the very perversity of the notion of a ladder of sins. One writer has suggested: 'The *descensus* is an experience of the moral sense, every step of which is recorded and may therefore be retraced upon a familiar *scala ascensus*'.[7] That particular *scala* would have been familiar enough to Bernard's audience. Indeed, it was an established staple of monastic reading, being drawn from a passage in the Rule of Saint Benedict.[8]

Benedict's ladder had twelve steps as well, but they were designed to illustrate an ideal to be achieved rather than errors to be avoided. These steps were neither as succinct nor as progressively ordered as were Bernard's, but the general resemblance is immediately evident:

1. *Timorem Dei sibi ante oculos semper ponere*
   (always to fear God)
2. *Non implere desideria sua*
   (not to be fulfilling one's own wants)
3. *Se subdare maiori*
   (to be subject to one's superior)

4. *Patientiam amplexari in obedientia*
(to embrace patience as regards matters of obedience)
5. *Confiteri mala sua*
(to confess wrong doings)
6. *Se judicare malum et indignum*
(to have conviction of one's wrongfulness and unworth)
7. *Se credere vilem esse*
(to believe oneself to be lowly)
8. *Nihil agere nisi quod cohortantur regula vel maiores*
(to do nothing not ordered by the rule or by superiors)
9. *Taciturnitem habere*
(to keep silence)
10. *Non facilem in risu esse*
(not to be too ready to laugh)
11. *Humiliter loquari et pauca verba*
(to speak humbly and in few words)
12. *Se indicare ipso corpore humilem esse*
(to show humility in one's bearing)[9]

The rhetorical *coup* which Bernard accomplishes results from inverting this model. That he underscores a present good which is capable of loss in preference to an as-yet-unattained goal is perhaps suggestive of a certain optimism concerning human nature which Bernard characteristically displays. In any case, in thus aiding his monks to view a familiar pattern in a new light, the sobriety of the original is lightened by gentle humor.[10]

Just prior to the steps of pride in the *De gradibus humilitate*, we find an interesting transition. Bernard has been alluding to Saint Paul's rapture in the third heaven[11]—another sort of climax, no doubt—from which heights he brings the reader abruptly back to earth:

What business has a poor wretch like me to do prowling about the two higher heavens? ...I have quite enough for my hands and feet beneath the lowest heaven. Thanks to the help of him who called me I have built a ladder *(mihi scalam erexi)* to take me to it.[12]

This passage is meant to prepare us for the next topic, a recollection of Jacob's well-known ladder, the scriptural antitype of Saint Benedict's steps of humility.

To draw upon Holy Writ at just this point is

to announce a matter possessing special authority. To cite the typology is, in itself, to evoke its allegory. Even more it is the quasi-biblical diction which signals the presence of a *typos*. The passage contains an almost verbatim citation from Genesis 28 as it continues: *Jam Dominum desuper innixum suscipio...* (Already I see God, resting on top of the ladder...).[13] The typology, let it be said, does not originate with Bernard. He had it right at hand in Benedict's treatment of the original twelve steps: *Actibus nostris ascendentibus scala illa erigenda est, quae in somnio Iacob apparuit* (By our ascending acts that ladder which appeared to Jacob in his dream must be erected).[14] Yet Bernard does not fail to bring this into his argument because he has nothing of his own to add; he does it because he is emphatically announcing that his *scala* is none other than that which his predecessor had cited, and that the one and the same ladder is—as was Jacob's—a ladder of salvation. In the event, the reader is shown salvation as much by recognizing what he must avoid as by remembering the goal he should seek. As Bernard notes, the ladder is 'for those who come down, the way of iniquity; for those who go up, the way of truth'.[15]

We noted that the form of the *De gradibus humilitate* is binary. While the second section is perhaps the more arresting, the first has the greater profundity. Indeed, it is this theoretical consideration that gives the twelve steps of pride their full significance. What we find here is 'three steps of truth'. In these steps we proceed from the world of appearances to the realm of glory.[16] To extend a metaphor, we are given the foundation—the metaphysical foundation, if you will—on which the very idea of a ladder to heaven must stand.[17]

That foundation lies on three distinct levels, each of which is a different grade of knowledge. To have the fulness of such knowledge is to have humility, the very subject of the whole treatise. The levels are as follows:

1. SELF-KNOWLEDGE
   Attendas quod es, quia vere miser es
   (Pay attention to what you are, because you are truly full of misery).[18]

2. KNOWLEDGE OF ONE'S NEIGHBOR
   Veritatem in proximus inquirunt dum ex his, quae patiuntur, patientibus compati sciunt
   (They seek the truth in their neighbors and from the things they themselves

have   suffered   they   learn   compassion).[19]

3. KNOWLEDGE OF GOD
   Beati mundo corde, quoniam ipsi Deum
   videbunt
   (Blessed   are   the   clean   of   heart   for   they
   shall see God—Mt 5:8).[20]

In   the   actual   treatise,   the   steps   are   presented   in
a   less   obviously   schematic   fashion;   still,   this   is   the
underlying   plan   of   Bernard's   exposition.   Once   again,
we   find   that   he   has   employed   a   familiar   theme   from
Scripture—in   this   case   the   so-called   'summary   of   the
law'   (Mt.   22:37-39   and   parallels).

This   latest   gradation   is   a   triad   which   originated
with   Jesus'   conflation   of   two   texts   from   the   Pentateuch,
Deuteronomy   6:5   and   Leviticus   19:18—a   compression
of   the   Decalogue   and   yet   a   new   emphasis   in   ethical
norms:

1. *Diliges Dominum Deum tuum...*   Love your God
2. *Diliges proximum tuum—*   Love your neighbor
3. *sicut teipsum*   as yourself

It   is   not   usually   acknowledged   that   this   too   is   the
work   of   a   gifted   rhetorician,   one   whose   mind   perhaps
operated   on   principles   not   far   removed   from   those
informing   Bernard.   In   any   case,   we   are   fortunate
in   that   Bernard   did   not   hold   this   extremely   sacred
text   in   such   reverence   that   he   was   prevented   from
adapting   it   freely   to   match   his   own   insight.

There   are   two   emendations   from   the   original:
the   inversion   of   order   and   a   substitution   in   the   governing   verb.   In   his   choice   of   verb,   Bernard   perhaps
drew   upon   1   John,   which   so   clearly   envisages   a   correla-
tion   of   love   and   knowledge.   Since   these   are   the   preëmi-
nent   modes   by   which   rational   beings   relate   to   one
another,   the   exchange   of   *agnoscere*   (to   know)   with
diligere   (to   love)   is   a   natural   one.[21]   Actually,   while
love   involves   a   subjective   sentiment,   it   is,   in   a   certain
way,   more   objective   than   knowledge.   This   is   because
the   latter   is   a   kind   of   gathering   unto   oneself,   while
the   former   implies   a   movement   toward   another,   as
Bernard   notes   elsewhere.[22]   The   implication   is   that
intellection   of   the   Good   will   inevitably   lead   to   an
affection   for   it,   an   idea   going   back   to   Plato.

As   to   the   inversion,   Bernard's   motive   seems   to
have   been   as   much   to   secure   clarity   as   to   promote
novelty.   He   will   educate   his   audience   by   drawing
them   in   easy   steps   from   the   familiar   to   the   unknown.
In   this   he   shows   a   predilection   for   the   concrete   and
psychological   over   the   speculative.   The   self   is   the
one   entity   of   which   everyone   living   has   first-hand

knowledge. A little experience suggests that others
must feel something of what I feel, and thus I can
begin to know another. This is, in turn, related to
reaching out further to know God. It is parallel to
the point raised in 1 John 4:20: 'One who has no
love for the brother he has seen cannot love the God
he has not seen' (New American Bible). This idea
will be more fully expounded in the *De diligendo Deo*,
but even in this treatise, the interrelation of knowledge
and love is strongly affirmed:

> These are the three steps of truth. We climb
> to the first by the toil of humility, to the
> second by a deep feeling of compassion,
> and to the third by the ecstasy of contempla-
> tion. On the first step we experience the
> severity of truth, on the second its tenderness,
> and on the third its purity. Reason brings
> us to the first as we judge ourselves; compas-
> sion brings us to the second when we have
> mercy on others; on the third the purity
> of truth sweeps us up to the sight of things
> invisible.[23]

Note how the progression of concrete terms (self/neigh-
bor/God) has given way to one of abstractions (reason/
affection/purity). Underlying the second triad is another
sequence, that of the soul's faculties: mind, heart,
and will.[24] Bernard could have taken the further
step of noting that when *caritas* pervades these faculties, we have a paradigm of the Blessed Trinity.[25]
Surely it is no accident that his next subject (chapter
7) is the Trinity.

In the steps of truth lies the germ of much of
Bernard's teaching. It depicts the progression from
the carnal to the eternal. There is, to be sure, a
vast gulf between the two, but Bernard does not perceive
it as infinite. This is because he thinks, not in terms
of dichotomies, which were to become the hallmark
of dialectical scholasticism, but in hierarchies, as
a metaphysician in the platonic tradition. Gradation,
not antithesis, is therefore very prominent in his
thought and expression.[26]

This does not, however, mean that Bernard is
a crypto-pantheist or emanationist. He held that there
is a real continuum from the here to the beyond is
possible only because of Christ the Mediator. In the
hypostatic union of divine and human is to be found
the path by which we move from the miserable to
the sublime, from the contingent to the absolute.[27]
Should it seem an impossible distance from the brother

one has seen to God whom one has not, this is only
because we fail to take into account that Christ is
our brother as well as our Lord. For Bernard the
concept of neighbor incorporates 'Christ according
to the flesh'—*secundum carnem.*[28] Only because God
became incarnate can there be such ladders, whether
of knowledge or of love or of humility.

We see then that the figure of gradation is not
so much an accident of Bernard's speech as it is
the matrix of some of his most penetrating thought.
In the later treatises, we see the archetype—for such
it is—of the ladder in a yet more extended image.
In *De diligendo Deo,* the operative progression
is four- rather than three-fold. An increase of one
element may seem a small matter, but in reality it
broadly increases the resulting field-of-vision. This
new gradation has to do with the desire for God,
dilectio, the most powerful force in the universe.
The content of the treatise as a whole has been well
summarized by Robert Walton:

> After considering man's motives for loving
> God, St Bernard analyzes this love, which
> he divides into four degrees. The first degree
> is that in which man loves himself for natural
> reasons. Later he learns that he cannot subsist
> without his neighbor, he has to rely on divine
> help when facing life's hardships, and he
> needs God's pardon when he sins. Thus man
> loves God for the good he has received, which
> constitutes the second degree of love. Since
> only a heart of stone could fail to see how
> lovable such a benefactor is, man moves
> on to the third degree of love in which God
> is loved for his own goodness. The fourth
> degree of love is different from the preceding
> ones. It is so perfect that the soul cannot
> love anything but God, it cannot even love
> itself except for God's sake.[29]

Again, we schematize the steps indicated herein
by title. Note that it is possible to define the first
three steps affirmatively, but that the ultimate step
requires a negation:

1. *Amor carnalis*   natural affection for self
2. *Amor Dei propter se*   God, on account of his
                              gifts to oneself

3. *Amor Dei propter Ipsum*   God, for God's own sake
4. *Nec seipsum amare nisi*   divine affection reflected
   propter Deum[30]   toward oneself

Beyond the obvious added fourth stage, there are
two main departures from the type of gradation found
in the steps of truth. First, the love of neighbor
cedes itself to the love of God for his gifts—understanding, of course, that the neighbor may be counted
among those gifts. The second change is concerned
with the complication of the pattern of arrangement
which has come in with the fourth element.

In the steps of truth, there was one subject (the
self) and three objects: the self as experienced reflexive-
ly, the neighbor, and God. Here there are, in addition
to the self as the single subject, two objects—the
reflexive self and God[31]—plus two causal agents which
happen to be identical in name, but not in function,
with the objects. The reasoning bears a kind of resemblance to the double accusative in grammar. It can
best be shown in a diagram, understanding that in
each case the subject is the self-as-lover:

Step	Object of the Love	Cause of the Love	Abstract Sign
1.	The self	The self	A:A
2.	God	The self	B:A
3.	God	God	B:B
4.	The self	God	A:B

The gradation which emerges here takes the form
A:A/B:A/B:B/A:B. It is perhaps an unexpected progression
because it is less symmetrical than the more likely
A:A/B:A/A:B/B:B, beginning, that is, with self-for-
the-sake-of-self and ending with God-for-the-sake-of-
God. Why did Bernard incline toward the less predictable
alternative? He did not necessarily visualize it abstractly
as we have done here, but he must have had an intuitive
sense about the shape of the progression.

Perhaps the turn of Bernard's mind can be traced
in the fact that the first three steps here—A:A/B:A/B:B
—are exactly parallel to the pattern suggested by
the incarnation of Christ, which may be stated as
'humanity (equivalent to the self)/divinity *and* humanity
(equivalent to Christ the mediator)/divinity (equivalent
to God the Wholly Other).' All that is needed to complete
the progression is the 'A:B' term: humanity subsumed
into the divinity, which is the ultimate meaning of
loving oneself for God's sake.

Furthermore, as we have noted, there is a formal
difference between the first three and the last of
the steps, for step four is expressed as a negative
rather than a positive element. It is as if the rhythm
of Bernard's mind were counting out, 'One, two, three...
and four'. That pause, just before the fourth step,
is as significant as the order of the steps. It is
an 'eschatalogical' pause, because the fourth step

has to do primarily with the life of the age to come. It marks the boundary of what is normally attainable under the conditions of this mortal life and what characterizes the final consummation. Bernard says as much in chapter ten of the treatise.[32]

To ascend even to the third degree, the love of God for God's own sake, is to attain to such a state of purification that the soul's deification has begun.[33] Its eventual fruit would be the renewal of the *similitudo Dei*, the likeness of God, and thus return to one's pristine state. Only when that has taken place can one expect to love--or even to know--oneself in a truly selfless way. The name for this state, which--if it is to occur at all in this life--can only be a momentary flash, is ecstasy, *excessus*.[34] The promise of eternal life is that the ecstasy will be permanently enjoyed.

Returning, however, to our rhetorical analysis, we should note that the ultimate stage of love in this four-fold scheme confirms the beginning. The gradation has verisimilitude because it is grounded in the observable fact that our self-love is natural.[35] We proceed from the known to the as-yet-unknown, just as we did in the three steps of truth. But here, when we arrive at the goal, we find that it is, in one sense, the starting place: *from* love of self *to* love of self, though a much more elevated love at the end. How encouraging this is morally! How aesthetical- ly reassuring, rhetorically! We see that love of self is to be, not destroyed, but transformed.

Clearly this undercuts any notion that the love of the self is an unqualified evil. Such a view tacitly assumes that all that can really be said about human nature is comprehended in the term 'original sin'. While Bernard never undervalued this aspect of human existence, he also knew that without something worthy of being redeemed there never would or could have been the Redemption. Thus, the four-fold gradation of *De diligendo Deo,* rhetorical though it may be, encompasses the solution to the key theoretical problem of moral theology: human worth. It cuts through the dilemmas which arise out of the Augustinian/Pelagian antithesis, and it does so concretely, in the context of the common human struggle in which we are all engaged. The spirit of Bernard's insight here is conveyed in a very personal way in a prayer which he frames as an expression of universal hope:

> My God, my help, I shall love you as much
> as I am able for your gift. My love is less
> than your due, yet not less than I am able,

for even if I cannot love you as much as
I should, still I cannot love you more than
I can.36

We turn now to a quite different sort of work.
De consideratione was composed as a series of practical
admonitions for the reigning pope, Eugenius III (1145–
53). While touching on matters ascetical here and
there, it is primarily a work of pastoral theology.37
In it, Bernard again has recourse to gradation. Indeed,
this pattern virtually governs the entire work.38
The treatise encompasses many topics concerned
with the government of the Church, but our focus
is confined to what may be called the 'steps of consideration'.39 These are themes which Bernard commends
to the Pope for his reflection and guidance. Not surprisingly, the steps commence with the self. Note the
order in which they occur:

1. *Te consideranda quae*   things concerning yourself
   pertineat ad te ipsum
2. *Quae sub te*   things which are beneath you
3. *Quae circa te*   things which are about you
4. *Quae supra te*40   things which are above you.

Unlike the gradation in *De diligendo Deo,* which apparently is Bernard's own invention, this progression was
already something of a commonplace. Its immediate
source would be Hildemar, a ninth-century commentator
of the Benedictine Rule; its ultimate source is probably
Saint Augustine. Bernard could be drawing on either
or both.41
As it existed before Bernard's version, the progression moved from things above the self to the self,
then to things next to the self (on the same plane
as oneself), and finally to things beneath the self.42
A comparison of the two schemes shows that the original
was linear, whereas Bernard's is spherical in effect.
Bernard places his addressee at the bottom of the
ladder, not to denigrate the Supreme Pontiff, but
to emphasize his status as servant of servants. The
context of the treatise here shows that from his vantage,
looking up the ladder, the Pope must recognize that
even those persons and affairs which he rules *(quae
sub te)* possess an importance greater than his own,
at least in relation to his official role as Chief Pastor.
Therefore, paradoxically, no matter which way he
turns his gaze—beneath, around, or above himself
—the direction from a moral point of view will be
up. It is an elegant conceit, not without its gentle
irony, inasmuch as it concerns some one virtually

at the apex of medieval human society.

Each of the four books which follows the introductory book treats in turn one of the foregoing steps. It is in this sense that gradation actually governs the treatise as a whole. In Book II, under the heading of self, Bernard reminds his reader of who he is (a man), of what he is (the pope), and of what quality he is. In Book III, the term *sub te* covers the various categories of persons under papal jurisdiction and care. *Circa te* (Book IV) deals with the Romans, the Curia, and the immediate papal household. In the final book stand the things *supra te,* and here the theologically most significant topics are found: the hierarchy of angels, the Blessed Trinity, and the Incarnate Christ.

The inclusion of the angelic hierarchy here is both a sign of twelfth-century concerns and yet another instance of gradation. Each of the nine traditionally-recognized orders of angels is designated in ascending degree, and is assigned a distinctive ministry in accordance with its rank:

1. Angels—guardians of individual human beings
2. Archangels—messengers to the same
3. Virtues—instigators of cosmic portents
4. Powers (*potestates*)—wardens over evil forces
5. Principalities—controlling national destinies
6. Dominions—controlling the lesser ranks of angels
7. Thrones—beings upon which God is enthroned (in a non-corporeal manner)
8. Cherubim—purveyors of the Divine Wisdom
9. Seraphim—spirits burning with Divine Love and Knowledge.[43]

Each order is, in itself, an allegory of graces received in the created world, but the very arrangement speaks of the goodness of the universe. Its order and orderliness extends even to the realm of unseen things—indeed it is preëminently found there. This order reveals the coordination of power and value in a unifying hierarchy and is exemplary for defining the function and status of the pontifical ministry.

In Book Five (5.11-12), Bernard reiterates the ministries of the celestial powers according to their tropological or moral significance. Here the values appear in descending order, lending a pleasing variety to the presentation and possibly evoking an awareness of the fact that the ladder to heaven allows descent as well as ascent.

Why Bernard places consideration of the Incarnation after that of the Trinity is not entirely clear. It

may reflect the retroflexion we have already encountered
in the fourth step of loving God. That is, we begin
with a man, the pope; we also end with Man, the
human Lord. Where the one is mortal and fallible,
the other is eternal and divine. This means that the
top rung of Bernard's archetypal ladder, every time
it is invoked, signifies that most perfect occurence
of the *Imago Dei*, the person in whom it is alone
possible for us to love God *propter Ipsum* and ourselves
propter Deum.[44]

One further point: in a brilliant epilogue, Bernard
considers the very nature of God under a new set
of terms, a progression which resembles, but does
not precisely duplicate, the pattern *te/sub/circa/supra*.
Here he draws upon Ephesians 3:8, recasting it in
a way that brings out God's chief attributes. God's
length is his eternity. His *breadth* is his charity.
His *height* is his majesty (or unattainability). His
depth is his inscrutable wisdom. These four, in turn,
stand for two human qualities or virtues most to be
desired in the Vicar of Christ: holy fear *(sanctus
timor)* and holy love *(sanctus amor)*. They correspond
respectively to (a) the height and depth and (b)
to the length and breadth.[45] Yet for all of these complica-
tions, the Pope is reminded that truth is finally simple.
God is one. *Divisus hic est, non ille* (Divisions exist
in our understanding, not in God).[46]

Gradation, a characteristic mark of Saint Bernard's
thought and expression, better serves the poetical-
allegorical style of the monastic tradition than it
would the dialectical method of the scholastics. What
gradation is able to do is, first of all, aid the memory,
for in an age of few books and frequent sermons,
this was an important function. But it also promotes
persuasion and even analysis. Bernard is noteworthy
not so much for his originality as for his perceptiveness.
He exemplifies the gift of discretion, the capacity
to see things in due proportion and order. This is
because he, as few others, was able to see things
in God. We do well to conclude with a maxim of his
which demonstrates this:

I said above that God is the reason for loving
God. That is right, for He is the efficient
and final cause of our love.[47]

Fordham University
New York

NOTES

1. Edd. Jean Leclercq OSB and Henri M. Rochais OSB, *Sancti Bernardi Opera* (SBOp) (1963) 3:13–59; ET by Ambrose Conway OCSO, in CF 13:25–82.
2. SBOp 3:121–54; ET by Robert Walton OSB, CF 13:93–132.
3. SBOp 3:394–493; ET by John Anderson and Elizabeth T. Kennan, *Five Books on Consideration: Advice to a Pope,* CF 37:23–179.
4. These devices are summarized in Jean Leclercq, *Receuil d'études sur Saint Bernard et ses écrits* 3, 'Raccolta di studi e testi' 114 (Rome: Edizioni di Storia e Letteratura, 1969) 117. See also, Augustine of Hippo, *De doctrina christiana,* 4.7.11.
5. George Bosworth Burch, ed., *The Steps of Humility: By Bernard Abbot of Clairvaux* (Cambridge, Mass.: Harvard Univ. Press, 1940) 181–225.
6. CF 13:12f. The satirical vignettes which illustrate certain of the steps lend additional force to the argument.
7. Barton R. V. Mills, ed., *Select Treatises of S. Bernard of Clairvaux* (Cambridge, Mass.: Cambridge Univ. Press, 1926) 116n.
8. RB 7:10–66.
9. The *scalae* are compared in a diagram in CF 13:26f. The treatment here is my own.
10. Compare the discussion in Burch, 53–55.
11. 1 Co 12:2: *Scio hominem in Christo...raptum eiusmodi usque ad tertium caelum.*
12. Hum 9.24; CF 13:53.
13. *Ibid.* Cf. Gn 28:13: *Vidit Dominum innixum scalae dicentem sibi: Ego sum Dominus Deus....*
14. RB 7:6.
15. Hum 9.27; CF 13:56.
16. My own inference.
17. On Bernard's Christian Platonism, see Jean–Marie Déchanet OSB, 'Aux sources de la pensée philosophique de S. Bernard', *Saint Bernard théologien: Actes du Congrès de Dijon, 15–19 Septembre 1953,* Analecta SOC 9 (1953) 56–77. See especially p. 61, n. 1.
18. Hum 4.13; CF 13:41.
19. Hum 5:18; CF 13:46.
20. Hum 6.19; CF 13:47.
21. Bernard's vocabulary is, in this matter, non–technical. He employs *dilectio, amor,* and *caritas* synonymously and at random; so also with *noscere, cognoscere, scire, attendere, considere,* and *intellegere.* No doubt this reflects a desire for euphony and varia-

tion as opposed to strict logical precision.

22. See Dil 7.17: *Caritas affectus est, non contractus...*
    sponte afficit, et spontaneum facit. See also 7.18:
    Inest omni utenti ratione naturaliter prope sua
    semper aestimatione atque intentione appetere
    potiora....

23. Hum 6.19; CF 13:47: *Cum sint itaque tres gradus*
    seu status veritatis, ad primum ascendimus per
    laborem humilitatis, ad secundum per affectum
    compassionis, ad tertium per excessum contemplation-
    is. In primo veritas reperitur severa, in secunda
    pia, in tertio pura. Ad primam ratio ducit, qua
    nos discutimus; ad secundum affectus perducit,
    quo aliis miseremur; ad tertium puritas rapit,
    qua ad invisibilia sublevamur.

24. Cf. Burch, 10–14.

25. Bernard holds the union of the Holy Spirit and
    the human will to be a giving of birth to charity.
    See Hum 7.21; CF 13:49.

26. However, see Elizabeth T. Kennan, 'Antithesis
    and Argument in the *De consideratione'*, *Bernard*
    of Clairvaux: Studies Presented to Jean Leclercq,
    CS 23 (1973) 91–109. This essay concerns Bernard's
    ethical and political ideas more than his strictly
    theological and ascetical thought.

27. Csi 5.10.22f.; CF 37:166–168.

28. Hum 7.21; CF 13:48f.

29. CF 13:87f.

30. Watkin W. Williams provides a more technical
    treatment in Mills, p. 46, n. 1; further, see
    p. 47, n. 6.

31. The close association of the self and God approxi-
    mates the concept of *unio mystica.* See Dil 10.27;
    CF 13:119f.

32. Ibid.: Beatum dixerim et sanctum, cui tale aliquid
    in hac mortali vita raro interdum, *aut vel semel....*
    (italics mine.)

33. See Pacifique Delfgaauw OCR, 'La nature et les
    degrès de l'amour selon S. Bernard', *Saint Bernard*
    théologien, 234–252.

34. See M.-D. Chenu OP, 'L'éveil de la conscience
    dans la civilisation médiévale', *Conférence Albert-*
    le-Grand, 1968 (Montreal: Institute d'Études Médié-
    vales, 1969) p. 35f. See, also, Étienne Gilson,
    La théologie mystique de saint Bernard (Paris:
    Vrin, 1947) 166.

35. Dil 15.39; CF 13:130f. Cf. Cicero, *De amicitia*,
    21.80.

36. Dil 6.16; CF 13:109: *Deus meus, adiutor meus,*
    diligam te pro dono tuo et modo meo, minus quidem
    iusto, sed plane non posse meo, qui, etsi quantum

debeo non possum, non possum tamen ultra quam possum.

37. CF 37:15.
38. A detailed plan of the work is given in Leclercq, *Receuil d'études* 3:120f. It is also summarized in CF 37:11–16.
39. My own designation, but see also Csi 2.3.6; CF 37:52f.
40. Leclercq, *Receuil d'études* 3, 120f.
41. *Ibid.* pp. 130–133.
42. Cf. Augustine, *De doct. christ.* 1.23.22.
43. Csi 5.4.7f; CF 37:146–149. The order given is that of Gregory the Great, not that of the Pseudo-Dionysius. See Edmond Boissard OSB, 'La doctrine des anges chez S. Bernard', *Saint Bernard théologien,* 114–135.
44. Csi 5.9.20; CF 37:164f.
45. Csi 5.14.31; CF 37:178.
46. Csi 5.13.27; CF 37:173–175.
47. Dil 7.22; CF 13:116: *Dixi supra: causa diligendi Deum, Deus est. Verum dixi, nam et efficiens, et finalis.*

THE COMPOSITIONAL STRUCTURE OF BERNARD'S EIGHTY-FIFTH SERMON ON THE SONG OF SONGS

Dorette Sabersky

In his eighty-fifth sermon on the Song of Songs,[1] based on Sg 3:1 (*quaesivi quem diligit anima mea*), Bernard suggests seven[2] reasons why the soul seeks God, and they form the theme of this last complete text of the *Sermons on the Song of Songs*. These reasons are enumerated at the beginning and represent a dynamic series of steps which lead to God:

> Quaerit anima Verbum,
> cui consentiat ad correptionem,
> quo illuminetur ad cognitionem,
> cui innitatur ad virtutem,
> quo reformetur ad sapientiam,
> cui conformetur ad decorum,
> cui maritetur ad fecunditatem,
> quo fruatur ad iucunditatem.[3]

The concept of a spiritual development places Bernard in the literary tradition of the gradual ascent,[4] and appears in many of his works.[5] It is characteristic of his psychological and pedagogical interest, and enables him to put all things in the order established by God, yet see them under ever-varying aspects.[6] This procedure is also noteworthy because many of the *Sermones de diversis* and the *Sententiae* consist only of such a skeleton, common for mnemonic purpose. Reading the eighty-fifth sermon, one can get an idea of how Bernard created an artful composition from a basic structure.

Following the seven steps and their arrangement, the coherency of the text is accomplished by stylistic elements like metaphors, word plays, sound associations, and expressive compact sentences. Their function is to enhance statements, to establish antithetical and dialectical relations, transitions, and summaries. Bernard's structuring seems so natural and effortless that we are not aware of its complexity and highly artistic quality unless we take a closer look. In addition to these fascinating stylistic features, the compositional structure also implicitly includes many themes important in Bernard's work. All of this is essential to the understanding of his poetic text, as I intend to show in this paper.

In the preface, constructed according to rhetorical tradition,[7] Bernard mentions that he does not wish

to repeat himself, but to complement the preceding
sermon, and he means it quite literally. For the eighty-
fourth sermon sets the necessary condition for the
contents of the following sermon by describing how
the soul can only seek and love God because it was
first sought and loved by him, and that it is love
which is the reason for the never-ending search.[8]
Now, in the eighty-fifth sermon, Bernard confines
himself to demonstrate the actual realization of this
search. The text is strictly adapted to the spiritual
need of his audience. Bernard consistently adjusts
his point of view to the respective step and emphasizes
the moral aspect which is directed by its mystical
objective.[9]

Bernard begins by explaining how the soul consents
to correction and cites Mt 5:25: *Esto consentiens adversario tuo.* This quotation furnishes the two keywords
for Bernard's reasoning: *consentire* (to agree) and
adversarius. The adversary is interpreted as the Word,
because he is the adversary of our carnal desires.[10]
Confronted with the divine wrath to come, the soul
can only escape by agreeing with the adversary;
and in order to do this, one's own will has to be
changed so that man becomes his own adversary: *At
istud [consentire adversario] impossibile, nisi dissentias
tecum, nisi tibimet adverseris.*[11] Bernard makes this
countermovement evident by the language itself: *dissentias
tecum* refers to *consentias* and *tibimet adverseris* to
adversario. In this struggle against one's self one's
own effort is vain, as is illustrated in two images:
it is like trying to stop a raging torrent with one
finger or to make the Jordan run backwards. Therefore
the solution of the problem is that the soul seek the
Word to be enabled to agree with him, because only
the divine adversary can transform the will to the
good so that it will no longer be an adversary of
the soul: *Quaere Verbum cui consentias, ipso faciente.
Fuge ad illum qui adversatur, per quem talis fias
cui iam non adversetur....*[12] Bernard's precise wording
stresses here again the two keywords *consentire* and
adversarius and thus describes literally the transformation of the will.

Consensus is an essential concept in Bernard's
work. The free will which constitutes the dignity and
responsibility of man, can, supported by grace, manifest
itself only in the voluntary consent to the good.[13]
This represents the spiritual life of the soul.[14]

In order to attain the indispensable knowledge,
zeal for God is not sufficient, the soul is told again

to turn to the Word. In this second step, he will
direct the soul to the right way so that it does not
go astray. The metaphor of way leads into the terminology of light, for the Word is the light that illuminates
both the way and the blind soul, bestowing on it
the vision to see the way, which in itself is God.[15]

The concluding comparison between the two steps
concerning will and reason is stressed by the similarity
of sound between the corresponding words: *immutata-
illuminata*, *vitam-visum*.[16]

With the parallel of will and reason, used to
construct the second step, Bernard prepares the third.
The two feet, devotion and knowledge, on which the
soul now stands in the good relate to the preceding
metaphor of way, changing it from horizontal to vertical,
as is characterized by the terms 'stand', 'raise',
'ascend', but also by the opposite term 'fall'.

The soul has been raised by the hand of the
Word,[17] and it must realize that it does not stand
in its own strength; otherwise it will fall. Moreover,
man is pushed by three attackers: by the devil, by
the world, and by man himself. However, the attack
is only successful if man gives his consent. Thus,
man's greatest threat is himself. His carnal self causes
his own fall,[18] but without his consent neither devil
nor world can succeed.[19] Therefore, man alone is
held responsible for the fall.[20]

The detailed account of the three attackers (one
page in the Latin text) is presented in circular structure. The summary above is the starting point as
well as the conclusion of Bernard's thinking. It is
an effective reasoning: by repeating the theme he
tries to emphasize the essential point and thus to
persuade the audience of its menacing reality.

Consenting to God in the first step requires dissent
with oneself, which means a change in the intention
of the will toward the good. But here, in the third
step, consenting implies yielding to temptation and
has a perjorative meaning; it stands in opposition
to resisting.[21] The will should not only aim at the
good, but also do good by resisting the attacks of
sin. This distinction between the two levels of the
will is more clearly stated in the eighty-fourth sermon
and in other texts by Bernard.[22] The two contrary
meanings of *consensus* make apparent the ambivalence
of free choice.[23]

In order for man to gain stability or, as Bernard
says (changing his image), to control himself, he
needs strength,[24] strength from above: *virtute ex
alto* (Lk 24:49).[25] This moral vigor can direct everything

to reason.[26] It enables the soul to bring the quadriga of the four affects under the control of reason and to put it in the service of virtue.[27] This traditional allegory, favored by Bernard,[28] connects the theme of controlling the carnal desires with the metaphor of way.

Opposed to the image of the fall is not only that of standing, but also the dynamic ascent to the perfection of virtue, an impossible task without the support of the Word. Thus, the ascending soul leans on the beloved (Sg 8:5). With the word 'leaning', *inniti*, Bernard introduces the second term of importance for this step which is entitled 'leaning on the Word in pursuit of virtue'.

It is characteristic of Bernard's style that he immediately picks up the word *inniti* to take full advantage of its potential. With the opposition *niti-inniti* he condenses the preceding to an effective formula: *frustra nititur, si non innititur*[29]--'unless it leans on him its effort is in vain'. But he also uses *inniti* to lead to the image of self-control. He continues: 'But it will gain force by struggling with itself'--*contra se innitens*.[30] *Inniti*, followed by *contra se*, has the meaning of resistance against the self. The use of the same word signals that only the Word, on whom the soul is leaning, makes human virtue possible.[31] If the soul leans on the All-powerful, everything is possible for it as well.[32]

The last sentence of the fifth paragraph is a beautiful combination of the elements with which Bernard previously dealt successively; *Verbo*, the most important, stands in the initial position: *Verbo innixum et indutum virtute ex alto, nulla vis, nulla fraus, nulla iam illecebra poterit vel stantem deicere, vel subicere dominantem.*[33]

This step concludes with the fall of the devil, the prototype of pride.[34] Here the question is not one of consent of the weak will, but of its cause, that is, pride relying on its own strength rather than on the Word.[35] Bernard alludes to the image of sitting, adapting it to the context. Usually, the devil's intention of sitting illustrates the zenith of his arrogance, namely, to be equal to God, for it is becoming only to majesty to sit.[36] Here, however, the devil wants to sit down, being incapable of standing upright.[37] By this device, Bernard seems to reveal that the devil's idle claim to power is nothing but weakness. Three words having similar sound, show the descending movement of the devil: *nec stetit, nec sedit, sed cecidit.*[38]

Looking at the textual structure of this step,

we are struck by how Bernard moves in a spiral,
adding one link to the next, enriching the text and
bringing it to life. Comparison with other texts of
Bernard makes it apparent that he integrates here
several aspects under the topic of virtue.[39]
    As we could see, this integration is accomplished
stylistically by the coherency of the metaphors, typical
of Bernard's use of the images in general. He adheres
to his chosen imagery and adds further related figura-
tions which arise spontaneously, mostly from the riches
of the Bible. This procedure by association shows
that the original contents of these images are still
present with all their connotations. At the same time,
the metaphors are characterized by their transparency.
A specific image does not become so preponderant
as not to be replaceable by another if the train of
thought demands it. Even then, Bernard likes to preserve
continuity either by the metaphors themselves or by
sound and word associations.
    Up to this point the soul as Bernard describes
it has been addressed in the second person, and thus
identified with the reader.[40] Obviously, Bernard assumed
that his audience had reached this third stage of
spiritual development, where the crucial confrontation
between flesh and spirit, pride and humility takes
place and can be resolved thanks to the virtue granted
by God. This would also provide an explanation why
Bernard devoted so much space to the treatment of
virtue, which extends into the fourth step by its relationship to wisdom.

    Wisdom, the subject of this fourth step, is compared
with virtue, based on 1 Co 1:24: *Verbum virtus, Verbum
sapientia est.*[41] Both are gifts to man, originating
in the Word. They are the same in the Word, but
have a different effect in the soul. Virtue is akin
to wisdom. Although to a certain degree contemplative,[42]
virtue consists in activity and struggle; its efforts
are laborious: *honor quidem, sed labor est.*[43] On
the other hand, wisdom, being also strong (*potens*),[44]
is defined as love of virtue and replaces *labor* with
sapor: Ubi autem amor est, labor non est, sed sapor.[45]
Wisdom is connected with love, and its contemplative
characteristics, leisure[46] and spiritual enjoyment (*frui,
in suavitate deliciari*)[47] already point toward *fruitio*
in the last step. *Sapor* as spiritual taste is also
aimed at enjoyment. It acts as seasoning for a tasteless
and bitter virtue.
    Deriving *sapientia* from *sapor*, according to etymologi-
cal tradition,[48] Bernard now defines wisdom as a
taste for the good. This leads to *reformari*, the second
component of this step entitled 'reformation through

the Word to wisdom'. The preceding deformation necessi-
tated a reformation. For the palate of the heart, infected
by the poison of the serpent, acquired a taste for
evil. This perversion is made evident in the folly
--*insipientia*--of Eve. With Mary the symmetrical countermovement is initiated[49] which leads to the re-establishment of wisdom--*sapientia*. When the palate becomes
healthy, it has once again a taste for the good and
for wisdom, the best possible good. By noting the
derivation of *sapientia* from *sapor*, Bernard makes
it clear that wisdom cannot be grasped rationally.
It must be tasted, in other words, experienced, and
this is what matters to Bernard.[50]

The repeated juxtaposition of wisdom and virtue
at the end of the fourth step introduces the recapitulation
of all the foregoing steps.[51] As we saw, the four
progressing steps are organized in two pairs. The
coordination of the two steps on different levels forms
an important structural component of this text, stating
the collaboration of two faculties.[52] Besides the quantita-
tive increase, there is a distinct intensification. More
closely related than will and reason in the first two
steps, virtue and wisdom supplement each other. Virtue
itself, as a sign of co-operation with the Word, brings
about the enjoyment of wisdom and anticipates the
final encounter. What wisdom counsels, virtue accomplishes. In addition, will and reason both participate
in virtue as well as in wisdom, for virtue is strength
of will directed by reason, and wisdom is knowledge
determined by love. Furthermore, virtue through its
strength upgrades the mere intention of the will, and
wisdom, rooted in the experience of the good, proves
to be a knowledge superior to reason. These many-
sided relations erect a complex system on the linear
sequence of the steps, differentiating and adapting
the sequence to the continuity of spiritual growth.
At the same time, the arrangement of the steps is
loosened and compensated by their individual treatment.

At the beginning of the fifth step, the previous
stages are once more enumerated, this time not in
retrospect, as seen from wisdom at the end of the
fourth step, but in prospect, looking ahead and forming
a transition to the next step.[53] This causes a division
distinguishing two parts. In the list of the seven
reasons for the search of the Word, this division is
already emphasized by the two verbs 'reform' and
'conform'. In a wider sense, reformation denotes the
whole first part,[54] whereas conformity relates to the
second part of this conversion of the soul to God.[55]

By the concept of form, Bernard alludes to the

doctrine of image. The purpose of reformation is to
remove the unlikeness of the soul to God. It is thus
conspicuous that Bernard stresses the aim of each
of the first four steps by using opposites. This method,
beginning with the negative pole, takes into consideration
the realistic situation of man.[56] Spiritual life, consisting
in consent to the Word, is opposed to spiritual death;[57]
the illuminated reason is contrasted with blind ignorance.
To describe reformation, Bernard starts from deformation.
This procedure is especially clear in the third step:
to illustrate standing and ascending in virtue, Bernard
deals more extensively with the impending fall.[58]
This quadruple reformation is the condition for conformity, the re-establishment of man's likeness to God.[59]
Therefore the artfully varied antithetical structure
of the steps is no longer used in the second part.

The fifth step consists in 'the conformity with
the Word to obtain beauty'. The likeness of the soul
to God is described as an aesthetic experience.[60]
The Word, clothed in beauty (Ps 92:1), wants a like
garment for his bride, who is also his image. Note
that the soul qualifies here for the first time as the
bride whose beauty and love the Word desires.
It is significant for this text that Bernard moves
over to the area of ethics expressed by beauty, calling
the beauty of the soul the honorable: *honestum*.[61]
It has its origin in the conscience, the evidence of
which is its clarity. In accordance with tradition,
the aesthetic quality is revealed in the luminosity
of light.[62] Inner, spiritual beauty cannot but radiate
outward and become physically visible in human behavior.[63] Since God is light in a proper sense, beyond
a mere metaphor, human luminosity is an image of
divine light.[64] This reflection, in which the nobility
of the soul resides, expresses conformity with the
Word.
Noteworthy again is the coherency of the terminology,
which could be seen as an enhancement of the metaphor
of light in the second step. While there, reason illuminated begins to see; here, owing to the moral improvement,
the splendid beauty of the likeness to the Word shines
forth.

This beauty, founded on conformity with the Word,
prepares the bride for marriage,[65] since the nubility
of the soul corresponds with its degree of likeness
to the Word. The betrothal of the soul confirms the
ascetical act of leaving all behind in order to adhere
to the Word and to love him more than anything else.[66]
A rhythmically dense sentence, characteristic of Bernard's

evocative style, lists the essential aspects of the soul married to the Word:

> *Ergo quam videris animam,*
>   *relictis omnibus* (Lk 5:11),
>   *Verbo votis omnibus adhaerere* (cf. Ps 72:28),
>   *Verbo vivere,*
>   *Verbo se regere;*
>   *de Verbo concipere quod pariat Verbo,*
>   *quae possit dicere:*
>   *Mihi vivere Christus est et mori lucrum* (Ph 1:21),
> *puta coniugem Verboque maritatam.*[67]

This sentence expresses strikingly the exclusive nature of the relationship between the soul and the Word and leads from the ascetical state of detachment to the subject of giving birth.[68]

Note that Bernard does not think here, as in other sermons,[69] of spiritual matrimony as a mystical union but as a fruitful association. With marriage, the soul following the example of Paul, takes over the role of a mother responsible for feeding her children.[70] In this spiritual marriage, there are two kinds of birth and thus two different but not opposite children:[71] by preaching, souls are born, while meditation engenders spiritual knowledge. These two functions appear as two equivalent manifestations of the one love to God[72] forming a dialectic relation.[73]

I should like to point out that fecundity also implies contemplation here, whereas traditionally it is only part of the active life.[74] Since this concept of fecundity is never used for the profit of one's own soul, but is already directed toward one's neighbor, fecundity of contemplation must signify its inspiring power and emanation, urging the soul on to preaching and unselfish fraternal care.[75]

Immediately following this, in the seventh step, where contemplation culminates in mystical ecstasy and the knowledge of meditation is changed into the affective experience of enjoying the Word, Bernard alters the perspective of the metaphor. Now the fruitful mother is opposed to the bride enjoying the Word. With the sound association *fructificans Verbo–fruens Verbo,*[76] Bernard alludes to the tension between oneness and separateness of mother and bride.

The fact that Bernard, a master in the use of images, here substitutes the metaphor of the mother for the image of the mother–bride cannot be explained simply by oversight, but hints at the importance of this passage and at certain innovations in the tradition. Since Bernard extends the imagery of the spiritual marriage to its fecundity, the soul becomes a mother, also of contemplation. On the other hand, in accordance with the augustinian tradition and with his own mystical doctrine determined by the bride, pre-eminence belongs to the *fruitio* that crowns the ascent of the soul to God. For this mystical enjoyment shows transcendental features by anticipating the ultimate union to come.[77] Therefore, motherhood has to precede the bridal stage; this is achieved by the separation between marriage and mystical union. Yet this is against the logic of the image and leads to an inconsistency in the metaphor:[78] the transition from the mother to the bride who is also mother but prefers to be bride.[79]

The mother-bride represents the enhancement and fulfilment of the terms virtue and wisdom, which in turn are based on the soul's faculties, will and reason. The ascetical effort of virtue is aimed at the achievement of purity of heart, which is the preparation for action fruitful for others. Enjoyment in wisdom is a dynamic movement oriented toward mystical ecstasy. By this increasing order of the three ascending pairs forming opposing poles of a unit, Bernard is able to connect the idea of gradual ascent with the dialectic experience of human life.[80]

The question of the meaning of *Verbo frui*,[81] with which Bernard probes the limit of the utterable, introduces the conclusion. The hint at the inadequacy of language passing ultimately into the area of silence goes well beyond a rhetorically effective closing of the sermon.

Citing Paul (2 Co 5:13 and 2 Co 12:4), Bernard shows the intention and the limit of his sermon. Mystical experience is not communicable: *non docet hoc lingua: docet gratia*;[82] and it is not understandable as long as the soul has not reached this point. As we mentioned before, Bernard assumes realistically that his audience finds itself within the third stage. Bernard is here not interested in theoretically treating the problem of the communication of mystical experience[83] or in the dilemma of the preacher caught between speaking and keeping silence,[84] but only in directing his public to grace, namely, by way of humility.[85] Bernard seems to act in humility himself when he first denies his own mystical experience of which he cannot speak[86] and refers to Paul as an expert.[87]

As a counterpart to pride, which is considered the cause of man's fall, humility is especially related to that third step, from which the audience is supposed to move on to a higher level.[88] There, however, the word 'humility' is not mentioned; it is used just once at the end, in spite of the fact that the whole sermon is imbued with the spirit of humility. What until now was tacitly present is now put into focus by its explicit designation.

In consequence of the paradox of humility—'worthy to attain what it is not able to learn'[89]—the soul might be dignified with the grace of mystical ecstasy. Since this paradox is rooted in the will of God—'because it pleases him' (cf. 1 Jn 3:22)—, the way of humility includes not only each of the steps, but also the apparent tension between them. Ultimately, the dynamism of spiritual life consists in the progressive assimilation to God's will.[90]

As we can see, the compositional structure of this text is established by a system of intricately arranged elements.[91] We add to this humility as a further dimension, related to Bernard's audience and corresponding to the moral perspective of this sermon. Humility, pre-figured in the human nature of Christ,[92] forms the basis of Bernard's monastic spirituality. It is the subject of his early treatise *De gradibus humilitatis et superbiae*, which follows the Rule of St Benedict. Recurring throughout his work, humility is also the end of this last complete sermon on the Canticle. The conclusion was rightly called Bernard's literary testament.[93]

Center for Medieval and Renaissance Studies, UCLA

NOTES

1. SC 85; SBOp 2:307-316 (CF 40:195-210).
2. Following Ps 118:164 ('Septies in die laudem dixi tibi, Domine') Bernard says about the number seven: 'Videte hunc septenarium. Sacer numerus est: non vacat' (SC 15, 8; SBOp 1:88, 17f.). Seven as a number of perfection lends authority to the enumeration. But on the other hand, Bernard stresses that there are many more reasons to seek God, since the needs of the soul and its anxieties are countless. The number seven is common and can be found in other writings by Bernard: see, for example, Div 40, Div 41, Div 118. Obviously, all texts referring to the seven gifts of the Holy Spirit contain the number seven, see, for example,

Div 14, VII SS, III Sent 98. Similarly the seven steps of SC 85, based on a christological concept (see below, note 41), could be understood as the seven gifts of the Word (see also below notes 11, 24, and 54). On the number seven, see Margot Schmidt, *Rudolf von Biberach, Die siben strassen zu got,* Spicilegium Bonaventurianum 6 (Quaracchi, 1969) 248*ff.

3. SBOp 2:307, 14–17: 'The soul seeks the Word to consent to receive correction, to be enlightened to recognize him, in order to lean on him in pursuit of virtue, to be reformed by him to wisdom, conform--ed to his beauty, to marry him to become fruitful, to enjoy him in bliss' (translation adapted from CF 40:195f.).

4. On the gradual ascent, see Schmidt, 184*–194*, Emile Bertaud and André Rayez, 'Echelle spirituelle', DSp 4 (1961) 62–86, Karl Rahner, 'Ueber das Problem des Stufenweges zur christlichen Vollkommenheit' in *Schriften zur Theologie* (Einsiedeln ³1959) 3:11–34.

5. The best-known examples are Hum and Dil. Following Gregory the Great (*Moralia in Iob,* 22, 19; PL 76:240CD), Bernard confirms the theory of gradual ascent: 'nemo repente fit summus, sed gradatim quisque ascendit' (Hum 26; SBOp 3:36, 25).

6. See Maur Standaert, 'Le principe de l'ordination dans la théologie spirituelle de saint Bernard', Coll. 8 (1946) 212ff.

7. Bernard uses, for example, the rhetorical topics *taedium* to be avoided and *brevitas* (SBOp 2:307, 10–13). On the topics related to the *exordium,* see Leonid Arbusow, *Colores rhetorici* (Göttingen, ²1963) 97ff.

8. Cf. SC 84, 5 and 1; SBOp 2:305, 12ff. and 303, 10ff.

9. This conception could also explain why the terminology of love is so sparingly used. Bernard hardly ever mentions love explicitly, yet the seven steps are a sign of progressing love. *Amor* occurs three times (SBOp 2:312, 20 and 315, 10), *amare* and *caritas,* however, not at all; *diligere* and *dilectus* are mentioned only in the quotations of SC 3:1 and 8:5; there is only one instance of *amplexus* (316, 5) and of *oscula* (316, 6).

10. Augustine (compare, for example, *Sermo de Vetere Testamento* 9, 3; CC 41:109) and Gregory the Great (*Moralia in Iob* 9, 89; CC 143:520) interpret the adversary as *sermo Dei* (or *veritatis*), as does Bernard in Div 124; SBOp 6/1:402, 11–13. See also below note 26. Bernard's christological exegesis

is characteristic for this text, see below note 41.

11. SBOp 2:308, 6. Fear is the motivation for the consent. Likewise, *timor* is the first gift of the Holy Spirit.

12. SBOp 2:308, 11f.

13. See Aimé Forest, 'Das Erlebnis des *consensus voluntatis* beim heiligen Bernhard', in *Bernhard von Clairvaux, Mönch und Mystiker: Internationaler Berhardkongress 1953* (Wiesbaden, 1955) 120–27, and Standaert, 'Ordination', 199ff. Cf. Gra 19; SBOp 3:180, 18–20: 'Est autem ordinatio, omnimoda conversio voluntatis ad Deum, et ex tota se voluntaria devotaque subiectio'.

14. See SBOp 2:313, 29. On the spiritual life of the soul see SC 81, 4ff.

15. The connection between the way and God is not made here, but see Hum 1; SBOp 3:17, 3ff.: 'Si imitaris eum, non ambulas in tenebris, sed habebis lumen vitae....Ego sum via [Jn 14:6], quae ad veritatem duco'. On the theory of illumination, see Hans Blumenberg, 'Licht als Metapher der Wahrheit', *Studium Generale* 10 (1957) 440f., and Etienne Gilson, *Introduction à l'étude de saint Augustin* (Paris, 41969) 103ff.

16. SBOp 2:308, 24–26: 'Nec parum profecit anima tua, cuius immutata voluntas, cuius illuminata ratio est....In altero vitam, in altero visum recepit'.

17. 'Manu Verbi levata' (308, 29). The image of the hand is used again at the end of the third step (311, 17). The supporting hand of the Word is contrasted with man's own hand consenting to temptation (309, 10: 'Manus tua, consensus tuus') and with *manus impellentis* (311, 6f.). Likewise, the metaphor of the feet is picked up again at the end (311, 17: Ps 39:3) and opposed to *pes superbiae* (311, 6: Ps 35:12).

18. The text indicates that Bernard means here the carnal aspect of man (309, 24 and 310, 1f. and 26, see also Ws 9:15), and this is confirmed by other texts as well: Quad 5, 1; SBOp 4:372, 15ff.: 'Ubique proprium circumferimus inimicum: carnem hanc loquor de peccato natam....Hinc est quod tam acriter adversus spiritum concupiscit....' In Div 23, 3f., Bernard lists *spiritus carnis, spiritus mundi, spiritus malitiae* (SBOp 6/1:180f.). II Sent 2 begins: 'Quattuor sunt, quorum in hac vita obsequiis deservimus: caro, mundus, diabolus, Deus' (SBOp 6/2:23, 10f.). Cf. also Rog 2; SBOp 5:122, 15ff., where Bernard distinguishes between *ratio, voluntas,* and *caro.* See also Augustine,

Sermo 344; PL 39:1512: 'Hic propositus nobis agon, haec lucta cum carne, haec lucta cum diabolo, haec lucta cum saeculo'.

19. The free will can only be forced by itself, which means it consents. Thus Bernard says, referring to Peter's denial: 'Quem sua denique ad negandum voluntas compulit, compulsus est quia voluit: immo non compulsus est, sed consensit, et non alienne potentiae, sed propriae voluntati...' (Gra 39; SBOp 3:194, 11-13).

20. Bernard Piault, 'Le désir de la sagesse. Itinéraire de l'âme à Dieu chez S. Bernard dans le sermon LXXXV sur le Cantique des cantiques', *Coll.* 36 (1974) 29, stresses Bernard's attitude toward personal responsibility.

21. '...sed consentientes, non resistentes' (SBOp 2:309, 27f. concerning Adam and Eve). The keyword *consensus* and its variants *assensus, consentire,* and *consentaneus* determine this passage. Together with the term 'attack' (*impulsor, impulsus, impellere*) they structure and enrich the image of standing and falling.

22. SC 84,3; SBOp 2:304, 14ff.: 'Palam est, quia vult et non potest...ut qui dedit velle, det et perficere pro bona voluntate'. In Div 124, the first degree of *bona voluntas,* that is *recta voluntas,* also refers to Mt 5:25: 'anima mente legi Dei consentit, sed, carne repugnante, bonum quod diligit perficere non invenit, sed saepe malum quod odit per infirmitatem facit. In hoc tamen recta est eius voluntas, quod adversario suo consentiens, in se odit quod ille reprehendit'. The second degree describes *voluntas valida:* 'anima non solum malum quod odit non agit, sed etiam bonum quod diligit, licet cum gravedine, fortiter tamen, perficit...' (SBOp 6/1:403, 7ff.). In Gra 46f., Bernard distinguishes between *bonum velle* and *bonum perficere:* 'immutando etiam malam vountatem, sibi per consensum iungit; ministrando et consensui facultatem...innotescit' (SBOp 3:199, 12ff.). '...sanat, cum mutat affectum; roborat, ut perducat ad actum' (*ibid.* 199, 29f.). See also SC 3,3f.; SBOp 1:16, 3f.: 'Qui autem dedit voluntatem paenitendi, opus est ut addat et continendi virtutem...'. In Gra 18, there are three grades of the will: 'Si enim velle malum defectus quidam est voluntatis, utique bonum velle profectus eiusdem erit, sufficere autem ad omne quod volumnus bonum, ipsius perfectio' (SBOp 3:180, 2ff.), the last step being only partly attainable in this life, see Gra 26: 'peccato, etsi non ex toto carere,

certe non consentire' (SBOp 3:185, 10f.).

23. 'Only the will, then, since, by reason of its innate freedom, it can be compelled by no force or necessity to dissent from itself, or to consent in any matter in spite of itself, makes a creature righteous or unrighteous, capable and deserving of happiness or of sorrow, insofar as it shall have consented to righteousness or unrighteousness' (Gra 6; CF 19:61).

24. Div 72,2; SBOp 6/2:308, 7ff.: 'Quidam enim trahuntur inviti....Invitis necessaria est fortitudo, qua resistant usque ad mortem minis, cruciatibus et damnis...'. See also Rog 2; SBOp 5:122, 5ff. For SC 3,3f. and Gra 46f. see above, note 22. *Fortitudo* as the fourth gift of the Holy Spirit is opposed to the vice of *consensus* or *concupiscentia*; see, e.g., III Sent and 98, Div 14, III Sent 19 and 20.

25. SBOp 2:310, 11.

26. The struggle between reason and the depraved will has to be resolved in favor of reason. In Ded 2.3; SBOp 5:377, this subject is based on Mt 5:25, whereby in this case reason is the adversary. See also Gra 3; SBOp 3:168, 1–6.

27. On the four affects *timor, laetitia, tristitia, amor* (here: *ira, metus, cupiditas, gaudium,* SBOp 2:310, 24), see Augustine, *De civitate Dei* 14,8f.; CC 48:425ff. The four affects can turn into either virtues or vices: *affectiones ordinatae=virtutes, inordinatae=perturbationes* (see Div 50; SBOp 6/1:270–72).

28. On Bernard's use of the allegory of the chariots and its literary tradition, see Jean Leclercq, *Recueil d'études sur Saint Bernard et ses écrits* (Rome, 1962–1969) 3:150–158 and 1:207:212, 288.

29. SBOp 2: 310, 22f.

30. *Ibid.* 310, 23.

31. The virtuous man strives to moral unity: 'Est unitas potestativa, quo homo virtutis non instabilis, non dissimilis, sed unus sibimet semper nititur inveniri' (Csi 5,18; SBOp 3:482, 22f.). See also Asc 3,1; SBOp 5:131, 19ff.

32. Bernard quotes Ph 4:13 ('Omnia possum in eo qui me confortat') and Mk 9:22 ('omnia possibilia sunt credenti').

33. SBOp 2:311, 4f. 'So, I say, neither power, nor treachery, nor lure, can overthrow or hold in subjection the mind which rests upon the Word and is clothed with strength from above' (CF 40:201). Note that the two verbs *de-icere* and *sub-icere* combine the idea of standing with that

of controlling the affects.
34. On the fall of the devil, see E. Mangenot, 'Démon d'après les Pères', DThC 4 (1911) 355–58, 364–76, 379–84.
35. Bernard says in Dil 4 that knowledge without virtue turns into arrogance. 'It is pride, the greatest of sins, to use gifts as if they were one's by natural right and while receiving benefits to usurp the benefactor's glory' (CF 13:97). In Mor 19, however, Bernard distinguishes between *superbia caeca: intelligentiae* and *superbia vana: voluntatis* (SBOp 7:114f.). Therefore, consent could be understood as *superbia voluntatis* and pride as *superbia intelligentiae*.
36. Hum 31; CF 13:60: 'All else in heaven's court are standing: you alone presume to sit....In that court none has a right to sit save him who sits above the Cherubim, waited on by all'. See also O Pasc 2,1; SBOp 5:118, 13ff., SC 69,3f; SBOp 2:203f. and SC 17,5; SBOp 1:101, 6ff.
37. '...sedere voluit, quia stare non valuit' (SBOp 2:311, 10f.). Thus, to sit can also mean humiliation: 'Sedere enim praesidentis est, sedere dominantis est et regnantis. Maxime vero sedere super solium dominationem notat; nam sedere simpliciter, aliquando humiliationem' (1 Nov 5,4: SBOp 5:320, 18–20).
38. SBOp 2:311, 12.
39. In addition to the themes already mentioned I note the following: Bernard's exposition of the command of love as in Dt 6:5 ('Diliges Dominum Deum tuum ex toto corde tuo, ex tota anima tua, ex tota virtute tua'—Vulg.: 'fortitudine tua'): 'amor quidem cordis ad zelum quemdam pertinere affectionis, animae vero amor ad industriam seu iudicium rationis, virtutis autem dilectio ad animi posse referri constantiam vel vigorem...scientes amorem cordis, quem et affectuosum dicimus, absque eo qui dicitur animae, dulcem quidem seducibilem, illum vero absque illo qui virtutis est, rationabilem, sed fragilem' (SC 20,4; SBOp 1:116, 26ff.). The parallel with the first three steps in SC 85 is obvious. The same applies to the following text: Dil 2–6 proposes three gifts to the soul: dignity, knowledge, and virtue. Dignity is the free will, through knowledge man recognizes his dignity. Through virtue man seeks God and adheres to him. Ignorance makes beasts of us, but reason without virtue leads to arrogance and associates us with demons. Virtue is the fruit of dignity and knowledge. The virtuous man ascribes all the gifts to God and does not keep them for himself

as his own. This is not possible for man by his own free will (see SBOp 3:121-24).

40. There is one later instance in a higher step, where within a biblical citation, the soul is addressed directly: SBOp 2:314, 2 and 5: 'concupiscet rex decorum tuum' (Ps 44:12). The future tense supports the interpretation given.

41. According to Wilhelm Hiss, *Die Anthropologie Bernhards von Clairvaux* (Berlin, 1964) 22f. and 111, this is the foundation of the christological structure of the soul, consisting only of will and reason in contrast to the trinitarian structure of will, reason, and memory: 'Habet et ipsa anima similiter duo labia, quibus osculatur sponsum suum, id est rationem et voluntatem. Rationis est percipere sapientiam, voluntatis virtutem' (Div 89.2; SBOp 6/2:336, 13-15).

42. '...et virtus suavis existat' (SBOp 2:312, 7). On Bernard's position that virtue is not only necessary for contemplation, but is already a sort of contemplation, see Hans Urs von Balthasar, 'Aktion und Kontemplation' in *Die Deutsche Thomas-Ausgabe* (Heidelberg-Munich-Graz-Vienna-Salzburg, 1954) 23:445, and Emero Stiegman, 'Action and Contemplation in Saint Bernard's Sermons on the Song of Songs', CF 31 (Kalamazoo, 1979) xvi.

43. SBOp 2:312, 12.

44. SBOp 312, 7.

45. SBOp, 312, 20f. The connection *labor-amor* seems to go back to Augustine: 'Non ergo recusetur labor, si adest amor; nostis enim quoniam qui amat non laborat' (*In Iohannis Ev. Tractatus* 124,48; CC 36:413. See also *De bono viduitatis* 21,26; PL 40:448. Bernard adds *sapor*. The similarity of sound of the two-syllable words with the vowels a-o is evident.

46. 'Ergo sapientiae otia negotia sunt' (SBOp 2:312, 17f.). This paradox describes the activity of wisdom; see Brian Stock, 'Experience, Praxis, Work, and Planning in Bernard of Clairvaux: Observations on the *Sermones in Cantica*' in *The Cultural Context of Medieval Learning*, edd. John E. Murdoch and Edith D. Sylla, Boston Studies in the Philosophy of Science 26 (Dordrecht, Boston, 1975) 246f. In Asspt 2,9; SBOp 5:237, 21, Bernard applies the term *negotium* to Martha, whereas Mary's leisure is called *non otiosum otium*. Augustine uses the expression *otiosum negotium*, see Jean Leclercq, *Otia Monastica. Etudes sur le vocabulaire de la contemplation au moyen âge*, SAn 51 (1963) 40.

47. SBOp 2:312, 14f. and 312, 6.
48. See Isidore, *Etymologiarum sive originum liber* 10.240, ed. W. M. Lindsay (Oxford, 1911). For further references see Schmidt, 156* note 2. See also Balthasar, 445.
49. '...ut qui per feminam deformati in insipientiam sumus, per feminam reformemur ad sapientiam' (SBOp 2:313, 2f.). Bernard calls the symmetrical order of fall and redemption *ordinis pulchritudinem* (Miss 2,13; SBOp 4:30, 11). 'Notandum de reditu animae ad Deum, quia quo ordine a Deo discessit, eo ordine redeundum est ei ad Deum' (III Sent 69; SBOp 6/2:101, 9f.); see also Div 66,1; SBOp 6/1:299, 13, and Pent 2,3; SBOp 5:167.
50. See SC 23,14; SBOp 1:147, 24ff.: 'Instructio doctos reddit, affectio sapientes...tunc primum animae Deus sapit, cum eam afficit ad timendum, non cum instruit ad sciendum...sapor sapientem facit, sicut scientia scientem...'.
51. 'It is right to put wisdom after virtue, for virtue is, as it were, the sure foundation above which wisdom builds her home (Pr 9:1). But the knowledge of good should come before these, because there is no fellowship between the light of wisdom and the shadows of ignorance (2 Co 6:14). Goodwill, too, should come before them, because wisdom will not enter a soul disposed to ill (Ws 1:4)' (CF 40:205f.).
52. This is equally valid for the third pair formed by the sixth and seventh step, see below p. 94. These pairs evolve from the christological structure of the soul, see above note 41.
53. See Arbusow, 62, n. 37 (*transitio*).
54. The first part is framed by Ws 7:30: victory of wisdom over malice. In the introduction (SBOp 2:307, 22), Wisdom stands for the Word who initiates this process, whereas in the second instance (313, 17), wisdom means the restored gift granted to man. This citation is also used at the beginning of a text describing the seven gifts of the Holy Spirit, wisdom being the seventh gift; see Div 14; SBOp 6/1:134–39. For references to Bernard's citation of Ws 7:30 which departs from the Vulgate, see Leclercq, *Recueil*, 1:124f. and 3:242.
55. 'Iam vero animae reditus, conversio eius ad Verbum, reformandae per ipsum, conformandae ipsi' (SC 83,2; SBOp 2:299, 17–19).
56. The treatise Hum, wherein Bernard explains the steps to humility by the degrees of pride, is the main example for this structuring. In Hum 57, Bernard states that he can teach only what

he knows himself (see SBOp 3:58f.). On the composition of Hum, see Leclercq, *Recueil* 3:113–17.

57. SBOp 2:308, 26. On spiritual death, see SC 81,4; SBOp 2:286, 20ff.

58. Note also the dynamic aspect of these antitheses. According to Bernard, there is only progress or relapse, in other words, stagnation means regression, see Pur 2,3; SBOp 4:340, 8–12, and Ep 254,4; SBOp 8:159, 10–12.

59. Maur Standaert, 'La doctrine de l'image chez saint Bernard', ETL 23 (1947) 90, indicates that there is also an ethical aspect to image. The part of likeness or image within the virtues is called *rectitudo*. Hiss, 74–76, notes that the terminology is inconsistent: In SC 24,5–7 and SC 27,7f., the easily lost *rectitudo* is related to likeness; in SC 80, however, to image. In Gra 26, where image means *liberum arbitrium*, likeness containing *liberum consilium* and *liberum complacitum*, is re-established by virtue and wisdom, though only partly in this life (see SBOp 3:184, 25ff.).

61. On the connection *decorum–honestum*, see, e.g. Ambrose following Cicero: 'Illud quod decorum dicitur, quod ita cum honesto iungitur, ut separari non queat' (*De officiis clericorum* 1,218: PL 16:95A).

62. See, e.g. Otto von Simson, *Die gotische Kathedrale. Beiträge zu ihrer Entstehung und Bedeutung* (Darmstadt, [2]1972) 78ff.; Rosario Assunto, *Die Theorie des Schönen im Mittelalter* (Cologne, 1963) 59; de Bruyne, 3:3–29 (regarding the thirteenth century). In SC 71,1f., virtue is called white and radiant (*candida*), and its beauty is described with metaphors of light (see SBOp 2:215). In SC 45,9, the beauty of Christ appears as radiating light. The periods of this lyrical text are introduced in this way: 'Quam pulcher es....Quam mihi decorus es....Quam clara mihi oriris stella...quam lucidus flos...quam iucundum lumen....Quam spectabilis.... Quam denique rutilans....quam formosus...' (SBOp 2:55, 7ff.). His beauty is his love which precedes the soul. By calling the soul beautiful, he infuses into it the power to love (*ibid.* 54, 25ff.).

63. The idea of the body as a mirror of the soul could indicate that this passage is based on Ambrose's *De officiis clericorum:* 'Speculum enim mentis plerumque in verbis refulget' (1,67; PL 16:47 CD). 'Itaque vox quaedam est animi corporis motus' (1,71; ibid., 49A).

64. See Joseph Ratzinger, 'Licht und Erleuchtung. Erwägungen zu Stellung und Entwicklung des Themas in der abendländischen Geistesgeschichte',

Studium Generale 13 (1960) 369; Blumenberg, 440;
and Alois Haas, 'Der Lichtsprung der Gottheit
(*Parz.* 466)' in *Typologia litterarum*, Festschrift
Max Wehrli (Zurich, 1969) 219ff. for further references. On the term *claritas*, see Christine Mohr-
mann, 'Observations sur la langue et le style
de saint Bernard' in SBOp 2:xv.

65. 'Talis conformatio maritat animam Verbo' (SC
83.3; SBOp 2:299, 21). On the subject of marriage,
see Leclercq, *Monks on Marriage. A Twelfth-Century
View* (New York, 1982).

66. On the term *adhaerere*, see Standaert, 'Ordination',
209.

67. SBOp 2:315, 17-20. 'When you see a soul leaving
everything and clinging to the Word with all
its will and desire, living for the Word, ruling
its life by the Word, conceiving by the Word
what it will bring forth by him, so that it can
say: "For me to live is Christ, and to die is
gain", you know that the soul is the spouse and
the bride of the Word' (CF 40:208f.).

68. According to the context of Ph 1:21, Bernard
combines this citation with the subject of fecundity.
This connection is explicitly stated in SC 51,2;
SBOp 2:84, 17f. ('...mater praegnans et fructificans,
cui vivere Christus est et mori lucrum'), and
SC 58,1; SBOp 2:127, 24f.

69. See SC 61,1f.; SBOp 2:148f., and SC 83,3; SBOp
2:299, 27-29, where 1 Co 6:17 ('Qui adhaeret
Deo, unus spiritus est') is mentioned.

70. As long as the bride has not developed breasts,
she is not nubile, she is not yet ready for the
guidance of souls or for the duty of preaching
(see SC 10,1; SBOp 1:49, 2ff.). In connection
with Ga 4:19—'Filioli mei, quos iterum parturio,
donec formetur Christus in vobis' (SBOp 2:315,
24f.)—Bernard mentions occasionally the birth
of Christ in the soul, V Nat 6,11; SBOp 4:243
(*fecunda virgo*) and Div 51; SBOp 6/1:273, 11f.
See Denis Farkasfalvy, *'L'inspiration de l'Ecriture
Sainte dans la théologie de saint Bernard*, SAn
53 (1964) 72. In contrast to Eckhart, this subject
is only of marginal importance for Bernard who
emphasizes the relationship of bride and groom.

71. '...diversas soboles, sed non adversas' (SBOp
2:315, 27). Bernard several times stresses that
Martha and Mary are sisters living together.
See Henri de Lubac, 'A propos de la formule
"diversi, non adversi"', Rech. SR 40 (1951-1952:
Mélanges Jules Lebreton II) 27-40, and Joseph
de Ghellinck, *Le mouvement théologique du XIIe*

siécle (Bruges, Brussel, Paris, ²1948) 517–23. This formula which is used to harmonize contradictory biblical and patristic passages, suggests that Bernard tries to reconcile the opposition of action and contemplation.

72. See SC 18.6; SBOp 1:107, 14ff. (107, 27: 'Deus caritas est'); see also Stiegman, x.

73. On the one hand, the necessary active life is a precondition for the privilege of contemplation (see, for example, SC 46,5; SBOp 2:58, 16ff.), on the other hand, the latter creates a reservoir out of which the preacher draws spiritual wealth (see SC 18,3; SBOp 1:104, 19ff.). On the many-faceted relationship between action and contemplation in Bernard's work, see Thomas Merton, *On Saint Bernard*, CS 9 (Kalamazoo, 1980) 23–104 and Bernardin Schellenberger, *Bernhard von Clairvaux* (Olten and Freiburg, 1982) 18–27.

74. Ever since Augustine, the sterility of contemplation is opposed to the fecundity of action as typified in Rachel and Leah. See, for example, Gregory the Great, *Homilia in Hiezechielem* 2,2,10; CC 142:231f. In Bernard see, e.g. SC 9,8 and SC 46,5. See Dietmar Mieth, *Die Einheit von vita activa und vita contemplativa in den deutschen Predigten und Traktaten Meister Eckharts und bei Johannes Tauler: Untersuchungen zur Struktur des christlichen Lebens* (Regensburg, 1969) 42.

75. 'But if the bride is enticed by the Bridegroom this is because she receives from him the desire by which she is enticed, the desire of good works, the desire to bring forth fruit for the Bridegroom' (SC 58,1; CF 31:108). 'It is characteristic of true and pure contemplation that when the mind is ardently aglow with God's love, it is sometimes so filled with zeal and the desire to gather to God those who will love him with equal abandon that it gladly forgoes contemplative leisure for the endeavor of preaching' (SC 57,9; CF 31:103). See also Schellenberger, 25f. According to Balthasar, 455, the concept of fecundity of contemplation appears in Bernard. A beginning of this idea shows in Gregory the Great, *Homilia in Hiezechielem* 2,2,11; CC 142:232.

76. SBOp 2:316, 3f. Describing the mystical ecstasy in the preceding sentence, Bernard combines *frui* with *furari:* '...quodammodo se sibi furatur, immo rapitur atque elabitur a seipsa, ut Verbo fruatur' (*ibid.* 316, 2f.). Imbedded is another similarity of sound so that the movement culminates in *frui.* The two different sound associations

of *frui* are used to lead from the theme of ecstasy to the comparison between mother and bride.

77. See Mieth, 84ff.

78. The treatise *De quattuor gradibus violentae caritatis*, attributed to Richard of St Victor, advances this idea further so that it concurs with the sequence of the imagery: 'In primo gradu fit desponsatio, in secundo nuptiae, in tertio copula, in quarto puerperium' (Richard von St Viktor, *Ueber die Gewalt der Liebe. Ihre vier Stufen*, intro. and trans. Margot Schmidt, Veröffentlichungen des Grabmann-Institutes NF. 8 [Munich, Paderborn, Vienna, 1969] 44).

79. 'A mother is happy in her child; a bride is even happier in her bridegroom's embrace. The children are dear, they are pledge of his love, but his kisses give her greater pleasure. It is good to save many souls, but there is far more pleasure in going aside to be with the Word' (CF 40:209). The evaluation of the comparison is reversed in SC 9,8: 'The favor you demand is rather for your own delight, but the breasts with which you may feed the offspring of your womb are preferable to, that is, they are more essential than, the wine of contemplation. What gladdens the heart of one man cannot be placed on equal terms with that which benefits many' (CF 4:59). The affective love (*caritas affectualis*), that is contemplation, is estimated higher than love in action (*caritas actualis*), but in this life, the opposite and preposterous order often prevails SC 50,5f.; SBOp 2:81).

80. On Bernard's experience of tensions and contradictions, see G. R. Evans, *The Mind of St Bernard of Clairvaux* (Oxford, 1983) 218ff.

81. SBOp 2:316, 11 and 316, 17.

82. *Ibid.* 316, 18. Cf. Div 95,2; SBOp 6/1:354, 7-10: 'Potest namque praedicator monita salutis auribus circumstantibus insonare; sed nemo, nisi solus. Deus, valet saporem caritatis palato cordis infundere. Unde Gregorius: "Nisi sit intus Spiritus qui doceat, doctoris lingua exterius in vacuum laborat"'; Cs 5,5; SBOp 3:470, 6f.: 'Ergo quae supra sunt, non verbo decentur, sed Spiritu revelantur'.

83. See, for example, SC 41,3; see also Farkasfalvy, 59ff. and 73ff. (regarding SC 67).

84. See, for example, SC 62,3, SC 57,5, and SC 74,1-5.

85. Hum 1; SBOp 3:16, 23f.: 'Viam dicit humilitatem, quae ducit ad veritatem'.

86. On Bernard's attitude toward his mystical experience, see John R. Sommerfeldt, 'The Epistemological Value of Mysticism in the Thought of Bernard of Clairvaux', in *Studies in Medieval Culture*, ed. J. H. Sommerfeldt (Kalamazoo, Michigan, 1964) 48–58.

87. Bernard quotes 2 Co 5:13 and then bases his own mystical experience on 2 Co 12:4. It is characteristic for Bernard to consider Paul an authority and at the same time to identify with him. See also SC 74,1–5. On Bernard's relationship to Paul, see Gertrud Frischmuth, *Die paulinische Konzeption in der Frömmigkeit Bernhards von Clairvaux* (Gütersloh, 1935) 42f., and Friedrich Ohly, *Hohelied-Studien. Grundzüge einer Geschichte der Hoheliedauslegung des Abendlandes bis um 1200* (Wiesbaden, 1958) 144.

88. 'Anyone who strives forward toward the spiritual heights must have a lowly opinion of himself; because when he is raised above himself he may lose his grip on himself, unless through true humility, he has a firm hold on himself. It is only when humility warrants it that great graces can be obtained, hence the one to be enriched by them is first humbled by correction that by his humility he may merit them. And so when you perceive that you are being humiliated, look on it as the sign of a sure guarantee that grace is on the way. Just as the heart is puffed up with pride before its destruction, so it is humiliated before being honored. You read in Scripture of these two modes of acting, how the Lord resists the proud and gives his grace to the humble (Jn 4:6)' (SC 34,1; CF 7:160f.).

89. Bernard uses again the figure of sound similarity to express the paradox: 'digna adipisci quod non valet addisci' (SBOp 2:316, 20f.).

90. Standaert, 'Ordination', 205: 'L'humilité revient, somme toute, à cette sujétion parfaite de la volonté de l'homme de celle à Dieu', see also 209ff. '...ut in consensu duorum integrum stet perfectumque connubium' (SC 83,6; SBOp 2:302, 12f.). Essentially, the soul in its tension between bride and mother is anxious to comply with God's will: 'Quite often though the mind is tossed to and fro amid these changes, fearful and violently agitated lest it cling more than is justified to one or the other of these rival attractions and so deviate from God's will even momentarily' (SC 57,9; CF 31:103f.). Balthasar, 460f., emphasizes that the Bible requires to place God's will above the ideal of contemplation.

91. On the composition of Bernard's works, see Leclercq,
     Recueil, 3:56–67, 105–135, 137–62, 180–88.
92. See, for example, SC 47,5ff. and Csi 2,18. See
     also Erich Auerbach, 'Sermo humilis' in *Literatur-
     sprache und Publikum in der lateinischen Spätantike
     und im Mittelalter* (Bern, 1958) 36.
93. See Jean Leclercq, *The Love of Learning and
     the Desire for God. A Study of Monastic Culture*
     (London, New York, 1978) 328.

THE PRE-CISTERCIAN BACKGROUND OF CÎTEAUX AND THE CISTERCIAN LITURGY

Chrysogonus Waddell, OCSO

In 1961 Fr Bruno Schneider, a young monk from the 'Clairvaux of Austria', Heiligenkreuz, began publishing in the pages of *Analecta Sacri Ordinis Cisterciensis*[1] a doctoral dissertation of considerable importance for our understanding of early Cîteaux. This dissertation, *Cîteaux und die benediktinische Tradition: Die Quellenfrage des Liber Usuum im Lichte der Consuetudines monasticae* broke into print, sad to say, at a somewhat inauspicious time. By 1961 the attention of most cistercian monks and nuns had already begun focussing more on what was about to happen at the Second Vatican Council than on what was supposed to have happened in the marshlands outside Dijon towards the close of the eleventh century. Fr Bruno's scholarly study of the sources of the early cistercian usages in the light of customaries of the same period served nonetheless to correct that popular myth which recounts the origins of Cîteaux primarily in terms of a systematic opposition to Cîteaux's opposite number, Cluny and its empire. Important though this opposition is, suggested Fr Bruno, it is much less important than those similarities of observance which ensured first for the New Monastery and then for the nascent Order at large a place well within the mainstream of the more general *ordo monasticus*.[2]

Fr Bruno had the good fortune to have for his mentor Dom Kassius Hallinger, general editor of the monumental *Corpus Consuetudinum Monasticarum;* and the methodology adopted for Fr Bruno's carefully crafted thesis is a credit to master and disciple alike. For his study Fr Schneider had some seventeen customaries at his disposal, chiefly though not exclusively 'benedictine'; and his comparison of cistercian and non-cistercian points of usage bore on some one hundred-fifty details. The general emergent revealed the cistercian customary as lying well within the orbit of Cluny, at least in a general way. For when viewed more particularly, the cistercian usages seemed to be more directly in line with those of the nearby adopted daughter of Cluny, St-Bénigne de Dijon, than with Cluny herself. Was there a *direct* connection between early Cîteaux and the ancient abbey in Dijon? Probably not, decided Fr Bruno, for the evidence suggested intermediary links between Cîteaux and St-Bénigne. Assuming that the earliest cistercian usages had been imported from

Molesme, he noted that abbot Robert of Molesme, the chief architect of the Molesme observance, had been abbot of St-Michel de Tonnerre before being abbot-founder of Molesme in 1075. Now St-Michel de Tonnerre had itself been reformed at an earlier date by the 'second founder' of St Bénigne, the Bl. William (+1031), styled variously of Volpiano or Fruttuaria or Fécamp or Dijon; and under William's aegis, the first administrators and superiors of the reformed community of St-Michel had been, first, Letbald, monk of St-Bénigne; and then, Hunald I, who had been even more closely associated with William in his reforming activity at St-Bénigne. It would have been at St-Michel, then, that abbot Robert had been familiarized with the usages of the great abbey at Dijon, an abbey which, though 'cluniac' and though reformed by one of the greatest disciples of St Mayeul of Cluny (959–994), had nevertheless maintained its own characteristic physiognomy. In brief, early Cîteaux shared a family resemblance with St-Bénigne by way of Molesme and St-Michel de Tonnerre.3

This hypothesis of a 'chain of tradition' linking early Cîteaux with Dijon by way of Molesme and Tonnerre is in no way an essential feature of Fr Schneider's dissertation. For Fr Schneider, the important thing is that, whatever the tensions between Cîteaux and Cluny, the early White Monks remained within the benedictine family—a thesis I myself would like to see re-affirmed and re-affirmed again. As for Cîteaux's indirect contacts with St-Bénigne, this is a fine working hypothesis. But, like every working hypothesis, it remains tentative until proved or disproved by the emergence of new evidence. And new evidence, I believe, is now emerging.

This paper, then, is no more than the sketchiest of progress reports about an area of research opened by recent research into the origins of some of the early cistercian liturgical books. Not modesty, but simply honesty requires that what follows be prefaced by an apologetic note. For, logically, the first thing in the order of priorities should be an edition of all the pertinent documentation; next, a series of monographs dealing with dozens of particular points; and only then, a final synthesis. The recently inaugurated *Cistercian Liturgy Series*, in which each major text edited has a corresponding volume of commentary, represents an initial attempt to speak to this need. But the amount of material to be edited is immense; and the terrain to be explored is largely virgin territory. In an ideal survey, each statement concerning new acquisitions should be supported by concrete proof

--something impossible within the limitations of the present report. I should like, for instance, not only to state that the Molesme responsory-series for the Sundays after Pentecost is identical with that of Montier-la-Celle, but to prove it with the help of comparative charts and detailed references to precise folios. The best I can here do, however, is simply to share with the reader a few general emergents based on reams of comparative charts of material excerpted from unedited and hitherto unstudied manuscripts. In particular, I mean to invite others to join me in exploring regions which call for team-research rather than exploration by isolated individuals; and I accordingly intend to identify, from time to time, areas which seem to beckon for more immediate investigation. Finally, though my interest was originally brought to bear on the material under discussion chiefly because of my love for early Cîteaux, and though it is from this optic that I here envisage my subject, I am no believer in monastic pan-cistercianism. The pre-cistercian monastic milieu about to be discussed would be of immense interest and relevance had the Cistercian Order never come into existence.

STATEMENT OF AN HYPOTHESIS

Let me state straightaway that the chain of tradition which ensures Cîteaux a place well within the *ordo monasticus* has nothing to do, I believe, with St-Bénigne de Dijon; nothing to do even with St-Michel de Tonnerre. The chain indeed links early Cîteaux with Molesme; but from Molesme the chain stretches, not to Tonnerre, but to Troyes and its ancient abbey of Montier-la-Celle; and from Montier-la-Celle the same chain stretches still farther back to Tours and to the even more ancient abbey founded by the poor and humble St Martin: Marmoutier.

PERSONAL PROLEGOMENA

As a young student much interested in the early liturgy of the White Monks, I had assumed--not without encouragement from more than one monastic historian --that the liturgical reforms inaugurated at the New Monastery not long after its foundation in 1098 had been undertaken in part by way of reaction against the cluniac excesses of Molesme, whence came the founding fathers. Back in those days I was foolish enough to presume that, within the benedictine family, whatever wasn't cistercian must be 'cluniac'; and 'cluniac' meant, of course, all that was prolix, ornate, overly dramatic.

It was, of course, a reasonable enough assumption that, prior to the first systematic reforms at the New Monastery, the liturgical books of the fledgling monastery had been basically the same as those of Molesme. After all, in an age when the celebration of the monastic liturgy was still largely a matter of oral tradition involving only a handful of liturgical books for the community at large (with Mass and Office antiphonaries serving chiefly as memory–aids for chants already familiar), it was rather unlikely that a score of pioneering monks would leave Molesme and its liturgy one day and, upon arriving in the forest of *Cistercium* a few days later, would begin chanting a new repertory of texts and melodies from an alien tradition. Indeed, there was one bit of documentary evidence which rendered almost certain the working hypothesis of a basic continuity between the liturgy of the two monasteries. For in his letter dealing with the return of the founder Robert to his former community at Molesme, Hugh, archbishop of Lyons and *quondam* papal legate *(quondam* because of the interregnum following upon the death of Urban II) specified that the 'chapel' (liturgical books of furnishings) brought by the pioneers from Molesme to Cîteaux were to remain with the brethren at Cîteaux, though with the exception of 'a certain breviary' which, with the permission of the monks of Molesme, was to be copied at the New Monastery and then returned before the feast of St John the Baptist.[4] Here is not the place to discuss the nature of this *breviarium*, which was more likely a lectionary with Night Office readings rather than a 'breviary' in the modern sense of the word. Here the important thing is that, according to the terms of Archbishop Hugh's letter, the liturgical books of the New Monastery consisted of either books brought from Molesme or else books copied from a Molesme model.

Later on, of course, most of this Molesme–derived repertory was to be jettisoned by the reformers in keeping with their understanding of fidelity to the Rule and with their passion for the authentic: their hymnal was now to be the 'ambrosian' hymnal from Milan (for Benedict had frequently referred to hymns under the technical term *ambrosianum*); and the Mass and Office chants were to be those of Metz (which boasted sincerely but mistakenly of having faithfully retained the texts and melodies fashioned by Pope St Gregory I). Precisely how long the Molesme chant books remained in use at early Cîteaux is a moot question. At least two or three years would be a reasonable conjecture, however, seeing that the official founding date of the monastery was 21 March 1098, but that the concrete and systematic implementation of the reform already accepted chiefly in principle but not yet worked out in fine detail began only after the brethren had received the papal privilege *Desiderium quod,* dated 19 October 1100.[5] How long it took to decide to appeal to Milan and Metz for help in things liturgical, how long it took to transcribe the material, and how long it took to introduce the rather esoteric repertory in actual practice—all this is a matter largely of guesswork. But between the departure from Molesme and the day on which the Molesme chants were sung for the last time at the New Monastery, there must have been an interval of at least several years.

Any comprehensive historical survey of the cistercian liturgy, such as I ambitioned, ought as a matter of logic to include those first years at the New Monastery. So as a matter of logic I set about discovering what I could about the liturgy at early Molesme.

THE MOLESME LITURGICAL BOOKS

Back in 1907, Jacques Laurent, whose edition of the Molesme cartularies[6] represents a remarkable scholarly achievement of the highest order, had noted in passing that already in the early eighteenth century there were only a few Molesme manuscripts, and that of these only two were known to have survived down to the present day. Unfortunately for my own purposes, neither of these two manuscripts concerned things liturgical.[7] But more Molesme manuscripts survived than Laurent had realized. In his bibliography of breviary manuscripts in French public libraries, Vincent Leroquais succeeded in identifying two breviaries of Molesme provenance. Troyes, Bibliothèque municipale, ms 807,[8] had been assigned by scholars, first with hesitation, then with full assurance, to the church of Langres.[9] Since Molesme was, after all, located in the ancient diocese of Langres, this putative provenance was not so much wrong as imprecise. The second Molesme manuscript is now at Evreux, Bibliothèque municipale, ms 127.[10] While noting the composite nature of this manuscript—calendar, psalter, some missal formularies, sections of breviary material—and while also noting that the manuscript had been adapted for use at the benedictine monastery of Lyre (diocese of Evreux), Leroquais failed to note that, besides being composite, the manuscript is made up of material from two *different* sources. Only the calendar and psalter are from Molesme.

Both manuscripts were written long after the foundation of Cîteaux. The Evreux manuscript (calendar and psalter) is from the thirteenth century, and closer to the middle than to the beginning. The Troyes ms (breviary without notes) Leroquais dated from the first half of the twelfth century; but, on paleographical grounds, a date closer to around the 1170s seems much more likely. For our present purposes, the breviary manuscript is by far the more valuable of the two, which is all the more reason to lament the fact that it is, in its present state, only half of what it once was. The original manuscript was a complete breviary, whose thickness probably made for clumsy handling. Sometime in the thirteenth century it was dismembered and the gatherings were rearranged so as to form a winter season breviary and a summer season breviary. Only this latter has survived, supplemented by a few thirteenth-century folios which make good some of the material retained in the lost winter season volume but also needed in the summer season. Thanks to the scribe's numbering of the gatherings, the organization of the original manuscript can easily be inferred; but this is slight consolation for the loss of all the texts belonging to the period from Advent to Easter in the temporal cycle, and from December 26 to early April in the sanctoral cycle.

A satisfactory beginning had been made. But was it possible to make good the missing material so as to have an integral repertory of the Molesme Office texts?

My attention then turned to manuscripts from the many Molesme dependencies, of which there were some fifty-four priories of monks and nine communities of nuns, to say nothing of a half-dozen abbeys of monks or of nuns in some way affiliated with Molesme.[11] The gleanings were disappointingly meager. From the important priory of nuns, Jully-les-Nonnains, there survive from the thirteenth century two important psalter-hymnals, both of which include calendars: Verdun, Bibliothèque municipale, ms 149;[12] and Lyon, Bibliothèque municipale, ms 539.[13] But from the dozens of other Molesme dependencies I could discover nothing.

Still, the Molesme material now at hand was by no means negligible: nothing at all, musically; but the calendar was recoverable, as was the psalter; the hymn repertory could now be studied in its virtual integrity, as well as the summer season (and even some of the winter season) texts of the breviary. Since the Office collects of the breviary were in part those of the corresponding Mass, some little light was thrown on the non-extant Molesme sacramentary. And though the breviary manuscript contains, by way of Night Office readings, only snippets of the integral texts of the lectionaries used in choir, these snippets suffice for the identification of at least some of the readings in use at Molesme in the twelfth century, if not earlier. Still missing, however, was so much as a single note of music, to say nothing of the bulk of the winter-season repertory of Office material. Could the lacunae be made good from indirect sources other than Molesme's dependencies?

THE SOURCE OF THE MOLESME LITURGICAL BOOKS

Mindful of Fr Bruno Schneider's hypothesis that St Robert had imported the St-Michel de Tonnerre usages into Molesme, I attempted, unsuccessfully, to find whatever might have survived from the liturgical books of St-Michel. Since, however, St-Michel and St-Bénigne would have been monastically of a single piece, according to Fr Bruno, I collated the Molesme material with corresponding sections of two extant breviaries from St-Bénigne.[14] The results were negative, but in a positive sense. Molesme and St-Bénigne belonged to two quite different traditions. If St-Michel really were in line with St-Bénigne, then it was clear that Molesme had broken with this tradition, and that the St-Bénigne books could *not* be used to make good the missing portions of the Molesme repertory. But consider: St Robert's two or three unhappy years as unsuccessful abbot-reformer of St-Michel (1068/1070) were no more than a brief parenthesis in his long monastic career. Why would Robert have adopted for Molesme monastic and liturgical usages from a problematic community of merely episodic importance for Robert's *curriculum vitae*?

Almost inevitably, my attention now turned to the abbey where Robert had been initiated as a youngster into monastic life (towards 1043, and perhaps earlier), and where he had lived as monk and prior for at least a quarter-century before his ill-starred interlude at Tonnerre. I refer to Montier (or Moutier)-la-Celle, the ancient merovingian abbey implanted on the outskirts of Troyes.[15] Was there evidence to be found of any kind of continuity, be it ever so tenuous, between the liturgical observances at Molesme and those of Robert's original monastic family at Montier-la-Celle?

No sacramentary or other Mass book from Montier-la-Celle is known to have survived; but for the Office we have no fewer than three breviary manuscripts —though none earlier than the late thirteenth century.[16] Making due allowance for the inevitable evolution within any local tradition, it seems reasonable to suppose that the substance of the material presented by these late manuscripts would be in line with the same tradition in the mid–eleventh–century form it had had when Robert was at Montier–la–Celle. Such traditions can be interrupted during times of sweeping reform of the sort carried out in so many abbeys when new colonies of monks were introduced to re-invigorate the life of a community in decline; but there were no signs whatsoever of such a switchover of observances at Montier–la–Celle during the period in question. Whatever *a priori* reserve I may have entertained was speedily dispelled, however, as soon as I began my work of collating the material, formulary by formulary. Apart from accidental variants, the texts of the Office chants were so identical that I felt obliged to re-verify the provenance of the Molesme summer–breviary as being indeed from Molesme, and not from Montier–la–Celle. I found the hymn repertory to be all but identical, too—the chief differences being due to additions introduced either at Molesme or at Montier–la–Celle after around 1075. Comparison of collects and short readings or *capitula* proved more interesting. The substance of the repertory was quite the same; but the evidence began pointing to the fact that at Molesme more of an evolution had taken place than at the markedly conservative Montier-la-Celle. Much of the material admitted, too, of only uneasy comparison; because, at the period of Molesme's foundation, some liturgical formulas were not always assigned to a specific formulary. One finds in early manuscripts, for instance, a lengthy series of Advent or Christmastide or Eastertide collects and *capitula;* and it was left to the individual concerned to choose an appropriate text from among the many provided by the manuscript. Thus, two later manuscripts with basically the same collects and *capitula* might assign the material to different formularies; or one manuscript might retain the earlier practice of providing non-assigned texts, while another manuscript assigns the formulas to precise formularies. Another group of formulas requiring finesse on the part of the analyst is that of the Night Office readings. In manuscripts such as we are dealing with, only a tiny part of the integral text can be excerpted by the scribe. A scribe about to 'abbreviate' the four readings of the third nocturn of the First Sunday of Advent might, for instance, decompose the first reading of the four-lesson formula into four brief readings, and forget about the other three of the complete formulary; or he might decide to take as his starting-point a line in the middle of the second lesson in the original group; or he might pick and choose a snippet here, a snippet there. The collation of the same material abridged by two different scribes can therefore be a bit tricky.

It must be remembered, too, that breviaries of the sort which here concern us are a relatively late phenomenon. They are pieced together from material taken from independent and quite separate books: antiphonaries, collectaries, lectionaries, hymnals, psalters. The manner in which the resulting 'breviary' was organized became standardized only at a relatively late date, long, very long after the foundation of Molesme.

All in all, the concordance between the parts of manuscripts common to Montier-la-Celle and Molesme is impressive, and even—in the case of the antiphons and responsories—all but phenomenal. The practical consequence with respect to the antiphons and responsories is this: the antiphons and responsories missing, together with most of the other winter-season material in the Molesme breviary, may be recovered with a reasonable degree of security from the Montier-la-Celle winter-season material. And since it is all but logistically impossible for the texts of a largely oral sung tradition to pass elsewhere without the melodies, or with different melodies, the presumption must be that the melodies recoverable from the Montier-la-Celle books are close if not quasi-identical to those of the Molesme tradition. Here great caution is needed. For Molesme, whose foundation dates back to 1075, also dates from a period when most chant-manuscripts were being notated without clear indication as to precise pitch-relationships. The transmogrification of melodies is all too easy when they pass from an oral tradition to a tradition of imperfect chant notation (a notation without indication of precise pitch-relationships) and then to a tradition of perfect chant notation (with indications of precise pitch relationships). Accordingly, prudence suggests that we see in the late-thirteenth-century noted melodies of Montier-la-Celle merely the general shape rather than the precise version of the melodies sung also at Molesme.

It might be thought that at this stage the mustering of Molesme and Molesme-related *liturgica* had gone about as far as it could. In point of fact, I was simply at the starting-point of a new stage in my survey of the background of primitive Cîteaux.

THE ROOTS OF THE EARLY CITEAUX-MOLESME-
MONTIER-la-CELLE TRADITION

From what little I could learn about Montier-la-
Celle, I concluded, on the basis of its hoary antiquity
and its many monastic dependencies, that the liturgical
tradition of this great abbey must have been pretty
much *sui generis*, rooted in the distant past, and
doubtless reflecting elements proper to the region
of which Troyes was the principal city. I was wrong.

Quite early in my work with the manuscripts
of Montier-la-Celle I had been puzzled by the fact
that in a comparative study of the antiphons for the
Night Office responsories *de psalmis* for the period
between Epiphany and Septuagesima, Fr Raymond Le
Roux, monk of Solesmes, had established an identity
for the material under consideration between the noted
breviary of Montier-la-Celle (Troyes 109) and two
other documents, the one a thirteenth-century noted
breviary from Ste-Trinité de Vendôme (between Blois
and Tours), the other a printed breviary from St-Melaine
de Rennes (Brittany).[17] I was soon able to obtain
a microfilm of the Ste-Trinité breviary, and was more
than a little surprised to note that the identity between
Montier-la-Celle and Ste-Trinité de Vendôme (a monastery
founded only as late as 1032) extended to virtually
the complete repertory. Night Office readings were
clearly drawn from a common source; the basic repertory
of collects and short readings or *capitula* was the
same; the hymn repertory was practically identical;
and even the melodies differed in only minor details.
Surely one must depend on the other, I theorized;
and since Montier-la-Celle was old by half a millenium
before Ste-Trinité was even founded, the presumption
was that Ste-Trinité was somehow beholden in matters
liturgical to the ancient abbey in Troyes. I was wrong
again.

I wasted a considerable amount of time in a vain
attempt to establish some kind of a connection between
Ste-Trinité de Vendôme and Montier-la-Celle; and my
puzzlement grew when, in the course of further comparative studies of particular formularies in various manuscripts, the group constituted by Montier-la-Celle,
Molesme, Ste-Trinité de Vendôme, and St-Melaine de
Rennes expanded to include still other monasteries
such as St-Florent de Saumur and Josaphat in Chartres.
Attempts to link Montier-la-Celle with any of these
other monasteries proved as fruitless as in the case
of Ste-Trinité. Was there some other connection, direct
or indirect, which lay behind the remarkable homogeneity
of these disparate monasteries? There most certainly
was.

MARMOUTIER. *Maius Monasterium,* the Greater Monastery, founded by the humble monk-bishop Martin of Tours in 372, rendered glorious by the presence of the carolingian liturgist *par excellence,* Alcuin, destroyed by the Normans in 853, re-inhabited soon after by the chapter of canons of St Martin, but subsequently restored as a monastery of reformed monks by a colony of monks introduced around 982 under the high authority of St Mayeul, abbot of Cluny. The newly formed community was quick to break its ties with Cluny; but as an independent abbey it flourished, and then flourished still more, becoming itself a center from which colonies of monks went to found new communities (such as Ste-Trinité de Vendôme, in 1032) or to reform and assist communities already founded under different auspices (such as St-Florent de Saumur).

Indeed, the time came soon enough when Marmoutier rivalled Cluny itself as a center of monastic reform. When, for example, Ordericus Vitalis formulated the case against Cîteaux in his *Historia ecclesiastica,* he summed up the Molesme spirit of fidelity to tradition by referring to both Cluny and *Marmoutier:* 'As long as we find the monks of Cluny and Tours [=Marmoutier] ...maintaining these institutions, we shall not depart from them'.[18] Around the same time we find St Bernard himself speaking of the two in the same breath as he asked the rhetorical question: 'What then? Must the monks of Marmoutier [*in Maiore Monasterio*] adopt the customs of Cluny, or should Cluny give place to Marmoutier?'[19] What is here important is that Bernard refers to the two great abbeys on the basis of contrasting monastic customs. Just as significant is a decision made earlier at the council held at Meaux in 1082, which decreed that underpopulated abbeys with less than ten monks should be reduced to non-abbatial rank and subjected either to Cluny or to *Marmoutier.*[20] Popular repute waxes and wanes; and many an amateur medievalist, if asked to name the three most important monastic centers in the eleventh century, might not get beyond 'Cluny'; and even in the case of the professional medievalist, Marmoutier might not be accorded second or even third place. In point of fact, however, the prestige and influence of the abbey was prodigious.

The bibliography for Marmoutier in standard works such as Cottineau's *Répertoire*[21] or Beaunier-Besse's *Abbayes et prieurés de l'ancienne France*[22] is immense. But two areas of research which have remained virtually untouched are those of the Marmoutier liturgy and of their usages. So far as the liturgy is concerned, there is no dearth of material; and for the Office there are no less than three breviary manuscripts still extant, two of them with chant notation.[23]

Now for the Office, there is a virtual identity between Marmoutier and Montier–la–Celle. How does one explain this phenomenon in the case of an abbey like Montier–la–Celle, which was never even remotely subject to Marmoutier in any juridical sense whatsoever? A serious history of Montier–la–Celle has yet to be written;[24] and such a history is, believe me, well worth the writing. On the basis of presently available documentation, however, the fact is that no less than two eleventh–century abbots of Montier–la–Celle had been monks of Marmoutier: Bernard or Bénard, abbot for more than a half–century, from around 1038 to around 1089; and Bernard's immediate successor, Gausmard, who died in December of 1103.

Upon first reading in Mabillon's *Annales Benedictini*, under the year 1038, that Bernard, monk of Marmoutier, was chosen abbot of Montier–la–Celle in virtue of the counsel and authority of Albert, abbot of Marmoutier, I was more than a little puzzled—so much so that I failed to grasp the import of Mabillon's further remark that Albert had been commissioned for this purpose by Count Odo or Eudes.[25]

The reference is, of course, to Eudes II, count of Blois in 1004 and count of Champagne in 1019 (it was in this eleventh century that the title of count of Champagne passed from the house of Vermandois to the house of Blois). Eudes II was nothing if not conscientious and energetic in the exercise of his rights and duties of patronage with respect to the monastic establishments within his vast territory; and in his efforts to assist communities in need of help—of which there were many—he consistently drew on the resources, not of Cluny, which was well outside his domains, but of Marmoutier, his favorite abbey, where, he, like other members of the noble family, was to be buried. Indeed, Eudes II's death in battle occurred only a short time after the preliminaries to the Montier–la–Celle election had been undertaken, so that it was the Count's widow and his boy–heir from whom the abbot–elect, Bernard, received his temporalities.[26]

Not a single shred of extant evidence suggests that the initiative of Eudes II in commissioning Albert of Marmoutier to supervise the election was taken amiss by the brethren of the ancient merovingian abbey at Troyes. They needed help, apparently needed it badly; and their patron and protector, Eudes, was merely doing his job. There is an indication of this in a fascinating letter concerning the election of Bernard, and written in the name of the community to the bishop of Chartres.[27] In the letter the brethren of Montier–

la-Celle explicitly refer to themselves as *nos pauci fratres,* 'we few brethren'; and from the lengthy exordium based on the theme of the superior as the sole means of ensuring peace and concord among the brethren, we may infer that these brethren, few though they were, were not remarkable for their mutual concord and unity of spirit. What was needed was an outsider to ensure, if not to restore, peace and order.

The sources are silent on the point, but I suspect that Albert of Marmoutier provided not only an abbot for the depopulated abbey at Troyes, but other monks as well. For within ten years of Bernard's accession the abbey was able to take over and staff--at the instigation of the Count of Champagne and Blois--the large and important priory of St-Ayoul de Provins, and to embark upon a remarkable program of expansion. Indeed, if one looks objectively at cartularies of the abbey and other sources, the picture is that of an ancient but small abbey which, all of a sudden, takes on a new lease of life around 1038, rapidly expands, and becomes the center of a veritable monastic congregation. It cannot be demonstrated that the introduction of the Marmoutier liturgy at Montier-la-Celle coincided with the advent of abbot Bernard, former monk of the great monastery at Tours; but neither can it be denied that Molesme, founded in 1075, had, in the mid-twelfth century, a breviary compiled from sources quite the same as those used at Montier-la-Celle and Marmoutier. The only working hypothesis which fits the evidence is this: that when Robert left Montier-la-Celle for the brethren at Collan, whom he subsequently transferred to Molesme in 1075, he took with him Montier-la-Celle *liturgica* derived in some manner from Marmoutier. The arrival of abbot Bernard at Montier-la-Celle in 1038 at a critical juncture in the history of the small community may well have been the occasion for the introduction of the Marmoutier liturgical books. Hence the 'chain of tradition' which runs from Molesme through Montier-la-Celle back to Marmoutier (and ultimately to early Cluny of the late tenth century?).

It was also at this juncture that there arrived at Montier-la-Celle a fifteen year-old youngster by the name of Robert. The chronology of Robert's early years is still less than certain, since various authors have him being born as early as around 1017 or as late as around 1029; but whatever the date of Robert's birth, his formative years as a young monk would have coincided with the period of renewal *à la Marmoutier* inaugurated at Montier-la-Celle under the aegis of abbot Bernard. Robert himself must doubtless have played a role in this renewal, for he was Bernard's prior, and--according to his biographer--prior at an early date.[28] Formed as a monk under Bernard, and later, as prior, Bernard's active collaborator in a community only recently involved in the process of reform and renewal, Robert could hardly have remained unmarked by the great tradition of Marmoutier as mediated by abbot Bernard.

This was a tradition he could scarcely have sloughed off when introducing the hermits of Collan into life according to the Rule; and it should come as no surprise that the liturgical life of Molesme was, to the extent we can reconstruct it with the help of the Molesme breviary, of a single piece with that of Montier-la-Celle and Marmoutier.

A SECOND LOOK AT FR SCHNEIDER'S HYPOTHESIS

We now have to return to Fr Schneider's hypothesis about St-Bénigne de Dijon, by way of St-Michel de Tonnerre and Molesme, as a major source of the early cistercian customary. We should recall, in particular, that Fr Schneider himself postulated a link or links between Dijon and Cîteaux, since the evidence--evidence, in point of fact, concerning relatively few points of observance--suggested an indirect rather than a direct link. Unfortunately, for the verification of this hypothesis, nothing remains of a Molesme customary; nothing remains of a St-Michel de Tonnerre customary; the St Bénigne customary is late (thirteenth century); the points of comparison relatively few. What can be verified, however, is this: the Office characteristic of St Bénigne is wholly distinct from the Office character- istic of Molesme--an Office we can trace directly back to Marmoutier. Could it be, then, that we should look, not to Dijon, but to Molesme and Montier-la- Celle and Marmoutier for the more immediate sources of the early cistercian customary?

The terms in which this question is formulated presupposes that monastic usages normally have a history parallel to that of the liturgy. This is, in general, quite true. There are certainly exceptions --and here the Cistercians are an excellent case in point. Their characteristic hymnal (the one which replaced the Molesme hymn-repertory) came straight from Milan; and their Mass and Office chants came from Metz; but their monastic customary was rooted in a tradition in which Milan featured not at all, nor did Metz. Thus, speculatively considered, it is at least possible that the Marmoutier monk Bernard, upon arriving at Montier-la-Celle, brought with him the Marmoutier Office texts and chants, but not the

observances. Normally, however, liturgy and usages
are of a single piece; and since Molesme is at odds
with St-Bénigne in things liturgical, while being very
much at one with Montier-la-Celle and Marmoutier
in things liturgical, it is by no means unreasonable
to examine the hypothesis that Molesme had its monastic
usages from the same sources, and transmitted them
to the New Monastery.

It is doubtful that such a hypothesis will ever
be fully verified: nothing remains of a Molesme or
Montier-la-Celle Customary; and the same is true of
Marmoutier itself, despite the fact that source documentation connected with the abbey is so abundant as to
constitute a veritable library. Should it ever be possible
to recover a sufficient amount of material from Marmoutier
customary sources, direct or indirect, then only would
we have the means of testing the working hypothesis
of a link running from Marmoutier to the New Monastery
for the customary as well as for the liturgical books.
But because of the undeniable linkage in things liturgical, such a parallel linkage in monastic observances
seems considerably more likely than Fr Schneider's
suggestion of an indirect link with St-Bénigne de
Dijon.

THE SURVIVAL OF MOLESME LITURGICA
AT THE NEW MONASTERY

It may rightly be objected that, though it is
well and good to talk about the Marmoutier background
of the Office books at Montier-la-Celle and Molesme,
there is no evidence that, after the initial reforms
carried out at the New Monastery, any of this earlier
tradition managed to subsist in the reformed community,
and that the same could well hold true of the customs
from the same milieu. My answer is that the premise
is quite wrong. For there *is* evidence that, despite
the massive upheaval caused by the adoption of the
Ambrosian hymns and the Metz Mass and Office chants,
something of the earlier tradition survived as a basis
of further reform. The question calls for a detailed
presentation with a lengthy monograph for each point
studied. Here all I can do is formulate a few of the
tentative results of my own research.

In the case of the KALENDAR, the evidence speaks
clearly: for the classification of feasts Cîteaux adopts
the brutally simple norms of the Rule of Benedict
(while also allowing for commemorations of saints
after the dismissal verse of Lauds and Vespers); but
the kalendar as a whole is only a simplification of
the Molesme kalendar, which in turn is a simplification

of the even more ample Montier–la–Celle kalendar. For the moment I have not carried this research farther back than Montier–la–Celle.[29] The major differences in the list of saints included in the sanctoral cycle of these several monasteries are due largely to geographical factors: the kalendar of Montier–la–Celle abounds in saints peculiar to Troyes; Molesme, lying in a different diocese, abandons most of the saints of Troyes, while adopting the favorite saints of the region around Tonnerre; and the New Monastery does precisely the same in the diocese of Châlons–sur–Seine. Further differences between Montier–la–Celle and Molesme result from the practice of celebrating the feasts of the patrons of their respective priories and churches. Thus, St Ayoul (in Provins) features large only in the Montier–la–Celle kalendar, whereas St Aniane (patron of an entire village owned by Molesme) is especially prominent in the Molesme kalendar. The dependence of the New Monastery on Molesme for its kalendar is particularly interesting in that the earliest extant manuscripts reveal that the sanctoral in the body of manuscript breviary, sacramentary, gradual, epistolary and evangeliary was that of the ancient Franco–Roman books, even though the kalendar contained many other entries of a more local regional stamp. (Formularies for these regional saints were relegated to the Common.) It would have been relatively simple for the early Cistercians to limit themselves to the sanctoral cycle of the earlier carolingian books with a few necessary adjustments. But they preferred to remain quite in line with the Molesme tradition.

The cistercian NIGHT OFFICE LECTIONARY is basically that of Molesme and the antecedent tradition, but purged of all readings by authors who failed to qualify, in keeping with the exigencies of the Holy Rule, as 'well–known and orthodox Catholic Fathers'.[30] In point of fact, the earliest extant breviary–manuscript, from around 1132,[31] is somewhat lax in this regard; and the series of readings excerpted by the scribe for the period after Pentecost is suspiciously close to that of the Molesme breviary.[32] One particularly curious detail of cistercian practice is noted by Fr Réginald Gregoire, OSB, in his analysis of the cistercian homiliary in its shape of around 1175: lessons 9–12 of the third nocturn often give the opening passage of a homily, while passages from later sections of the same homily occur partially or wholly as lessons 1–8 of the first two nocturns. This inversion of sequence is, Fr Grégoire says, a specifically cistercian phenomenon.[33] Not so. We find the same curious practice at Montier–la–Celle.

The cistercian EVANGELIARY seems to point, in its earliest recoverable form, to only a slight re-working of the system we find in part at Molesme and wholly at Montier-la-Celle. The most peculiar feature of the early cistercian gospel-series is the use of Luke 4:14–22 for the Sunday preceding Septuagesima Sunday. Dom Kassian Lauterer, in a provisional edition of the earliest extant cistercian breviary, called attention in a note to the untraditional character of this pericope in this particular place, and pointed out that Henri Barré had found the same pericope similarly placed in only a single Bavarian homiliary.[34] Just so. But the same oddity occurs at Montier-la-Celle. It would seem that for the evangeliary early Cîteaux remains, once again, in the line of Molesme and Montier-la-Celle. For the EPISTOLARY we have nothing from the two older monasteries to compare to the earliest extant cistercian epistolary; so it is no more than an informed guess (but a reasonable one) to suggest that the history of the early cistercian epistolary was parallel to that of the cistercian evangeliary.

The early cistercian system of OFFICE COLLECTS is also in line with that of Molesme and Montier-la-Celle. It should be remembered that the general practice of the period was to provide, not just one collect for a particular day, but three: the principle one for the Night Office, Lauds, Terce and Vespers; but also a different one for Sext, and a still different one for None. The basis of the collect-repertory in the Marmoutier milieu was a 'gregorian' sacramentary with the Supplement now generally ascribed, thanks to the brilliant detective work of Fr Jean Deshusses, OSB, to Benedict of Aniane.[35] But this basic repertory was further supplemented with extraneous material. Compared to the late but relatively sober Montier-la-Celle manuscripts, the Molesme breviary of around 1175 appears distinctly innovative. As for the Cistercians, they seemed to have purged their collect-repertory of its non-gregorian elements, making relatively few errors in the process. Clearly, they must have had some objective norm to help them identify the gelasian and other extraneous formulas foreign to the 'gregorian' books of an earlier date. But even after this 'purge' of the collect-repertory, the cistercian series remains remarkably in line with that of Montier-la-Celle. This suggests that at the time of the secession of the cistercian pioneers from Molesme, the Molesme collect-series was closer to Montier-la-Celle than it was when the single extant Molesme breviary was written around 1175.

But the early cistercian books contain other reminiscences of Molesme and Montier-la-Celle even in the Office antiphonary, despite the fact that this book was based directly on the Metz books, which had the reputation (undeservedly, alas) of being authentically 'gregorian'.[36] Whereas all the recoverable Office manuscripts from Metz provide multiple choices for most of the many *Magnificat* and *Benedictus* antiphons in the post-Pentecost season, the cistercian reformers eliminated this flexibility and, as often as possible, chose those antiphons already familiar to them from the Molesme repertory. A particularly noteworthy instance of this discreet continuity with Molesme is evident in the series of Saturday *Magnificat* antiphons based on texts from the books of Kings. In the Marmoutier series, there are eleven such antiphons, as also at Montier-la-Celle (and at Ste-Trinité de Vendôme). The identical antiphons also appear—all eleven—at Molesme; but the order has been reworked, in the case of antiphons 3-8, in an attempt (not wholly successful) to arrange them in a more coherent chronological order. The Metz sources have a somewhat different series still differently arranged. While having, as a matter of principle, to draw from Metz sources, the Cistercians nonetheless followed, as much as they could, the unique order of the Molesme series. Something similar obtains, by way of further example, for the Annunciation Office. Metz sources offer a proper Office of relatively late and non-classical vintage; whereas the older tradition draws the Annunciation material from the Advent cycle —as at Marmoutier and Montier-la-Celle (and probably at Molesme, though this is not demonstrable because of the lacunose state of our Molesme breviary manuscript). Early Cîteaux followed the classical tradition. While drawing the texts from the Metz Advent material, however, it chose them and arranged them in a manner astonishingly close to the Montier-la-Celle model. Given the wide range of Advent material to draw from, and the countless possibilities for arranging this material in different sequence, the parallelism between early Cîteaux and Montier-la-Celle cannot be fortuitous. Something similar obtains in the case of the St Benedict Office—though, in this instance, there is a good chance that even the music of Montier-la-Celle-Molesme was retained.[37]

CONCLUSIONS

In summary, my impression is that the first Cistercians were far from disdaining their liturgical patrimony from Molesme. Out of fidelity to the Rule as they understood it, and out of their passion for the 'authentic', they courageously went to Milan for their hymnal and to Metz for the Mass and Office chants. But for the rest, they seem to have used the Molesme patrimony (itself transmitted from Marmoutier by way of Montier-la-Celle) as their point of departure for a reworking and 'purification' of that same tradition. To understand the earliest cistercian liturgical practices during the first few years at the New Monastery we must look to Molesme, but also to Montier-la-Celle, and finally to Marmoutier; and an awareness of this background remains important for us even at a later date, when the Milanese hymnal and the Metz chant books replaced those inherited from Molesme.

Since the liturgical 'chain of tradition' goes from early Cîteaux back to Marmoutier by way of Molesme and Montier-la-Celle, totally ignoring St-Bénigne de Dijon, it is possible if not likely that the 'chain of tradition' in monastic usages and observances linked exactly the same monasteries within the same general tradition. But this is a working hypothesis which has to be verified.

The vaguely 'cluniac' stamp of the early cistercian usages would, in this hypothesis, be readily explicable, seeing that the Marmoutier observance had been first inaugrated under the aegis of St Mayeul, abbot of Cluny, a colony of his hand-picked monks. But Cluny itself underwent a considerable evolution, so that by the late eleventh century the usages of Marmoutier could be spoken of as distinct from the usages of Cluny.

At this stage, the two areas I most wish to see explored by competent scholars are those of early Marmoutier and of Cluny in the corresponding period. It is astonishing how often, for instance, 'rare' antiphon or responsory texts in the Marmoutier-Montier-la-Celle-Molesme tradition are found also at St-Maur-des-Fossés and (to a much lesser extent) even at St-Denis. Despite their fierce spirit of independence a vis-à-vis Cluny, Marmoutier, St-Maur, and St-Denis all passed through a brief perid of dependence on the abbot of Cluny.

In our attempts to study a particular phenomenon such as early Cîteaux, it is not only understandable but essential that we consider those features unique and most particular to the object of our study. But we shall never come to a real understanding of early Cîteaux unless we also appreciate the equally important areas in which the New Monastery remained in profound continuity with Molesme and Montier-la-Celle and Marmoutier and even, perhaps, early Cluny. Fr Bruno Schneider's working hypothesis of a 'chain of tradition' linking the New Monastery with St-Bénigne de Dijon

may well be, given the emergents from a comparative
liturgical analysis, less than likely; but the place
of Cîteaux well within the *ordo monasticus*--and this
is the essential part of his thesis--is amply and emphatically confirmed.

Gethsemani Abbey

NOTES

1. The dissertation appeared in two issues, vol.
    16 (1960, fasc. 3-4) 171-254, and vol. 17 (1961,
    fasc. 1-2) 89-114; but it was also printed separately
    and re-paginated with continuous page numbers.
    References are to the latter version.
2. For a perceptive appreciation of the importance
    of Fr Schneider's dissertation, as well as a helpful
    summary of the methodology adopted, see the review
    by Fr Jacques Hourlier, OSB, in *Studia Monastica*
    4 (1962) 246-248.
3. Schneider, *Cîteaux*, 123-126.
4. The letter forms the bulk of Chapter VII of the
    Exordium Parvum in any of the many editions
    of this narrative of the foundation and early
    years of the New Monastery. The most practical
    edition is the one by Fr Jean de la Croix Bouton
    and Fr Jean-Baptiste Van Damme, *Les plus anciens
    textes de Cîteaux. Cîteaux-Commentarii Cistercienses.*
    Studia et Documenta. Vol. II (Belgium: Achel,
    1974), where the pertinent paragraph of Hugh's
    letter is on p. 65: 'De capella etiam praedicti
    abbatis Roberti, et de ceteris rebus quas a molismen-
    si ecclesia recedens secum tulit, et cum eis Cabilonen-
    si episcopo atque novo monasterio se reddidit,
    id statuimus ut omnia fratribus novi monasterii
    salva permaneant, praeter breviarium quoddam,
    quod usque ad festivitatem sancti Johannis Baptistae
    retinebunt, ut transcribant assensu molismensium'.
5. The text of the Roman Privilege is followed, in
    the *Exordium Parvum,* immediately by Chapter
    XV, which deals with the general principles and
    some particular points of the New Monastery obser-
    vance. The adverb *dehinc* forms the connecting
    link with the text of the Roman Privilege immediately
    preceding: *Dehinc,* 'From this time forth', 'hence-
    forth', 'since then', 'afterward', 'hereupon',

or any other of the many dictionary meanings. However clearly the principles of reform had been previously agreed upon, it was only after the reception of the Roman Privilege that the reformers felt free to implement their program systematically.

6. Jacques Laurent, *Cartulaires de Molesme*. 2 vols. (Paris: Alphonse picard et Fils, 1907–1911).

7. Laurent, *Cartulaires* I: p. 6, note 5. Eighteenth-century sources refer only to 'quelques manuscripts en papier et en vélin', i.e., to 'some', 'a few'. The two identifiable surviving manuscripts are both in Paris: Bibliothèque Sainte-Geneviève, ms 73; and Bibliothèque de l'Arsenal, ms 776.

8. Vincent Leroquais, *Les bréviaires manuscrits des bibliothèques publiques de France* IV (Paris, 1934) 220.

9. See the bibliographical references at the end of the description of the manuscript, *ibid.*, 220.

10. Leroquais, *Les bréviaires* II: pp. 106–107, where many of the details call for correction.

11. List of houses with bibliographical notes in Laurent, *Cartulaires* I: 207–266, 272–275.

12. Description in Vincent Leroquias, *Les psautiers manuscrits des bibliothèques publiques de France* II (Mâcon, 1940) 264–265.

13. *Ibid.*, Vol. I: pp. 232–236.

14. Paris, Bibliothèque d'Arsenal, ms 274 (non-noted breviary, 14th cent.); description of ms in Leroquais, *Bréviaires* II: 324–326; Dijon, Bibliothèque municipale, ms 113 (non-noted breviary, prob. 14th cent); description in Leroquais, *Bréviaires* II: 23–25.

15. For an extensive bibliography, see L. H. Cottineau, *Répertoire Topo-bibliographique des Abbayes et des Prieurés* II (Mâcon, 1939) 1952–1954.

16. Châlons-sur-Marne, Bibliothèque municipale, ms 360, 14th-cent. non-noted winter-season breviary, but with 16th cent. additions so as to make it complete breviary; partly mutilated and lacunose; description in Leroquais, *Bréviaires* I: 253–255. Troyes, Bibliothèque municipale, ms 109, late 13th-cent. noted winter-season breviary; description in Leroquais, *Bréviaires* IV: 212–214; ms 1974, late 13th-cent. non-noted breviary; description in Leroquais, *Bréviaires* IV: 253–256.

17. 'Les Répons de Psalmis pour les Matines, de l'Epiphanie à la Septuagésime', in *Études Grégoriennes* VI (1963) 39–148, with special reference to p. 107.

18. *Historia ecclesiastica* III. viii. 25; PL 188:640.

19. *De praecepto et dispensatione* 48; PL 182:386;

Leclercq, *Sancti Bernardi Opera* III (Rome, 1963) 286.
20. Mabillon, *Annales Ordinis Sancti Benedicti*...V (Lucca: 1740) 173: 'In praedicto concilio Meldensi statutum est ut minores abbatiae, in quibus duodecim monachorum numerus cum abbate sustentari non poterat, Cluniacensis vel Majoris-monasterii abbatum procurationi subjicerentur...' Cf. Mansi, *Sacrosanctorum Conciliorum...collectio...*20:587.
21. Cols. 1762-1766 of the volume referred to above, note 15.
22. Tome VIII (Ligugé-Paris, 1920) 26-32.
23. Evreux, Bibliothèque municipale, ms 119 (13th cent., lacunose, beginning only with Palm Sunday); Rouen, Bibliothèque municipale, ms A. 164 (11th cent., with non-diastematic chant notation); Tours, ms 153 (13th cent., sanctoral, diastematic chant notation).
24. Neither the *Histore abrégée de l'ancienne et illustre abbaye de Montier-la-Celle-lèz-Troyes* by Dom S. Dieudonné, OSB (Troyes, Bibliothéque municipale, ms 2688), nor Dom Titon's *Histoire de l'abbaye de Montier-la-Celle* (Troyes, Bibliothèque municipale, ms 2663) satisfies the exigencies of serious historical writing, even by eighteenth-century standards. C. Lalore's useful edition of the abbey's cartularies, *Cartulaire de Montier-la-Celle* (Paris-Troyes, 1882) contains a great deal of helpful material, but in no way replaces the need for a comprehensive history of the ancient abbey.
25. '...Haec electio facta est consilio atque auctoritate Alberti Majoris-monasterii abbatis, qui ab Odone comite ejus rei curam susceperat...' *Annales OSB* IV: p. 390.
26. 'Electione facta, idem Albertus electum obtulit Hermengardi comitissae, sub cujus ditione locus ipse consistit, et Stephano comiti ejus filio, a quibus donum rerum temporalium, ad idem pertinentium coenobium, suscepit'. *Ibid.* The Countess Ermengarde d'Auvergne, sister of King Robert's wife, Constance, was the second wife of Eudes II.
27. The letter survived chiefly because it found its way into the register of letters of Bishop Fulbert of Chartres, and was included in early editions of Fulbert's correspondence--as in the 1618 edition of Tome XI of the *Bibliotheca magna veterum patrum*, p. 27CD, where the text appears as Epistola 107. Once the error was detected, the letter--transcribed almost *in extenso* in Dom Dieudonné's *Histoire abrégée*, pp. 150-151--was excluded from editions of Fulbert's correspondence.

28. The early thirteenth-century *Vita* has been edited with a detailed introduction by Fr Kolumban Spahr, O.Cist., *Das Leben des hl. Robert von Molesme. Eine Quelle zur Vorgeschichte von Cîteaux* (Fribourg: Paulusdruckerei, 1944). The pertinent text, p. 5 of this edition, reads: 'ille, in cuius manu corda sunt hominum eiusdem domus fratribus inspiravit, ut virum Dei Robertum sibi eligerent in priorem'. This election of Robert as prior by the community is a bit suspect, since Lalore, *Cartulaire*, p. XXIV, included the prior in his list of five officials who owed their lifetime appointment to the abbot.

29. A detailed study of the kalendars of early Cîteaux, Molesme, and Montier-la-Celle will appear in the *Cistercian Liturgy Series*, incorporating material from an earlier unpublished monograph and a conference given earlier under the auspices of the Cistercian Institute at the 1983 International Congress on Medieval Studies.

30. St Benedict, *Rule for Monasteries* 9:8.

31. West Berlin, Prüssischer Kulturbesitz, ms lat. in oct. 402. The date of the ms is supplied chiefly by indications in the *computus* table at the end of the kalendar.

32. A comparison of the two manuscripts forms part of a lengthy monograph, *The Cistercian Night Office Lectionary in the Twelfth Century*, which will appear, revised and expanded, in the *Cistercian Liturgy Series*.

33. Fr Réginald Grégoire, 'L'Homiliaire cistercien du manuscrit 114 (82) de Dijon', in *Cîteaux. Commentarii Cistercienses* 18 (1977) p. 135: '...phénomène qui semble spécifiquement cistercien: les leçons 9–12...donnent souvent une homélie dont la suite constitue les leçons des deux premiers nocturnes, partiellement ou totalement...'.

34. 'Mirum est, unde R I hoc evangelium Lc 4, 14 sumpserit quod omnino differt a cetera pericoparum traditione. Barré unum exemplum adfert Homéliaire bavarois p. 322...' (p. 110 of the *hors de commerce* edition, a revision of which is in preparation for general distribution, under the main editorship of Fr Alberic Altermatt, O.Cist.).

35. Jean Deshusses, OSB, 'Le "Supplément" au sacramentaire grégorien: Alcuin ou s. Benoît d'Aniane?' in *Archiv für Liturgiewissenschaft* IX/I (1965) 48–71.

36. St Bernard, 'Prologue to the Revised Cistercian Antiphonary': 'Missis denique qui Metensis ecclesiae antiphonarium—nam id Gregorianum esse dicebatur

—transcriberent at afferent....' Text from F. J. Guentner, SJ (ed.), *Epistola S. Bernardi de revisione cantus cisterciensis et Tractatus scriptus ab auctore incerto cisterciense.* Corpus Scriptorum de Musica 24 (American Institute of Musicology, 1974), p. 21.

37. Extant Metz mss are here a bit problematic, since they either give, for St Benedict, only a few proper formulas for a minor feast (as in the Metz Cathedral antiphonary, Metz, Bibliothèque municipale, ms 461—a ms destroyed in World War II, but recoverable in photocopy) or else a rhymed office of recent vintage (as in the St-Arnould breviary, Metz, Bibliothèque municipale, ms 573). It is impossible to know, on the basis of extant mss, just what St Benedict material the early twelfth-century Cistercians found at Metz; but the 'corrected' Westmalle antiphonary fragments (no shelf-number), which include many folios from pre-1147 antiphonaries erased in part and overwritten with the new texts and melodies of around 1147, have relatively few emendations in the melodies of the St Benedict Office. Both text and melodies are much in line with those of the Montier-le-Celle books. But closer study is needed before concluding (or not concluding) that the early cistercian St Benedict Office derives, by way of exception, from Molesme rather than from Metz.

MECHTHILD VON MAGDEBURG:
EXILE IN A FOREIGN LAND

Odo Egres, O. Cist.
(1918–1979)

Few facts are known about Mechthild's life.[1] There are some autobiographical references in *The Flowing Light of God*. Events are mentioned which may have prompted her to take a stand, or to explain things in writing, perhaps with the unmedieval intention of escaping the anonymity which was the common fate of medieval women. About the last ten years of her life there is abundant information in the writings of Mechthild von Hackeborn and St Gertrude the Great. As witnesses of those years in the Convent of Helfta, these two cistercian nuns apotheosized her death as this earthly pilgrim's arrival in the Palace–Court of God.

According to the generally accepted reckoning of Emil Michael,[2] Mechthild von Magdeburg was born in 1210 in the vicinity of Magdeburg, a prosperous town governed by its own elected council. Magdeburg was also an important member of the Hanseatic League. During the troublesome years of the early sixteenth century, its archbishop, Cardinal Albert of Brandenburg, authorized the preaching of indulgences and thus became instrumental in launching Martin Luther's Reformation.

We learn from the opening dialogue of *The Flowing Light of God* that Mechthild was the daughter of well-to-do parents. Throughout the entire book she mentioned them only one more time: in a prayer for the repose of their souls. In this dialogue she complains that Lady Love had taken from her the happy days of her childhood, her friends and relatives, and her treasured possessions:

> *frowe minne ir hant mir benommen die welt*
> *weltlich ere un allen weltlichen richtuom.*
> Lady Love, you have taken from me the world,
> worldly honor and all my possessions....[3]

The Latin version of *The Flowing Light of God* also mentions that Mechthild had a younger brother who died as a Dominican friar in the city of Halle.

By her own admission, she was a happy child. She received a good education. Her knowledge of courtly manners, her independent spirit and her writings, rivalling with the best of her time, prove that during the tender years of her childhood she had had the advantage of all the available means of learning, without having entered a convent. Yet she frequently called herself an 'unlearned' and 'uneducated' woman. In the seventh book of *The Flowing Light of God*, written in her old age, she made excuses to the sisters of Helfta when they asked her to give them instructions. 'You expect me to teach you when I myself am unlearned' (VII.21). Such apologetic utterances, taken from the common stock of monastic parlance, should not, however, be taken literally because self–depreciations of this kind were common; they were used even by the brightest minds. Mechthild's note may have claimed 'inexperience' in spiritual guidance or it may have referred to the fact that she had no systematic training in scholastic theology, since as a child she did not attend one of the elite convent schools established for noble girls which competed with the best monastic schools for men in theological training. Mechthild had no knowledge of Latin. In a long poem which praised the simplicity of God's instruction, she suddenly interrupted the rhythmical flow of theological terms and helplessly complained about the inadequacy of the German idioms for the recording of God's teaching in human words. In her exasperation she wrote:

> *nu gebristed mir tutsches,*
> *des latines kan ich nit.*
> Here my German failes me
> and Latin I know not. (II. 3).

The story of Mechthild's childhood and youth, the typical medieval circumstances of her call to the monastic life, and the reasons for writing in a very un–medieval fashion about her personal experiences, are summed up in the second chapter of Book Four in *The Flowing Light of God:*

All my life, before I began this book and before a single word of it came from God into my soul, I was the simplest creature....Of the devil's wickedness I knew nothing nor of the evil of the world nor of the falseness of so–called spiritual people.
In the twelfth year of my life I, an unworthy sinner, was greeted by the Holy Spirit so overpoweringly when I was alone that I could no longer have given way to any daily serious sin....I knew nothing of God except the usual Christian beliefs and I tried to follow them diligently....God Himself is my witness that I never consciously

asked him to give me the things of which I have written in this book. I had never dreamt that such things could come to any human being. While I was living with relations and friends to whom I was most dear, I had no inkling of such matters....Then through the love of God I went to a town [Magdeburg] where I had no friends....But God never left me....For twenty years I was never but tired, ill, and weak, first from remorse and sorrow, then from good desires and spiritual effort. There after many days of bodily illness the almighty love of God struck me so powerfully with its wonders that I could no longer keep silent, although on account of my simpleness I was sorry for it. I exclaimed 'Merciful God, what have You seen in me? You know that I am a fool, a sinner, a poor creature both in body and soul. Such things as these You should have shown to the wise...'. Then I went in humble shame to my confessor...and asked for guidance. He said I should go joyfully forward; God who had called me would look after me. Then He commanded me to do that for which I often weep for shame when my unworthiness stands clear before my eyes, namely, that I, a poor and despised little woman, should write this book out of God's heart and mouth. This book, therefore, has come lovingly from God and is not drawn from human senses (IV.2).

According to this sketch of her early life, Mechthild moved to Magdeburg probably in 1235. As the Latin version of *The Flowing Light of God* put it, she lived there as an *exul in terra aliena,* as an 'exile in a foreign land', as a beguine in a semi-religious community of women who did not take the traditional religious vows.[4] She dedicated herself to works of piety and manual labor and cared for the sick and the poor.

Mechthild's prayer, *Dominice, lieber vater min,* 'Dominic, my dear father', proves that the Beguine house at Magdeburg had been entrusted to the spiritual guidance of the Dominican Order. Here, under the watchful eyes of a *Domini cane,* a 'hound of the Lord', as she called her confessor, Mechthild spent her life in a daily renunciation of the natural aspirations of a woman. What had been fulfillment to others, she repudiated as the source of all unhappiness. Of course, she experienced love in abundance, but God

never ceased to ask it back from her, to beg for
it in the manner of needy lovers. While he placed
her under the immediate radiance of his divine love,
he did not allow her a moment's rest under the shades
of human affections. The crushing burdens of poverty,
work and illness were the only visible signs of God's
love; life was to her like water under the heat of
the sun:

> When I came to the spiritual life,
> and took leave of the world,
> I looked at my body––
> it was heavily armed
> against my poor soul:
> With plenty of might
> and with the full powers of nature.
> It was clear to me: here is my enemy.
> I saw that were I to escape everlasting death,
> I must utterly conquer my own self
> and that would be a sore struggle.
> Then I looked at the armor of my soul,
> and saw that they were
> the sublime suffering and death of our Lord
>   Jesus Christ––
> That was my protection.
> I must be in constant fear
> for all my enemies aim heavy blows at my body.
> Sighing, weeping, confession, recollection,
> discipline and prayer––
> These I must constantly practice (IV.2).[5]

In these lines Mechthild characterized her life as
a struggle between body and soul. Then she turned
to prose and enumerated the implications of this spiritual
warfare:

> With these weapons of my soul I so painfully
> conquered the body that for twenty years I
> was never but tired, ill and weak, first
> from remorse and sorrow, then from good
> desires and spiritual effort....The mighty
> love of God struck me so powerfully with its
> wonders that I could no longer keep silent.
> (IV.2).

What she had to say netted her many enemies.
She openly criticised the 'false people in ruling posi-
tions' (V.35) and their shameful conduct. This caused
her to say 'outrageous' things even about the canons
of Magdeburg; she called these clerics 'goats...because
they reek of impurity regarding Eternal Truth. If
they are to become lambs, they must eat the fodder

which Master Dietrich[6] has laid in the manger for them, that is, holy penance and faithful counsel in confession' (VI.3). When one of these clerics questioned the orthodoxy of her visions, she gave him the nickname, 'my Pharisee'. She told him, 'your lies and your hatred will not be forgiven', but then, as a good Christian, she qualified her strong words by adding, 'without suffering' (VI.35). Such harsh critical utterances show Mechthild von Magdeburg as a fearless woman with a fiery temper. Wilhelm Preger therefore believed that she was a thirteenth century female Martin Luther. Preger also compared the strong and fiery words which Mechthild used against certain Church officials with the poems of Walther von der Vogelweide (d. 1230), whose biting irony, brilliant imagery, and violent denunciation of clerical abuses must have been known to her. Certain passages of *The Flowing Light of God*, for instance,

> your gold is dimmed in the filth of evil desires; you must become poor; you have no true love; your purity is burned up in the consuming fire of greed; your humility is sunk in the swamp of your flesh...the flowers of all the virtues have fallen from you...you make war upon God and upon his chosen friends (VI.21),

could indeed have been inspired by the bitter attacks of Walther's political poems, written at a time when, in opposition to the political designs of Pope Innocent III, patriotic feelings flared up and called for German self-assertion.[7] Other scholars, among then Heinrich Denifle and Wilhelm Oehl,[8] argued on the other hand that the indignation in Mechthild's writings was the sure voice of an emerging individualism which, however, did not call for an outright repudiation of ecclesiastical authority. In the very first sentence of *The Flowing Light of God*, God says: 'This book I now send forth as a messenger to all spiritual people both good and bad--for if the pillars fall, the building cannot stand'. Its meaning is that in the eyes of God the pillars, i.e., the Church authorities, are still standing and throughout the entire book Mechthild's prevailing attitude is not one of bitter antagonism, but sincerity, generosity and whole-hearted forgiveness. 'If I see my friend and my enemy in equal need, I shall help both equally' (V.22).

As a beguine, Mechthild devoted her life to the alleviation of the needs of the poor and the suffering: 'We seek and find the stranger, the sick and the

prisoner, and comfort them with friendly words and
prayers'. To these simple words describing the beguine's
vocation she added the incomparable couplet:

> *du solt die siechen laben*
> *und solt doch selbe nit haben.*
> Comfort the weary
> without finding comfort for yourself (V.22).

The Convent of St Agnes, originally a cistercian
foundation, was Mechthild's home for more than thirty
years at Magdeburg. As an angel of mercy, she gave
love and consolation to those who in their misery
looked for a ray of hope; she helped and consoled
the *edlen armen,* 'the noble poor', and the sick,
by offering them human compassion.

While pursuing this service, she was 'struck
by the mighty love and wonders of God'. She wrote
down her soul's encounter with God on loose sheets
of paper in her Low German dialect, thus entrusting
her inmost thoughts and feelings to poetic permanence.
This was not easy for her:

> Some [people] may wonder, how I, a sinful
> being, can dare to write about such things.
> I say truly that had not God bestowed a
> singular grace on my heart seven years ago,[9]
> I should have kept silence and never dared
> to write. But thanks to God's mercy, the
> writing did me no harm (III.1).

But the encouragement of her confessor, whose name
she does not mention, dispelled Mechthild's reluctance
to commit her thoughts to writing. It was this confessor
who circulated the first poems written on loose sheets
of paper among the religious houses of the Magdeburg
area.

These highly personal revelations, charged with
the emotions of a passionate woman, also caught the
attention of Heinrich von Halle, who had once been
a student of St Albert the Great and was now lector
at Neuruppin, the first dominican house in Saxony,
founded by the great Wichmann von Arnstein (d. 1270).
Wichmann's letters, which circulated among convents
and houses of beguines under the auspices of the
Dominican Order, are the first indications that the
bridal mysticism of St Bernard of Clairvaux had by
this time already become known in certain parts of
Germany. Hence, it is not surprising that this lofty
poetic imagery of western spirituality went on to flourish, with a German flavor, in the writings of Mechthild

von Magdeburg, Mechthild von Hackeborn, and St Gertrude the Great. After Wichmann's death, Heinrich joined the newly founded community of Halle in 1271; hence his name *Henricus Hallensis* in the annals of the Dominican Order. He had the reputation of a scholar, based on his book *Wider die Keczir (Against the Heretics)* now lost, but widely known still in the sixteenth century as a firm apology of traditional christian doctrine. Its uncompromising logic greatly aided the German Dominicans in their fight against various heresies. A document from the year 1273 additionally reveals that Heinrich had been a close friend of the most influential cistercian abbots in Saxony and frequently met Hermann von Walkenried, Reinhard von Pforta, Dietmar von Volkerode, and Edmund von Reifenstein.

Heinrich von Halle heard about Mechthild von Magdeburg most probably from his sister Oda, a beguine herself, who lived in or not far from Magdeburg and must have provided her brother with the first writings of Mechthild, which by then had been severely criticized by many of his confrères. Heinrich, too, must have had doubts about the orthodoxy and the theological accuracy of these visionary writings, because prior to his decision to arrange them into books and translate them into Latin, he wrote a letter to Mechthild asking her to explain how her visions and their description, often touching the fringes of unmistakable sensuality, should be understood. The beguine's answer apparently assured Heinrich that her visions and poems were compatible with scholastic teaching. He even included Mechthild's letter in the Latin translation of *The Flowing Light of God* with the introductory remark, *Frater Henricus dictus de Hallis, lector Rupinensis, admiratus de dictis et scriptis Sororis Mechtildis tale ab ipsa recepit responsum.* Then he faithfully copied it, perhaps for the sake of justifying his translation:

> Master Heinrich, you are surprised at my bold words which are found in this book? I wonder why that surprises you? But it grieves *me* to the heart that I, a sinful woman, had to write. Yet I cannot otherwise describe to anyone the true knowledge and glorious holy revelations save in these words alone, which seem to me all too poor in the face of Eternal Truth. I asked the Lord Everlasting what he would say to you and he answered: 'Ask Master Heinrich how it came to pass that the Apostles, who at first were so weak, became strong and fearless after they had received the Holy Spirit? And ask

further where Moses was when he saw nothing
but God? And ask yet further, how it was
that Daniel was able to speak so wisely
in his youth? (V.12).

Master Heinrich von Halle, convinced about the
sincerity of Mechthild's 'bold' vocabulary, diligently
collected the scattered pieces of poetry into the six
books of *The Flowing Light of God.* Before his death
in 1292, he undertook a similar, but much easier,
editorial task when, at the request of St Gertrude
the Great, he corrected and sanctioned the circulation
of her latin work called *Insinuationes.*[10]
In 1270, at the advise of Heinrich von Halle,
whose Latin translation of *The Flowing Light of God*
evoked almost the same unfriendly reactions on the
part of the clergy as had the controversial original
text, Mechthild, advanced in age and almost blind,
left Magdeburg, where she had always been a stranger,
and asked for admission into the cistercian community
of Helfta, which was about a half hour's walking
distance from Eisleben, the future birthplace of Martin
Luther. Here she hoped to find kindred souls with
whom she could live in peace and praise the great
deeds of God for the rest of her life. The beguine
who had dedicated her whole life to the needs of beg-
gars, now became herself a beggaress. Helfta took
her in for the last stretch of her *hoverise (Hofreise).*
The cistercian community at Helfta had been founded
in 1229 by Elisabeth, Countess of Mansfeld, out of
gratitude to St Elisabeth of Hungary at whose tomb
Elisabeth's prayers for the recovery of her sick child
had been heard. The original site of the foundation,
the palace of Countess Elisabeth in Mansfeld, proved
ill-suited for the monastic life however, whereupon,
five years later, the community moved to Rodarsdorf.
Its first abbess, the pious Kunigunde von Halberstadt,
was succeeded by Gertrude von Hackeborn in 1251.
Gertrude was only nineteen years old at the time of
her election, but her understanding and kindness,
her wise exercise of authority and profound learning
in things divine, made her one of the most admired
women in thirteenth-century Germany. But when the
drinking water at Rodarsdorf turned out to be hazardous
to the community's health, the sisters had to look
for yet another home. In 1258, they finally settled
at Helfta.
Helfta soon became the most famous cistercian
convent in Germany. There four remarkable women,
driven by their feminine desire *gode unde der werlde
gevallen,* 'to please God and the world', introduced

a new spiritual devotion from which the popular cult of the Sacred Heart developed. These four women were Gertrude von Hackeborn, her sister Mechthild von Hackeborn, St Gertrude the Great, and, of course, Mechthild von Magdeburg. Their writings are eloquent proofs of the heights attained by the medieval spirit.

The charismatic leadership of Gertrude von Hackeborn (1232–1292) made Helfta the home of a *devotio moderna* which drew its themes from the Church's liturgy. The daily rhythm of the liturgical celebrations perfectly fulfilled the inner needs of these medieval women, who conversed with God in ecstatic visions. The sister of the reform-minded abbess, Mechthild von Hackeborn (1240–1298) was only seven years old when she entered the convent school at Rodarsdorf. In 1258, when the community moved to Helfta, the charming and highly talented Mechthild, nicknamed because of her beautiful voice 'the Lark of God', followed her sister to their new home already as a professed nun. She became the choir mistress and directress of the monastery school which, under her leadership, became a renowned school for girls from the German nobility. Her book, *Liber specialis gratiae*, the *Book of Special Graces*, is a joyful account of her spiritual experiences. Her visions are based on the liturgical year, and her elegant Latin reveals her erudition and doctrinal orthodoxy. Mechthild von Hackeborn's most famous pupil was St Gertrude the Great (1256–1302), who had been entrusted to the school at the age of five, and who is the best known among the women who brought fame to Helfta. Inspired by St Bernard's *connubium spirituale*,[11] Gertrude saw the main objective of the religious life in the human soul's bridal union with Christ; in this union, love grows 'naturally' into the life of 'the resplendent and completely tranquil Trinity'. Gertrude herself wrote three Latin spiritual classics: *Exercitia spiritualia*, a collection of meditations; *Insinuationes*, also known as *Legatus divinae pietatis*, a book of visions and daily divine favors which are 'heralds' of the Sacred Heart, with instructions about the mysteries of the liturgical seasons; and *Preces Gertrudianae*, a collection of prayers.[12]

These three noble and learned nuns were familiar with the writings of Mechthild von Magdeburg; they had admired her courage and power of expression. Hence, when Mechthild, almost totally blind, knocked at the monastery door asking to be given 'the wedding dress of her soul', they gave her a loving welcome.

The old beguine had come to Helfta as a helpless and poor woman. Yet, she saw loving-kindness every-

where, 'in the morning dew, in the song of the birds'.
She asked God with fervent prayers to let her know
how she could be useful to the community. God's answer
was that, in spite of her blindness, she was to enlighten
others. This prompted her to dictate the seventh book
of *The Flowing Light of God*. With weakening desires
and ebbing strength, with the calm waning of the
evening star, she extolled from the threshold of the
invisible realities the blessings of her new-found
monastic environment where each day brought her
nearer to the Sacred Heart of God. Already at Magdeburg
where her 'enemies' had accused her of being misled
by poetic fancies instead of guided by sound christian
doctrine, she had found that her 'treasures', her
poetry, had become a heavy burden, a barrier
between her good will and the distrust of others:

> Soul: Lord, I bring you my treasure,
> It is greater than the mountains,
> Wider than the world,
> Deeper than the sea,
> Higher than the clouds,
> More brilliant than the sun,
> More manifold than the stars—
> It outweighs the whole earth!
>
> Lord: What is your treasure called?
>
> Soul: Lord! It is called my heart's desires!
> I have withdrawn it from the world,
> Denied it to myself and all creatures.
> Now I can bear it no longer.
> Where, my Lord, shall I lay it?
>
> Lord: Place your heart's desire
> in my own Divine Heart—nowhere else—
> and on my human breast.
> There alone will you find comfort
> and be kissed by my Spirit. (I.39).

The theme of this dialogue, the 'placing' of her
heart's desire into God's own heart, expressed Mechthild's surrender to Divine Love. Once, as a young
beguine, she had wished to be courted, like a noble
lady, by her Heavenly Knight. 'The Holy Trinity must
obey me', she wrote with a noble lady's delight in
her rank. At Helfta, she no longer had such youthful
aspirations. From St Gertrude the Great[13] she learned
that suffering must be viewed as the Savior's *herzeblut*,
as blood from the Savior's heart, as the continuation
of his redemption. Now the image of the heavenly

Knight and the 'handsome Young Man' changed into the figure of a Suffering Servant:

> During the days of my great suffering God
> revealed himself to my soul; showing me
> the wounds of his heart, he said: 'Look,
> how greatly they have hurt me!' (VI.24).

In Helfta she wrote the long and thoughtful poem on 'how a religious should turn his heart away from the world'. In it she compares all pleasure-seekers to a fish and their unquenchable thirst for pleasure to the bait and hook of the fisherman. 'The fish looks eagerly to the red fly wherewith the fisherman will catch it, but does not see the hook' hidden in the bait. The hook of suffering is hidden in every pleasure, even in the *grosse minne gotes*, even in 'the great love of God'. Whoever swims after this bait must be prepared to bite the cross-shaped hook of the soul's Fisherman. She concludes her allegorical poem with a hymn to the suffering Savior:

> If you really wish to follow him
> with holy thoughts
> Look up! See how he hung on the Cross
> lifted up on high
> for all the world to see
> his body covered with blood.
> His garment shall be the treasure of your heart,
> his royal eyes overflowing with tears,
> his sweet Heart pierced for love.
> Now hear the voice
> which teaches you the love of God—
> How the hammers of the smiths
> drove in the nails
> through his hands and feet on the Cross.
> Think also of the wound of the spear
> Which pierced his side to the heart
> And confess him all your sins!
> This is how you will come to know God (VII.27).

In the monastic atmosphere of Helfta, Mechthild also wrote hymns in praise of the Divine Office. These poems do not have the tempered solemnity of the well-known liturgical hymns; they are passionate *minne-viessen*, passionate 'outpourings of love', in the vernacular of these *moniales litteratae*, these educated nuns, expressing an acceptance of God's will and of his invitation to reap the harvest of a life-long service. Her Vespers-Song, for instance, is filled with a poetic power most uncharacteristic of old age:

O secret outpouring of love!
O faithful giving of the heart!
O sacred Body killed for my sake,
Dearly loved Jesus Christ!
Let my five senses ceaselessly rejoice
in the bloody spear and the wounds of your Sweet Heart.
Let my poor soul rejoice in them
with all those for whom I must and want to pray
from all my heart. Amen. (VII.18).

The so-called 'blind poems' collected in the seventh book of *The Flowing Light of God* tell us that old age should not be viewed as 'a shameful secret', but be seen rather as a natural phenomenon when the body which enfolds the soul 'as a fruit enfolds its stone' (Rilke) is growing weaker. She is grateful to God for the loss of her eyesight, for this gives him the opportunity to be good to her through the eyes of others:

> *sit mir benommen hast die maht miner ougen*
> *daz du mir nu dienest mit froemden ougen.*
> Lord! I thank you that since you have taken
> from me the sight of my eyes
> You serve me through the eyes of others (VII.64).

At the end she welcomed death as a life-long friend:

> When I think of death, my soul rejoices so
> greatly at the thought of going forth from
> this earthly life, that my body soars in
> a supernatural peace beyond words; and
> my senses recognize the marvels which attend
> the passing hence of the soul; so that I
> would most gladly die at the time forseen
> by God. At the same time I would gladly
> live till the last great day and in my heart
> I long for the days of the martyrs that I
> might have shed my blood for Jesus whom
> I love. That I dare to say I love God is
> because a special gift forces me to do so.
> For when my burdens and sufferings are
> held before me, my soul begins to burn in
> the fire of true love of God in such blissful
> sweetness, that even my body soars in divine
> bliss. But my senses still continue to lament
> and pray for all who have injured or maligned
> me, that God would keep them from sin (VI.26).

Mechthild remained a compassionate woman to the very end of her life. Worn out, blind and forgotten by the world, the nun of Helfta 'still continued to be concerned' about others. She remained the kind of a woman who could not leave the world without saying a last good-bye. In her farewell prayer one still feels the tenderness of a kiss from the distance of seven centuries:

When I am about to die
I take leave of all from which I must part.
I take leave of Holy Church;
I thank God that I was called to be a Christian
and have come to real christian belief.
Were I to remain longer here
I would try to help Holy Church
which lies in many sins.
I take leave of all poor souls now in purgatory.
Were I to be longer here I would gladly help to
   expiate their sins
and I thank God that they will find mercy.
I take leave of all those in hell
and thank God that he exercises his righteousness
   on them.
Were I to be longer here
I would ever wish them well.
I take leave of all sinners who lie in mortal sin.
I thank God that I am not one of them.
Were I to be longer here
I would gladly carry their burden before God.
I take leave of all penitents working out
   their penance.
I thank God that I am one of them.
Were I to be longer here
I would always love them.
I take leave of all my enemies.
I thank God that I have not been vanquished by them.
Were I to be longer here
I would lay myself under their feet.
I take leave of all earthly things.
I lament before God
that I never used them according to his
   holy ordinances.
I take leave of all my dear friends.
I thank God and them
that they have been my help in need.
Were I to be longer here
I should ever be ashamed of the lack of virtue they
   must have seen in me.
I take leave of all my wickedness.
I lament before God
that I have so greatly spoiled his bold gift to
   my soul

so that there was never so small a sin,
but would be seen in my soul in heaven.
Even though the sin were expiated,
the stain remains.
Lord Jesus! I lament it to you,
for you bear the shame of it.
I take leave of my suffering body.
I thank God that he has preserved me in many things
    from many sins.
Even were I to remain longer here
the sins of the body are so manifold
that I could never be quite free of them (VI.28).

Mechthild von Magdeburg died in the cistercian community of Helfta, at the time 'foreseen by God', between the years 1281 and 1283. As she had said, she was ready for 'the marvels which follow the passing of the soul'.

Adapted and edited by Bede K. Lackner, O. Cist.
Our Lady of Dallas Abbey

NOTES

1. See, by way of introduction, Odo Egres, 'Mechthilde von Magdeburg: *The Flowing Light of God*', in *Cistercians in the Late Middle Ages,* edited by E. Rozanne Elder, Cistercian Studies Series, 54 (Kalamazoo: Cistercian Publications, 1981) 19–37.
2. Emil Michael, *Geschichte des deutschen Volkes* (Frankfurt, 1897–1915) vol. III: p. 188. See also Jeanne Ancelet-Hustache, *Mechtilde de Magdebourg* (Paris, 1926) 46: 'Elle a reçu la première grande grace...en 1219, et comme elle avait alors douze ans, elle est donc née en 1207'.
3. I, 1. These numbers indicate Book and chapter of *The Flowing Light of God,* as found in the Einsiedeln codex.
4. J. Greven, *Die Anfänge der Beguinen* (Münster, 1912).
5. Translations of poetry usually lose the magic of the original language which clearly distinguishes poetry from prose. A good example is the phrase 'When I took leave of the world' (*zu der welte urlop nam*). Originally *urlop* meant the feudal lord's (or lady's) permission given to a knight to leave his (or her) presence. The translations

merely serve as a key to a better understanding of the Middle German text.

6. Master Dietrich was elected a canon of the chapter of Magdeburg in 1260. Mechthild spoke kindly of him and saw in him a protector against her 'enemies'.

7. Wilhelm Preger, *Geschichte der deutschen Mystik* (Leipzig, 1874) vol. 2.

8. Heinrich Denifle, *Die Offenbarungen Mechthilds von Magdeburg* (1875), and W. Oehl, *Die Lieder Mechthilds von Magdeburg* (München, 1911).

9. A Reference to Mechthild's twenty-fifth year when she dedicated herself to the religious life as a beguine.

10. See R. Hünicker, 'Studien über Heinrich von Halle', *Thüringisch-Sächsische Zeitschrift für Geschichte und Kunst* 23 (1935) 102–117.

11. It was St Bernard of Clairvaux who made the *connubium spirituale* an ever-recurring theme of his 86 Sermons on the Song of Songs. These sermons were known to Mechthild through the circular letters of Wichmann von Arnstein, a famous dominican spiritual director of the time. The *connubium spirituale* theme was as old as christian mysticism, but no one had developed it as daringly as St Bernard. He offered his monks as a theme that basic factor in human life which is forbidden to every monk by virtue of his profession and which is sinful for him to desire. Bernard saw beyond the centuries-old list of lust, perversion, and corruption which result from man's uncontrolled nature. In sexual union he saw an image of God's inner life and of his love for man's immortal soul. Thus he told his monks in the fifty-second Sermon: 'I cannot restrain my joy that this majesty did not disdain...to enter into wedlock *(inire connubia)* with the soul in exile and to reveal to her with the utmost ardent love how affectionate was this bridegroom whom she had won'. Bernard of Clairvaux, *On the Song of Songs,* III; CF 31: 50–51.

12. The works of Mechthild von Hackeborn and Saint Gertrude the Great were published, with the Latin version of Mechthild von Magdeburg's *The Flowing Light of God,* by the Benedictines of Solesmes under the title *Revelationes Gertrudianae et Mechtildianae* (Paris, 1877–1878).

13. 'On dit que sainte Gertrude fût la sainte de l'humanité de Jésus-Christ...On a dit également qu'elle a été la théologienne du Sacré-Coeur'. *Dictionnaire de théologie catholique,* 9 (Paris, 1920) 133.

NOTES ON CISTERCIAN ARCHITECTURAL REMAINS
AND DAILY LIFE IN LOWER SAXONY

Nicolaus Heutger

The chapter houses are preserved at both Loccum and Walkenried. There the entire community met each day, usually early in the morning, and heard the holy Rule read through, chapter by chapter. There, too, benefactors were commemorated and each monk was assigned his work for the day. Outside chapter the monks generally communicated by a sign language, a fragment of which has survived at Loccum. In the cloister near the church the monks did their reading, giving the area its German name *Lesegang*, which survives to this day at Loccum.

In winter the *calefactorium*, or warming house, was the one place in the monastery—especially at Loccum and Wienhausen, where the monks, or nuns, were allowed a fire to warm themselves, although in the Later Middle Ages other rooms were heated in winter. The *lavatorium*, or fountain room, is preserved at Walkenried and the site is known at Loccum. There the monks washed their hands before entering the refectory for meals. A splendid late Gothic refectory survives at Loccum, and the lutheran Abbot of Loccum once a year invites very important guests from Lower Saxony to dinner where once the white monks ate their simple meals. At Walkenried the old refectories are being restored—refectories, in the plural, because the monks and lay brothers had separate refectories, as we can still see at Loccum and Amelungsborn. Better than average fare was served at the abbot's house, for guests, and in the infirmary. Fish was eaten instead of meat in the early centuries (though not on fast days), and fish ponds formed an important part of the monastic economy. They remain at Riddagshausen, Walkenried, Loccum, and Marienrode. In many manuscripts we find mention of extra allowances of food, called pittances. This might be an extra dessert, white—rather than the usual grey—bread, eggs, good beer, or even meat given in memory of a benefactor. The best beer was produced at Hude. New excavations at Walkenried have also uncovered a whole system of canals, attesting to the excellent water supply of the monastery.

The *scriptorium* of Amelungsborn produced a fine bible in the fourteenth century and the Wigaloistext of 1372. This beautifully illustrated adventure book, written for a duke, is now at Leyden. The illuminated

books of Wöltingerode (now at Wolfenbüttel) are also
extremely important. In the Late Middle Ages the cistercian monasteries of Lower Saxony had good libraries,
especially Amelungsborn, of which we have a list
of holdings. They also borrowed books at nearby Corvey
without always returning them.

The *conversi* worked in the western range of the
monastery, as we see at Walkenried, Loccum, and
Amelungsborn. At Loccum the western range has a
cellarium, a place for stores. At Amelungsborn we
find a special lane between the main building and
the western walk of the cloister. This lane had existed
at Cîteaux and Clairvaux, and was connected with
some special occupations of the lay brothers. We have
reports from Marienrode and Amelungsborn of trouble
between *conversi* and the monasteries' neighbors.

The gateway at Loccum and Walkenried are fine
architectural structures. Over the gateway was a room
for the porter, who was to be a wise old man, who
'shall know how to receive a reply and to return
one' (RB 66). All the monasteries had a chapel near
the gateway for guests, especially for women. At Loccum
and Riddagshausen, these chapels are preserved, and
at Loccum we can still see the small door by which
the monk-priest approached from the monastery. Near
the gateway was an alms house, where the poorest
travellers were lodged and food was distributed to
the needy of the district.

All the cistercian monasteries of Lower Saxony
had infirmaries. At Loccum we still find this building,
with its own chapel, outside the eastern range. The
most famous patient at Walkenried was Duke Henry
the Lion, whose broken thigh the monks failed to
cure.

The monks slept in the dormitory, which was
approached from the church by a staircase at Loccum,
Riddagshausen, and Walkenried. At Walkenried the
old dorter is preserved, but elsewhere the dormitory
was divided into separate chambers in the Late Middle
Ages, something entirely against early practice.

New discoveries at Wienhausen have cast light
on the daily life of the nuns there. Small rosaries,
toys for the pupils in the nunnery school, fragments
of letters, extremely old spectacles, eggs as symbols
of fertility, and even traces of superstition, on the
whole more than a thousand objects, have been discovered
there, mostly under the planks of the nuns' sanctuary.

In the churches the seats had misericords to
allow the monks, or nuns, to half-sit during the long
services. In Wienhausen there is a hole under each
seat, scratched away by bored feet. In addition to

community services in men's monasteries there were private Masses said by the monks who were priests at numerous side altars, as at Loccum, Riddagshausen, and Marienrode.

At some abbeys special cistercian items can be seen: at Loccum an altar reliquary in the form of a church, and a crucifix of painted wood rather than sculpture. Each cistercian church had a statue of St Mary, protectress of the community and of the whole Order. In the beginning the windows held only grey glass, but early simplicity gradually broke down until in the fourteenth century, Amelungsborn received a splendid painted glass window, one of the largest in Europe. This was unfortunately destroyed in 1945. In the beginning, too, cistercian churches had no ornamentation, as we can see at Loccum. But as time went on this also changed, and the ruins of Hude contain important ceramic ornaments.

Cistercian towers were supposed to be small and to contain only one bell, small enough to be rung by a single person. These *Dachreiter* can be seen, for example, at Loccum, Marienrode, Mariensee, and Rinteln.

The church had a small lychgate for the extremely simple funerals of Cistercians: this *porta mortis* is preserved at Loccum. The churchyard was to the north of the church, but monks of special reputation were buried in the cloister, as at Loccum and Amelungsborn, where human bones have been found under the cloister site, so passing monks could remember their virtues.

A number of economic buildings still exists from Lower Saxony cistercian monasteries, especially at Walkenried, Loccum, Amelungsborn, and Marienrode.

Hildesheim, 1984

THE CISTERCIAN SOURCE:
AELRED, BONAVENTURE, AND IGNATIUS

Marsha L. Dutton

The medieval growth of affective spirituality and its close association with the school of Cîteaux is by now almost a commonplace. Ewert Cousins describes this approach in the intro- duction to his 1978 translation of Bonaventure:

> The most characteristic form of Christian spirituality in the West focuses on the mystery of Christ, who is seen as the Mediator between God and man and the Savior freeing man from the burden of sin and leading him to salvation. In the Middle Ages this spirituality took the form of devotion to the humanity and passion of Christ, with concentration on vivid details, an awakening of human emotions, especially compassion, and the imitation of Christ in his moral virtues. This devotion is rooted in the fundamental orientation of Western culture toward the concrete, the particular, the human and the moral. Grounded in classical Roman culture, this orientation developed in the spirituality of the Middle Ages and blossomed in the 13th century into a complex form of religious sensibility, with Francis of Assisi as its chief expression.[1]

The flowering of that affectivity in Francis, and in franciscan spirituality in the Middle Ages, is also generally acknowledged, but the significant role played in its development by the twelfth-century english cister- cian Aelred of Rievaulx, his new approach to meditation and its popularity throughout western Europe, have gone almost entirely unrecognized. Aelred's influence on franciscan and ignatian spirituality has largely escaped the notice of scholars. Because of the great importance of the franciscan tradition of affective spirituality and of the ignatian imaginative approach to meditation and because of the attention given both by modern scholarship their common origins in the contemplative writings of Aelred should be recognized. Both Bonaventure's *The Tree of Life* and Ignatius' *Spiritual Exercises* find their ultimate source in Aelred's single treatise on the contemplative life, *De institutione inclusarum* or *On Reclusion*.[2]

In about 1160 Aelred, abbot of Rievaulx, wrote
On Reclusion, a work of spiritual direction for an
anchoress. In it he provided guidance for her life,
its quotidian details, virtue, and loving search for
God. Although in 1155 at the request of a young monk
for contemplative direction he had used one story
from the life of Jesus to set forth the journey toward
God in *On Jesus as a Boy of Twelve,*[3] the later treatise,
On Reclusion, was unique in its concern with the
life devoted to contemplation. It alone of his works
was written for a woman, it alone exalted the life
of Mary over that of Martha. Further, it guided the
contemplative toward union not, like *On Jesus,* through
imitation of Jesus but through intimacy with him.
This approach to contemplative union depended on
the imaginative involvement of the contemplative in
the human life of Jesus.

On Reclusion begins with attention to the anchoress'
daily life, then turns to the three virtues that define
her life: chastity, humility, and charity. As the contemplative life has to do centrally with the love of God,
Aelred devotes the larger part of the entire work
to three meditations, on the past, present, and future.
He intends these to nourish the contemplative's affections,
to enable 'the sweet love of Jesus to grow in' them.[4]

The first of the three contains an extended narrative
of Jesus' life. In it Aelred directs the contemplative
to participate in the events of that life, to love Jesus
with those who loved him then, to minister to him
with those who ministered to him, and finally to know
him and to become one with him in his crucifixion.
This meditation ends with the post-Resurrection appearance of Jesus to Mary Magdalene in the garden and
with her finally being allowed to 'come close and
clasp his feet'.[5] In the third meditation, that on
the future, Jesus appears again, but this meditation
concentrates less on Jesus than on the Judgment and
the beatitude prepared for the blessed. It is the first
meditation with its presentation of the life of Jesus
and the contemplative's participation in that life
that was so new in christian spiritual writing; it
is this approach to contemplation and the search for
union with God as seen in the meditation on the past
that influenced all who followed Aelred.

Aelred's first meditation is one extended narrative,
interrupted by occasional spontaneous prayers. The
narrative itself is largely imperative or third person
subjunctive, 'let the contemplative'. It includes little
theological explanation or exposition, gives no attention
to an imitation of Christ, and concentrates primarily
on the contemplative's imaginative going forward to

love and to minister to Jesus. Aelred's constant gentle
exhortation and admonition, an approach to meditation
imitated by Bonaventure in *The Tree of Life*, functions
within *On Reclusion* as guidance toward contemplative
union; it is the keystone in Aelred's approach to
meditation and contemplation.

Aelred's *On Reclusion* probably became known
to Bonaventure in Paris between 1257 and 1267. By
that time he had completed his studies at the University
of Paris and been elected Minister General of the
Franciscan Order. He is thought during this period
to have written his spiritual works; Ewert Cousins
says in the introduction to his translation of three
of these that this time in Bonaventure's life 'flowers
in a host of spiritual writings which have a distinctive
Franciscan flavor'.[6]

The three most important of Bonaventure's 'mystical
opuscula' are *The Triple Way*, *The Soul's Journey
into God*, and *The Tree of Life*, which Cousins describes
as 'his classic meditation on the life of Christ'.[7]
In the first of these Bonaventure most systematically
sets forth his understanding of the three stages of
the spiritual life; the second is abstract, highly speculative, and heavily influenced by Richard of St Victor's
discussion of the ascent to the vision of God in *The
Mystical Ark*.

The Tree of Life is a very different kind of work.
It is a much simpler work of affective spirituality,
devoted to the life and passion of Jesus and to his
glorification. This is Bonaventure's primary work
of affective spirituality; it must be central in any
consideration of franciscan influence in that tradition.[8]
Its indebtedness to Aelred's *On Reclusion*, almost
exclusively to the first of the three meditations, is
overwhelming.

The influence of *On Reclusion* on Ignatius and
his *Spiritual Exercises* has been more widely recognized
and therefore demands less attention here. The link
between Aelred and Ignatius is Ludolph of Saxony,
a carthusian monk who in about 1330, probably while
at Mainz, wrote a work sometimes referred to as the
most influential work of popular spirituality of the
Middle Ages. Ludolph's *Vita Jesu Christi*, a lengthy
compilation of patristic writings, contains among other
things the entire first meditation of *On Reclusion*—
credited to Anselm, to whom Aelred's three meditations
were long attributed from the fourteenth century on
—some of the third meditation, and large pieces of
On Jesus as a Boy of Twelve, credited to Bernard.[9]
In 1502–3 Ferdinand and Isabella of Spain commissioned
a translation of the *Vita Christi* by Ambrose Montesino,

a Franciscan; he translated about two-thirds of the work into Castilian.[10]

After receiving his leg wound in the siege of Pampelona in 1521, Ignatius asked his sister-in-law for chivalric romances to read while recuperating. When she could find none in the family castle at Loyola, she substituted two popular—and hence easily available—books of piety, a *Flos Sanctorum* (probably Voragine's *Golden Legend)* and Ludolph's *Vita Christi.* Ignatius was so delighted with these books that he copied extracts from them into a quarto volume of three-hundred leaves. 'The words of Christ he wrote in red ink and those of Our Lady in blue, on polished and lined paper in a good hand, for he was an excellent penman'.[11] All discussions of Ignatius and of the *Spiritual Exercises* insist on the role played by the *Vita Christi* in their composition.[12]

Not only did the *Vita Christi* effect Ignatius' conversion, but it—and so its sources—directly influenced his later writings, most recognizably the *Spiritual Exercises.* In the *Dictionnaire de Spiritualité* article on 'Application des sens', the characteristic meditative approach of the *Spiritual Exercises,* Jean Maréchal traces this method so associated with Ignatius from Bernard through Aelred, Richard of St Victor, Henry Suso, and Ludolph to Ignatius. Of Aelred Maréchal cites *On Jesus as a Boy of Twelve* and *On Reclusion,* saying that in them Aelred 'gives counsel and example of a concrete contemplation of the Gospel events, one that here and there becomes an application of the senses, whether imaginative or spiritual'.[13]

As Maréchal's words indicate, Aelred's influence on Ignatius and even on Bonaventure has not gone unnoticed by scholars. In 1944 Sr Mary Immaculate Bodenstedt published her Catholic University dissertation, *The Vita Christi of Ludolphus the Carthusian.* In it she noted that Ludolph occasionally attributed passages incorporated into his work to Anselm when they had in fact originated with Aelred, but as she had no text of *On Reclusion* available, she was unable to be specific about either the extent of Ludolph's borrowing from Aelred or his treatment of the borrowed passages.

In 1958 Anselm Hoste mentioned that at least four exact citations from *On Reclusion* appeared in Ludolph's *Vita Christi.* He repeated the observation in the introduction to his 1958 parallel text edition of *On Jesus as a Boy of Twelve* and again in his 1962 *Bibliotheca Aelrediana.*[14]

Following Hoste, Charles Dumont discussed Aelred's influence on Ludolph and through him Ignatius at length in the introduction to his 1961 French-Latin parallel text edition of Aelred's treatise, *La Vie de Recluse*, saying: 'Ludolph the Carthusian, while writing his *Vita Christi*, had the text of Aelred's meditation constantly under his eyes. He believed it to be by Anselm, but that matters little....To conclude his work, he quotes the last lines of Aelred's treatise'. Regarding the meditative technique of Aelred, that seen later in both *The Tree of Life* and *Spiritual Exercises*, Dumont says:

> Saint Bernard was doubtless the originator of this new method, but he was too intellectual, too speculative to do all with it that one might do. It was up to Aelred, imaginative and sensitive, to accomplish this little master-piece and in it to apply the method, following its creator but with an ease and freedom that gave it the richness of his own experience.[15]

Not surprisingly, in light of Ludolph's care to acknowledge his sources and Bonaventure's failure to do so, scholarly recognition of Aelred's influence on *The Tree of Life* has been much slighter. In 1923 André Wilmart, in his introduction to D. A. Castel's French translation of Anselm's meditations and prayers, commented, 'I believe that [Bonaventure] had direct recourse to Aelred's *De institutis inclusarum*, perhaps already attributed to St Augustine (viz. *Lignum vitae*, par. 9)'.[16] In 1958 Anselm Hoste, in the same article as that mentioned above, said that five citations from *On Reclusion* appeared in *The Tree of Life*.

The long-time attribution of Aelred's meditations to both Augustine and Anselm is part of the problem for both bonaventuran and ludolphan studies. J.-P. Migne printed most of *On Reclusion* among the works of Augustine in the *Patrologia Latina*, though he noted there that it was in fact Aelred's, as Lucas Holstenius had recognized in his 1661 *Codex Regularum*. In the same note he pointed out that roughly a third of the work (the three meditations, in fact) appeared in the *Patrologia* among the meditations of Anselm as numbers 15, 16, and 17. But in that volume he made no mention of Aelred, saying merely in a footnote to meditation 15, 'S. Anselm wrote this to his sister'.[17]

In 1924 Wilmart discussed the history of printing and attribution of *On Reclusion*, and in 1927 he again identified the three meditations as Aelred's. Because of his work there should no longer be any confusion about the authorship of the various 'Anselmian' meditations.[18]

As a further complication, not only are Aelred's

meditations often attributed to Augustine and Anselm, but passages attributed by modern scholars to Anselm may in fact have been written not only by Anselm or Aelred, but also by a number of others. Wilmart lists thirteen authors, six named and seven unnamed, for the twenty-one meditations printed in the *Patrologia* as Anselm's. Of the nine passages that the Quaracchi edition of *The Tree of Life* attributes to Anselm and three others noted as resembling his (eight of which are attributed in Cousins' translation to Pseudo-Anselm), only one is by Aelred;[19] the other eleven come from the meditation printed by Migne as meditation nine, 'On the humanity of Christ'. The author of that meditation was actually the twelfth-century Ecbert of Schönau in the diocese of Trier.[20]

Despite the occasional recognition of Aelred's influence on Bonaventure and Ludolph and the now-general awareness that some of what has long been considered anselmian meditation originated with Aelred, franciscan scholars have remained unaware of Aelred's role.[21] In the preface to Cousins' 1978 translation Ignatius Brady says about *The Tree of Life*, 'The opuscule is, quite evidently, a highly original work. Apart from frequent anonymous use of the meditations once ascribed to Saint Anselm, it reveals no dependence on other writers...'.[22]

Brady's statement of course depends on Cousins' analysis of the work's sources. Unfortunately, although Wilmart in 1924, 1927, and 1932 showed Anselm to have written only three of the meditations long attributed to him, Cousins in 1978 apparently merely accepted the 1882-1902 Quaracchi edition's attribution of eight passages to Anselm.[23] Nor does he appear to have sought out non-biblical sources other than those familiar from the Quaracchi edition. His neglect of the question of sources for Bonaventure's treatise and of the implications of the pseudo-anselmian passages within it has caused him and Brady to regard *The Tree of Life* as essentially original and to leave that impression with their readers.

Cousins has recognized the similarities of method between *The Tree of Life* and Ignatius' *Spiritual Exercises*, but he attributes their origin to Bonaventure, saying in the introduction to his translation:

> Bonaventure can be seen in relation to the *Spiritual Exercises* of Ignatius of Loyola. Bonaventure's *The Tree of Life* is in many respects a forerunner of Ignatian meditation, in both its subject matter and its techniques.... From one point of view, the Ignatian *Exercises*

can be seen as an initiation into the contemplative vision that Bonaventure proposes in
The Soul's Journey; and from another point
of view, one could follow Bonaventure's suggestions as how to open [sic] the meditation
on the humanity of Christ in the *Exercises*
to a more mystical contemplation of Christ.[24]

In a Franciscan Studies session at the 18th annual
Congress of Medieval Studies at Kalamazoo on 7 May,
1983, Cousins combined these two comments in a paper
titled 'St Bonaventure's *Lignum Vitae:* Mysticism of
Historical Events'. In his paper he argued that in
The Tree of Life Bonaventure invented a new kind
of affective approach to God, an approach which he
termed 'mysticism of historical events', and suggested
again that this meditative approach directly influenced
Ignatius in his writing of the *Spiritual Exercises.*[25]
Cousins is quite right in recognizing the influence
of this form of spirituality in the *Spiritual Exercises;*
his error lies in considering Bonaventure its originator
and in failing to recognize him as, like Ignatius,
a beneficiary of cistercian affective spirituality and,
specifically, of Aelred's unique contribution to that
tradition. In fact, Bonaventure's *The Tree of Life*
is largely derivative, truly original only apparently
in its external structure and not at all in content
or meditative approach and style.
Bonaventure's *The Tree of Life,* written about
a hundred years after Aelred's *On Reclusion,* declares
two purposes. First, it is intended to create in the
Christian an ability to declare with Paul in Galatians,
'With Christ I am nailed to the cross',[26] that is,
to guide the Christian to imitate Christ. In a characteristically bonaventuran understanding, Christ appears
from the beginning of the treatise as the exemplum
of the christian life.
After beginning his work with this general statement
of purpose, Bonaventure continues with greater specificity
to define the purpose and subject matter of his treatise.
Where in the first paragraph he refers to Christ crucified
as the 'bundle of myrrh' whom the contemplative will
'carry about continuously, both in his soul and in
his flesh', in the second the bundle of myrrh becomes
the work itself, now understood as the life of Christ,
to be used as a stimulus to devotion and faith.
He is no less specific about his source: 'the
forest of the holy Gospel'. Unfortunately for later
scholars, Bonaventure does not follow either of the
two familiar medieval patterns of source acknowledgment,

either alluding to all the Fathers as the inspiration and source or neglecting to mention any source at all. Had he either modestly and conventionally acknowledged widespread assistance in his literary and spiritual task or admitted to none, readers and scholars in all subsequent periods would have searched intently for the literary origins of *The Tree of Life*. Rather, he acknowledges a source, the obvious, necessary, and, one would think, sufficient one. While the ubiquity of medieval plagiarism is a byword of medieval scholarship, this work is unusual in disguising its heavy reliance on an important source through apparent forthrightness of acknowledgement. In this Bonaventure is, I would argue, disingenuous, intentionally misleading.

Finally Bonaventure details the full complexity of the large image that shapes his treatment of the life of Christ, one not biblical in origin (and also not aelredian: it may well be original with him), a tree of life with twelve branches and twelve fruits:

> To enkindle in us this affection, to shape this understanding and to imprint this memory, I have endeavored to gather this bundle of myrrh from the forest of the holy Gospel, which treats at length the life, passion, and glorification of Jesus Christ. I have bound it together with a few ordered and parallel words to aid the memory. I have used simple, familiar, and unsophisticated terms to avoid idle curiosity, to cultivate devotion, and to foster the piety of faith. Since imagination aids understanding, I have arranged in the form of an imaginary tree the few items I have collected from among many, and have ordered and disposed them in such a way that in the first or lower branches the Savior's origin and life are described; in the middle, his passion; and in the top, his glorification.[27]

The work is divided into a prologue and three main divisions, devoted to the origins, passion, and glorification of Christ. Within each of these divisions appear four sections, 'fruits', each of which contains four separate meditations. At the end of the whole comes a prayer to obtain the seven gifts of the Holy Spirit.

Of the forty-eight meditations, forty begin with short narrative passages, sometimes only a sentence or two, followed by a lyrical prayer, exhortation, or exclamation. Most are exhortations to the soul, though the intended audience is most clearly defined

in the prologue to the work: 'The true worshipper
of God and disciple of Christ, who desires to conform
perfectly to the Savior of all men crucified for him'.[28]
Almost all of the borrowings from Aelred come in these
lyrical exhortations.

Throughout *The Tree of Life* Bonaventure moves
rhythmically from third person indicative narration
of Jesus' life to second person conditional—'if you
could'—or imperative and back again. The pattern
is not quite regular, however, for sometimes he addresses
God in these passages or speaks cohortatively. The
rhetorical function of these passages in *The Tree of
Life* is not altogether clear, but they reflect the perva-
sive influence of *On Reclusion* upon *The Tree of Life*
and indicate Bonaventure's desire in this work to
imitate Aelred's meditative approach while not fully
understanding its purpose.

In his discussion of *The Tree of Life* Cousins
describes the meditative approach of the work and
addresses the question of its purpose:

> In *The Tree of Life*, however, Bonaventure
> provides a meditation that touches the very
> heart of Franciscan devotion to the humanity
> and passion of Christ....In each specific
> meditation, Bonaventure summarizes the narrative
> details of an event in Christ's life, with
> references to the foreshadowing in Old Testament
> texts. There is a vivid application of the
> senses, an imaginative re-creation of the
> Gospel scene, a drawing of the reader into
> the drama of the event as a witness and
> a participator. Most of the meditations contain
> a prayer or direct address to the reader,
> evoking strong emotions through graphic,
> dramatic imagery....In this type of meditation,
> one applies the senses to a vividly imagined
> scene and evokes human emotions ranging
> from tender love to anguish.[29]

In *The Tree of Life* all aelredian passages come
from *On Reclusion*, all but three from the first of
the three meditations. These three are not in fact
certain borrowings—they are similar in language and
function, but that similarity could be coincidence
or simply reflect the gospel accounts that underlie
both works. Two of these come from the third meditation,
that on the Judgment, and one from the section on
humility just before Aelred's three meditations.

The passages in *The Tree of Life* revealing influence
from Aelred fall into four rough categories: (1) near-

identity with slight variation in phrasing, (2) extensive verbal parallels with embellishment or rearrangement, (3) some verbal similarity and likeness in technique and purpose but with considerable independence in phrasing, and (4) stylistic imitation of Aelred with little overlap of content or phrasing. These classifications are highly inexact and fluid; they indicate a continuum between passages unmistakably taken from *On Reclusion* and minimally adapted in *The Tree of Life* and passages merely reminiscent of Aelred's meditative approach as seen in *On Reclusion.*

However, Aelred's influence is markedly greater than this description would indicate, because it seems clear that Bonaventure's purpose in writing this work and his internal structure, the movement from a third person indicative narrative of Christ's life to second and third person exhortation, comes directly from Aelred. Bonaventure surely intended in *The Tree of Life* to follow Aelred's lead in writing a work of affective spirituality based on the life of Christ, using Aelred's style and often words, but in so doing to transform what was for Aelred only one portion of a work written for the specific needs of a very specific audience, an anchoress, into a single, unified work of spiritual direction drawn from the life of Christ, expanded and adapted for a much more general audience.

There are nine instances of category one. These include Aelred's direction to the contemplative to accompany Mary to visit Elizabeth, to embrace the manger at the nativity, to 'let love overcome bashfulness, affection dispel fear',[30] to accompany the holy family to Egypt, and so on. These appear with minor variants —a word inserted, an embellished phrase, a verb replaced by another of the same root, all changes which might but probably do not reflect minor manuscript variants. Frequently Bonaventure inserts a sentimental word or two or a brief theological statement into Aelred's direction. Usually, though not always, the borrowed passages appear in the same position in *The Tree of Life* as in *On Reclusion.* For example, most of the words in which Aelred speaks of the nativity are directly transferred to Bonaventure's meditation on the nativity, but one phrase of direction, that mentioned above, is transferred from Aelred's nativity passage to Bonaventure's Presentation in the Temple.

An instance of this category appears in the Visitation passage. Aelred says:

> But now with your most sweet Lady go up
> into the mountains and gaze at the sweet
> embrace of the barren one and the virgin

and at their greeting, in which the little
servant recognized and greeted with unspeakable
joy the lord, the herald the judge, the voice
the word, the one confined in the old woman's
womb, the other enclosed in the womb of the
virgin.

Bonaventure's version says:

If you might hear with joy the virgin singing,
if you might go up with your lady into the
mountains, if you might gaze at the sweet
embrace of the barren one and the virgin
and at their greeting, in which the little
servant recognized the lord, the herald the
judge, the voice the word, I believe that
then with the most blessed virgin you would
sing in sweet measure that sacred song, 'My
soul magnifies the Lord'. And you, at one
with the little prophet, will adore the marvelous
virginal conception, rejoicing and exulting.[31]

Here Bonventure changes Aelred's imperative mood
to a conditional followed not by direction but by a
result clause: Aelred urges the imaginative participation
of the contemplative, Bonaventure the consideration
of what it would be like for the contemplative if only.
    In this passage Bonaventure adds to the aelredian
passage the suggestion that the soul sing with Mary,
in the words of the *Magnificat*. In *On Reclusion* Aelred
four times asks the contemplative to sing with those
hymning Jesus' coming: once at the Annunciation,
twice at the nativity, and once at the entry into
Jerusalem on Palm Sunday. But in Aelred's work the
contemplative who so joins her voice always associates
herself with worshipers of Jesus divine and human,
never with Mary or Jesus himself. Bonaventure, in
imitation and adaptation of this meditative technique,
advises the soul to sing—or says that the soul will
sing—with thirteen others in six passages: with Mary
at the Visitation, with angels at the nativity, with
the spouse from the Song of Songs and with Simeon
at the Presentation, with six recipients of miracles,
with Peter at the Transfiguration, and with the Psalmist
(from Psalm 41) at the Last Supper. Aelred's instruction
to the contemplative has her singing as one among
worshipers, while Bonaventure's various such passages
are disparate, incorporating the idea of the contemplative's imaginative involvement but without such clear
sense of purpose or definition of the contemplative's
role in the biblical scene.

In the Visitation passage, then, Bonaventure not only directly incorporates Aelred's Visitation scene, but also imitates an aelredian feature Aelred himself omits, exemplifying category four as well as category one. This combination of direct verbal borrowing and imitation of technique indicates the ubiquity of Aelred's influence on Bonaventure in *The Tree of Life*.

Another nine passages fall into category two, those containing marked verbal parallels to Aelred's but with a rearrangement of phrases and a conflation of what are in *On Reclusion* separate passages, discrete narrative events. In these the inspiration and the words both clearly come from Aelred's parallel passages. For example, Aelred's nativity concentrates on the birth, then considers Mary's joy at the birth and the assistance of the contemplative at that birth, next the contemplative's embracing the crib and kissing the infant's feet, and finally the angels' visit and the coming of the Magi. After the angels' song—with which the contemplative is asked to sing along—Aelred directs her attention in one sentence to the Magi and the flight to Egypt. He says nothing about the gifts or worship of the Magi. The movement is straightforward and unbroken; it occupies three and a half sentences and seven imperative verbs.

In his parallel treatment of these scenes Bonaventure gives only narrative space to the fact of the birth, placed within a theological statement perhaps in imitation of Aelred's passage on humility well before the meditation on the past.[32] He devotes one sentence in the lyric to the soul's embracing the manger and kissing the infant's feet, then moves rapidly to the shepherds' watch and the angels' song. The Magi's coming is distinct from the nativity passage (the fourth meditation of the first fruit, the Magi the second meditation of the second fruit). In *The Tree of Life* Jesus' circumcision, an incident not included by Aelred, intervenes. Still later, as the fourth meditation of the second fruit, Bonaventure conflates the flight to Egypt with the story of the twelve year old Jesus in Jerusalem.

Another example of category two comes from Peter's denying Jesus. Aelred directs the contemplative's attention in this scene primarily to Jesus and his response to Peter's denial, then acknowledges his own guilt and asks Jesus' compassion on him. He identifies himself with the sinner as one in need of grace, and the contemplative washes Jesus' face out of love and compassion for him rather than a desire to atone. Her compassion precedes and is separate from the guilt and repentance of Peter and the author.

Bonaventure reports Peter's denial in a lengthy

narrative paragraph and turns the more lyrical one
toward the guilt and personal atonement of the listening
contemplative; for him the emphasis is not on compassion
for Jesus' suffering, Jesus' mercy toward the sinner,
or his own guilt; rather, he concentrates on his audience's guilt and ability to make satisfaction. Aelred
says to the contemplative:

> Follow him rather 'to the courtyard of the
> prince of priests', and with your tears wash
> his most beautiful face, which they are smearing
> with spittle. Regard how compassionate his
> eyes, how mercifully, how effectually he
> looked back at Peter denying him for the
> third time when Peter, turned about and
> returned into himself, 'wept bitterly'. Good
> Jesus, would that your sweet eyes might
> look upon me who so often at the voice of
> the shameless serving girl, that is, my flesh,
> have denied you by evil deeds and affections.

Bonaventure says here:

> 'Yet Peter', more faithful, 'followed at a
> distance even to the courtyard of the prince
> of priests', where at the voice of a serving
> girl, he with an oath denied that he knew
> Christ and repeated it a third time. Then,
> the cock crowing, the gentle master looked
> back at the beloved disciple with a look
> of compassion and grace, by which Peter,
> reminded, 'going outside, wept bitterly'.
> O, whoever you are, who at the voice of
> an insistent serving girl, that is, your flesh,
> have shamelessly denied Christ, either by
> will or by act, Christ who for you suffered,
> remember the passion of your beloved Master
> and go out with Peter to weep most bitterly
> over yourself. When the one who looked upon
> the weeping Peter looks upon you, you will
> be inebriated with 'the wormwood' of a twofold
> bitterness: remorse for yourself and compassion
> for Christ, so that having atoned with Peter
> for the guilt of your crime, you will be
> filled with the spirit of holiness.[33]

Ten passages fall into category three. They contain
similarities with parallel passages in *On Reclusion*
and are clearly influenced by Aelred's meditative
style, but they might not be recognized as influenced
by him did they not appear in this heavily aelredian

context. For example, Aelred says to the contemplative
in the Passion narrative:

> And what of you? It is not surprising if
> when the sun mourns you mourn with it,
> if when the earth trembles you tremble with
> it, if when rocks are rent your heart is
> rent, if with the women weeping at the cross
> you weep as well.

Bonaventure says:

> And you also, redeemed man, consider...at
> whose passing over heaven and earth mourn
> and hard rocks rend as if from natural compas-
> sion. O human heart, you are harder than
> any hardness of rocks if at the recollection
> of such great sacrifice you are not struck
> with terror nor moved with compassion nor
> rent with compunction nor softened with devo-
> tion.[34]

Category four, containing roughly seven to twelve
passages, shows Bonaventure's imitation of Aelred's
meditative approach. An example comes after his sentence-
long summary of miracles done by Jesus (a topic intentionally avoided by Aelred):

> To him our sinning conscience calls out like
> the faithful leper, 'Lord, if you wish, you
> can make me clean'. Now like the centurion,
> 'Lord, my servant boy is lying at home paralys-
> ed and is suffering intensely'. Now like
> the woman of Canaan: 'Have mercy on me,
> Son of David'. Now like the woman with the
> issue of blood: 'If I touch the hem of his
> garment, I will be cured'. Now with Mary
> and Martha: 'See, Lord, the one you love
> is ill'.[35]

This passage attempts in pedestrian fashion to provide
an aelredian meditation where none is available.

Aelred's influence on *The Tree of Life* is not
limited to instances of parallel usage; Bonaventure's
repeated borrowing reveals an enormous stylistic debt
to Aelred. The work as a whole--its style and approach
of imaginative involvement in Jesus' human experience,
intimacy with him, and growing nearness to God,
continuously resonates of Aelred's first meditation.
Knowledge of the regularity with which Bonaventure
relies on Aelred for language and style allows the

reader to recognize Bonaventure's dependence on him in the individual instance. For example, at the beginning of *The Tree of Life* Bonaventure defines his audience as:

> one who, not unmindful of the Lord's passion nor ungrateful, contemplates the labor, suffering and love of Jesus crucified, with such vividness of memory, such sharpness of intellect and such charity of will that he can truly say with the bride: 'A bundle of myrrh is my beloved to me; he will linger between my breasts'.[36]

Immediately after this sentence, Bonaventure defines his purpose in *The Tree of Life*, saying 'To enkindle in us this affection, to shape this understanding and to imprint this memory, I have endeavored to gather this bundle of myrrh from the forest of the holy Gospel'.[37] In both cases Bonaventure uses Song of Songs 1:12 in reference to Jesus crucified, as he does in *The Life of St Francis (Legenda Maior)* when he says 'Jesus Christ crucified always rested like a bundle of myrrh in the bosom of Francis' soul'.[38]

Bernard of Clairvaux had also used this verse to refer to Christ in sermons forty-three and forty-five on the Song of Songs, in the former case defining Christ as the lover of the bride and speaking of his humility, the suffering of the present time, and the anticipation of glory to come. In sermon forty-five Bernard explicitly identifies the myrrh as Christ crucified: 'And yet when reproved [the bride] repented and said: "My beloved is to me a little bundle of myrrh that lies between my breasts". As much as to say: It is enough for me: I desire to know nothing any longer except Jesus and him crucified'.[39]

Bonaventure might well have taken his understanding of this verse from Bernard, but awareness of his intimate acquaintance with and constant reliance on *On Reclusion* leads the reader to examine Aelred's work for the immediate source—and apparently to find it. At the moment in *On Reclusion* when Joseph of Arimathea takes Christ down from the cross Aelred says to the contemplative, 'Then could that holy man say, "My beloved is a bundle of myrrh for me, he shall rest upon my breast"'.[40] It is surely Aelred's use of this verse that influences both of Bonaventure's identifications of the crucified Christ as a bundle of myrrh upon the believer's breast.

Some thirty-five to forty instances of the four categories of borrowing appear in *The Tree of Life*.

Aelred's life of Christ in the first meditation of *On Reclusion* is clearly Bonaventure's primary source; it and Ecbert's meditation on the humanity of Christ ('Anselm's' meditation nine) shape the content and style of the work. If the structure of the tree is acknowledged to be original with Bonaventure, his only other important source is probably the Gospels themselves.

At the same time *The Tree of Life* is very different from Aelred's life of Christ in overall structure and purpose. Although Bonaventure apparently wrote his life of Christ out of admiration for Aelred's first meditation and used it as the core of his own work, he was not satisfied merely to duplicate it; he chose to add to it on both ends—largely extra-canonically —and in the middle, with attention to Gospel events that showed forth Jesus' ministry and divinity. Bonaventure's life of Christ begins with a theological statement about the begetting of Jesus and ends with fourteen meditations after the Resurrection, including the Ascension and providing a number of theological summaries of Jesus' identity in glory, such as Jesus' Extraordinary Beauty and Jesus Given Dominion Over the Earth. He includes the Transfiguration, as Aelred does not, and concentrates on the Last Supper not, like Aelred, as a human event whose immediate interest lies in the relationships of those present at it, in its provision of a eucharistic model for contemplative union, or in it as an incident in Jesus' human life, but as a theological and sacramental event.

Aelred's life of Christ begins with the Annunciation, ends with the Resurrection, and omits the Transfiguration, miracles, and most of Jesus' ministry. He includes some events that Bonaventure omits: Jesus' washing the disciples' feet, the paralytic man let down through the roof, dinner with Mary, Martha, and Lazarus, and Mary's anointing of Jesus. He treats separately some stories conflated by Bonaventure, such as the woman taken in adultery and her later anointing Jesus, but treats the details of the Passion as part of a whole, a narrative that picks up speed and coherence as it develops, rather than as a series of individual events, as does Bonaventure.

Further, Bonaventure's contemplative theology as enunciated in *The Tree of Life* is radically different from Aelred's. Bonaventure insists on coming to God by imitation of Jesus rather than by intimacy with him. Where Aelred regularly directs the soul to minister to, to anoint, to love Jesus, Bonaventure's emphasis is always on following Jesus' lead, on reaching toward identification with him, likeness to him, through meditation on his life and its meaning for humankind rather

than on coming to union with him, even in passages
in which the soul must naturally identify herself with
those who love Jesus rather than with Jesus himself.
While in the meditation on the Magi he urges veneration
of Jesus with gifts of gold, myrrh, and frankincense,
he concludes, 'You will return to your country in
the footsteps of the humble Christ'.[41] When Jesus is
nailed to the cross he asks, 'Who will grant me that
my request should come about and that God will give
me what I long for, that having been totally transpierced
in both mind and flesh, I may be fixed with my beloved
to the yoke of the cross?'[42]

In the parallel passages Aelred says nothing
about the Magi except to note their coming, but he
urges the contemplative to weep at the Passion, to
stand with Mary and John, and finally to drink the
blood and water from Jesus' side, to enter into his
wound, and finally to bear up his limbs and save
the falling drops of blood. Aelred guides the contemplative toward spiritual union with Christ through love
of him, not toward perfection through imitation of
him, suggesting that such perfection, such imitation,
is neither possible nor necessary.

Bonaventure's treatise finally is less concerned
with the humanity of Jesus and with the events of
his human life than with a theological understanding
of that humanity, placed within the context of his
divinity. Thus he leads his reader to Jesus through
two statements about his origins, statements not taken
from the Gospel accounts, titled 'Jesus Begotten of
God' and 'Jesus Prefigured'. Neither of these passages
allows any human involvement with Jesus, neither
has the usual lyrical passage. The top four branches
on Bonaventure's tree again contain meditations from
outside the human life of Jesus, with scenes from
his glorification. Even within the events of Jesus'
life Bonaventure is concerned to provide theological
definition and explication.

Bonaventure's concern, then, is more speculative
and didactic than affective or contemplative. He is
essentially concerned with leading his reader to understand and perhaps to effect a change in his behavior
as a result of that understanding. His treatise appears
more truly concerned with a moral reading of the
Gospel than a contemplative one; its center is cognitive,
not contemplative, its concerns doctrinal and moral.
Because of a radically different purpose in the work,
Bonaventure uses Aelred's direction to the contemplative,
his constant urging her forward, not as a way of
bringing her to closeness with Jesus in his humanity
and thus to God, but rather as a stylistic variant,

a different way of explaining Christ's dual nature
and of leading his audience to imitate it so as to
come to God. His treatise on the life of Christ emerges
from a radically different understanding of the road
to mystical knowledge of God.

At the same time *The Tree of Life* is consciously
emotive, urging the reader, the soul, ever to greater
levels of emotional intensity in hearing and responding
to the Gospel events. It accomplishes Bonaventure's
moral and theological goals through emotional appeal,
a familiar and valuable heuristic approach. The reader
is led to feel as well as to think, to become involved
in order to understand.

Cousins misunderstands the work, though, when
he tries to present it as a contemplative work, one
leading toward mystical knowledge of or union with
God. He comments in his Introduction that 'Bonaventure
meditates on Christ as the beginning, the middle and
the end of the journey; but in each case he focuses
not on the historical Jesus in the concrete details
of his earthly life as an example of moral virtue,
but on the mystical Christ who opens the deeper dimen-
sions of the soul and leads to union with God'.43
That statement is hard to support on the basis of
the work itself, and in fact Cousins' own suggestion
that *The Tree of Life* cannot stand alone as a contemplative treatise, that it requires combination with either
The Soul's Journey into God or *Spiritual Exercises*
to allow such a passage to union, bears more convic-
tion.44

Like Bonaventure, Ludolph the Carthusian directs
the reader of his *Vita Christi* to imitation of Christ;
it is his work and his emphasis on this meditative
approach which is generally understood as underlying
the *imitatio* school of spirituality, notably in the
works of Thomas à Kempis and Francis of Sales.

Each of the eighty-nine chapters of Ludolph's
Vita Christi is given to a different aspect of the life
of Jesus (some actually to Mary), and each ends with
a brief appended prayer, essentially the only parts
of the whole thought actually to have originated with
Ludolph. That pattern of narrative followed by semi-
spontaneous prayer, seen also in *The Tree of Life*,
may itself have been influenced by the similar brief
prayers interjected by Aelred into his life of Christ
in *On Reclusion*, but it is of course a pattern not
restricted to any one author. Anselm LeBail has suggested
it as a characteristic of cistercian spirituality:

> These men...find it necessary to interrupt
> their exposition with prayers, with flights

upward to God, with chants of praise....Here perhaps we see the quintessence of the style of the Cistercian spirituality of the twelfth and thirteenth centuries. It is a search for God and the moment the insight is attained the heart bursts forth in chants of praise.[45]

While such movement from third person objective narration to first person prayer is perhaps characteristic of cistercian spirituality, it is clearly a natural one and not restricted to any one school. It need not depend on any non-biblical source, but if one were sought it might be as well Augustine as Aelred.

Ludolph, unlike Bonaventure, makes no pretense of having drawn his lengthy life of Christ from the Gospels alone. He appears to have used every author and every manuscript available to him, and he cites every borrowed passage both before and after its use. Passages quoted from *On Reclusion* begin *Hic dicit Anselmus* and end *Haec Anselmus*. A few times, at the appropriate place in his narrative, he quotes from *On Jesus as a Boy of Twelve*, known to him as written by Bernard, and before and after those passages he writes *Hic dicit Bernardus* and *Haec Bernardus*. His treatise is finally more a carefully annotated florilegium than an independent work.

Like Bonaventure, Ludolph breaks Aelred's uninterrupted narrative into brief topical blocks, on the Annunciation, the Visitation, the Nativity, and so on. Like Bonaventure, he begins at the beginning of time and ends with the Judgment, so not all of Aelred fits into his scheme. Further, he puts much more emphasis on the public ministry of Jesus than does Aelred, so has no material from Aelred for those portions of his treatise. It is clear, however, that he wrote with a manuscript of Aelred at hand, for the entire first meditation, almost word for word, appears in blocks at the appropriate places in his work. He omits only words in which Aelred indicates a transition from one scene to another--'Now, sister', 'linger no longer here'--or too great specificity of audience, 'O, virgin'.

Ludolph's access to Aelred is unquestionably independent of Bonaventure. Not only does he include all of the first meditation, as Bonaventure does not, but he does not ever adapt, rearrange, embellish, or conflate Aelred's narrative as Bonaventure always does. It is also clear that Ludolph has more than one 'anselmian' manuscript available to him. In his account of the Annunciation he begins *De hac Verbi Incarnatione, sic dicit Anselmus,* and follows that with a prayer to the Son not taken from *On Reclusion*. After the prayer he adds *Idem ad sororem suam* and continues with Aelred's urging the contemplative to await with Mary the coming of the angel.[46]

Both Bonaventure and Ludolph used the first meditation of Aelred of Rievaulx's *On Reclusion* extensively in the composition of their own lives of Christ. The evidence of their use argues that perhaps they wrote in direct response to that meditation, out of deep admiration for it and desire to replicate it in a work devoted to that one purpose. That desire is more clear in the case of Bonaventure than that of Ludolph, given the great number of authors represented in Ludolph's work. Both later writers were perhaps frustrated with what they saw as Aelred's truncated treatment of the gospel account, beginning only with the Annunciation and ending with the meeting in the garden after the Resurrection, and both wanted more theological definition.

Not only had Aelred both begun too late and ended too early in his portrayal of Christ, he had not even dealt with all of his human experiences, especially those that showed forth divinity—miracles, teaching, and so on. Aelred was much more interested in *On Reclusion*, as in all his works, in Jesus' human relationships during his life and the model they suggested for men and women of all times to come into relationship with him. Bonaventure and Ludolph, then, added not only to the beginning and end of Aelred's account of Jesus' life, but to the middle as well.

Both also failed to understand Aelred's concern for the contemplative's life and purpose, the yearning effort to come into union with God. Because Aelred writes his work not as a theological treatise or as an allegorized re-presentation of the Gospel, but rather as a simple work of guidance in the life of contemplation toward the goal of that life, his meditation on the life of Christ exemplifies that purpose.

And Aelred's understanding of the way to come to union with God was like his understanding of human union: it comes through love, through intimacy. His meditation exemplifies that understanding of contemplative union throughout, and his meditative method of imaginative involvement in the human life of Jesus—the only life in which a contemplative can involve himself (that being the point of the Incarnation, after all) —grows out of that understanding.

Bonaventure and Ludolph were able to use his words and, in the case of Bonaventure, imitate his method, but in the absence of his particular purpose and understanding—and with their own understanding of Christ as exemplar and of contemplative union as emerging from imitation of Christ—they were never able really to understand what Aelred had in mind. It did not matter so much in Ludolph's *Vita Christi*, because he merely quoted Aelred, but in Bonaventure the passages borrowed from Aelred sometimes fit awkwardly, as in the passage on the Magi. Aelred's *On Reclusion* is, finally, contemplative, theirs devotional and theological, given over to meditation and exposition.

Ludolph's effect on Ignatius was also devotional and theological, finally leading toward exemplarism; the *Spiritual Exercises* reflect his stylistic and didactic influence. The resemblance of Bonaventure and Ignatius has clearly been misleading; it is far too easy to trace Ignatius to Bonaventure and to his *application des sens* in *The Tree of Life*, even though Ignatius, like Ludolph and unlike Bonaventure, acknowledged the origin of his spiritual insight. Oddly, then, franciscan and ignatian spirituality resemble one another more than they do Aelred and cistercian spirituality. Nonetheless, both schools trace their heritage to the cistercian Aelred.

Aelred said in the second meditation of *On Reclusion* (the one never borrowed or imitated, so far as I know, and omitted almost entirely from many manuscripts):

> In men's opinion the graciousness of the giver and the good fortune of the recipient are so connected that they praise not only him to whom praise alone is due, the giver, but also him who has received the gift. What does a man possess that he has not received? And if he has received freely, why is he praised as if he had deserved the gift?[47]

Well might he ask. Aelred's gift of the meditation on the humanity of Christ has been the good fortune of Bonaventure, Ludolph, Ignatius—and all of western christian spirituality.

The University of Michigan

NOTES

In the following notes LV=*Lignum Vitae*, the Latin text of St Bonaventure's work as it appears in the Quaracchi edition of 1882–1902; TL=*The Tree of Life*, in Ewert Cousins' 1978 translation; A=Aelred; B=Bonaventure; PL=*Patrologia Latina*, ed. J.-P. Migne.

1. *Bonaventure: The Soul's Journey into God, The Tree of Life, The Life of St Francis*, translation and introduction by Ewert Cousins, preface by Ignatius Brady (New York: Paulist Press, 1978) p. 34.

2. C. H. Talbot, 'The "De Institutis Inclusarum" of Aelred of Rievaulx', *ASOC* 7 (1951) 12–217, reprinted CCCM 1:636–82, is the standard edition of this work. It appears in translation by M. P. Macpherson, 'A Rule of Life for a Recluse', CF 2 (Spencer, Mass.: Cistercian Publications, 1971) 43–102. The notes give line numbers from the CCCM text and page numbers from the CF 2 translation, but in cases of compared passages I have provided my own translations. I am using a straightforward rendering of the Latin title, one that better defines the work. Biblical phrases within quoted passages will appear within quotation marks.

3. Ed. Anselm Hoste, CCCM 1:247–78; trans. Theodore Berkeley, *Jesus at the Age of Twelve*, CF 2:1–39.

4. Inst incl 29; CCCM 1:883–84; CF 2:79.

5. Inst incl 31; CCCM 1:1237; CF 2:92.

6. Cousins, p. 10. Three manuscripts of *On Reclusion* are still to be found in Paris, though all postdate Bonaventure. In view of Aelred's popularity and the number of cistercian houses in France, manuscripts of *On Reclusion* must have been widespread in France for many centuries.

7. Cousins, p. 10. The standard edition of Bonaventure is the Quaracchi critical edition, *Doctoris Seraphici S. Bonaventurae Opera Omnia*, ed. studio et cura pp. collegii a S. Bonaventura, 10 vols. (Quaracchi: Collegium S. Bonaventurae, 1882–1902). *The Tree of Life, Lignum Vitae*, is in vol. 8, 'Opuscula varia ad theologiam mysticam', pp. 68–87. The notes give line numbers from this edition and page numbers from Cousins' translation, but in all cases of compared passages I have provided my own translations. Biblical phrases within quoted passages appear inside quotation marks.

8. John V. Fleming, in *An Introduction to the Francis-*

can Literature of the Middle Ages (Chicago: Franciscan Herald Press, 1977), says: 'What are usually
called his "mystical *opuscula*"...are among the
most beautiful and most influential of all the
hundreds of spiritual books in the Middle Ages....
The *Lignum vitae*...demonstrates the pleasing
harmony of the visual and verbal imaginations
of Bonaventure's pastoral writings' (pp. 203–204).

9. *Vita Jesu Christi*, ed. L. M. Rigollot, 4 vols.
   (Paris & Brussels: 1878). *Vita Christi's* translation
   history has been examined in two studies: Mary
   Immaculate Bodenstedt, *The Vita Christi of Ludolphus
   the Carthusian*, The Catholic University of America
   Studies in Medieval and Renaissance Latin Language
   and Literature, vol. 16 (Washington, D.C.: The
   Catholic University of America Press, 1944), and
   Elizabeth Salter, 'Ludolphus of Saxony and His
   English Translators', *Medium Aevum* 33 (1964)
   26–35. Salter points out that since its printing
   in 1472 it has been edited sixty times and that
   during the fifteenth and sixteenth centuries it
   was translated into almost every European language.

10. Bodenstedt, p. 22.

11. Ignatius Loyola, *St Ignatius' Own Story as Told
    to Luis González de Cámera*, trans. William J.
    Young (Chicago: Henry Regnery Co., 1956) 7–11.
    See also 'Ignace de Loyola', *Dictionnaire de Spiritual-
    ité*, 7 (1971) 1267.

12. Besides Bodenstedt and Salter, e.g., Emmerich
    Raitz von Frentz, 'Ludolph le Chartreux et Les
    Exercises de S. Ignace de Loyola', Mélanges
    Marcel Viller, *Revue d'ascétique et de mystique*
    25 (1949) 375–88, and Henri Watrigant, *La genèse
    des exercises de saint Ignace de Loyola* (Amiens:
    Yvert & Tellier, 1897).

13. 'Application des Sens', *Dictionnaire de Spiritualité*
    1 (1937) 823–24. Regarding Bernard's role in
    the development of this approach, Maréchal cites
    the Third Sermon on the Nativity, saying, 'Nothing
    very remarkable from our point of view, except
    the affective and imagistic genre of devotion
    to the incarnate Word, a new genre in patristic
    literature'.

14. Hoste, 'Marginalia bij Aelred's De Institutione
    Inclusarum', in *Cîteaux in de Nederlanden*, 9
    (1958) 133; *Quand Jesus eut douze ans*, trans.
    Joseph Dubois (Paris: Editions du Cerf, 1958),
    p. 32; *Bibliotheca Aelrediana* (Steenbrugge: In
    Abbati sancti Petri, 1962) 145.

15. Dumont, *La Vie de Recluse*, Sources Chrétiennes
    76 (Paris: Cerf, 1961), pp. 35–36.

16.   André Wilmart, 'Le recueil des prières de S.
       Anselme', p. xvi, *Méditations et Prières de S.
       Anselme*, trad. D. A. Castel, Pax XI (Paris: Abbaye
       de Maredsous, 1923). I have also noted Aelred's
       influence on Bonaventure and Ludolph in my 1981
       dissertation and a 1983 article: Marsha Stuckey,
       'An Edition of Two Middle English Translations
       of Aelred's *De Institutione Inclusarum*' (Ph.D.
       dissertation, The University of Michigan, 1981)
       p. 28; 'A Prodigal Writes Home: Aelred of Rievaulx's
       De institutione inclusarum', CS 68:35.
17.   PL 32:1451–74 (Augustine); 158:785a–98b (Anselm).
18.   André Wilmart, 'La tradition des prières de S.
       Anselme', *Revue Bénédictine*, 36 (1924) 52–71;
       'Les Méditations VII et VIII attribuées à Saint
       Anselme: La Série des 21 Méditations', *Revue
       d'ascétique et de mystique*, 8 (1927) 249–82. Wil-
       mart's attention to the corpus of devotional works
       traditionally attributed to Anselm has identified
       as his, three out of the twenty–one meditations
       in PL 158; these three have been printed in a
       critical edition by Franciscus Schmitt, *S. Anselmi
       Cantuariensis Archiepiscopi: Opera Omnia*, vol.
       3 (Edinburgh: Thomas Nelson and Sons, 1946).
       See also Wilmart, *Auteurs spirituels et textes
       dévots du moyen âge latin* (Paris: 1932) 162–201.
19.   That one passage, identified by the Quaracchi
       editors and by Cousins as coming from Anselm's
       meditation fifteen, is in paragraph nine of *The
       Tree of Life*, the passage on The Nativity. One
       additional passage not idicated by the Quaracchi
       editors as anselmian is identified by Cousins
       as coming from one of the three authentic anselmian
       meditations, med. two in PL, 'About the terror
       of judgment, to excite fear', PL 158:724–725=Schmitt
       Med. 1, 'Meditatio ad concitandum timorem', pp.
       76–79.
20.   Wilmart, 'Méditations', p. 273.
21.   Dunstan Dobbins, *Franciscan Mysticism*, Franciscan
       Studies, no. 6 (New York: 1927) 82, states that
       Bonaventure's 'principal sources...are the Gospels,
       the writings of St Anselm and St Bernard, and
       the characteristically Franciscan traditions begun
       by the "Poverello"...it is to these that he is
       indebted for his conception and presentation of
       the mystical value of this practical devotion to
       Christ....Both in the dogmatic and in the scriptural
       treatises already mentioned, and in the *Opuscula*,
       he constantly appeals to the earlier writers for
       confirmation'.
22.   Cousins, p. xvi. Brady's phrase 'frequent anonymous

use' appears to contradict his conclusion of 'no dependence'. In fact, besides the 'anselmian' passages noted by him and Cousins and the multiple aelredian usages that Cousins does not recognize, Cousins footnotes two passages in the work from Bede and one from Boethius. Further, there is some evidence that Bonaventure may have known and been influenced by Robert Grosseteste's *Moralia super Evangelia,* probably delivered to the Franciscans of Oxford in about 1230 (see S. Harrison Thomson, *The Writings of Robert Grosseteste* [Cambridge: 1940] 134; this work may have been the immediate source for Bonaventure's use of the authentic anselmian meditation.

23. Cousins does not follow the Quaracchi editors in attributing to 'Anselm's' med. nine some lines in LV 29, titled 'Iesus, sol morte pallidus'.
24. Cousins, p. 37. See also below, fn. 44.
25. As Cousins notes Bonaventure's use of one passage from the authentic Anselm and eight from the Pseudo-Anselm, as well as the two from Boethius and one from Bede, it is hard to explain his suggestion that Bonaventure invented the method. Of the nine passages attributed by him to Anselm or Pseudo-Anselm, six urge the soul to participate imaginatively in the historical events of Jesus' life. Despite his ignorance of Aelred's influence, Cousins clearly knew that Bonaventure followed at least two previous authors, Anselm and Ecbert (his Pseudo-Anselm), in his use of this approach to meditation through the historical events of Jesus' life. The immediate impact of Cousins' paper and its coining of a new term of reference for the meditative approach that Bonaventure found in Aelred may be seen in a paper presented at the 19th Congress of Medieval Studies in Kalamazoo, May 1984. The program booklet of the conference for 11 May 1984 includes a paper by William Hood, 'Franciscan Pilgrimage Sanctuaries of the Renaissance: A Case of Cousin's [sic] Mysticism of the Historical Event'.
26. Gal 2:19; LV Prol. 1, p. 68; TL p. 119.
27. LV Prol. 2, p. 68; TL pp. 119-20.
28. LV Prol. 1, p. 68; TL p. 119.
29. Cousins, pp. 35-36.
30. A: *uincat uerecundiam amor, timorem depellat affectus.* (Inst incl 29; CCCM 1:926; CF 2:81)
     B: *vincat verecundiam amor, depellat timorem affectus* (LV 7, p. 72; TL p. 131)
31. A: *Iam nunc cum dulcissima domina tuo in montana conscende, et sterilis et uirginis suauem intuere*

*complexum, et salutationis officium, in quo seruulus
dominum, praeco iudicem, uox uerbum, inter anilia
uiscera conclusus, in Virginis utero clausum agnouit,
et indicibili gaudio salutauit.* (Inst incl 29;
CCCM 1:910–914; CF 2:81)
B: *Si Virginem canentem cum iubilo posses audire,
si cum Domina tua in montana conscendere, si
sterilis et Virginis suavem intueri complexum
et salutationis officium, in quo servulus Dominum,
praeco Iudicem, vox Verbum agnovit: puto, quod
canticum illud sacrum: 'Magnificat anima mea
Dominum'* etc., *cum beatissima Virgine suavi tunc
modulatione concineres mirumque conceptum virginem
una cum Propheta Parvulo exsultans et iubilans
adorares!* (LV 3, p. 71; TL pp. 127–28)

32. *Qua enim fronte de diuitiis uel natalibus gloriaris
quae illius uis sponsa uideri, qui pauper factus
cum esset diues, pauperem matrem, pauperem
familiam, domum etiam pauperculam, et praesepii
uilitatem elegit?* (Inst incl 24; CCCM 1:684–87;
CF 2:71)
B: *qui, cum magnus esset et dives, pro nobis
effectus parvus et pauper, extra domum in diversorio
nasci elegit, panniculis involvi, lacte virgineo
pasci et inter bovem et asinum in praesepio reclin-
ari.* (LV 4, pp. 71–72; TL p. 128)
This passage may not have resulted from Bonaventure's familiarity with Aelred; it is a natural
kind of exposition of the details of the nativity,
and by the thirteenth century it was commonplace
in all devotional literature. But in view of Bonaventure's constant use of Aelred, it may occur here
through his influence. It suggests familiarity
with more of *On Reclusion* than just the three
meditations.

33. A: *Sequere potius eum 'ad atrium principis sacerdotum', et speciosissimam eius faciem, quam illi
sputis illiniunt, tu lacrymis laua. Intuere quam
piis oculis, quam misericorditer, quam efficaciter
tertio negantem respexit Petru, quando ille conuer-
sus, et in se reuersus, 'fleuit amare'. Vtinam,
bone Iesu, tuus me dulcis respiciat oculus, qui
te totiens ad uocem ancillae procacis, carnis
scilicet meae, pessimis operibus affectibusque
negaui.* (Inst incl 31; CCCM 1:1121–28; CF 2:88)
B: *'Petrus, tamen', tanquam fidelior, 'secutus
est a longe usque in atrium principis sacerdotum',
ubi ad vocem ancillae, se Christum nosse cum
iuramento negavit tertioque repetit, donec, gallo
cantante, respexit benignus Magister praedilectum
discipulum respectu miserationis et gratiae; quo
commonitus Petrus et 'foras egressus flevit amare'.*

O quisquis es, qui ad vocem impetentis ancillae, carnis videlicet tuae, Christum pro te passum negasti procaciter vel voluntate vel actu; rememorans passionem dilectissimi Magistri, foras cum Petro egredere, ut te ipsum amarissime defleas, si quando te respeciat qui Petrum lacrymantem respexit, geminae quoque amarictionis 'compunctionis' scilicet pro te et 'compassionis' ad Christum, inebrieris absinthio, ut, expiatus cum Petro a reatu sceleris, replearis cum Petro spiritu sanctitatis. (LV 21, p. 76; TL pp. 144–45)
Aelred is always aware that the sinner cannot make recompense, that he is dependent on God's unmerited mercy. Note also that for Aelred *inebriate* is an essentially contemplative word; one who receives God's grace, one who knows union with him, experiences inebriation. Cf. Acts 2:13; Inst incl 31; CCCM 1:1091–94; CF 2:87.

34. A: *Quid tu? Non mirum si sole contristante, tu contristaris, si terra tremiscente, tu contremiscis, si scissis saxis, tuum cor scinditur, si flentibus iuxta crucem mulieribus, tu collacrymaris.* (Inst incl 31; CCCM 1:1161–64; CF 2:89–90)
    B: *Considera et tu, homo redempte,...cuiusque transitum et caelum luget et terra, et lapides duri quasi naturali compassione scinduntur. O cor humanum omni lapidum duritia durius, si ad tanti rememorationem piaculi nec terrore concuteris nec compassione afficeris nec compunctione scinderis nec pietate molliris!* (LV 29, p. 79; TL p. 154)
35. LV 11, p. 73; TL p. 135.
36. LV Prol. 1, p. 68; TL p. 119.
37. LV Prol. 2, p. 68; TL p. 119.
38. *Legenda Sancti Francisci*, Quaracchi 8:9.2; Cousins, p. 263.
39. Bernard, *On the Song of Songs II*, trans. Kilian Walsh (Kalamazoo, Mich.: Cistercian Publications, 1976) CF 7:223, 234.
40. Inst incl 31; CCCM 1:1198–1200; CF 2:91.
41. LV 6, p. 72; TL pp. 130–31.
42. LV 26, p. 78; TL p. 149.
43. Cousins, p. 35.
44. Cousins in fact recognizes the heavy moral emphasis of *The Tree of Life* despite his attempt here to deny it as central, saying on the next page: 'In this type of meditation, one applies the senses to a vividly imagined scene and evokes human emotions ranging from tender love to anguish. In the history of Christian piety, this form of meditation has been problematic, especially in

its focus on the passion of Christ. Since it evokes human emotions, it can fall into a superficial sentimentalism. If it avoids this, it might remain exclusively on the moral level, proposing Christ's virtues for imitation in everyday life. It can, however, be a gateway into deeper mystical states of consciousness. Bonventure indicates how this can be done when in *The Soul's Journey* he speaks of Christ as the doorway into the Franciscan contemplative vision, then later as the Bridegroom of the soul and finally as the passage to mystical ecstasy. If one were, for example, to link Bonaventure's meditations on the life of Christ in *The Tree of Life* to these three points, he could integrate these two forms of meditation in an organic fashion' (Cousins, p. 37). Aelred's *On Reclusion* does in fact integrate the two forms of meditation, not sequentially but organically, leading the contemplative to mystical union through intimacy rather than imitation.

45. Cited in CF 2:80, fn. 8, from 'La Spiritualité cistercienne', *Les Cahiers du Cercle Thomiste Fémine*, 7 (1927) 491.
46. Ludolph, 1:5.27; vol. 1, p. 44.
47. Inst incl 32; CCCM 1:1319–23; CF 2:95.

NON–FIGURAL USES OF SCRIPTURE IN
SAINT BERNARD'S *SERMONS ON THE SONG OF SONGS*

Robert M. Dresser

Saint Bernard of Clairvaux's *Sermons on the Song of Songs* are known to be synonymous with allegorism. The extent to which non–allegorical (or, better, non–figural) interpretation of Scripture enters into this work has generally received all too scant attention. We wish to redress this oversight.[1] Our examination will be confined to a set of four sermons, those numbered twenty–five through twenty–eight; they are illustrative of our point and fairly representative of the work as a whole.[2] In this sequence Bernard comments upon *Song of Songs* 1:4: *Nigra sum, sed formosa, filiae Ierusalem sicut tabernacula cedar, sicut pelles Salomonis* ('I am black but beautiful, o daughters of Jerusalem, as the tents of Kedar, as the curtains of Solomon').[3]

Before looking at the text of these sermons, we need to set forth some preliminary assumptions. The first is the perhaps obvious fact that Bernard's notion of exegetical interpretation is the opposite of that prevalent today. Not only does he assume the literal inerrancy of Holy Writ, but he shows little more than passing concern with its historical context. To enter sympathetically into Bernard's experience of God's Word, we need lay aside for a time the inevitable preoccupations of the twentieth century and try to take the Sacred Page at its face value.

Secondly, a word about literal interpretation is necessary. Under this term must be understood attention, not only to the immediate content of the text in question, but also to the supposed circumstances of its composition. This approach had, in fact, been in eclipse ever since the fall of Christian Antioch in the seventh century—although it would re–emerge to some extent in the work of Abelard and Andrew of Saint Victor. For Bernard, at any rate, such an approach would have been either excessively narrow or else impious. As his great model, Saint Augustine, had abundantly shown, many a hard, dark passage can be explained only in terms which avoid the apparently plain sense.

Furthermore, Bernard had the advantage of an insouciance about historical (and linguistic) problems which we perforce lack. His implicit confidence in the substance and integrity of his text gave him a freedom to be inventive and even playful without ever

calling his own seriousness of purpose into question.
In this he was aided by the apparent conviction that
the Latin scriptures were as inspired as the original
tongues—though it is doubtful that the matter would
have been in need of discussion.[4]

Indeed, it was virtually axiomatic that the particular form of verbal revelation could never be accidental.[5]
The guidance of the Holy Spirit in shaping the Bible
was taken as such to mean that any given word or
phrase could be expected to contain latent meaning
worthy of devout exposition. It mattered little that
doctrine might shape exegesis, if only because the
christian faith was ultimately a seamless garment.[6]

Finally, before turning to the non-figural material,
we must say something about figuralism itself. There
are few more controversial topics for the student of
medieval letters than that of the functions of so-called
'allegory'. It may well be that the source of controversy
will in the end turn out to be a confusion over the
meaning of the word 'literal', for there are, in reality,
two quite distinct concepts covered under the one
term. These are not always separated in practice
as they should be.

On the one hand there is the *prima facie* content
of a passage, assuming that it is patent of a rational
and even useful explication.[7] On the other, there
is what is called the *sensus litteralis*, denoting not
so much the intentionality of the passage as its objectifi-
cation.[8] In this case, whenever a passage refers to
a thing, a person, or an event, that literal object
can become the point of reference for one or more
unexpressed ideas, which will be analogous in import,
but not at all identical in form. This notion of literal
implies transferral of meaning which is like metaphor,
only more concrete. To it we would give the name
'figuralism', although it is more conventionally designated 'allegory'. A good case could be made for reserving
the term allegory for that artifice of poetry which
relies upon personification to convey abstract qualities,
an artifice which is as much a cipher as it is a
metaphor. The term *figura*, however, would seem the
most exact way of describing an image in which various
degrees of associated meaning are capable of being
discovered.[9] The distinction here is roughly equivalent
to that between sign and symbol. Figuralism is simply
a concise name for the well-known 'patristic' scheme
of four-fold exegesis.

It follows that figuralism (like personification
allegory) is an extrinsic mode—the one being interpre-
tive, the other expressive. Literal interpretation,
by contrast, is an intrinsic mode; but lest we confuse

it with the so-called *sensus litteralis*, which is actually an aspect of figuralism, it is preferable to speak of non-figural interpretation rather than literal interpretation.[10] *A fortiori*, this terminology avoids any ambiguity which might arise as a result of the meaning that modern fundamentalists have given to 'literalism'. Whatever may have been his critical naiveté, Bernard was not a scriptural literalist of the sort that one encounters today.

Figuralism is usually based upon narrative. The literal fact, which will be subject to a process of association in order to get at its supposedly real meaning, is normally something that turns up in a story of some kind (whether an historical chronicle, legend, myth, or plain fiction).[11] Such is the case in the sermons on the *Song of Songs*. So long as the person, object, or event in question is depicted sufficiently concretely, the particular words employed are no more than incidental. Since what the story seemed to be saying was only an approximation--i.e., a sign --of what it was really saying, the narrative *per se* was inevitably devalued. This explains why Bernard seems only mildly interested in the historicity and even of the verisimilitude of the book he is interpreting. It also explains why there seems to be so little continuity from one sermon to the next, at least in terms of following the story-line of the *Song of Songs*.

This tendency toward a certain disjointedness is heightened by the obscurity of the original poem. Even more is it due, perhaps, to the incongruity of a theme which (in its plainest sense) scarcely exalts the virtue of erotic abstinence. One way of avoiding embarrassment here is to see everything *sub figura;* another is to treat the words as ends in themselves, thus mitigating the potentially lubricious impact of the story they tell. Still, Bernard's treatment of his text does not descend to a mere explaining away of it.

This is possible because of his mental habit of seeing things in a kind of platonic light.[12] What this means in principle is that graphic, as opposed to propositional, modes of cognition predominate in his work. This is the consequence, surely, of a sense that the authentically real is to be encountered through exemplarity. Words thus become the corporeal husk of a spiritual and living kernel of truth. When figuralism is employed, it means that the *sensus litteralis* must decrease in order that the *sensus spiritualis* may increase.

Yet not all scriptural passages yield readily to that kind of oblique construal. Some *genres*, such as legislations, exhortations, and proverbs, must be taken to mean what they say, and no more. These require, not transferral, but reiteration. This kind of 'literalism' possesses no special name, for it ordinarily requires no special notice. For want of a better term, we could call it verbalism *(or sensus verborum.)*

Often enough, Bernard treats the *Song of Songs* figurally; but equally often, his understanding of it is more precisely verbal. That is, he either ignores the actual story or uses it as a mere *point d'appui.* It is as if the very words, even when they depict an object which is the basis of a figural construct, have a primary, non-contextual message of their own. Which is to say that he sometimes treats his story as if it were not a story at all, but a collection of aphorisms and exhortations. He does this in a manner which anticipates the modern technique of free-association.[13] It could justly be said that the *Super Cantica* has the form of a long journey in the course of which there are many interesting detours. Bernard sees the figure within the letter, and then he goes on to see the letter within the figure.[14]

One scholar who was especially aware of the latter aspect of Bernard's work is Dumontier. As he has observed, 'From the turn of phrase, from the tone that we sense our orator has borrowed from the context [of his material], it becomes evident that Bernard is not totally at ease with allegory'.[15] He often substitutes for it what Jean Leclercq calls *le jeu biblique.* An example of this is the way Bernard expresses his ideas in 'successive waves' after the model of biblical poetry.[16] Or, again, Dumontier says, Bernard 'spoke Bible' the way people speak their mother-tongue.[17] This reveals an intimate love for the diction of Holy Scripture. Bernard would never be content with winnowing out the graphic images and leaving the particular words aside as mere chaff.

What is the relationship of the figural and the non-figural elements in Bernard's treatment of the *Song?* We could liken the figural portions to the walls of a room. They define the space which Bernard accords some topic. For example, he uses the Bride's blackness in *Sermon Twenty-five,* part four and following to stand for various kinds of involvement with the world. But in a room there is not only space, but also furnishing and ornament. Just so his non-figural interpretations fill in and give style to the basic area defined by the 'allegory'. Nevertheless, this fascination with diction is the outgrowth of the figuralism. He does not indulge in it until he has clearly deciphered the types and shadows. That is why we speak of 'the letter within the figure'.

Once the meaning of the controlling figure has been posited, it becomes the point-of-reference for a polyvalent interpretation. If the reader knows that the Bridegroom signifies Christ or the Blessed Trinity (according to context), and he further knows that the Bride must be either the Church Militant or the individual soul in its spiritual journey, the specific details of the figure tend to be self-revealing. It is then, and only then, that Bernard draws our attention to the fact that God has used some highly significant language with which to convey his story to us. The method here is to state what the figure means, comment upon it in non-figural (i.e., didactic) terms, digress at will, and finally return to the figure for additional reflection thereon before bringing the sermon to an end.

To look more closely at *Sermon Twenty-five,* this time the sixth section, we see that the Bride's reputedly dark skin is taken as a blemish *(decolorare videtur),* and that this is presented as the consequence of a rigorously penitential life. Obviously, this is a tropological reference, viz., that the Bride is an exemplary adept of the *via purgativa.* The commentary which follows consists of personal observations on the subject of ascetical practices. None of this need be taken to suggest that Bernard was innocent of the original significance of the beloved's dark-skinned beauty, but only that he assumed that God meant the commentator to go below the superficial meaning. As a consequence, nearly all of *Sermon Twenty-five,* parts six through seven, is dedicated to a straightforward lesson on humility and penance. The coexistence of the two hermeneutical modes (extrinsic and instrinsic) is apparent even in a brief passage like the following:

> The outward blemishes that we may discern in holy people are not to be condemned, because they play a part in the begetting of interior light, and so dispose the soul for wisdom. For wisdom is described by the wise man [Solomon] as a reflection of eternal life [cf., Wisdom 7:26], and brightness befits the soul in which it decides to dwell.[18]

The allusion to the book of Wisdom here marks a transition between the two modes. What follows is a catena of verses, taken largely from the pauline epistles, which espouse the attitude of *contemptus mundi* as a key to spiritual advancement.[19] Bernard weaves the words of the biblical authors together with his own to achieve an elevated and authoritative tone.[20]

We can best epitomize the difference between figural and non-figural patterns by the concept of 'substantiality'. The *sensus litteralis,* in its commonly accepted force, is necessarily insubstantial. That is, its function as a gate to some higher level of signification requires that it be self-effacing or even transparent.[21] A far better designation for it would be *signum figuralis.* The way it works can be demonstrated by reference to the word 'curtain' *(pelles)* in its occurence at *Song of Songs* 1:4. Bernard takes this to be a type of heaven itself.[22] The reader is expected to lay aside the normal denotation of a curtain. This is a case not of ambiguity, but of substitution. The *signum* 'curtain' is offered as the shadow of a greater reality, and that reality is complex.

Not only does the curtain signify heaven (typology, the specifically allegorical sense), it is also the Bride's virtue (tropology, the moral sense), and, at the same time, the communion of saints (anagogy, the supernatural sense).[23] This is a classic instance of drawing three degrees of spiritual significance from a single literal referent.

It is not our purpose to elaborate on the so-called allegorical method, for that has been done abundantly already.[24] We do, however, wish to note in passing that non-figural, strictly verbal, elucidation is univocal, whereas figuralism is, by definition, polyvalent. The *signum,* in the former is substantial, then, because it signifies itself. Like the word of the Lord it abides forever.[25] In the latter mode, the *signum* is expected to withdraw once it has announced itself, leaving only its concept behind to guide us to its archetype. When Bernard treats a sign verbally rather than figurally, this has the effect of leading us to encounter Christ as Logos in the particular and unique words of Scripture.[26]

This principle is manifest in *Sermon Twenty-eight,* section four. Here Bernard reassumes a theme already announced (SC 25:5), the contrast between appearance and reality. Again we meet the allegory of the black skin––but this time it is applied to the Bridegroom rather than the Bride:[27] the Son of God, though essentially beautiful by virtue of his divinity, has, nevertheless, the appearance of ugliness by having been subject to his cruel and unjust death. Thus far we have figuralism, based on the poem of the Suffering Servant in Isaiah 53. In an apparent *non-sequitur,* however, Bernard abruptly takes us to a new vantage point where we may see the Lord's true beauty through the eyes, not of the Bride, but of the centurion at the foot of the cross.[28] The centurion's *persona* could be said to be an extension of the Bride's because fundamental to Bernard's understanding of the *Song of Songs* is the conviction that the Bride is any individual soul in quest of God. Certainly the centurion may qualify as such. In any case, the reference, by its unexpectedness, arrests our attention as yet another catena of verses begins.

The reference to the centurion evokes the broad image of the entire crucifixion event. It brings to mind Christ's being suspended between two thieves and his receiving the derision of the crowd. How, Bernard asks, can there be any element of beauty in so grim a scene? In response, he sends forth a stream of scriptural references well-calculated to stimulate affectivity.[29] The familiar passages, in their cumulative effect, elicit admiration for the humanity and vulnerability of the Saviour. None of this is remotely allegorical. While the chain of references happens to be appended to an allegory, literal statement, not figuralism, dominates the section.[30]

Emotional appeal is not the sole reason why Bernard employs intrinsic reference. While it is true that in this mode of discourse there is but one intended level of signification—not four—a variety of emphases are still possible within it. These can greatly enhance its utility. These uses may be classified in three broad categories: the affective (just demonstrated), the asservative, and the prescriptive. Subsumed under these categories can be numerous embellishments: plays on words, exploitations of sonority, and lexical invention.[31] Not least in importance is the perhaps unconscious adoption of a quasi-scriptural diction which, by process of association, lends a forcefulness that may be the most potent of all the considerable array of persuasive arts at Bernard's command.[32] Yet, these are simply stylistic variations, and what must concern us here are the three basic types of direct statement.

The three types are, in a certain way, analagous to the three higher levels of figuralism. Thus, the asservative use, which reports a fact or propounds a thesis, conveys a message not unlike the end-product in typology. In the end, typology is concerned with declaring who God is and what he has done. As such, it addresses primarily the intellect.

By extension, the prescriptive statement is parallel to tropology. It invokes expression of obligation or describes the means of obtaining ascetical proficiency. Sometimes there may even involve a narrative passage, since they can consist in edifying *exempla* drawn

from life or from biblical history. In this respect
they are narratives of direct statement rather than
figuralism. Prescriptive *dicta* are addressed primarily
to the volition.

Finally there is the affective use, which we have
seen Bernard skilfully employ. It consists in the
use of charged diction or in the graphic depiction
of events so as to arouse wonder, compassion, or
even yearning. It would be difficult to decide whether
this is directed more to the emotions or to the imagination; presumably it aims at both in tandem. We should
note, however, that the affective use is only partly
like its counterpart in figuralism, i.e., anagogy.
Anagogy normally concerns the last things, the eschatalogical dimension of what God has in store for us, whereas
affectivity is oriented toward the here-and-now. The
analagous factor here—so characteristically bernardian
—is love. In the final analysis, all human virtue
inclines toward its highest fulfillment in *charitas*.
It can be confidently asserted that love is that good
most basic to all human teleology; indeed it is the
very energy which leads one to the vision of God
and contemplative rapture. It is the brief anticipation
of the eschaton achievable under the conditions of
mortality. When Bernard speaks with affectivity, he
prepares us to know God as he is.

In contrast to the affective use, the asservative
is the least colored. Yet it is admirably useful. It
encompasses the full sweep of evangelical proclamation
from creation to redemption and the final fulfillment;
indeed, it is capable of approaching the field of meta-
physics as well:

> Though this visible material heaven, with
> its great variety of stars is unsurpassingly
> beautiful within the bounds of the material
> creation, I should not dare to compare its
> beauty with the spiritual loveliness the bride
> received [Rm 8:18] with her first robe when
> arrayed in the garments of holiness [Rv
> 7:14].33

Thus far it is traditional allegory, but now comes
the asservation:

> But there is a heaven of heavens to which
> the Prophet refers, 'Sing to the Lord who
> mounts above the heaven of heavens, to the
> East' [Ps 67:33-4, Vulg.]. This heaven is
> the world of the intellect and the spirit;
> and he who made the heavens by his wisdom

[Ps 133:5 Vulg.] created it to be his eternal dwelling place [Is 35:5].34

There is a distinctively platonic cast in the passage. The Creator is most fully to be encountered in the noetic order—a theme which underlies Bernard's mystical theology at all times. At first glance this passage could be seen as metaphorical, if not allegorical. What makes it finally literal is the fact that it makes a direct observation characteristic of the science of contemplation. It tells us where God is to be found and locates heaven, not as a place 'out there', but as a state within. The same passage then shifts to the prescriptive vein:

> You must not suppose that the bride's affections can rest outside of this heaven, where she knows her Beloved dwells: for where her treasure is, there her heart is too [Mt 6:21]. She so yearns for him that she is jealous of those who live in his presence; and since she may not yet participate in the vision that is theirs, she strives to resemble them in the way she lives. By deeds rather than words [1 Co 4:5] she proclaims: 'Lord, I love the beauty of your house, the place where your glory dwells' [Ps 25:8 Vulg].35

Throughout the foregoing, of course, the framework is the tropological figure of the Bride as devout contemplative. Yet none of the scriptural citations is given for allegorical reasons. They are, rather, forthright statements to the effect that the life of holiness is based above all on ardent desire.

What we have just examined is typical of the way that the figural and the verbal modes may be found inter-woven. In some places, however, the verbal mode stands completely alone. *Sermon Twenty-six*, the elegiac meditation occasioned by the death of Bernard's brother, Gerard, is of this type. In it familiar words from Scripture are adapted to circumstances far removed from their original context; but somehow the entire composition has a special authenticity —perhaps because it reveals so much human feeling in Bernard. It is, in fact, more than a personal expression of grief; it is a theodicy on mortality. That it could fall within the series of the *Super Cantica* without doing violence to the general sequence of its thought is because it is an *exemplum* of an individual's endowment with *capax Dei*, with the soul's ability to desire and, in some measure, comprehend its Maker.36

Finally, we note that Bernard's use of direct statement is never remote from the actual words of Holy Scripture. The practice of heaping up citations and allusions is neither gratuitous nor haphazard. It owes much, surely, to the custom, so deeply ingrained in monasticism, of accumulating *florilegia*, quotations gleaned from the Bible and the Fathers.[37] It is also the fruit of a prodigious memory. Most of all, it is a valid instance of letting Scripture interpret Scripture. This method stems, of course, from the New Testament itself and from the midrashic literature of the early rabbis.[38] One might justifiably regret its demise in our own age. It both expresses and shapes the consensus of Holy Tradition in a way that a more historically-based exegesis, with its inevitable reservations and doubts, can never quite achieve. In any case, our intention has been fulfilled if we have been able to suggest that the power of Bernard's understanding of Scripture lies as much in his sensitivity to words as it does to the Word itself.

Fordham University
New York

NOTES

1. A study which does acknowledge this side of Bernard's work is P. Dumontier, *Saint Bernard et la Bible* (Paris, 1953); it concentrates more on the saint's spirituality than on his literary craft.
2. Bernard of Clairvaux, *Sermones super Cantica Canticorum* [abbr. SC] 25–28; *Sancti Bernardi Opera*, edd. J. Leclercq, H. M. Rochais, C. H. Talbot (Rome, 1957) 1:163–202; ET *On the Song of Songs II,* CF 7 (Kalamazoo, 1976) 50–101.
3. Biblical quotations, other than those cited in CF 7, are from the Douai version, slightly modernized.
4. Jean Leclercq *OSB, The Love of Learning and the Desire for God* (New York, 1982) 79 [Original French, Paris, 1957].
5. Henri de Lubac, *Exegèse médiévale* (Paris, 1959) 1:480.
6. Dumontier, p. 68f.
7. See Beryl Smalley, *The Study of the Bible in the Middle Ages* (Oxford, 1952, 1978) 23.

8. Neither of these alternatives takes into account the emotional and connotational elements in a given passage, factors which play a considerable role in Bernard's art.
9. See Eric Auerbach, *Scenes from the Drama of European Literature* (New York, 1959) 53–54. [Original German, *Neue Dantestudien* (Istanbul, 1944.)]
10. The ambiguity in the word 'literal' parallels that in the word 'sentence', which can mean either a grammatically complete thought or 'the sense, substance, or gist' of any such thought (*Oxford English Dictionary*, s.v.).
11. De Lubac, 1:428f.
12. M.-D. Chenu, *Nature, Man, and Society in the Twelfth Century* (Chicago, 1968) 113–14 & 159–61 [original French, Paris, 1957.]
13. See Étienne Gilson, *La théologie mystique de Saint Bernard* (Paris, 1934) 167.
14. See de Lubac, 1:396–408.
15. Dumontier, 136.
16. Jean Leclercq *OSB, Recueil d'études sur Saint Bernard et ses écrits,* 3 (Rome, 1969) 241.
17. Dumontier, p. 155.
18. SC 25:6; CF 7:54; translation by Killian Walsh *OCSO.*
19. The passages are 2 T 4:8, 1 Co 2:6–8, 2 Co 10:10 & 11:23; also, 2 Co 4:16, Gn 1:26, Ps 44:14 (Vulg.), 1 P 1:24, 2 Co 1:12, Ga 6:4, Rm 8:28 & 5:23, 2 Co 12:9–10.
20. Of incidental interest is the way in which Bernard contrasts Saint Paul's reputed unattractiveness with his sanctity and inner beauty. This is a case of moral *exemplum,* rather than of figural typology, even though it subserves the figure of the Bride's blackness.
21. De Lubac, 1:128f.
22. Sg 1:4: 'Nigra sum...sicut tabernacula cedar...sed formosa...sicut pelles Salomonis' (text intentionally rearranged by Bernard). See SC 27:2 (CF 7:75).
23. SC 27:3, 27:13; CF 7:76, 85.
24. See Gilson, 136f.
25. Dumontier, p. 172: 'On se rend compte maintenant de la valeur et des richesses du sens littéral bien compris, celui-ci embrassant tout ce que les Pères demandaient au sens spirituel, et bien plus...'.
26. Gilson, pp. 34–36.
27. In keeping with his lack of concern for historical verisimilitude and with his (as I believe) greater penchant for asservative than for narrative statements, Bernard readily takes license to rearrange

the facts of his text as needed, but within reasonable limits.

28. In this case a narrative technique has been co-opted for the purposes of straightforward verbal elucidation. The reason for this seeming inconsistency is that the centurion is a transitional element in the rhetorical scheme here. He is, as it were, the hinge on which the non-figural material depends.

29. Mk 15:39–40, Jn 19:37, Lk 23:33, Mt 27:39, Is 53:12, (direct citations); also Si 40:22, Jb 12:4, 2 M 12:22 & Hb 3:5 (allusions).

30. SC 28:4; CF 7:91.

31. See Leclercq, *Receuil*, 3:163–210.

32. See Dumontier, 157–64 & Leclercq, *Love of Learning*, 75f.

33. SC 27:4; CF 7:77.

34. *Ibid.*

35. *Ibid.*

36. See M. Corneille Haflants in his introduction to CF 4, *On the Song of Songs I*, pp. xi–xiv.

37. Leclercq, *Love of Learning*, pp. 184–86.

38. De Lubac, 1:337.

CISTERCIAN MIGRATIONS IN THE LATE MIDDLE AGES

Gerhard Jaritz

The Order of the Cistercians and the phenomenon of migration are connected in many ways and under various aspects: mother-abbeys send new communities to regions often far away, abbots make annual journeys to General Chapters, and father-abbots visit their affiliated monasteries; even the laybrothers' trek to granges where they worked may be seen as an example of, though usually very regional, migration. The migration this paper wants to deal with is of still another kind.

A problem for the Order from its beginnings seem to have been the *monachi vagantes,* members of cistercian communities, who—for some reason, left their monastery, travelled through the secular world, joined or wanted to join another community of the Order or even intended to stay in the world. Statutes of the General Chapters sometimes refer to the Rule of Saint Benedict and call them *gyrovagi,*1 who 'spend their whole lives wandering from province to province, staying three days in one monastery and four in another, ever roaming and never stable'.2 From the twelfth century until modern times cistercian documents demonstrate the difficulties and problems inherent in their occurence.3 Two examples may be given. At about 1150 the abbot of Ebrach (Franconia) sent a letter to the abbot of Sittichenbach (Thuringia) complaining about one of his monks who had left the community without permission and gone to Sittichenbach.4 He asked the abbot there to send the monk back to prevent further harm. More than five-hundred years later, in 1693, another abbot of Ebrach wrote to the abbot of his daughter-house Rein (Styria) and dealt with scandals which migrating monks had provoked in the past and still provoked in his day.5 We may ask ourselves, therefore, whether we are here confronted with a situation which had not changed much over the centuries of cistercian history.

Looking at the statutes of medieval General Chapters which refer to *monachi vagantes* and the problems evoked by them, we can discern at first sight that developments and changes must have taken place. In the number of statutes referring to our topic we already find remarkable differences. Until the end of the fourteenth century and again from the beginning of the sixteenth century onwards we occasionally come across statutes condemning migrations of monks into

the secular world. Their number, however, is low.
The problem seems to have existed, but not to have
been of remarkable importance. Sometimes there is
a concentration of cases of individual monks dealt
with by the General Chapter. We find, for instance,
five cases in the first half of the thirteenth century
and three cases in the thirties of the fourteenth cen-
tury.6 Statutes on migration issued for the entire
Order are almost entirely missing.7

If we look at the fifteenth century, we find a
situation almost completely different. Already in the
first half of this century we find, on one hand, a
number of statutes on *monachi vagantes* concerning
the entire Order, and, on the other hand, increased
dealings in cases of individual monks.8 The latter
are almost always dealt with in the same way: a
monk had left his community—often without being authorized—and had provoked 'scandals' in other monasteries
or in the world. The Chapter ordered him to be sent
back to the monastery where he had made profession
and the abbot there was advised to deal with his
case.9 An even more decisive change in the number
of statutes regarding migrating monks can be proven
after 1450. Especially from the fourteen-fifties to the
seventies almost each of the General Chapters makes
mention of the problem of monks roaming through the
world.10 It is continuously repeated that only really
serious reasons might allow to send a monk to another
monastery.11 Disputes inside communities should not
be solved by dismissing the monks who had picked
the quarrel.12 If a monk was sent to another community
for good reason and could not be kept there, he should
only be sent back to the monastery from which he
came and not on to yet a third community.13 Other
examples could be given; the statutes often go into
great detail. In the same way, the number of individual
cases of monks dealt with by General Chapters increased
in the second half of the fifteenth century.14

We might, therefore, ask whether this extraordinary
fifteenth-century situation might be taken as a culminating point in the decline of cistercian monastic stability
or even in monastic life as a whole. Does it reveal
a low in obedience to the General Chapter, which
year by year was repeating its claims and statutes,
and not being heard or followed by many cistercian
monks and communities?

Without any further reflection on our problem
we could be tempted to accept this hypothesis. Given
the one-sidedness of the information we have at our
disposal when looking only at statutes, we would
do well to retain a bit of scepticism. Another group

of sources widens the view and offers possibilities
for compasison: the letters of recommendation which
were given to monks by the abbots of the monasteries
they had left. In our research we have concentrated
on those letters which have survived from austrian
cistercian communities of the Late Middle Ages. There
we come across not only individual letters, but also
formularies which contain whole collections of such
letters and offer a much wider view of the problem
of migrating monks. Their contents go far beyond
the austrian territories and make it possible to interpret
the situation on an 'international' basis. Formularies
of this kind have survived from the monasteries of
Lilienfeld (Lower Austria), Wilhering (Upper Austria)
and Neuberg (Styria).[15] They contain letters mainly
from the fifteenth century and a few from the fourteenth
century.

The structure of the letters is quite similar.
Each contains information on migrating monks going
to or coming from one, two, three, or sometimes even
more, monasteries of the Order. A typical formula
is: The abbot of A sends a monk of B, who came to
him from the monastery of C to the community of D
and asks the abbot to keep the monk there. Two examples
may be given:

In 1439 Abbot Stephan of Lilienfeld informed Abbot
Paul of Neuberg that brother Augustin, a monk of
Heinrichau (Henrikow/Silesia), whose monastery had
been devastated by the Hussites, had been sent to
him by the abbot of Baumgartenberg (Upper Austria)
who was unable to keep him. For *serious reasons*--
here we see the influence of General Chapter--Lilienfeld
also cannot keep Augustin.

The abbot of Neuberg is therefore asked to allow the
silesian monk to join his community (see figure 1).[16]
The second example may show how long monks sometimes
'roamed' through the world, in this certain case obviously not by his own choice. Between 1470 and 1474 the
monk Walthasar of Wilhering was sent to Fürstenzell
(Bavaria) because heavy damages his monastery had
suffered forced a large part of the community to leave.
From Fürstenzell he had to go to Aldersbach (Bavaria);
from there--because too many people were living in
the monastery--he went back to Wilhering (Upper Austria). In 1477 he had to leave the community again,
travelled to Raitenhaslach (Bavaria) and from there
to Ebrach, the mother-house of Wilhering. In agreement
with the statutes of the General Chapter he was once
more sent back to Wilhering. Two weeks later the
Abbot of Ebrach, on his way to visit his Styrian
filiation Rein, met Walthasar, who obviously also

wanted to go to Rein, in the small town of Rottenmann
in Upper Styria. Once again forced to return to Wilhering, Walthasar had to leave yet another time in 1480,
when he went to Heiligenkreuz, caused trouble in
the community there and was sent back to Wilhering.
One month later he was on his way again, this time
to Lilienfeld (Lower Austria) and, because Lilienfeld
had too many guests and the Turks were threatening
the area, further on to the Lower Austrian monastery
of Säusenstein (see figure 2). There we lose track
of him.[17]

The formularies and some individual documents
yield about two hundred such letters, most from
the fifteenth, a few from the fourteenth century,
which contain information on migration. They show
that migrating did indeed play a decisive role in
the history of the Order in the fifteenth century and
that the statutes of the General Chapter against it
were not successful. The letters in the formularies
can be proven to be mainly copies of actual letters
and not fictional, as these in other surviving formularies
sometimes are.[18]

A relatively large number of documents of the
same or similar structure allows us to look for more
general results reaching beyond the information we
would be able to deduce from single letters or could
get from the statutes of the General Chapter. Especially
questions concerning the *reasons*, and *distances* and
the *directions* of migrations and the changes of these
components may be answered.

Reasons for the migrations of monks, for their
dismissal, for sending them away or further on are
mentioned in about a hundred cases: some ten percent
concern disputes within a community; another ten
percent the high number of persons or guests living
in a monastery; ten percent bad harvests or other
economic reasons; about ten percent 'serious' reasons
not detailed; another ten percent the wish of the monks
themselves; five percent refer to business for the
monastery. The remaining reasons, which cover a
bit less than half the cases mentioned, concern devasta-
tions of monasteries by fire or other natural forces
and/or serious troubles caused by some kind of war,
by fighting parties of the aristocracy, the Turks,
or the Hussites. The ravages of the Hussite wars account-
ed for about a third of the reasons given in the letters
at our disposal. From the 1420s until far into the
second half of the fifteenth century they played the
decisive role in motivating monks to leave monasteries,
where they had been professed. Communities from as
far north as Pelplin (south of Danzig), as far south

as Baumgartenberg (Upper Austria), and as far west as Langheim (Franconia) were directly affected,[19] not to mention the insecurities indirectly evolving at many other monasteries.[20]

Interpreting the reasons for migrations, we can see that they generally result only to a slight degree from situations within the communities (as disputes), something we might have expected from the information given by the statutes. The major motives came from outside, that is, from the secular world, and were obviously often destructive not only of a flourishing material culture, but also of an acceptable monastic life. We may assume that in the main disobedience and neglect were not the reasons for not observing the statutes of General Chapter, but that the material and economic means of living the monastic life were lacking, having been lost through influences from outside. That 'scandals'--as the General Chapter puts it ever and again--inevitably arose when whole communities were dispersed into an insecure world to look for other monastic communities to live in, seems quite obvious. And the effect of more or less sudden descent of numerous guests on life in the abbeys they came to must also be recognized.

If we look, for example, at the letters of recommendation concerning migrations to the abbey of Neuberg in Upper Styria which have survived, particularly from the 1430s to the 1450s, we observe that the origin of monks coming to them are concentrated in the North (and Northwest) (see figure 3).[21] They often travelled to the Danube valley and along the river usually trying to join an easily accessible nearby community. Refusal by monasteries in or around the Danube valley seems to have forced them to go further south to the Upper Styrian abbey much more off the beaten track. The Neuberg situation may be assumed to be typical of the regions we are dealing with. It shows that monks were migrating mainly south from areas like Poland, Silesia, Bohemia, Moravia, even parts of Brandenburg, Franconia, and Upper Bavaria. The reasons they left their communities were particularly war, the complete or partial devastation of their monasteries or lands, especially by the Hussites, and therefore insecure political and economical conditions. The southern route of many monks led to an overcrowding of the austrian abbeys along the Danube, which were then forced to accept no more guests or even faced with no other alternative than that of sending their own monks away.

These problems could be increased by difficulties within the austrian abbeys themselves. Between 1410 and 1412 Lilienfeld was struck by fire, destruction, and plundering; the community had to leave the abbey for a time.[22] In 1473, Wilhering was involved in controversies between Austria and Bohemia which again became the motive for monks to be sent away.[23] Comparing the Neuberg results with the situation we find in the sources of Wilhering, and concentrating more on the second half of the fifteenth century, we can, with some exceptions, recognize similar trends:[24] a North-South movement, though not as pronounced as in the case of Neuberg; a concentration on the Danube valley; and, especially relevant, a very strong connection with Ebrach, Wilhering's mother-house (see figure 4). The documentation on monks leaving Wilhering in the same period again shows a concentration on the Danube valley and the mother-abbey Ebrach, but an easily explainable trend towards the south. Almost nobody migrated to the insecurities of the North (see figure 5). The same phenomenon can be demonstrated by the sources of Lilienfeld (see figure 6 and 7).[25]

Therefore, we have to emphasize not only that the main reasons for migrations to the areas we have dealt with were serious incidents hitting the communities from outside, but also that the direction of cistercian migrations seem, consequently, to have followed quite explicit principles. The migration of late medieval cistercian monks was no uncertain roaming through the world, but a planned and organized move comparable to the migrations of travelling artisans, for whom we could cite similar trends.[26]

Relative to the number of monasteries in certain areas forced to send away monks at one time, the distances covered seem to change. Particularly in the period of the Hussite wars we come across monks who certainly travelled for more than a thousand miles through Europe. In more quiet times there seems to have been more regional migration between neighbouring communities. But even when the migrations covered very long distances, some parts of Europe remained completely or nearly untouched by monks from the areas we have been considering; this is particularly true of Italy, France, and of course far-away regions like Spain, England, or Scandinavia. Because of the political situation, the late medieval process of territorialisation and already perhaps language-problems, the monks stayed more or less within the German-speaking parts of the Empire. This cannot, of course, mean that migrations of cistercian monks in Italy, France or England were less common than in the areas we have dealt with. What further research should concentrate on, therefore, is the investigation of cistercian migrations in other parts of Europe and especially the differences of reasons, directions, and distances between those areas and Austria and Germany.

Institut für mittelalterliche Realienkunde
Krem/Danube, Austria

NOTES

1. See, for instance, Josephus-Maria Canivez, *Statuta Capitulorum Generalium Ordinis Cisterciensis* I (Louvain, 1933) 130 (1190:60); IV (Louvain, 1936) 371 (1432:9), 372 (1432:11).
2. Regula Benedicti, cap. 1.
3. Cf. Otto Grillnberger, 'Kleinere Forschungen zur Geschichte des Cistercienser-Ordens', *Studien und Mittheilungen aus dem Benedictiner- und dem Cistercienser-Orden* 16 (1895) 600–603.
4. Werner Ohnsorge, 'Eine Ebracher Briefsammlung des XII. Jahr-hunderts', *Quellen und Forschungen aus italienischen Archiven und Bibliotheken* 20 (Rome, 1928/29) 37–38, n. XI.
5. 1693 June 4, Nurenberg: Rein archives, Hs. 137/11, n. 214.
6. Canivez, *Statuta* I, 325 (1206:30), 374–375 (1210:374), 445 (1215:49), 511 (1219:40); II (Louvain, 1934), 49–50 (1226:12); III (Louvain, 1935), 443–444 (1336:9), 446 (1337:5), 452 (1338:9).
7. See, for instance, Canivez, *Statuta* I, 90 (1182:90); III, 445–446 (1337:4), 509 (1348:3).
8. General statutes for the Order: Canivez, *Statuta* IV, 34–35 (1402:14), 249 (1422:26), 337 (1429:70), 371–372 (1432:9). Statutes concerning individual monks and monasteries or certain regions: Canivez, *Statuta* IV, 298 (1425:72), 311 (1427:11), 339 (1429:75), 353 (1430:58), 372 (1432:11), 507 (1441:36), 519 (1442:35).
9. It must be stressed, though, that the term 'scandal' is used in a wider sense in the statutes than we use it today; often rather mild cases are called 'scandalous' so we may not automatically assume a very severe offence.
10. General statutes: Canivez, *Statuta* IV, 672 (1452:103); V (Louvain, 1937), 9 (1457:48), 55 (1460:34), 101 (1461:148), 112 (1462:58), 119 (1462:101, 250 (1469:56), 289 (1471:42), 302–303 (1472:20), 373–

375 (1478:31), 568–569 (1487:8).

11. See, for instance, Canivez, *Statuta* V, 112 (1462:58).

12. See, for instance, Canivez, *Statuta* V, 302 (1472:20).

13. See, for instance, Canivez, *Statuta* V, 9 (1457:48), 119 (1462:101), 568–569 (1487:8).

14. Statutes concerning individual monks and monasteries or certain regions: Canivez, *Statuta* IV, 635 (1450: 47), 646 (1451:28), 655 (1451:75), 691 (1453:88); V, 9 (1457:49), 12 (1457:61), 58 (1460:48), 65 (1460:82), 90 (1461:84), 92 (1461:99), 100 (1461:144), 102 (1461:102), 119 (1462:102), 133 (1463:44), 179–180 (1466:14), 214 (1467:39), 252 (1469:65), 323 (1473:30), 367 (1478:11), 458 (1483:22), 477–478 (1484:28), 614 (1487:89), 616 (1487:98); VI (Louvain, 1938), 133–134 (1496:16), 142–143 (1496:35), 211 (1499:24).

15. See Valentin Schmidt, 'Ein Lilienfelder Formelbuch', *Studien und Mitteilungen aus dem Benedictiner- und dem Cistercienser-Orden 28* (1907) 392–407, 577–596; Johannes Hurch, 'Aus einem Wilheringer Formelbuche', *ibid.* 11 (1890) 104–114, 275–289; Otto Grillnberger, 'Kleinere Quellen und Forschungen zur Geschichte des Cistercienser-Ordens', *ibid.* 16 (1895) 599–610; 17 (1896) 41–59, 256–269, 437–443; Idem, 'Das Wilheringer Formelbuch "De kartis visitacionum"', *ibid.* 19 (1898) 587–601; 20 (1899) 127–137, 482–495; 21 (1900) 119–127, 384–392; Gerhard Jaritz, 'Die Konventualen der Zisterzen Rein, Sittich und Neuberg im Mittelalter' (Diss. Graz, 1973) I:109–122.

16. 1439 September 14, Lilienfeld: Jaritz, 'Die Konventualen' I:119.

17. (1470–74 – –, Wilhering): Grillnberger, 'Kleinere Quellen' 262, n. 129; (1470–76 – –, Aldersbach): *ibid.* 41, n. 29; 1477 April 13, Ebrach: *ibid.* 47, n. 59; 1477 May 1, Rottenmann: *ibid.* 46, n. 55, 56; 1480 July 2, Heiligenkreuz: *ibid.* 604, n. 2, 3; 1480 July–August, Lilienfeld: *ibid.* 42, n. 35. See also *ibid.* 601.

18. Cf. Grillnberger, 'Kleinere Quellen' 600.

19. For the problems of cistercian monasteries caused by the Hussites, see Valentin Schmidt, 'Zur Leidensgeschichte der Cistercienser in den Hussitenkriegen', *Cistercienser-Chronik* 20 (1908) 129–135, 170–175, 205–208.

20. We need only think of monks from different communities coming to one monastery, each of them certainly used to a different way of monastic life, to realize that problems could occur.

21. The basis for figure 3 are the letters listed by Jaritz, 'Die Konventualen' 109–122.

22. For effects on migrations, see Schmidt, 'Ein Lilien-felder Formelbuch' 583–584, nn. 129, 130, 136.
23. Therefore, in the 1470s a large number of monks left the monastery; see Grillnberger, 'Kleinere Quellen', *passim*. For an explicit reference to the effect on migrations, see *ibid.*, 43–44, n. 42. See also above the mentioned case of the monk Walthasar of Wilhering.
24. The basis for figure 4 and 5 are the letters listed by Hurch, 'Aus einem Wilheringer Formelbuche' and by Grillnberger, 'Kleinere Quellen' and 'Das Wilheringer Formelbuch' (see note 15).
25. The basis for figures 6 and 7 are the letters listed by Schmidt, 'Ein Lilienfelder Formelbuch' (note 15).
26. See, for instance, Gerhard Jaritz, 'Gesellenwanderung in Niederösterreich im 15. und 16. Jahrhundert unter besonderer Berücksichtigung der Tullner "Schuhknechte"', *Internationales Handwerksgeschicht-liches Symposium*, Veszprém 20.–24.11.1978 (Veszprém, 1979) 50–61.

Explanations of figures 3–7:

The monasteries marked in figures 3, 4 and 6 show communities, from which monks originated and/or which they touched on their way to Neuberg (Wilhering, Lilienfeld). For reasons of clarity, we make no distinction between monasteries where monks had professed and those at which they stayed only intermediately during their migrations. Figures 5 and 7 demonstrate destinations and/or intermediate stations of monks who had left Wilhering or Lilienfeld. Again we have not distinguished between final destination and intermedi-ate stations. Ciphers in connection with monasteries refer to the number of monks coming from or to there (directly as well as after/before intermediate stations). In the case of Lilienfeld (figures 6 and 7) we have not used numbers because of the relatively few surviving examples. The contents of some letters in the fomularies which seemed obviously fictions and some others where diverse doubts arose have not been marked in the figures.

List of Abbreviations

(The names of the monasteries usually refer to those which are used in the sources)

A	=	Aldersbach	Nk	=	Neukloster
P	=	Pelplin	O	=	Osseg
Al	=	Altzelle	Pi	=	Pilis
An	=	Andrejov	Po	=	Porno
B	=	Baumgartenberg	R	=	Rein
Be	=	Bebenhausen	Ra	=	Raitenhaslach
Bu	=	Buch	Re	=	Reifenstein
C	=	Chorin	Ri	=	Riddagshausen
E	=	Ebrach	(Ro	=	Rottenmann)
En	=	Engelszell	S	=	Säusenstein
F	=	Fürstenzell	Sa	=	Salem
G	=	Gotteszell	Sch	=	Schöntal
Go	=	Goldenkron	Se	=	Sedletz
H	=	Heiligenkreuz	Sel	=	Seligenthal
Ha	=	Herrenalb	SG	=	Sankt Gotthard
Hai	=	Haina	Si	=	Sittich
Hb	=	Heilsbronn	Sk	=	Skalitz
Hba	=	Heisterbach	ST	=	St Thomas/Venedig
He	=	Heinrichau	St	=	Stams
Ho	=	Hohenfurt	SU	=	St Urban
K	=	Koprzywnica	Sz	=	Szczyrzycs
Ka	=	Kamenz	To	=	Toplica
Kb	=	Königsbronn	V	=	Viktring
Ks	=	Königsaal	W	=	Wilhering
L	=	Lilienfeld	Wb	=	Walderbach
La	=	Langheim	We	=	Wettingen
M	=	Mogila	Wi	=	Wisowitz
Ma	=	Marienberg	Wo	=	Wongrowitz
Mb	=	Maulbronn	Ws	=	Waldsassen
Mo	=	Morimund	Z	=	Zwettl
N	=	Neuberg	Zi	=	Zips
Nb	=	Neuburg			
Ne	=	Neuzelle			

WAS BERNARD A FRIEND?

Brian Patrick McGuire

Bernard of Clairvaux might seem to be one of the least likely candidates in twelfth-century western Europe for the title of friend. Political organizer, theologian, founder of cistercian abbeys, even saint, he is so much larger than life that it is difficult to imagine him as a friend and companion to other men. Recent studies have tried either to emphasize the all-embracing sanctity of Bernard or else to show how one-sided and ungenerous he could be to other men. According to Jean Leclercq, one can either hate Bernard or love him: there is no middle ground. A hated Bernard can be seen as manipulating men for the purposes of his political and monastic programs, while a loved Bernard can easily be reduced to a man who in nearly all situations acted as a man of God should act. Either extreme leaves little room for a human being with strengths and weaknesses of character, for contradictions in his words and actions, for moments of inspiration and regrettable acts. It is my contention that by looking at Bernard in terms of the friendships he actually experienced in his life, we can find a middle way with him. So long as we see him in the context of the twelfth century and do not judge him as if he belonged to our own time, his words and actions can be understandable to us. In what follows I shall neither try to debunk the saint Bernard nor to praise him to the skies. He was a human being as we all are human beings, and by looking at the content and language of his personal relations we can touch upon an aspect of this humanity. I shall leave Bernard the saint to others, but perhaps through such a pedestrian portrait of the man, even the saint will become more apparent. For saints are the result of the impression they make on people in their own time, and by looking at Bernard as a potential friend we can perhaps better grasp why it is the man engendered such fierce loyalties and enmities.

A point of departure for any understanding of friendship is a definition of the phenomenon that was current in the Middle Ages and which still can be conceived in terms of modern life. Here we are much better off than with many other terms that are modern coinage about medieval life (as 'courtly love', 'feudalism', 'scholasticism'). *Amicitia* was a well-known concept among medieval intellectuals, and the first

place they looked for a definition of the term was
the treatise *Laelius de amicitia* of Cicero. 'Friendship
is nothing other than an identity of all things divine
and human in mutual goodwill and affection' (V.20:
*Est enim amicitia nihil aliud nisi omnium divinarum
humanarumque rerum cum benevolentia et caritate
consensio.*) The central word here is *consensio*, which
implies a simultaneity of experience or awareness
in the friends of the same phenomena, a coming together
in agreement and harmony. But friendship in Cicero
also implies good acts proceeding from goodwill, as
well as a climate of affection, perhaps even bordering
on tenderness.

Medieval intellectuals, since they in the twelfth
century were almost all clerics or monks, were not
always satisfied with a definition of friendship that
came from a non-Christian writer, and it was natural
for writers on friendship to include quotations or
examples of it from the Bible. One of the phrases
that constantly appears is taken from the Acts of
the Apostles, where the community of early Christians
is described as being one heart and soul (Ac 4:32
--*cor unum et anima una*). The passage has been
used in recent times by socialist thinkers in order
to emphasize the 'natural communism' of these men
and women, and even in the Middle Ages the poverty
and sharing of all goods in common indicated in the
passage did not pass unnoticed. But in most cases
the phrase was taken out of its immediate socio-religious
context and seen as a description of the harmony
among human beings that arises out of friendship,
a friendship linked to Christ and the christian community. It is this kind of friendship which we will pursue
in Bernard in the coming pages, one that is at one
and the same time individualized and particularized
and yet can be coordinated to the needs and demands
of community life. Could any monk, especially an
abbot with all his obligations, ever be of one heart
and mind with other members of his community and
with men outside his monastery? Is there any room
for friendships in a human living situation where
the most important goal is to maintain harmony among
the members of the community?

Centuries earlier, John Cassian had shown great
optimism about the possibility of friendships in the
monastic and even in the eremitical life, but if we
look at his famous sixteenth conference on friendship,
we find it is more concerned with the stability and
peace of the community as a whole than with individual
friendships. For him the one mind and soul dealt
primarily with the whole of the monastery and not

with particular monks' mutual relations.

If Bernard had followed Cassian alone and not Cicero as well, it is likely that he would have argued only for the friendship of community and not of individuals, but this does not seem the case. A review of his writings suggests the following conclusion: *Friendship is something natural in human affairs and as seen in Bernard's sermons and letters is worthy of literary expression.*

The fullest statement of this idea in Bernard comes in the twenty-sixth sermon *On the Song of Songs*, preached in 1138:

> It is but human and necessary that we respond to our friends with feeling: that we be happy in their company, disappointed in their absence. Social intercourse, especially between friends, cannot be purposeless; the reluctance to part and the yearning for each other when separated, indicate how meaningful their mutual love must be when they are together.[1]

Non erit otiosa socialis conversatio, praesertim inter amicos: the words are so self-confident and matter-of-fact that it is easy to forget how significant they are in a monastic context. Bernard is telling his brethren that it is quite in order that they cultivate friendships with each other, and he is answering a long tradition going back to the Fathers that insisted on distance as being of no importance for real friends, for they would love each other no matter what. Bernard accepts human needs, such as that of being together, as something natural and desirable.

'For a long time now we have been united in the closest friendship', Bernard wrote in 1149 to Peter the Venerable, abbot of Cluny: '...an equal affection has rendered us equals'.[2] In earlier letters Bernard had emphasized his unworthiness to come up to the same level as Peter and to deserve his love. Bernard's expression of humility may have been more a literary pose than a genuine feeling, but here he is saying that because of friendship the two men now are equals. His doctrine of equality in friendship, regardless of one's own status in the world, is derived ultimately from Cicero (*De amic.* XX.71). Bernard can cast away the traditional apparatus of humility and speak to Peter directly and immediately about a misunderstanding that has arisen between them. One of his letters to Peter had apparently contained expressions that might have been offensive. Bernard insists that his secretaries sometimes misunderstand his intentions when he has

them write letters for him. The passage has been
noticed because it gives us insight into the process
of composition at Clairvaux: Bernard had become so
busy that he apparently had to leave a major responsibility to his secretaries in order to answer his correspondence. But just as significant as this glimpse of Bernard
and his secretaries is his insistence on maintaining
goodwill towards his friend Peter the Venerable: 'Believe
me who love you that nothing could have come from
my heart or left my lips which would have offended
your ears'. Bernard wanted to keep his friendship
with Peter. This was a goal in itself, not subordinated
to any other purpose. A sceptical historian might
reply that it was in Bernard's best interest to maintain
good relations with Cluny and its powerful abbot,
and there is no doubt that Bernard was aware of
the importance of such a bond. But in this letter
he wanted most of all Peter to know that he loved
him as the person he was, and to do so he drew
on the entire tradition of classical and christian friendship, where friends want to share themselves completely
with each other: 'Would that I were able to express
in this letter all that I feel towards you!'

Is Bernard here trying to repeat and reflect
the classical tradition on which I claim his concept
of friendship builds? Bernard, like Anselm, is difficult
to catch making direct quotations from the Fathers
or from classical literature, and there is no special
reason to claim that he as a boy at school in Châtillon
definitely read Cicero. His language is always his
own, with faint echoes of a thorough and intense
training in Latin grammar but without the mark of
any single authors. But in Bernard's boyhood scholars
in German and French schools, from Worms to Chartres,
were making, or could have made, use of letter collections that dealt with the theme of friendship and
related it to classical models. The last half of the
eleventh century is a golden age for the reformulation
of the idea of friendship in classical and Christian
terms, and it is likely that Bernard the eager young
student, who preferred the schoolroom to the battlefield,
would have been affected by this renewal of the expression of friendship in clerical letters and life. Bernard's
school training apparently encouraged him to accept
friendship as something worth writing about: classical
ideals were finding a rich christian mould in Bernard's
youth.

But in entering the monastery of Cîteaux in 1112,
the young Bernard, now in his early twenties, could
easily have been convinced that the process of conversion
meant that he had to leave friends and friendship

behind. After all, Christ himself had indicated more than once in the Gospels that in order to follow him, one must leave everything—and not just one's material possessions, also family and friends. The Eastern Fathers had understood this message well and found great virtue in the men who refused to see their mothers or brothers after they had gone into the desert for good. But this Eastern Model of breaking all family bonds is now replaced by what I would call a *bernardian model: In the process of conversion friendship is not abrogated: it is transformed into something even better, monastic friendship.*

William of Saint Thierry's description of Bernard's conversion to the monastic life describes this process in such a natural and inevitable manner that it is easy to forget how original Bernard was in insisting on entering Cîteaux not alone but in the company of about thirty fellow members of his family and old friends. If we look at the Vita Prima carefully, we can see that Bernard's decision to enter Cîteaux did not take place from one day to the next. First he decided on the monastic life, then he went about convincing his brothers and near relations and friends to accompany him, and afterwards he gathered the whole band in one place, probably his family's castle at Châtillon, where for six months the group prayed and talked and made themselves ready for the great move. Only then did Bernard and his brothers and friends come knocking on the door of Cîteaux. Abbot Stephen Harding was not confronted with a few individuals who had by chance gotten together in the last stages of the decision to become monks. He had to deal with a well-coordinated and absolutely determined group of men who had prepared themselves not just to enter a monastery but also to maintain their bonds to each other and yet to alter them radically because of the new context of monastic life. Stephen took on friends who intended to continue being each other's friends in new and more exciting ways than they could ever experience in the world of the school or of the castle.

The story of the conversion of Bernard's brothers is well-known in the account of William of Saint Thierry, and instead of retelling it, I would only insist that we have to lend a certain amount of credence to it. What is important for us is not the miraculous content but the evidence the stories provide of the strength of Bernard's will. He insisted on getting all his brothers, except the youngest, with him. He did not care if they were married, if they were on duty as soldiers, or if they had economic commitments. Everyone had to come, because they were his brothers and because the process of conversion was for Bernard a family affair.

The most striking indication of the importance of bonds of friendship for the young Bernard and his insistence on converting them into bonds of monastic life in friendship is the story of how Bernard convinced Hugh of Vitry to come with him. The first narrator of the incident is Geoffrey of Auxerre, who in his rough draft for a Life of Saint Bernard includes the incident and provides an emotional account of a man driven by the need to include his friend in the most momentous decision of his life:

> He said one day to his brothers: 'I have a friend at Macon, Hugh of Vitry. We have to get hold of him so that also he will become one of us'. This man was a cleric of noble birth who had reached a mature age. He was well off both in terms of lay and ecclesiastical possessions.[3]

Bernard was not to be stopped, even though 'those who knew him began to accuse Bernard of being too rash'.

Hugh must have heard something about Bernard's decision to change his way of life, and he wanted to do whatever he could to make sure that the brilliant young man instead made his career in the secular church, as he intended to do:

> When Hugh saw Bernard he wept and rushed to embrace him, but the man of God paid no attention to his tears. After Hugh became calmer, Bernard revealed his intention to him, and so Hugh's sorrow returned and the fount of tears flowed all the more, so that during that entire day his eyes did not have rest.

Bernard, who became so well known for his tears, is here in a situation where he refuses to weep. He cannot see any reason for sorrow in his decision to become a monk, and he intends to do everything possible to see to it that Hugh joins him. This must be why he decided to spend the night together with Hugh. They slept 'in a very narrow bed so that there was hardly room for both of them'. Hugh's sobs kept Bernard from falling asleep for a long time. Geoffrey makes no attempt to hide his master's irritation with these superfluous tears:

> In the morning when Hugh again was weeping,

Bernard was irritated and began to reproach
him all the more harshly. But he replied
to Bernard: 'The reason why I cry is not
the same today as it was yesterday. Yesterday
I wept for you, today I weep for myself.
For I know your way of life and am aware
that a conversion to the monastic life is
more necessary for me than for you'.

Hugh had been convinced: a night of fitful and interrupted sleep had paid off for Bernard! 'Weep', he said,
'as much as you wish, for these tears are excellent.
Don't stop'. The friend would now follow Bernard
into the monastic life, and so Bernard could lavish
on him all the outward signs of friendship. Bernard
and Hugh 'walked about together in sharing each
other's joy, and did not leave each other for a moment'.
They were bosom friends again, to the anger and
scandal of the secular clerics who wanted to keep
Hugh in the world.

The rest of this story is better known than the
first part: how the clerics did manage to separate
Hugh from Bernard for a while, but how Bernard managed
to summon up a rainstorm on a field where Hugh was
surrounded by his 'bodyguard' so that he could get
to speak with his friend and confirm Hugh's promise
to become a monk. Once again Geoffrey makes use
of intimate details: how Bernard even though he could
not at first get to speak to Hugh still managed to
move close enough to him to shed tears that landed
on his friend's neck, and how the two of them, after
'having confirmed a bond of spiritual union...returned
hand in hand'.

Hugh's tears, his embraces of Bernard, the narrow
bed, Bernard's tears on Hugh's neck, and the final
hand-in-hand scene are all missing in William of
Saint Thierry's version of the episode. He concentrates
the narrative on the way Bernard succeeded in convincing
Hugh to become a monk. But even if the outward emotional signs of friendship are missing in William's account,
he makes the same point, that Bernard and Hugh shared
a close friendship. He is even more specific about
the nature of the relationship, for he calls it *familiaris
amicitia*.[4] William may have found Geoffrey's enthusiasm
for the way in which Bernard was physically close
to Hugh a distraction from the central content of the
story, but like Geoffrey, William could see how Bernard
was able to transform a close friendship outside the
monastery into one that led into the monastery. The
friendship in the world could become more permanent
and true 'in a pact of new life', and William appropriate-

ly ends the passage with a reference to the key phrase
from the Acts of the Apostles: 'they became far more
worthily and truly of one heart and one mind in Christ
than they had been in the world'. William like his
mentor Bernard, does not deny the value of friendships
outside the monastery. He sees them as a point of
departure and inspiration for the much richer and
deeper friendships of the cloister.

Perhaps the main problem with William of Saint
Thierry's narration is that it is so smooth and literary
that one is not jolted into a realization of what is
happening here in Bernard's experience of other people
and influence on them. He is not just getting them
into the monastery because he sees the monastic way
of life as the best way to salvation: he is converting
people because they are his friends. Friendship requires
consensio, to return to Cicero, and in Bernard's mind
the best way to live in harmony is to live within
the monastery, where all can be one in Christ. Thanks
to Geoffrey of Auxerre's much less literary and more
anecdotal description of the process with Hugh of
Vitry, we can see how absolutely determined Bernard
was to make sure that his friends did come with him.
He could not imagine a community of monks without
the inclusion of his friends and relatives. In Bernard's
life and writings, friendship received an independent
value within the christian, and especially the monastic,
life. This is not just a process of friend first and
then monk. It is the transformation of the friend of
the world into the even stronger friend of the monastery.
Bernard was satisfied with nothing less!

In Bernard the western monastic ambiguity about
the value of friendship was resolved. For Bernard
this was probably not a question of choice but of
some inner necessity. He could not imagine living
without having friends. At the same time, however,
Bernard did not lose sight of the place friendship
had to assume within the monastery. *Despite its intrinsic
value friendship has to be subordinated and coordinated
to the goal of monastic community.* Thus Bernard makes
visible in his letters and treatises those friends who
contribute to this goal. As Adriaan H. Bredero has
pointed out, Bernard's actions can best be understood
if they are seen as working towards the spread of
the Cistercian Order. To go a step further than Bredero,
one could claim that any person who helped Bernard
with this purpose deserved to be qualified as his
friend, whether or not Bernard knew this person well
or not.

In a letter to the archbishop of Lund in Scandinavia, probably written in 1151 and not, as usually

thought, in 1152, Bernard expressed the degree of his affection:

> I believe I owe you and you owe me all the favour and affection that absent friends can bestow on one another....I cannot repay you for your affection, but I have one, whose mercy endures for ever, who will repay for me. I speak of the Lord in whom and for whom you love me with such devotion and bind me to you with such affection.[5]

Eskil had apparently written Bernard about his problems in opposing the power and influence of the archbishop of Hamburg-Bremen, and now Bernard was showing all his sympathy. But Eskil had also informed Bernard of his own intention to found a cistercian monastery at Esrum in Northern Zealand. The bearer of the letter and Eskil's messenger, William, the first abbot of the new Danish house, would proceed to the pope in December to get a foundation document for Esrum. Eskil had already provided a gift of property at the site, and now Bernard could look upon the archbishop as a man who was contributing to the spread of the Cistercians in the North. Eskil may well have written Bernard an affectionate letter, but the latter seems mainly to be responding to the fact that the archbishop of Lund is championing 'his' Cistercians in Denmark. Because of this cooperation, Eskil became a friend, even if Bernard had never seen him. The two were united in mutual affection stemming from their common effort, and because of this unity, Bernard could pour upon Eskil all the power of his pen:

> Would that I had the power from on high to say all this to you and not write it, so that I might open my heart to you by word of mouth rather than by the written word. Certainly the living word is more welcome than the written word, and the tongue more eloquent than the pen; for the eyes of the speaker lend credence to his words, and the expression of the face conveys affection better than the pen. But, being absent from you, this is beyond my power and so I must satisfy myself with the second best alternative of a letter.

The contrast between written and spoken word is perhaps one of the oldest clichés of letter writing, but the words seem to have had some effect on Eskil. Soon

after receiving this letter he went to Clairvaux and
met Bernard. Whatever the political motives for his
trip, it is hard to imagine he was not drawn by the
desire to see the man who could promise so much intensity in human contact and friendship.

Another close friend to whom Bernard can be
seen drawing near because of the willingness of the
friend to support the spread of the Cistercian Order
in his country is Malachy of Ireland, the only person
whose biography Bernard wrote. In what is called
a 'letter of confraternity' to Malachy as papal legate
in Ireland, dated after 1145 (and before his death
in 1148), Bernard managed to combine both the devotion
of friendship with his enthusiasm and gratefulness
for the good work that Malachy was doing. In the
very salutation of the letter Bernard summarizes this
double relationship, for he calls Malachy a 'great
priest and his best friend' (*summo amico suo*). The
first part of the letter starts out as a classical statement
of friendship which can exist even though the friends
are separated:

> Even though you are far away from us, you
> are still not far from our mind, since holy
> love admits to no inhibitions from time and
> place. Even if we are separated by the wide
> sea, we are still joined in charity.[6]

Such a sentiment could probably easily be traced
back to the letters of Seneca to Lucilius, and on the
way the idea can be seen in the sixth-century poetry
of Venantius Fortunatus. What is important here, however,
is the way Bernard quickly links this sentiment of
individual friendship with the unity of the friends
in Christ and in the brotherhood of the Cistercian
Order:

> In all matters I am joined to you by the
> kind reception of our sons and brothers,
> who lately have gone to those parts, and
> whom you cherish, love and help in an effica-
> cious manner. Although they did not come
> from our own house especially [Clairvaux],
> still they are not the less loved for being
> from one of our daughter houses, for we
> all, both near and far, are one in Christ,
> both these and those who come from our side
> to you, and we specially commend them to
> your fatherhood, asking that, what you have
> well begun, you will complete even better
> in the Lord.

The letter ends with an assurance to Malachy that he will be able to share in whatever good that is done in the Cistercian Order. This confraternal link was extremely rare in Bernard's time and not just a standard form of monastic prayer community, as it could be, for example, in the time of Saint Boniface. Bernard has managed in the course of fewer than twenty lines to go from expressing his special friendship for Malachy as a person to whom he was intimately joined, to a statement of the unity Malachy now enjoyed with the entire Cistercian Order and all its benefits. The link between individual friendship and monastic confraternity is the effort of Malachy to spread and protect the presence of the Cistercians in Ireland. For Bernard friendship and cistercian monasteries are intimately linked. Whether in Denmark or Ireland, he was willing to express his friendship to those who helped him in this process.

It might seem appropriate to end this paper here, in acknowledging Bernard's capacity for friendship and in seeing this as coordinated to his more important goal of spreading the Cistercians all over the known world of his day. But Bernard is not as simple as that: his need for friendship was so great that he seems to have sought out and maintained individual friendships for their own sake. Thus, *in Bernard's scheme individual friendships are both possible and desirable.* Here the strongest defense of such bonds can be found in Bernard's lament on the death of his brother Gerard, where he describes what a faithful support Gerard had been to him at Clairvaux and how difficult it is for him to accept the fact of Gerard's death.7 These passages I have analysed elsewhere: they are of central importance for an acceptance among monks of the value of tears for the loss of loved ones.

Another instance of a particularized friendship in Bernard's life is his relationship with Nicholas of Montiéramey. This bond has been exhaustively researched, but mainly in terms of Nicholas' great betrayal of his master and Bernard's virulent reaction. Recent writers tend to see Bernard as exaggerating the bounds of reasonable behaviour in accusing Nicholas of being a thief, and it is still not clear to what extent Nicholas was acting in good faith. But the finale of Bernard's and Nicholas' relationship should not distract us from the keen devotion Bernard showed him for several years. In Bernard's letters Nicholas can be seen as a bond and go-between for Bernard and Peter the Venerable, as when Bernard writes to Peter how he could on receiving a letter from Peter 'shut myself up alone with Nicholas, of whom you are so fond.

There I refreshed myself again and again with the charm which emanated from your letter'.[8] For Bernard there was no doubt that a letter from a friend was to have first priority over the daily obligations he had as abbot and political figure. Bernard wanted, moreover, to share the contents of the letter primarily with the friend whom he already shared with Peter, the Nicholas who had originally come from Peter and who could be allowed to add his own sentence to Bernard's letter to express his own individual affection for the abbot of Cluny:

> *Ego Nicolaus vester saluto vos in aeternum, et ultra, et domesticam illam familiam, quae lateri et spiritui vestro adhaeret.* And I Nicholas add my undying affection for you and for all your household.[9]

The work of Jean Leclercq has shown how much care Bernard put into his letters in order to make them works of literary art. One could go even further and say that the sensuality that some men invest in food, sex, or the pursuit of wealth Bernard placed in the pursuit of literary perfection. In allowing Nicholas to share in the process of writing a letter, and even adding his own explicit contribution to it, Bernard was showing confidence in a friendship. We tend to remember only how he was betrayed, or thought he was betrayed, but the letters we have make it clear that Bernard and Peter both loved Nicholas very dearly and wanted to be with him. Once again, Bernard could not be without his friends when he was doing what he loved to do: entering the monastic life, reading a friend's letter aloud, or responding to it. Like Augustine, as seen in his *Confessions,* Bernard could not be alone. He needed the acknowledgement and awareness and even physical presence of his friends.

One of Bernard's closest friends was the abbot of Cluny, Peter the Venerable. Once again it is the controversial part of this relationship, Bernard's attack on Cluny, that is best known, and not the later letters of friendship. The first of these are cautious and full of expressions of humility.[10] They date from 1138, the time when Bernard was returning to France after dealing with the schism of Anacletus. In the next years there were various disagreements with Cluny, such as that over the election of the bishop of Langres, but in 1143 Bernard wrote a letter to Peter which signalled that he wanted the two of them to share friendship. We do not have the letter of Peter to which Bernard was responding, but from what Bernard says, Peter had been poking fun at him in a most gentle way: 'So you are pleased to jest? Courteously and kindly I would admit, if I could be sure you were not ridiculing me'.[11] This time Bernard spoke directly to Peter and dropped the apparatus of humility: he chides him for not writing for a long time to him and says that now that a letter has come from Peter, he does not quite know how to take it. Peter has shown an 'unexpected esteem'—*inopinata dignatio*—for Bernard, and now Bernard wants to know what his exact meaning is in playing with language.

> I have only said this so as to be quite open with you and not to keep anything back from you, for this true friendship demands. Because charity believes all things, I have put away all my misgivings, and am glad that you have warmed to the memory of an old friendship, and recalled a wounded friend. Being recalled I am happy to return, happy to be recalled.

There has been some kind of misunderstanding between Bernard and Peter, between Cîteaux and Cluny, but Bernard is not addressing it as an official matter for the two Orders: it is a matter of friendship.

Bernard had felt offended by Peter's standoffishness, and now he did not know what to make of Peter's indication of affection. But he had decided to take it in the best possible sense. True friendship requires faith in the good intentions of the friend and complete openness with him. These enabled Bernard to forgive and forget whatever had passed between them, and he returned to his friend. The language here indicates that in 1143 Bernard considered his friendship with Peter an old one. Did it go back to the time when Bernard and Peter had resolved their differences in the 1120s? We do not know, for the collection of letters only allows us to focus on the relationship of the two men at selected moments. In 1143, at least, Bernard could again embrace the bond and characterize it in terms of true friendship. He implies, however, that there had been some trouble that now was over:

> Here I am, now as ever, your devoted servant, and full of gratitude for being once more your intimate friend, as you were kind enough to write. If I had perhaps grown cold towards you, as you reproach me for having done, there is no doubt that cherished by your love I shall soon grow warm again.

Bernard's references to Peter's letter allow us to reconstruct part of it: Peter had indicated, perhaps with gentle humour, that Bernard had stopped caring for him but that he, Peter, considered Bernard to be his friend: *intimus vobis.*

If Bernard had been following the rules of letterwriting, the *ars dictaminis,* this section would have included a statement of good will: the *captatio benevolentiae.* In general, Bernard shows his good will towards Peter here. But he does much more: he cuts through the polite superficiality of rhetorical good manners and describes to Peter something of what he has had to experience first because of the long silence and then because of Peter's remarkable letter. Only once he has described the development and setting back into place of his own relationship with Peter can Bernard accept the humour in a positive way and enjoy it:

> I must say I enjoy your fun. It is both pleasantly gay and seriously grave. I do not know how it is you are able to be gay and grave, so that your fun has nothing about it of frivolity, and your dignity loses nothing by your gaiety.

Every word is balanced carefully and contrasted with its opposite: *iucunditate gratus, et serius gravitate.* Bernard the artist of the phrase is at work: this is his way of expressing his decision not to be insulted by Peter's fun and games but instead to join in them as an indication of friendship. He then sets about describing his situation at Clairvaux and says that he will not be leaving it again, except for the General Chapter. Bernard is not well, but he is still able to join in on Peter's joking tone and to anticipate a possible humorous reply from Peter: 'I suppose you will not now dare to reproach me with my silence and, in the way you have, to call it sloth!' Bernard could not resist the temptation to return to Peter something of what he had received from him. Instead of being sour and displeased with Peter's disturbing mixture of silence and jokes, Bernard decided to return both in kind! Such passages are in my mind the mark of a real friendship and much more than a literary pose. The friend adapts and plays with the tone of the letter he has received and shows that he has understood and can respond to the nuances of affection that others might ignore or misunderstand. Just beneath the surface there is evidence of trouble and disagreement. Instead of suppressing this element, Bernard admits that it has been there but indicates his desire to renew an old and important friendship.

If we were to study all the letters between Peter and Bernard, it would be possible to trace their friend- ship into the early 1150s and to conclude that Peter was almost always the diplomat, while Bernard usually seemed to convey what was on his mind in a much more direct way. The two knew how far they could go with each other and respected boundaries, and the result is one of the few friendships in the twelfth century that can be illuminated from both sides. No matter how much we try to explain away this friendship in terms of the advantage of maintaining good relations between Clairvaux and Cluny, the language of Bernard is too powerful and affectionate to dismiss it as pure verbiage of a high literary quality. The only conclusion possible is that aside from all practical considerations, Bernard wanted and needed Peter's friendship. 'True friendships do not grow old: otherwise they were not true', he insisted elsewhere,[12] echoing Cicero and Jerome.

In the same letter, addressed to a 'W' who might be William of Saint Thierry, Bernard even borrowed from the language of the Song of Songs in order to express what he felt for a true friend: 'I shall hold him and not let him go, until I shall bring him into the house of my mother and into the chamber of her who conceived me' (Cant 3:4). Bernard is determined to hold onto the friend, come what may: '...since you still turn to me, I am yours and will be as long as I live'. In parting he tells this unknown friend that the sermons for which he had asked will soon be ready and will be sent off. The correspondent was thus interested in Bernard's literary and theological inspiration, but Bernard frames this bond in terms of friendship. Even the ecstatic language of the Song of Songs is appropriate here: this allegory of love can be applied boldly and immediately to one friend's need for another: 'I draw tight in my arms one who is joined to me in the marrow of his being, and there is no one who can snatch him from my grasp'.[13]

This last statement can be seen not just as an indication of the strength of Bernard's bonds with his friends. It also points to Bernard's determination to be the one to decide which human relationships were true friendships and how to go about cultivating these bonds. To put matters nakedly, *Bernard has to be in charge of his friendships.* He prefers to take the initiative in beginning a friendship or breaking it off, as we can see from a striking letter to a man who had promised to come to Clairvaux but had not kept his word. Bernard indicated that he is the one

who cares for his correspondent, and that the latter
has failed not only Bernard but also himself:

> Although you care not for yourself, yet I
> do not cease to care for you since I am
> fond of you and grieve over you. Because
> I am fond of you I grieve over you; because
> I grieve over you, I think of you.[14]

Bernard ties the continuation of his own personal
relationship to the man with his decision to enter
Clairvaux and become part of its fellowship. In rejecting
Clairvaux, the correspondent cut himself off from Bernard:

> If there lives in you the faintest spark of
> your old love for me; if you have any hope
> at all of eventually escaping from your wretched
> captivity: if you do not wish that confidence
> in the prayers and friendship of this community,
> which I am told you have even while living
> as you are, to be utterly empty and false,
> come at once to Clairvaux.

Here *amicitia* is placed together with prayer in the
context of the entire community of Clairvaux, not
just the friendship of Bernard alone. But for Bernard
the two can hardly be separated. If the man refuses
to come to Clairvaux, then he cuts himself off from
the 'friendship of good men, because by refusing
to take their advice, you will prove yourself unworthy
of their fellowship'. No compromise is possible for Bernard:
the promise once given must be kept. On its fulfillment
depended the continuation and renewal of his 'old
love' and the friendship of the entire community.

Once again we see that Bernard's individual
friendships were intimately linked to his goal of seeing
that as many good men as possible entered Clairvaux
and spread the Cistercian Order. He is here a man
without compromise, and so it is possible to imagine
that maintaining a friendship with Bernard was no
easy matter. This is the impression left by the long,
careful letters of Peter the Venerable to Bernard:
every phrase, every step had to be explained, for
Peter realized that Bernard would decide whether his
intentions and actions were acceptable. If we return
to the case of Hugh of Vitry, where Bernard was cross
at first because he could not control Hugh's tears
but was happy later because he had managed to make
him shed the right kind of tears, this scene of tension
and tenderness summarizes the way Bernard set the
tone. If Hugh was going to continue being his friend,

then he had to become a monk. Bernard did not care that Hugh had initially been shocked and disappointed by his own decision to choose another way of life and abandon the secular clergy.

Bernard would not take no for an answer, as can be seen in his letter to Aelred of Rievaulx ordering him to write a work on charity. Aelred had apparently objected that he was not fit for such a speculative work, for his life experience had been more with practical matters. Bernard took Aelred's arguments and made them his own:

> I most gratefully accept your excuses, they serve rather to inflame than extinguish the spark of my desire, because knowledge that comes from the school of the Holy Spirit rather than the schools of rhetoric will savour all the sweeter to me....[15]

There are no explicit declarations of friendship in this letter: Aelred is the pupil who has to follow the Rule of Saint Benedict and learn true humility and obedience. In humility he will accept that he is capable of doing what Bernard asks; in obedience he will follow the command of his master.

Aelred must have met Bernard at Clairvaux in the spring of 1142. It was probably then that Bernard had conceived his desire to Aelred. Once he did so, no compromise was possible. Outwardly everything conforms to the standard benedictine pattern of adherence to the Rule, but when one turns to the product of Bernard's conversations with Aelred, the result is a highly untraditional work of monastic theology, one that combines Aelred's personal experience with his interpretation of divine creation and love. Bernard must have recognized in Aelred a man who would be able to combine his own self-awareness with an understanding of the function of love in a christian context. The strength of Bernard's will in manipulating and making people conform to his desires and goals can easily be seen as a negative factor in his bonds with other men, but here in the case of Aelred the opposite is apparent. Bernard saw in Aelred a potential friend who could spread the doctrine of charity in monastic life by showing how it worked. As a man of will, Bernard could order Aelred to write a treatise on the subject. Aelred could only obey. The result is one of the most intense formulations of the workings of love in human and especially monastic life that we can find in the twelfth century. Without the strength of Bernard's will, Aelred might never have articulated

his ideas. Here friendship underlies the strict language
of command and subordination, for Bernard needed
Aelred to be his instrument in spreading the doctrine
of love in a cistercian manner.

Bernard had to be in charge, but he was not
a man who reduced friendship to sycophancy. He was
willing to respond to friends who had unflattering
things to say about him, and this is for me the most
convincing indication that Bernard was indeed a friend:
He was open to criticism and able to answer it. His
letters included many that reveal his receptivity to
criticism. Even if the letters to which he replies do
not survive, Bernard's review of their contents and
frequent quotation of individual passages enables
us to reconstruct the charges against him and to see
how Bernard dealt with them. Peter the Venerable
did the same, in even greater detail: he can be seen
moving carefully through letters from Bernard and
answering them point by point. Bernard was not as
meticulous, but he does not seem to be hiding the
essence of the complaints levelled against him when
he replies to a charge by William of Saint Thierry
that Bernard loved him less than William did Bernard:

> 'My affection for you is greater than yours
> is for me'. These are your very words, and
> I could wish they were not, for I do not
> know if they are true.[16]

Instead of dealing with this charge by protesting
the depth of his affection for William, Bernard pointed
out that only God knows what happens in the heart
of a man: 'You may be right...but I am certainly
certain that you cannot be certain'. The word play
on *certus* is intentional and makes the point well:
certitude about human dispositions is reserved to God
alone, and so Bernard can only be amazed at the
confidence with which William put forth his observation.

If Bernard had stopped here, it would look as
though he was trying to avoid answering the charge
by bringing up a theological point, thus intellectualizing
a matter of human emotion in order to avoid responding
in kind (as men have done both before and since!).
But Bernard was willing to assert his love for William:
his problem was that he did not know whether he
loved him sufficiently. He defined this love on the
basis of the Gospels as the willingness to lay down
one's life for one's friends. So Bernard was faced
by the dilemma that his love seems wanting:

> Woe is me, if (as I greatly fear) I am either

loved by this man more than I deserve or
love him less than he deserves.

The rules of letter writing and a zeal for edification
did not allow Bernard to leave William with a sense
of defeat. He ended the letter by reminding William
that he, Bernard, loves him to the limit of his capacity,
while he is sure that William can even increase his
love for Bernard:

> ...although you love more than I do, you
> do not love more than you are able. And
> I too, although I love you less than I should,
> yet I love you as much as I can according
> to the power that has been given me.

Do not ask me to be what I am not: try to find out
who I am, so that you can love me as I am. Was
Bernard trying to keep William at a distance? Or
was he telling a man for whom he cared deeply that
William has been mistaken and should reconsider what
it is that he seeks in Bernard and to what extent
Bernard can provide it? I cannot help thinking that
Bernard is being as frank and open with William
as he possibly could be, even belabouring his point
to near-repetitiveness.

The last part of this letter provides one of the
moments in the twelfth century where we are privileged
to see one man trying to speak nakedly to another.
Whatever the rhetorical and theological background
of this letter, it is a direct appeal from Bernard
to William not to expect too much of him, not to ask
for more than he can give, not to demand something
he cannot give at all. It is impossible to concretize
Bernard's message: he may have been reminding William
that he, as abbot of Clairvaux, could not take on
the needs and cares of William in more than a secondary
manner. William's own account of his stay with Bernard
at Clairvaux when the two were ill[17] shows how the
tension between them and the contest of wills at times
could only be resolved when Bernard got his way
and forced William to do as he wished. Bernard nevertheless gave William enough of himself that they could
remain friends, even after William, despite Bernard,
left his abbacy in order to become a cistercian monk.
The relationship between William and Bernard was
a contest of wills, but it also reveals Bernard's willingness to explain himself, to open his own sources of
motivation to his friend, and to share some of his
own inner life with those for whom he especially cared.
Again, it is easy to recall Bernard's relationship,

as that with Nicholas, because of the moments of tension in it, but in this letter we can see how friendship was so important for Bernard that he did his best to explain himself and to try to get the friend to understand why he acted and felt as he did.

A completely fair and objective characterization of Bernard's friendships would require as careful a review of his relationships with other men as Jean Leclercq has provided for his dealings with women. But since men were closer and more central to Bernard, while women remained at a distance, such a study would turn into a new biography of Bernard. I can only look forward to what Adriaan Bredero will say about Bernard's friendships in his coming biography, but for the moment I would conclude that *Bernard was a friend at least in his dealings with those who enhanced the monastic life at Clairvaux or the Cistercian Order as a whole.* With such men, as Peter the Venerable, William of Saint Thierry, Eskil of Lund, Malachy of Armagh, Bernard could be warm, open, responsive. While writing to them in careful literary formulae, Bernard could still manage to convey a unity of emotion and thought in the bond of love that is not only convincing to us today but which in its own time inspired strong loyalties from those to whom he addressed himself. One cannot help comparing Bernard's declarations of friendship with those of Anselm when he was still abbot at Bec and wrote to his former monks who had moved with Lanfranc to Canterbury.[18] Anselm was able to concentrate more exclusively than Bernard on the vocabulary of love and friendship: his letters are less often burdened by matters of business and the troubles of the world. But when Anselm spoke of his devotion to his friends, he spoke of an objective state of being having little or nothing to do with any particular feeling on Anselm's part. Anselm's friendships are part of a divine hierarchy of loves in the fullest platonic sense, where the friends are immediately subsumed into Anselm's yearning for divine love. Anselm expected the same progression from human to divine in his friends at times and could be surprised and even irritated by their demands for attention and more letters.

Anselm believed in and wrote about friendship, but it was Bernard who was the friend. Anselm had to hold back, to minimize friendship to the process of salvation through monastic obedience and humility, while Bernard could invest his passions and loyalties in friendships which he believed conformed to monastic requirements. Bernard could be a friend because he also could be an enemy: one was either for him and

all he stood for or against him, as Jean Leclercq
insists. This is not to contend that Anselm was a
passionless human being in comparison to Bernard.
Anselm's dealings with human beings are only shadows
of his yearnings for God, while Bernard could not
help getting inextricably involved and constantly
having to explain himself because he wanted and
needed to be understood and loved by his friends.
Anselm sought love through understanding, while Bernard
sought understanding through love.

*POSTSCRIPT: STEPHEN HARDING AND BERNARD'S MODEL
FOR FRIENDSHIP*

The careful reader may have noticed that almost
all of the friends mentioned in the preceding pages
lived outside of Clairvaux, and so no matter how
well we can describe Bernard's bonds with celebrated
churchmen like Peter the Venerable, we are at a loss
when we come to the practice of friendship at Clairvaux
itself. Only Nicholas was a friend at Clairvaux, and
with his special literary interests he remained outside
the context of monastic community. Should one then
conclude that we cannot say anything specific about
friendship in Bernard's time at Clairvaux? The problem
deserves further investigation, but for the moment
it is possible to touch on one aspect of this problem:
was the Bernard who entered Cîteaux in 1112 already
fully formed in terms of his views and practice of
friendship? Should we consider Bernard to have been
only peripherally influenced by the existing bonds
of the monks to each other? Is Bernard the originator
of the cistercian ideal and practice of friendship,
and should this be seen as a turning aside from a
more Eastern and ascetic ideal and way of life in
the earliest Cîteaux, where there was no room for
the cultivation of individual friendships?

Such a view might seem to gain support from
the text of the earliest draft of the *Carta Caritatis*
where there is nothing about friendship. The bond
of charity implied by the document is a legal one,
ensuring that the new group of monasteries maintain
mutual love not for the purpose of friendship but
for the sake of monastic discipline. There is much
here, as Chrysogonus Waddell has pointed out,[19] that
hearkens back to Cassian's Conference on friendship,
but it is the non-particularized friendship of monastic
harmony rather than any special bonds among individual
monks that are echoed in Cîteaux's text as we have
it.

As so often in dealing with early Cîteaux, we

are blocked by a lack of contemporary documents and
especially by a paucity of narratives. Again Father
Waddell provides help in his article exegeting a letter
from Stephen Harding to his former benedictine community
at Sherborne.[20] Dated 1131, the letter can be seen
as an assurance to an established english community
that it had nothing to fear from the coming of the
Cistercians to England. In the first sentence of the
letter, Stephen Harding provided a *captatio benevolentiae*
which provides a classical-sounding definition of the
purpose of letter writing in terms of maintaining love
among those who are separated from each other: 'The
function of a letter is to address the absent as though
they were present, and to bring together through
their fellowship of charity those still kept apart by
long distances'. A careful search through earlier
letter collections might reveal an exact source for
this statement: for the moment, however, it is enough
to characterize it as a statement of friendship and
love from one community of monks to another, but
especially from Stephen Harding to the monks of Sherborne, some of whom, he hoped, would remember him
as 'their' man.

By expressing himself in this manner, Stephen
must have sought to disarm the hostility of Sherborne
by appealing to a commonly accepted conception of
monastic life as a *contubernium caritatis*. But is it
possible to get even closer to the historical Stephen
Harding and to see if he was as dedicated to the
practice of friendship as Bernard was? There seems
to be no contemporary or near-contemporary material,
but in the Life of Saint Peter of Juilly, also an English-
man, we are told that he and Stephen were close friends
in their youths when they pursued their studies in
France before they became monks:

> Peter became aware of his way of life and
> approved of it, so he joined [Stephen] to
> himself as a friend and companion [*familiarem
> et socium*]. Thus both of them remained joined
> by the bond of holy companionship [*sanctae
> societatis*]....21

Since this biography was not written until after 1160
and perhaps as late as 1185,[22] its value as historical
evidence is limited. It refers to events that took place
in the 1070s and so would have had to draw on a
very long tradition. One cannot ignore the author's
interest in establishing a link to Stephen, the renowned
abbot of Cîteaux, in order to establish the holiness
of his own Peter.

But if we assume that there is some truth in this assertion of a strong friendship in Stephen's life as a cleric before he joined the reformed monastery of Molesme, then the pattern of his personal and religious development parallels that of Bernard: first there is the world of schools, friends, and competition for excellence in learning: only then does the youth turn to the monastic life. If Stephen and Bernard had such similar backgrounds, rooted in the flowering of learning and the expression of friendship in clerical circles at the end of the eleventh century, then Stephen would immediately have been able to recognize in the young Bernard at the gates of Cîteaux in 1112 the type of learned and enthusiastic young man that he himself had been at Molesme more than thirty years earlier. Because of Stephen Harding's own background in classical learning and clerical friendships, he could sympathize with the Bernard who brought his family and friends with him into the new life. Without the assent and encouragement of Stephen Harding, Bernard might never have been able to develop his practice and expression of friendship in the monastic life. Bernard might have done what he wanted in any case, but the presence of Stephen Harding still seems to have been essential for the new cistercian mode of friendship.

The transformation from desert asceticism to a greater appreciation of the worth of human bonds in the process of monastic salvation will perhaps always remain an obscure process at early Cîteaux, but once Bernard becomes visible to us, the development is clear. He was a difficult friend, a demanding friend, but a friend who could not imagine life without friends and friendship. He thus built on the tradition of Cicero as applied to monastic life by John Cassian but made the ethic and practice of friendship more personal, more individual, a rightful aspect of monastic society's conversion of the world into God's image in man.

BIBLIOGRAPHICAL NOTE

For Bernard the saint I am deeply indebted to the work of Jean Leclercq, and especially to his *Saint Bernard et l'esprit cistercien* (Paris, 1966) ET *Bernard of Clairvaux and the Cistercian Spirit*, CS 16 (Kalamazoo, 1976) and *Nouveau visage de Bernard Clairvaux* (Paris, 1976). The remark about hating or loving Bernard I have from my student, Lars Grunnet, in a conversation with Dom Leclercq during a conference at the Medieval Centre in Copenhagen in September 1983. I am much in debt to Lars Grunnet for many good talks on Bernard as a man, monk, and politician.

For the less sympathetic side of Bernard, Leif Grane, *Peter Abelard* (London, 1970) as well as the studies mentioned in Adriaan Bredero, 'Conflicting Interpretations of the Relevance of Bernard of Clairvaux to the History of His Own Time', *Cîteaux: Commentarii Cistercienses* 31 (1980) 53–81.

For the development of friendship in the Middle Ages, especially in a monastic context, see my forthcoming book, *Friendship in the Middle Ages: The Religious Experience* (to be published by Cistercian Publications), as well as a preliminary study, 'Love, Friendship, and Sex in the Eleventh Century: The Experience of Anselm', *Studia Theologica* 28 (Oslo, 1974) 111–52. Invaluable, but difficult to obtain, is Adele M. Fiske, *Friends and Friendship in the Monastic Tradition* (Cuernavaca, Mexico, 1970), a collection of articles on many of the central monastic exponents of friendship.

I have used the standard edition of Bernard, *Sancti Bernardi Opera,* edd. Jean Leclercq and Henri Rochais, in which the letters appear in volumes VII and VIII (Rome: Editiones Cistercienses, 1974 and 1977). For translations, *On the Song of Songs 2*, CF 7, trans. Kilian Walsh (Kalamazoo, 1976) and Bruno Scott James, *The Letters of Bernard of Clairvaux* (London and Chicago, 1953).

For Bernard's secretaries, Leclercq, 'Saint Bernard et ses secrétaires', *Recueil d'Etudes sur Saint Bernard et ses écrits* 1 (Rome: Edizioni di Storia e Letteratura, 1962) 3–25, and Leclercq, 'Lettres de Saint Bernard: Histoire ou littérature?', *Studi Medievali* 12 (Spoleto, 1971). I am more than grateful to Father Leclercq for generously making his work available to me in offprints, and here I can only mention a fraction of the number of his studies concerning Bernard.

For clerical expressions of friendship, see especially *The Letters and Poems of Fulbert of Chartres*, ed. Frederick Behrends, (Oxford, 1976) and *Briefsammlungen der Zeit Heinrichs IV,* Monumenta Germaniae Historica: *Die Briefe der deutschen Kaiserzeit* 5, edd. Carl Erdmann and Norbert Fickermann (Weimar: Böhlaus, 1950).

A pioneering study of the difference between early cistercian ideals and those of the eastern desert in Late Antiquity is Benedicta Ward, 'The Desert Myth', in *One Yet Two*, ed. Basil Pennington (Kalamazoo, 1976) 183–99.

Bredero's interpretation of Bernard in terms of his zeal for spreading the Cistercian Order is to be found in his 'Saint Bernard and the Historians', *Saint Bernard of Clairvaux*, CS 28 (Kalamazoo, 1977) 27–62, especially the last few pages.

For a fuller analysis of Eskil's letter to Saint Bernard, see my 'Why Scandinavia? Bernard, Eskil, and Cistercian Expansion in the North 1140–1180', in this volume. Also *The Cistercians in Denmark*, CS 35 (Kalamazoo, 1982).

Louis Lekai places the first formal cistercian confraternities in the thirteenth century; *The Cistercians: Ideals and Reality* (Kent State, Ohio: 1977) p. 388. The classic study of prayer confraternity in the Early Middle Ages is Adalbert Ebner, *Die klösterlichen Gebets-Verbrüderungen* (Regensburg, New York, Cincinnati, 1890).

Nicholas of Montiéramey is treated at length, with full bibliography, in Giles Constable, *The Letters of Peter the Venerable* 2 (Cambridge, Massachusetts, 1967) 316–30.

The remark on Augustine's inability to be alone is taken from Peter Brown, *Augustine of Hippo* (London, 1967) p. 61. I am also grateful to Peter Brown for his guidance and advice in considering the importance of kinship bonds in understanding friendship in Late Antiquity.

For the dispute between Bernard and Cluny, see Jean Leclercq's introduction to the *Apologia* to Abbot William, *Bernard of Clairvaux: Treatises* I, CF 1 (1970). Also Adriaan Bredero, 'The Controversy between Peter the Venerable and Saint Bernard of Clairvaux', *Petrus Venerabilis*, edd. Giles Constable and James Kritzeck (Rome, 1956) 53–71.

Jerome's adage on true friendship appears frequently in medieval contexts: *amicitia, quae desinere potest, vera numquam fuit* (ep. 3.6; p. 18 in I. Hilbert, Corpus Scriptorum Ecclesiasticorum Latinorum, 54 [Vienna, 1910]).

On Aelred and Bernard, see Aelred Squire, *Aelred of Rievaulx: A Study*, CS 50 (Kalamazoo, 1981), esp. ch. 2, 'A Way of Life'.

Jean Leclercq's study on women in Bernard is still being translated to English by Cistercian Publications: *La femme et les femmes dans l'oeuvre de Saint Bernard* (Téqui: Paris, 1982).

My remarks on Anselm are dependent on the work of R. W. Southern, *Saint Anselm and His Biographer* (Cambridge, 1966), esp. pp. 66–76.

For the 'postscript' on Stephen Harding and Bernard, I would be able to say very little at all without the published and unpublished work of Chrysogonus Waddell, as well as his private letters to me. He is in the process of reevaluating the sources for the early history of Cîteaux and giving them life and meaning again, and I look forward to a forthcoming article from him (of which he has shared an early draft with me) on Cassian and the *Carta Caritatis*. Not only my postscript, but also the body of my article, are meant only as a point of departure for a study of Bernard as a friend, and I have even thought of copying Father Waddell and calling it 'Notes Towards an Understanding of Bernard as a Friend'. My review of some of the available sources has convinced me that Bernard indeed could be a friend within the context of his monastic life and goals and so did participate and contribute to the flowering of monastic friendship in waiting for fuller statements in the coming years from Jean Leclercq, Adriaan Bredero, and Chrysogonus Waddell. To these and to all my cistercian friends, especially those in Kalamazoo, I dedicate this article.

Skamstrup/The Medieval Centre
Copenhagen University

NOTES

1. SC 26.10, trans. Kilian Walsh; CF 7:69.
2. Ep 387, SBOp 8:355–6, trans. Bruno Scott James, *The Letters of Bernard of Clairvaux* (London, 1953) 378.
3. 'Les fragmenta de *Vita et Miraculis S. Bernardi*', ed. Robert Lechat, *Analecta Bollandiana* 50 (1932) 94–5. (translation mine).
4. *Vita prima* 1.13; PL185:235.
5. Ep 390; SBOp 8:358 (trans. James, p. 493).
6. Ep. 545; SBOp 8:512–13 (my translation).
7. SC 26:3–14.
8. Ep 389; SBOp 8:356–7 (trans. James, 379).
9. Trans. James, 380.
10. Epp. 147, 148, 149; SBOp 8:350–53.
11. Ep. 228; SBOp 8:98–100 (trans. James, 375).
12. Ep 506; SBOp 8:506 (my translation).
13. My translation cf. Deut 32:39.
14. Ep 415; SBOp 8:398 (trans. James, 511).
15. Ep 523; SBOp 8:487 (trans. James, 246–7).
16. Ep 85; SBOp 7:221 (trans. James, 125).
17. *Vita prima* 1.59–60; PL 185:259.
18. As analysed in my "Love, friendship and sex in the eleventh century: The experience of Anselm", *Studia Theologica* 28 (Oslo: 1974) 111–52.

19.   Chrysogonus   Waddell,   'Notes   Towards   The   Exegesis
of   a   Letter   by   Saint   Stephen   Harding'   in   E.   R.
Elder,   ed.,   *Noble   Piety   and   Reformed   Monasticism,*
CS 65 (1981) 10–39.
20.   PL185:1259.
21.   See *Lexikon für Theologie und Kirche* 8:165.

THE SERMON AS GOAD AND NAIL:
PREACHING IN HÉLINAND OF FROIDMONT

Beverly M. Kienzle

Certain of Hélinand of Froidmont's sermons elucidate a medieval preacher's concept of the obligations of his office. Hélinand, monk of Froidmont,[1] was a renowned preacher in the early thirteenth century and for a time his feast was celebrated in the diocese of Beauvais.[2] While he has received scholarly attention primarily for his French poem, the *Vers de la Mort*,[3] he is the author of numerous Latin works, among them a *Chronicle* and twenty-eight edited sermons for the liturgical year.[4] In those sermons he discusses the preacher's duties, following a tradition dating back to Augustine, but established for the Middle Ages through Gregory's *Regula pastoralis*.[5] Hélinand echoes the obligations of knowledge and virtue that Gregory sets forth for the preacher, but modifies them to suit his own personality. For Hélinand, the three principal duties of the preacher are nurturing the divine Word, setting an example of virtuous living, and admonishing others. It is in the definition of this third obligation that Hélinand's advice is distinctive and personal. For Hélinand, the preacher ought to strike and puncture *(ferire et pungere)*, and to use words as goad and nail (Qo 12:11; PL 212:571C). Petulant by nature and fervent by conversion, Hélinand rebuked his contemporaries who had hardened their hearts to the Word.

In this study of Hélinand's preaching, various passages are selected from the edited sermons to illustrate his view of the preacher's responsibilities. Following is an examination of sermons where Hélinand goads the sinful and advises them to reform. These sermons reflect two periods of his life: first, his early criticism of Philip Augustus; and second, the later Toulouse sermons dealing with efforts to combat heresy. Finally, a third group of sermons, including one from Toulouse, contains denunciations of teachers and preachers whose lives are not consonant with the precepts of Scripture.

The preacher's duties are described with images which involve dispensing and nurturing. Admonishing others is an action of dispensing or transferring the divine Word from preacher to listener. As a dispenser of the divine Word, the preacher has many roles. Hélinand refers briefly to the preacher as an archer, *vir sagittarius* (PL 212:546), and a gardener (PL 212:716D). The archer penetrates the hearts of his listeners with arrows of the Word; the gardener employs tools of word and example to plant peace and holiness in the garden, that is, the hearts and bodies of his listeners. This planting is authoritative. The preacher is the mouth of the Lord *(os Domini)* inasmuch as he is a dispenser of the divine Word *(divini Verbi est prolator,* PL 212:679D). He is also a cloud from which the divine Word pours down, or a gate through which passes the grace of his teaching. That gate is closed if anything contemnible causes his preaching to be scorned (PL 212:504B).

Nurturing the divine Word and setting an example for others requires both a love of Scripture and a purification of self. In Sermon Six for the feast of the Purification, Hélinand applies maternal imagery to both preacher and listener. The listener ought to be a mother hen preparing a nest in his heart for the divine Word. There the chicks may be placed and tended in their proper home (PL 212:531D).[6] For his part, the preacher is the spiritual mother of the Word *(divini Verbi mater spiritualis)* and should revere the example of the mother of the living Word as he readies for preaching. He must prepare his heart, cleanse his life, and purge his conscience before reaching the purified state required for giving forth the Word (PL 212:534B). The Word is not to be offered in philosophical majesty, but in rustic simplicity. As the infant is wrapped in clean cloths, so the Word is treated with maternal sweetness, affectionately clothed *(affectuosissimis sententiis)* and sweetly or tenderly wrapped *(dulcissimis sermonibus)* (PL 212:534C). Since the heart is the hospice of God's word (PL 212:531D), so the preacher ought to direct his sermons to hearts,[7] not to purses in seeking money, to tongues and ears in seeking fame. The preacher of the word is to minister, with a pure, eucharistic tongue *(per linguam eucharim)* the salvific and persuasive Word (PL 212:534CD).

While the sweet language for the Purification describes the preacher's responsibility of nurturing Scripture, loving virtue, and reaching listeners' hearts, we often find in Hélinand a severity which both contrasts with and grows out of that gentleness. He frequently vituperates those who do not build a nest for the divine Word. If the preacher fulfills the first two duties of nurturing the Word with the example of his own life, he is justified in chastising unrepentant sinners. This chastisement is severe, not the blend of gentleness and severity that Gregory advises in the *Regula pastoralis*.[8] In a sermon for Palm Sunday, the six axe-wielding men of Ezekiel 9 become figures of the preacher who uses the Word as a weapon of

destruction against those who are merely listeners
and not doers. As the six men carry not lyres or
cithars, but axes, so the preacher ought not to caress
(palpare) sins. He should instead strike and puncture,
ferire et pungere, using the Word as a goad or a
nail like the words of the wise (Qo 12:11). Moreover,
he must follow the example of Christ's entrance into
Jerusalem. He provoked the Jews, evicting the money
changers and rebuking the corrupt (PL 212:571C).

This identification of self and preacher with the
rebuking Christ characterizes the tone of much of
Hélinand's preaching. His harshness was perhaps
influenced by his own dramatic conversion and renunciation of sinful living. He himself recounts most of what
we know about his life. According to his *Chronicle,*
his young father and uncle *(pueri nobiles et pulcherrimi)*
lost their inheritance in 1127 and were forced to flee
Flanders because of unjust reprisals following the
assassination of Charles, Count of Flanders (PL 212:
1028D). The uncle, Hellebaut, was to become chamberlain
of Henry, brother of Louis VII and archbishop of
Reims (1162–1175).[9] The year of Hélinand's birth is
unknown, but of the dates suggested, 1160 seems the
more reasonable.[10] At the end of a *Chronicle* entry
on Abelard for the year 1142, Hélinand identifies his
boyhood teacher as Ralph of Beauvais, Abelard's pupil.
Hélinand does not date the years he studied at Beauvais.
Ralph was at the height of his fame in the late eleven
sixties and seventies and was an old man around
1182–1185, when he was addressed in a letter from
Peter of Blois.[11] Following his studies, Hélinand acquired
fame as a poet and possibly entertained at the court
of Philip Augustus. Although Hélinand does not mention
entertaining at court, he writes in a later letter that
no spectacle was held anywhere without him.[12] The
poet's frivolous life ended with a sudden conversion
and entrance into the monastery at Froidmont around
1182.[13] Writing five years afterwards, he admitted
that many still doubted the authenticity of such an
abrupt change. Young, weak, and spoilt, he had wander-
ed seeking someone to flatter or chide. The world
had seemed a prison to him.[14] In a sermon, he again
describes his spiritual journey. Swayed by the devil,
he lived in the mire of self-indulgence. He was found
by Christ, who like a mother hen, led and cared
for him under protective wings (PL 212:592B).

The first outrage of a converted conscience seems
to have been directed at Philip Augustus. Hélinand's
denunciations of the powerful provide a link between
his vernacular poetry and his latin prose. In the
Vers de la Mort, the poet allies himself with a personified

Death, urging the wealthy and mighty, including his own friends, to reform their lives in preparation for the Judgment. Many of those visited by Death are ecclesiastic and lay figures involved in Philip Augustus' attempts to divorce Ingeburga of Denmark in 1193.[15] An assembly of French bishops affirmed Philip's false claim of consanguinity, but Celestine III revoked the annulment in 1195. The abbots of Clairvaux and Cîteaux were delegated by the Holy See as judges in the examination of Philip's claim. Philip defiantly took a new wife, Agnes, in 1196. Despite papal and episcopal pressure and despite Agnes' later death and a feigned reconciliation with Ingeburga, the stubborn king resisted recognizing his queen until 1213. An interdict decided upon in December 1199, was pronounced in January 1200. The year 1199 also saw an injunction from the Cistercian General Chapter against *Monachi qui rythmos fecerint, ad domos alias mittantur non redituri nisi per generale Capitulum.* Recent research affirms that the ruling was aimed at Hélinand for the *Vers de la Mort,* and at another cistercian poet, Bertran de Born.[16]

Although Hélinand must have refrained thereafter from writing such *rythmos,* he implicitly criticized Philip Augustus in at least one sermon although he did not refer to him by name. In the same passage where *ferire et pungere* are given as duties of the preacher, Hélinand cites the adultery of another king, Herod, and the chastisements of another preacher, John the Baptist. He also refers to Christ's treatment of the money-changers. With lively language he describes Christ's rebuke of the money-changers and John the Baptist's denunciations of Herod (PL 212:571C). Thus he establishes a comparison on the one hand between Christ, John the Baptist, and himself as preachers, and, on the other, Christ's enemies, Herod, and by implication, Philip. The money-changers and Herod were as recalcitrant as Philip Augustus who had obstinately refused to leave Agnes.

Following the pronouncement of the interdict and its enforcement by the French clergy, an outraged Philip took reprisals against the Church and people. He confiscated church property and revenues, claimed one third of his knights' goods and imposed intolerable taxes on the bourgeoisie.[17] Some of Hélinand's sermons denounce such actions as excessive taxation (PL 212:575D, 690D), pillaging in the provinces (PL 212:575CD) and the seizure of ecclesiastic property (PL 212:509C).

Sermon Three, along with its decrial of the seizure of church goods, refers to excommunicates withholding tithes in a time of famine.

What do the sons of Cain say in this matter...
who when asked not only refuse to pay the
tithes they owe, but when excommunicated
even presume to withhold them? When do
the wretches suppose God will accept the
voluntary gifts of those who, while not paying
what they owe, violently seize what is God's?

*Quid hic dicent filii Cain...qui decimas quas
debent, non solum rogati reddere nolunt,
sed etiam excommunicati retinere praesumunt?
quando putant miseri, quod Deus accepet
munera eorum gratuita, qui violenter rapiunt
illi sua dum non reddunt debita?* (PL 212:509D).

Spiritual food is the theme of the sermon: 'Et pluit
illis manna ad manducandum' (Ps 78:24); and there
are specific references to famine (PL 212:504D, 509CD).
Floods and eleven famines occurred in the reign of
Philip Augustus;[18] the worst famine began in 1195
and lasted four years. Along with the floods, it was
attributed by Innocent III to the wrath of God for
Philip's renunciation of Ingeburga.[19] The strong thematic
presence of famine in Sermon Three may indicate that
it dates from the final years of the twelfth century.
Hélinand seems again to criticize Philip Augustus
by implication; Philip's conduct was clearly considered
responsible for the years of famine. Whether Hélinand
imputed any responsibility to him for the withholding
of tithes by the excommunicates, or whether he is
counted in their number, is not clear. Philip himself
was formally excommunicated, not for his treatment
of Ingeburga,[20] but in 1216 for another matter.[21]
However, Philip's taking Agnes as a wife, or concubine
in the eyes of the Church, made him excommunicate
de facto, and undoubtedly so in the view of his op-
ponents. Thus, with the coincidence of famine, seizing
church property, and excommunication, it is possible
that Hélinand's anger in Sermon Three is directed
at Philip, although probably at other noblemen as
well.
    Thirty years after the height of the scandal,
around 1230, we find Hélinand in southern France,
involved in efforts to preach against heresy. The
1229 Treaty of Paris, which closed nearly twenty years
of warfare, contained clauses on the repression of
heresy. Among those was a provision for the foundation
of a university at Toulouse. Hélie, the abbot of Grand-
selve, the cistercian monastery closest to Toulouse,
was involved in peace-making between the king and
the count of Toulouse, and then in staffing the univer-

sity. The bishop of Toulouse, Foulques, had been a cistercian monk and abbot, and like Hélinand, was a former poet.[22] It is likely that the abbot, or perhaps the bishop, invited Hélinand to preach at Toulouse. Three of his sermons are titled as having been given in Toulouse and the content of a fourth indicates that it belongs with that same group. Of the edited sermons, one (Sermon Fifteen) was delivered on Ascension Day, possibly 24 May 1229.[23] Two others (Sermons Twenty-five and Twenty-eight) were given at a synod in November 1229, and were likely the opening and closing sermons.[24] The unedited sermon is for Rogation Day and titled as given in Toulouse in the Church of St James.[25] The four sermons address two broad purposes: defending the authority of the Church and her representatives; and advising the audience to be deserving of that authority by implementing the precepts of Scripture in their own lives and studies.

Affirmation of the Church's authority is the principal topic of Sermon Twenty-eight, *De potestate et probitate ecclesiae*. It was possibly the opening address to the 1229 Synod, called to promulgate legislation aimed at repressing heresy. Hélinand's remarks would have been delivered to an audience of clergy, nobility, and some members of the bourgeoisie, presided over by the papal legate.[26] Hélinand began the sermon with a description of the misery of the human condition. Life on earth is a proverbial plain overrun by thorny vines and menaced by wild beasts (PL 212:712A). As God set Jeremiah over people and kingdoms to destroy, build, and plant, so prelates are authorized to extirpate evil and plant good (PL 212:712D). Sharing in the prelates' responsibilities are the preacher and the papal legates. Here we find the image of the preacher or prelate as a gardener who uses word and example to plant peace and holiness in the hearts and bodies of listeners. That work is evangelical, and for a like purpose many legates have been sent from the Pope. But, the legates must be severe as well as gentle. They are to pluck out and destroy, as well as to build and plant (PL 212:716D). The new legate is owed reverence and obedience (PL 212:719-720). Here, the only reference to the heretics is metaphorical.

Hélinand does inveigh elsewhere against the heretical weeds choking God's garden (PL 212:549BC, 698C). Nonetheless, for the synod, his audience was composed, not of heretics, but of clerics, and he emphasized the preacher's duty to set an example with his life. He joins earlier cistercian and other preachers who had advocated virtuous example as a means of combating heresy in southern France.[27] In Sermon Twenty-six, probably the closing sermon of the synod, he sent the delegates away to examine their own lives. He developed his discussion of the dignity of the priesthood from Ps 132:9 and from the etymology of *sacerdos* as *sacrum dans*.[28] The priest is obliged to fear, honor, and love God, and to fight the devil, extirpating the latter's practices. What *sacrum* or holy thing does a priest give? Before his responsibilities of preaching and administering the sacraments stands the obligation of good example. Good example is essential for setting true priests apart from heretical priests of the devil. A virtuous life removes a true priest from suspicion and from the heretics' accusations.

The pursuit of virtue extends to university studies as well and Hélinand demonstrated an awareness of subjects occupying the intellectual circles of Paris. In his sermons, he warned against the dangers of study without a spiritual dimension. He voiced the same concern for learning and virtue which is expressed in the *Regula pastoralis* and in numerous thirteenth-century treatises.[29] Yet, he brought the acerbity of his own thrust to a traditional topic. In particular, he criticized parisian philosophers and teachers, many of whom were probably in his audience with their students. Because of that university's temporary closing, parisian masters were staffing the new university in Toulouse. The most notable of those, John of Garland, spent about three years in the city.[30] Certainly, Hélinand's presence in that city assured his familiarity with trends in Paris and his education with Ralph of Beauvais would have acquainted him with late twelfth-century currents in the schools. Furthermore, a recent article on Hélinand's use of Seneca's tragedies affirms that references to ancient and medieval writers are so extensive in the sermons and *Chronicle* that Hélinand himself quite likely worked in Paris at some point.[31]

In the Toulouse sermon for the Ascension, Hélinand directed his warnings to visiting Parisians when he spoke of scholars and students who traverse the country in pursuit of knowledge. True knowledge is found only in the book of divine wisdom, attainable in heaven alone. Learning that does not aid salvation is worthless, even harmful. Excessive study leads to insanity, loses sight of morality, and is frequently motivated by avarice. Both riches and worthless literature are impediments to salvation (PL 212:604B). The example of Benedict should be heeded; the students of his day were so corrupt that he withdrew from liberal arts studies. Their heirs are the clerics in Paris who seek everything but virtue. In an often-quoted passage, Hélinand laments: 'See how the clerics in Paris pursue liberal arts; in Orléans, authors; in Bologna, codices; in Salerno, medicine boxes; in Toledo, magic; and nowhere, virtue'. (PL 212:603B)

As the liberal arts are useless when not directed towards the love of God, so training in Scripture is pernicious when scriptural precepts are neglected (PL 212:633). University masters were criticized in other sermons than from Toulouse. In Sermons Eighteen for Pentecost and Twenty for the Assumption, Hélinand addressed his fellow monks and severely criticized teachers whom he called rosy doctors *(rosei...doctores;* PL 212:634B) and delicate masters *(delicati magistri;* PL 212:651). Teachers of Scripture are rosy, blushing doctors whose dress and comportment demonstrate that the world is topsy-turvy. Owls fly by day and no longer flee the sun. That literary *topos* is enlivened with vivid and even occasionally crude accusations of vanity and gluttony. Vain, the doctors reduce their tonsures to a minimal size and even curl their hair. They wear shoes on their hands and gloves on their feet, and look in mirrors all day. Gluttonous, they feed on the patrimony of the Church but serve their stomachs above Christ. Hélinand laments that virtue and learning rarely coexist (PL 212:633). He asks how anyone who demonstrates contempt for the cross and for apostolic poverty can teach about voluntary poverty and abstinence. The Church's preachers and teachers are *libidinosi,* pleasure-seekers whose teaching and studies are worthless because they do not practice good works (PL 212:634D). As damnable as those rosy doctors are the delicate masters. They debate about fasting with full stomachs, preach about chastity while surrendering to unchastity, and recommend poverty while well-clothed, wrapped in silver and stuffed with gold (PL 212:651BC). Their preaching is empty, like bark without sap, a lamp without oil, a wedding without a bridegroom, or food without seasoning. With a *sententia* taken from Chrysostom, Hélinand summarized his denunciation: 'He who lives well and teaches people well, instructs them how they ought to live; however, he who lives badly and teaches well God instructs as to how he ought to condemn himself'. (PL 212:651C) Hélinand's preaching rebukes those who live badly, but teach well or succeed otherwise in the eyes of the world.

In summary, Hélinand's preacher has three duties: nurturing the Divine Word, setting an example of virtuous living, and admonishing others. He nurtures and dispenses the divine Word. The affection expressed through the image of the spiritual mother leads the preacher to dispense the Word, often by severely goading

the sinful. The severity of Hélinand's preaching has
roots in his temperament and his conversion; his early
life exemplified vices he was later to denounce. Acquainted with the wealthy and powerful, he had spent years
in frivolous pleasures. Following his conversion, he
began to goad the conscience of the mighty, not excepting
the king. Near the end of his life, he had acquired
sufficient respect as a preacher to be invited to speak
at the opening of a university in the troubled region
of Toulouse. He distrusted current trends in university
teaching and counseled a return to Scripture as the
basis for learning, teaching, and preaching.

Hélinand's sermons interest us both for their
subject matter and for his effort to preach in accordance
with the advice he gives. His writing reflects the
controversies troubling the incipient thirteenth century:
struggles between church and king; turmoil surrounding
the Albigensian heresy; disputes in university teaching;
and conflicts resulting from the permeation of money
into all orders of society. In other sermons, Hélinand's
diatribes mirror conventional satire of the day. He
denounced the greed of the wealthy and the graft
and injustices of public officials (Sermons Eleven,
Twenty-three, Twenty-five). Bishops, proud and as
well-caparisoned as their fancy horses, did not escape
his attacks (Sermons Nine, Ten, Twenty, Twenty-five).
Against a background of change, Hélinand praised
the simplicity of monastic life and implored others
to pursue the virtues appropriate to their own lives.
Through his sermons, a distinct impression of Hélinand's
personality emerges. His advice to preachers, although
drawing heavily on tradition, is nonetheless personal.
Jean Leclercq has remarked that we should be grateful
to Hélinand for remaining himself.[32] As we read Hélinand
drawing extensively on Scripture and advising others
not to neglect its precepts, we discern that behind
the force of his goad was a great love for the divine
Word.

St Anselm College
Manchester, New Hampshire

NOTES

Research for this paper was supported by a 1983 Faculty Summer Research Grant from St Anselm College. A preliminary version was presented at the Fourteenth Conference on Cistercian Studies held in conjunction with the Congress on Medieval Studies, Western Michigan University, May 1984. I am grateful to Conference participants for their comments, and especially to Chrysogonus Waddell OCSO for his generous assistance, to Raymond Milcamps OCSO for bibliographic information, and to Eugene A. Green CO for his suggestions and careful reading of the paper's various versions.

1. Jean Leclercq *(The Spirituality of the Middle Ages* [New York: Seabury Press, 1982] p. 214) states that Hélinand was prior of Froidmont. However, Jean de Cirey lists Hélinand as 'monachus solennis historiographus', *Compendium sanctorum ordinis cisterciensis,* in *Privilegia ordinis cisterciensis* (1491; rpt. in *Les monuments primitifs de la règle cistercienne,* ed. Philippe Guignard [Dijon, 1878] p. 652.

2. Hélinand's feast was celebrated from 1854 until Pius X's reform of the Breviary. Anselme Dimier, 'Elinando di Froidmont', *Bibliotheca sanctorum* (Rome: Instituto Giovanni XXIII–Pontificia Università Laterense: 1964) IV: cols. 1073–1074; and Seraphin Lenssen, 'Aperçu historique sur la vénération des saints cisterciens dans 'Ordre de Cîteaux', *Collectanea* o.c.r. 6 (1939) 272.

3. *Les Vers de la Mort,* eds. Fr. Wulff and E. Walberg (Paris, 1905; rpt. NY: Kraus, 1965).

4. B. Tissier, *Bibliotheca patrum cisterciensium* (Bonnefontaine: 1669) VII:206–306; PL 212:481–720. All further references from PL 212 appear in the text.

5. See A. Wilmart, ed., 'Un sermon de saint Augustin sur les prédicateurs de l'Evangile', *Revue Bénédictine* 42 (1930) 301–315; Gregory the Great, *Regula pastoralis,* PL 77:9–126 *(Pastoral Care,* trans. Henry Davis, Ancient Christian Writers II [New York: Newman-Paulist, 1978]); Alan of Lille, *Ars praedicandi,* PL 210:109–198; *(The Art of Preaching,* trans. Gillian R. Evans, 23 [Kalamazoo, 1981]); Jean Leclercq, 'Le magistère du prédicateur au XIIIe siècle', *Archives d'histoire doctrinale et littéraire du moyen âge* (henceforth AHDL) 21 (1946) 59–67.

6. Hélinand cites Augustine as his source for the nest images (PL 212:531D). Caroline Bynum in *Jesus as Mother* (Berkeley: University of California

Press: 1982) discusses the association of the hen image (Mt 23:37) with male authority figures in cistercian writings (p. 147).

7. In contrast, Alan of Lille emphasized the mind: 'The fields ripe for harvest are said to be the minds of men, made ready to accept the word of God'. *Preaching;* PL 210:184C; CF 23:146.

8. Gregory, *Pastoral Care* II, 6; PL 77:38BC; ACW11:67.

9. PL 212:733B: 'De qua re certissimum retenebat exemplum patruus meus Hellebaudus, Henrici quondam Remensis archiepiscopi cubicularius'. Hellebaud's position probably explains Hélinand's friendships with Henry's nephews, first cousins of Philip Augustus: Philip of Dreux, bishop of Beauvais (1176 [1180]–1217); and Henry, bishop of Orléans (1186–1198). *Mort,* intro. p. VIII.

10. Dimier, col. 1073. 1170 was suggested by A. Lecoy de la Marche, *La chaire française au moyen âge,* 2nd ed. (Paris: Renouard, 1886) p. 157.

11. PL 212:1035D: 'Hujus etiam Petri Abaelardi discipulus fuit magister meus, qui me docuit a puero, Radulphus, natione Anglicus, cognomento Grammaticus, Ecclesiae Belvacensis, vir tam in divinis quam in saecularibus litteris eruditus'. On Ralph's life, see R. W. Hunt, 'Studies in Priscian in the Twelfth Century II', *Medieval and Renaissance Studies* 2 (London: 1950; rpt. Liechenstein: Kraus, 1969) 11–12.

12. PL 212:748CD: 'Ipse quidem spectaculum factus est, et angelis, et hominibus levitate miraculi, qui prius eis spectaculum fuerat levitatis; dum non scena, non circus, non theatrum, non amphitheatrum, non amphicircus, non forum, non platea, non gymnasium, non arena sine eo resonabat'. The idea that Hélinand performed at court is taken from the *Roman d'Alexandre,* where an Elinant is ordered to sing for the king, and is discussed by Florence McCulloch, 'The Art of Persuasion in Helinant's *Vers de la Mort',* *Studies in Philology* 69 (1972) 39.

13. Dimier, col. 1074. Hélinand, writing to Walter, describes himself as a young man at his conversion: 'Erubesce igitur, miserrime, te saltem non sequi istum praedecentem, juniorem, infirmiorem, debiliorem, delicatiorem', PL 212:749.

14. PL 212:749: 'Unde et tanta levitas, tam leviter mutata, apud plerosque nihil aliud putatur quam levitas. Hinc est, quod jam quinquennis ejus conversatio vix facit alicui fidem de futuro'. PL 212:748: 'Nosti Helinandum, si quis novit hominem, si tamen hominem neque enim tam natus

erat homo ad laborem, quam avis ad volandum
(Jb 7:1), circumiens terram, et perambulans eam,
quaerens quem devoraret (1 P 5:8) aut adulando,
aut objurgando. Ecce in claustro clausus est,
cui totus mundus solebat esse non solum quasi
claustrum, sed etiam quasi carcer'.

15. On Philip Augustus and Ingeburga, see Hercule
    Géraud, 'Ingeburge de Danemark', *Bibliothèque
    de l'Ecole des Chartes* 6 (1844) 3–27, 93–118;
    and William D. Paden Jr., *'De monachis rithmos
    facientibus'*, Speculum 55/4 (1980) 669–685, who
    clarifies and summarizes the controversy and
    Hélinand's role.
16. Paden, 672.
17. Géraud, 26–27.
18. Achille Luchaire, *Social France at the Time of
    Philip Augustus*, trans. E. B. Krehbiel (New York:
    Harper Torchbooks, 1967) p. 7. Rigord also mentions
    floods in 1195 and 1196. *Oeuvres de Rigord et
    de Guillaume le Breton*, ed. H. Francois Delaborde
    (Paris: 1882) 1, Rigord, *Gesta*, par. 105, 109.
19. See Géraud, 20.
20. Géraud, 19, 104.
21. *Oeuvres* II, G. le Breton, *Chron.*, par. 218.
22. Cyril E. Smith, *The University of Toulouse in
    the Middle Ages* (Milwaukee: Marquette Univ.
    Press: 1958) 31.
23. Smith (p. 38) feels that the sermon might have
    been preached in 1229, 1230, or 1231. A. Gatien-
    Arnould ('Hélinand', *Revue de Toulouse et du
    Midi de la France* [1866] 288) had dated the sermon
    to 24 May 1229. Gatien-Arnould's date is accepted
    by Yves Dossat, 'Les premiers maîtres à l'Université
    de Toulouse: Jean de Garlande, Hélinand', in
    Les Universités du Languedoc au XIIIe siècle,
    Cahiers de Fanjeaux 5 (Toulouse: Privat, 1970)
    197–201.
24. Gatien-Arnould, 349, 353; Dossat, 198–199.
25. The Rogation Day sermon is found in B. N. ms.
    lat. 14591, fol. 35vb[a]: *In rogacionibus apud
    Tholosam in ecclesia b'Jacobi.* See J-Th. Welter,
    *L'Exemplum dans la littérature religieuse et didac-
    tique du moyen âge* (Paris: 1927) 111. Dossat
    (p. 200) summarizes the sermon.
26. Smith, 48–49; Gatien-Arnould, 348.
27. On early cistercian involvement in Languedoc,
    see Smith, *The University*, 15–25; and Christine
    Thouzellier, *Catharisme et Valdéisme en Languedoc*
    (Paris: PUF, 1969) 183–203.
28. Gregory plays on *sacerdotes* and *sacrum ducatum*
    in *Pastoral Care* 11.7; PL 77:42A; ACW 11:74.

Beverly M. Kienzle

29. Jean Leclercq, 'Le magistère', 106–115.
30. Smith, 51–52.
31. Edmé R. Smits, 'Hélinand of Froidmont and the A-Text of Seneca's Tragedies', *Mnemosyne* 36, Fasc. 3–4 (1983) 339.
32. Leclercq, 'Pétulance et spiritualité dans le commentaire d'Hélinand sur le Cantique des cantiques', AHDL 31 (1965) 58. Although the Commentary was subsequently attributed to Odo of Cheriton ('Hélinand de Froidmont ou Odon de Chériton', AHDL 32 (1966) 61–69, Fr Leclercq offers interesting insights on Hélinand.

THE VOCABULARY OF CONTEMPLATION IN AELRED OF RIEVAULX' *MIRROR OF LOVE,* BOOK I

John R. Sommerfeldt

Almost at the beginning of Aelred's central treatise on love, which he names the *Mirror,* he prays:

> O Lord, I beg you, let just a tiny bit of your great sweetness fall into my soul so that it may sweeten the bread of bitterness for her. By the experience of a tiny draught of it, let her have a foretaste of what she should desire, what she should long for during this her pilgrimage. By her hunger let her have a foretaste; by her thirst let her drink. For those who eat you shall still hunger, and those who drink you shall still thirst. Yet they will have their fill when your glory shall appear, and when the great abundance of your sweetness, which you have kept hidden for those who fear you, shall be manifest; for you reveal it to no one save those who love you.[1]

This short passage is filled with appealing imagery —imagery which centers on the sense of taste. And this saporous imagery is appropriate, for Aelred is describing an experience—Aelred uses the word *experientia*—and all experiences are by their nature ineffable. And '...we must expect the contemplative to use poetic language when he attempts to convey the nature of his experience'.[2]

But is the experience Aelred describes in this passage a contemplative experience—a totally enraptured experience of the transcendent, yet imminent, Reality which he called God? I think not. Surely the fullness and manifestation of glory and sweetness which Aelred describes is not a contemplative experience of God in this life, but rather a description of the Beatific Vision, union with God in the life to come. But what of the sweet foretaste which Aelred also describes? Is this a contemplative union in this life? It may be, but one cannot be sure, for Aelred often describes experiences of God which we can enjoy in this life which fall short of enraptured union—and there are many levels of such experience for Aelred.

What I shall attempt to do in this paper is to examine the language of the first book of Aelred's

Speculum caritatis to discover not simply the words and images Aelred uses to express the experience of God, but to attempt to answer the question whether this part of the treatise does indeed speak of the rapturous union with God in this life, life which I have called 'contemplation'.

It would seem that a frontal attack on the question would be promising: does Aelred use the word 'contemplation' when he speaks of contemplation? He does indeed use the word—surprisingly, though, only three times. The first is in Chapter 21, section 59. Aelred writes:

> If you contemplate [*contempleris*] each creature more closely, from the first to the last, from the highest to the lowest, from the loftiest angel to the lowliest worm, you will surely perceive divine goodness—which we have said is nothing other than God's love—containing all things, encompassing all things, and penetrating all things, not by being communicated in any place or by being diffused spatially or by moving nimbly about, but by the stable and incomprehensible simplicity of its substantial presence, abiding in it constantly.[3]

This passage may be a moving metaphysical, perhaps cosmological, description, but it is action which Aelred requires us to take here. We must use our intellect—an intellect informed, to be sure, by grace—to see the nature of creation, not to experience the reality of the Creator. Only two sections later (in 21.61), Aelred uses the verb *attendas* in continuing to urge on us attention to the wondrous complexities of nature. *Attendas* and *contempleris* (at least here) require activity of the intellect, not the passivity of contemplation. Here, as in my previous work on this subject,[4] I refer to this activity as 'meditation', rather than contemplation.

Rather near the end of Book I of the *Speculum caritatis*, Aelred uses the word 'contemplation' as a noun—*contemplatione* is the form—and the context reveals a quite different meaning for the word. Aelred writes:

> And so true temperance, true prudence, and true fortitude are operative, respectively, in such a way that the rational mind may not be allured, deceived, or oppressed, and consequently may not exceed love's norm. Truly, when real love will have brought

all its followers into the realm of its tran-
quillity, when all the present allurements
of the flesh will have been consumed along
with the mortal flesh itself, when all the
darkness of errors will have been dispersed
by the contemplation of divine light, and
when true security has replaced the bothersome
troubles of this world, when, if I may say
so, the arms it uses in time of battle will
be set aside, love alone will refresh the
victors with its sweetness.[5]

I think I reveal no new startling truth when I remark
that this contemplation, though surely not the meditation
of the previously quoted passage, is not rapturous
contemplation in this life but the aveternal contemplation
of the Beatific Vision.

Shortly after this passage, still in Chapter 33,
now in section 97, Aelred, uses 'contemplation' for
the third and final time in Book I:

But if you contemplate [*contempleris*] more
loftily the rules of justice itself, no one
renders to each his due better or more perfectly
than a person who loves the things which
should be loved, and loves them only as
much as they should be loved....You see,
if I am not mistaken, the perfection of justice
depends on the perfection of love, so that
justice seems to be nothing else than well-
ordered love.[6]

Clearly, the contemplation which Aelred urges upon
us here is intellectual and rational in character and
not primarily experiential.

The passage I have quoted contains two instances
of the verb 'to see': *Vides* and *videatur*. And this
usage prompts my second attempt to elicit Aelred's
vocabulary of contemplation in Book I of the *Speculum
caritatis*. 'To see' is not an uncommon verb, of course;
indeed, it occurs in its various verbal, adjectival,
and other forms some seventy times in the Book we
are examining.[7] Not startling information, one might
think, but perhaps useful when we examine the contexts
in which the word occurs. For, as I have said before,
this word 'see' has a range of potential meanings
from the most literal to the most figurative.[8]

What does Aelred see when he 'sees'? Understand-
ably, for Aelred, seeing is often the simple act of
sight; this usage occurs some nineteen times.[9] More
often—some twenty-five times—Aelred means 'see' in

the common intellectual sense as when we say 'Do you see what I mean' or 'It seems that Aelred is an observant monk'.[10]

But sometimes Aelred uses sight in a sense more revealing. Near the beginning of Book I (1.2) there is a glorious passage on love:

> But what is love, my God. Unless I am mistaken, it is a wondrous delight of the spirit, all the sweeter because more chaste, more pleasant because more real, more joyous because more expansive. This is the palate of the heart which tastes that you are sweet, the eye which sees that you are good. This is the place capable of holding you who are infinite. Anyone who loves you grasps you, and grasps you in the measure that she loves you; for you are love, you are charity. This is that richness of your house, in which your dear ones become so drunk that, quitting themselves, they pass over into you. And how, O Lord, except by loving you, by loving you with all their being.[11]

Now this passage is doubly attractive to me because of its twin reference to sight and its twofold use of saporous imagery. Is the sight by which we see, the palate by which we taste, an evocation of a contemplative experience? Again it is not clear—again, at least not to me. The images of embracing the infinite, seeing the good, tasting the sweet, indeed, being drunk on sweetness, do indeed convey a sense of experience—surely of God. I am hesitant, however, to describe this experience as contemplative in the sense I have been using the word. For I detect process here, perhaps better: a progression. Please note that the soul grasps God 'in the measure that she loves you....' And surely not all who love are by that fact contemplatives. I think we have here a description of the fact—for Aelred—that God can be experienced at many levels, levels which he clearly indicates are directly related to the depth of the love the soul possesses.

And that possession clearly involves activity. Only a few lines later (in 1, 3), Aelred writes: 'In the meantime [until we reach the state of beatitude], O Lord, I shall seek you, and I shall see you by loving you'.[12] Love is an activity of the will, just as meditation is an activity of the intellect. Neither activity is by itself an adequate description of the totally consuming, essentially receptive experience of God which Aelred elsewhere describes as contempla-

tion.[13] Meditation and love lead to a state in which
the contemplative experience is possible. They are
not that experience.

I shall not burden you with this sort of detailed
analysis of all the other sixty-eight instances of sight
references in our treatise. Nor do you deserve to bear
the burden of my thoughts on all twenty-seven references
to hearing,[14] eighty-four references to taste,[15] two
references to smell,[16] one reference to touch,[17] and
six references to sensation in general.[18] I have also
counted three uses of *consideratio,*[19] four uses of
experientia,[20] three references to *meditatio,*[21] and
fourteen instance of embraces and kisses.[22] I think
it more profitable, however, to approach Aelred's
vocabulary of contemplation by viewing, with you,
a few key passages.

Let me quote one tantalizing passage; it is from
Chapter 7, section 22:

> Your knowledge is too wonderful for me,
> O Lord; it is very high, and I cannot reach
> it. I shall embrace you meanwhile, Lord
> Jesus...I shall run, O Lord, to the scent
> of your ointments....I shall follow you, O
> Lord, if not to the mountains of fragrant
> spices where your spouse found you, then
> to the garden where your flesh was sown.
> There you leap; here you sleep. Here, O
> Lord, you sleep, here you recline; here you
> keep the rest of a sweet Sabbath. O Lord,
> let my flesh be buried with you, that what
> I live in the flesh I may not live in myself,
> but in you who delivered yourself up for
> me. Let it be anointed with yours, O Lord,
> with the myrrh of modesty, that sin may
> no longer reign in my mortal body....[23]

Despite the complex yet delicate imagery Aelred uses
here, I think the most mystical--in the sense of allegori-
cal--interpretation likely indicates a description of
the activity of the soul--a soul informed, to be sure,
by the grace, the gifts of God.

The rest--save one--of my thirteen 'key passages'[24]
must wait for another day; they use poetic imagery
for purposes ranging from rhetorical device to descriptions of the Beatific Vision.

But, in my last example, I should like to focus
on an image Aelred only alludes to in the last passage
--the image of Sabbath. Aelred writes:

> Oh if only Pharaoh's task masters would

give me a little respite to permit my soul
to rest at least a half hour in the silence
of this sabbath....I shall look for that sabbath
--if perhaps you hear the longing of a poor
man, O Lord. When, one day, I am led out
of misery's pit and the mire of the swamp,
may you let me see 'how great is the sweetness
which you have hidden for those who fear
you', even by the experience of only a little
drop of it. For you do not reveal yourself
except to those who love you. Those who
love you find their rest in you; and true
rest is there, true tranquility, true peace,
the true sabbath of the soul.[25]

The central image here is Sabbath rest; the central
theme is experience. The very fact that Aelred longs
for but a half hour of rest, for but a drop of sweetness,
strengthens the case, as I see it, for attributing
to this passage a truly contemplative character. For
Aelred--and Bernard--often describe their contemplative
experiences as of short duration--Aelred, for example,
in his *On Jesus at Twelve Years of Age*, III.23[26] and
Bernard in his *Twenty-Third Sermon on the Song of
Songs*, 15.[27]
    Yet the context in which this passage is embedded
makes me cautious. Aelred continues:

But, O Israelite, what is the origin of your
sabbath? You answer: the fact that on the
seventh day God rested from all his works....Be-
cause of this, therefore, it is prescribed
that you should then be at rest....Oh, if
you only knew how to be at leisure and
see that Jesus himself is God, then certainly,
when the fog of unbelief would soon be lifted
and his face unveiled, you would recognize
in love the perfect sabbath. Then you would
not be so attached to the flesh-meat feasts
of your sabbath according to the flesh, as
you are now, but entering the place of the
awesome tabernacle, right up to the house
of God, among cries of joy and the sounds
of festivals of praise, you would overflow
with gladness and break into this song:
'We will exult and rejoice in you, praising
your love more than wine'. And at the height
of your joy you would take up the song of
Habakkuk: 'I will rejoice in the Lord, and
will exult in my God', Jesus.[28]

The phrase 'the fog would soon be lifted and his face unveiled' and its context strikes me as the condition of the soul at death. And so I am more secure in my belief that 'the awesome tabernacle', 'the house of God', in which Aelred hopes to revel 'amid cries of joy' and 'festivals of praise' is the Beatific Vision.

If I am right, the meaning of the penultimate passage I have quoted, the appealing Sabbath passage which I have said *could* describe contemplation, is in doubt. For my last two quotations follow one another in the text without any discernible transition. Again, if the second quotation describes the Beatific Vision, it is at least possible that the preceding passage does too.

And with what does this leave us? In the first third of a treatise which is often regarded as one of the masterpieces of twelfth-century contemplative writing, we have but one passage which *might* be describing contemplation—and there is at least some evidence from the context that Aelred is describing something else altogether.

I am not embarrassed by this. Contemplatives are notoriously loath to describe their contemplative experience and are coaxed out of their reluctance only when forced by love to serve their sisters and brothers in a pedagogical role. There is another reason why Aelred has no reference—or, at most, only one reference—to contemplation in the Book I have been studying. Aelred has saved the best until later and last. In a forthcoming paper, I hope to examine Aelred's vocabulary of contemplation in Books II and III of the *Speculum caritatis*.

The University of Dallas

248 John R. Sommerfeldt

NOTES

1. Spec car I.i.2; (edd. A. Hoste and C. H. Talbot, *Opera omnia, Corpus Christianorum, Continuatio medievalis*, I; Turnholt, 1971) pp. 13–14.
2. 'The Vocabulary of Contemplation in Aelred of Rievaulx' *On Jesus at the Age of Twelve, A Rule of Life for a Recluse*, and *On Spiritual Friendship'*, in E. Rozanne Elder, ed., *Heaven on Earth; Studies in Medieval Cistercian History*, 9, CS 68 (Kalamazoo, 1983) p. 73.
3. Spec car I.xxi.59; *Opera*, p. 37, lines 911–17.
4. 'Vocabulary', p. 72.
5. Spec car I.xxxiii.94; *Opera*, p. 55, 1601–609.
6. Spec car I.xxxiii.97; *Opera*, p. 56, 1653–56, 1658–60.
7. Spec car I, Praef., 1 (p. 5, 82); Praef., 1 (p. 5, 87); Praef., 2 (p. 5, 102); Praef., 4 (p. 6, 126); i.2 (p. 13, 23); ii. 5 (p. 14, 65); ii.5 (p. 15, 80); x.29 (p. 24, 425–26; four times); x.30 (p. 24, 436); x.30 (p. 24, 438); xi.31 (p. 25, 473); xii.36 (p. 27, 527–28); xii.37 (p. 27, 542); xiii.40 (p. 28, 585–96; seven times), xiv.42 (p. 29, 630); xv.44 (p. 30, 648); xv.46 (p. 31, 686); xv.47 (p. 31, 689); xvii.50 (p. 33, 757); xviii.51 (p. 33, 775); xviii.52 (p. 34, 784); xix.53 (p. 34, 811); xix.54 (p. 34, 817); xix.54 (p. 35, 822); xix.55 (p. 35, 840); xx.58 (p. 37, 903); xx.58 (p. 37, 904); xxii.63 (p. 39, 983); xxiii.67 (p. 41, 1061); xxiv.70 (p. 42, 1115); xxvi.72 (p. 43, 1143); xxvi.73 (p. 43, 1161); xxvi.76 (p. 45, 1224); xxvi.77 (p. 45, 1229); xxvi.77 (p. 45, 1207); xxvi.77 (p. 45, 1212); xxvi.77 (p. 45, 1224); xxvi.77 (p. 45, 1207); xxvi.77 (p. 45, 1231); xxvii.78 (p. 46, 1262); xxviii.79 (p. 46, 1274); xxix.83 (p. 48, 1351); xxxi.87 (p. 51, 1443); xxxiii.93 (p. 55, 1593); xxxiii.95 (p. 55, 1621); xxxiii.97 (p. 56, 1658); xxxiii.97 (p. 56, 1659); xxxiv.98 (p. 56, 1666); xxxiv.98 (p. 57, 1680); xxxiv.107 (p. 60, 1816); xxxiv. 108 (p. 61, 1830); xxxiv.109 (p. 61, 1866); xxxiv.111 (p. 62, 1908); xxxiv.112 (p. 63, 1925); xxxiv.112 (p. 63, 1940; twice); xxxiv.112 (p. 63, 1942); xxxiv.112 (p. 63, 1946); xxxiv.114 (p. 64, 1976); xxxiv.114 (p. 64, 1977).
8. 'Vocabulary', p. 73.
9. See, for example, Spec car I.x.29 (p. 24, 425–26) for *visus, visio, visus, visio*.
10. See, for example, Spec car I.xiii.40 (p. 28, 585–96) for *videat, videre, videt, videt, videat, videre, videat*.

11. Spec car I.i.2 (p. 13, 20–28).
12. Spec car I.i.3 (p. 14, 38).
13. For example, in Spir amic III.134; *Opera*, pp. 349–50, lines 1107–118.
14. Spec car I.i.2 (p. 13, 16); vi.18 (p. 20, 271); xi.34 (p. 26, 505); xii.37 (p. 27, 540); xii.37 (p. 27, 541); xii.38 (p. 27, 562); xvi.48 (p. 32, 714); xvii.50 (p. 33, 757); xviii.51 (p. 33, 773); xxiv.68 (p. 41, 1077); xxiv.68 (p. 41, 1081); xxiv.70 (p. 42, 1100); xxvi.75 (p. 44, 1194); xxvi.76 (p. 45, 1211); xxvi.77 (p. 45, 1212); xxvi.77 (p. 45, 1216); xxvi.77 (p. 45, 1227); xxvii.78 (p. 46, 1246); xxvii.78 (p. 46, 1247); xxvii.78 (p. 46, 1251); xxviii.79 (p. 47, 1279); xxviii.81 (p. 48, 1326); xxviii.82 (p. 48, 1339); xxxiv.101 (p. 58, 1742); xxxiv.108 (p. 61, 1847); xxxiv.108 (p. 61, 1848); xxxiv.108 (p. 61, 1854).
15. Spec car I.i.1 (p. 13, 8); i.1 (p. 13, 12); i.2 (p. 13, 23); i.2 (p. 13, 31 and 33; twice); ii.4 (p. 14, 62); ii.6 (p. 15, 85–86); ii.7 (p. 15, 96); ii.7 (p. 15, 101); ii.7 (p. 15, 104); iii.9 (p. 16, 123); iii.9 (p. 16, 124); iii.9 (p. 16, 126); iv.10 (p. 16, 136); vi.17 (p. 19, 247); vi.17 (p. 19, 248); vi.17 (p. 19, 250); vi.17 (pp. 19–20, 252–63; twelve times); vi.18 (p. 20, 265–75; fourteen times); vi.19 (p. 20, 276–87; eight times); vi.20 (p. 20, 294–96; three times); vi.21 (pp. 20–21, 300–305; four times); vi.22 (p. 21, 317); viii.26 (p. 23, 375); xi.33 (p. 25, 482); xii.37 (p. 27, 551); xv.46 (p. 31, 687); xvii.50 (p. 33, 758); xviii.51 (p. 33, 766); xxiii.66 (p. 40, 1043); xxiii.66 (p. 40, 1050); xxiii.67 (p. 41, 1061); xxvi.77 (p. 45, 1214); xxvi.77 (p. 45, 1215); xxviii.79 (p. 47, 1279); xxviii.79 (p. 47, 1293); xxviii.81 (p. 48, 1321); xxxii.90 (p. 52, 1506); xxxii.90 (p. 53, 1515); xxxii.91 (p. 53, 1529); xxxiv.98 (p. 57, 1680); xxxiv.100 (p. 58, 1710–11); xxxiv.100 (p. 58, 1717); xxxiv.102 (p. 58, 1745); xxxiv.102 (p. 58, 1746); xxxiv.111 (p. 62, 1897); xxxiv.112 (p. 63, 1935); xxxiv.113 (p. 64, 1964); xxxiv.114 (p. 64, 1973).
16. Spec car I.xvii.50 (p. 33, 759); xxvi.76 (p. 45, 1210).
17. Spec car I, xvii.50 (p. 33, 759).
18. Spec car I.v.16 (p. 19, 239); xii.37 (p. 27, 549); xvii.50 (p. 33, 756); xxviii.81 (p. 48, 1329–30); xxix.83 (p. 48, 1346); xxix.85 (p. 49, 1395).
19. Spec car I.vi.21 (p. 21, 302); xxiv.98 (p. 56, 1664); xxiv.98 (p. 56, 1666).
20. Spec car I.i.2 (p. 13, 31); xviii.51 (p. 33, 775); xxv.71 (p. 42, 1124); xxxiv.113 (p. 64, 1960).

21. Spec car I, Praef., 4 (p. 6, 121); v. 16 (p. 19, 229); vi.18 (p. 20, 265).
22. Spec car I.i.2 (p. 13, 18); iii.9 (p. 16, 28–29); v. 16 (p. 19, 227); vii.22 (p. 21, 311); vii.22 (p. 21, 315); xxxi.88 (p. 52, 1485); xxxiv.106 (p. 60, 1805); xxxiv.109 (p. 61, 1858); xxxiv.109 (p. 61, 1859–60); xxxiv.109 (p. 61, 1860); xxxiv.111 (p. 62, 1900); xxxiv.112 (p. 63, 1915); xxxiv.112 (p. 63, 1937); xxxiv.112 (p. 63, 1944).
23. Spec car I.vii.22 (p. 21, 310–11, 317–18, 320–29).
24. Spec car I.i.2 (pp. 13–14, 16–37); v.16 (p. 19, 227); vi.20 (p. 20, 294–96); viii.25 (p. 22, 357–64); xvi.49 (p. 32, 718–32); xvii.50 (p. 33, 755–60); xix.54–55 (pp. 34–35, 817–50); xxiii.67 (p. 41, 1059–70); xxviii.79 and 81 (pp. 47–48; 1279, 1293, 1321); xxxiii.94 (p. 55, 1606).
25. Spec car I.xviii.51–52 (p. 33, 766–69, 772–79).
26. Iesu III.23; *Opera*, p. 270, lines 148–49.
27. SC 23.15; SBOp 1:148.
28. Spec car I.xviii.52 (pp. 33–34, lines 779–80, 783–93).

WHY SCANDINAVIA?
BERNARD, ESKIL AND CISTERCIAN EXPANSION
IN THE NORTH 1140-80

Brian Patrick McGuire

If you arrive in Copenhagen on a sunny May morning and go directly across the street from the Central Station to the tulip beds and lakes of the Tivoli gardens, then Denmark, and all of southern Scandinavia, can seem like a fairy-tale straight out of Hans Christian Andersen. But if you live, as I do, far out in the countryside, and from November to April experience the alternation of freeze and thaw that punctuates the south scandinavian winter, then you begin to understand how surprising it is that the Cistercians managed to stay in the part of Europe that medieval Denmark once encompassed.[1] Southern Scandinavia is said to have the worst climate in Europe, and after more than a decade here, I am beginning to believe the truth of this assertion. There is no time of year, not even at the supposed height of summer in June, when one can count on warm, sunny weather. July can be cold, wet and windy. The Danes have a saying about 'the day it was summer last year', but even more important for a monastic order that preferred solid buildings, freeze and thaw for more than half the year mean that cracks and holes develop even in the best-built structures. The monks and especially their laybrothers must have had to spend a good part of their summers in repairing the ravages of their winters.

Besides the unpredictable and undependable weather of southern Scandinavia, another factor that mitigated against cistercian foundations here was the presence of well-established benedictine houses.[2] Denmark was a country that in wealth could hardly have supported the number of monastic foundations that Burgundy could harbour. At several locations, the Cistercians in the North ended up by replacing benedictine communities, which in some cases put up resistance to their removal. In cistercian literature from the end of the twelfth or the early thirteenth century, these benedictine houses are described as having been decadent, but this is almost certainly cistercian propaganda, legitimizing the cistercian replacement of these houses.[3] If we consider the dozen or so benedictine houses that existed in Denmark by the early 1140s, when the first Cistercians arrived, the areas of Jutland, Fünen, Zealand and Skane had a satisfactory number of monastic institutions to fulfill the need of local aristocrats for solid fortresses of prayer.[4] And yet the Cistercians came and found enough goodwill and material wealth to settle ten new houses by the end of the century.

Another factor which detracted from the chances of success the Cistercians had in Scandinavia is that they were not needed here to perform the function of missionaries in a non-christian land. This was the case on the south shores of the Baltic and in Northern Germany. The monks arrived from France in the 1140s and 1150s in a part of Europe that had been christian, at least in name, since the end of the tenth century. They thus came to Scandinavia with no clearly defined political or ecclesiastical role. They were invited as monks to a country that already had monastic foundations and had no need for missionaries.

Since the beginning of this century, danish historians have provided various explanations for the arrival and stay of the Cistercians in their part of Scandinavia. Since the beginning of the 1950s, these explanations have tended to minimize the role of the archbishop of Lund from 1138–1177, Eskil.[5] In a number of important studies, it has been pointed out that the material contribution made by Eskil to the new cistercian houses either cannot be established at all or was minimal. Eskil, who in the 1930s was seen as the strong churchman who defended Lund against royal encroachment and used the international order of the Cistercians as natural allies, has in recent years been reduced to a rather pompous old fool, who was good at telling tall tales to the writer Herbert at Clairvaux after his retirement there, but who exaggerated his own importance in the danish church and in power politics. Behind this analysis of Eskil is a perennial debate among danish and swedish historians concerning the veracity of the twelfth-century clerical historian and literary genius Saxo.[6] This formidable writer did not like Eskil at all and even made fun of him. It is as if modern danish historians subconsciously have felt obliged to choose sides between the clerical secular tradition represented by Saxo and the clerical monastic tradition found in Eskil and 'his' Cistercians. Usually Saxo wins, for his toughness and intelligence appeal to a modern materialistic mentality.

It is not my purpose here to defend Eskil or to attack Saxo, merely to provide some suggestions about the success of the Cistercians in settling in Denmark. In recent research, the monks are rightly no longer considered to have been Eskil's minions carrying out his ecclesiastical policies. Eskil's contributions to the spread of the order in Denmark is now distinguished from his involvement with the international order through his many stays at Clairvaux. In what follows, I shall show that even though Eskil's close bond to Clairvaux and especially to Saint Bernard has long been noted by researchers, the content and meaning of this friendship deserve further consideration. Eskil must be seen more fully in the context of cistercian spirituality and of bernardine friendship. In dealing with such factors I am not setting out to 'debunk' the usual materialistic analysis of Eskil and the early Cistercians in Denmark. I accept the most recent conclusions, which show how little land or money he actually gave most of the foundations that were made during his archbishopric. I also agree that it is misleading to speak of a cistercian party in mid-twelfth century danish politics with Eskil at its head. But I shall try to get behind the scenes and see what it is that could have motivated a man like Eskil to get involved with the Cistercians in the first place. I want to move our focus back from the late sources of the 1170s or 1190s to the events of the crucial decades when the Cistercians arrived in the North, the 1140s and 1150s.

Bernard the Friend

It is almost impossible to get behind Bernard to the very first Cistercians, but recent work, especially Chrysogonus Waddell's brilliant study of a letter by Stephen Harding,[7] enables us to see Bernard's first abbot at Cîteaux in a clearer light. The letter reveals a man steeped in the language of the Bible and able to use it in order to be a diplomat of the most subtle school. It also points to a man who used classical commonplaces about friendship as part of this diplomacy.[8] But the letter does not indicate that Stephen provided Bernard with the language of friendship and love that is so important in Bernard's writings and especially in his letters. Similarly, if we look at Stephen Harding's *Carta Caritatis*, we find love, but not Bernard's type of affectionate and emotional involvement with his brothers. Stephen's love is the type that binds the communities of monks together in clear legal terms. The central word is not *caritas*, but *carta*, the pact or agreement that is necessary so that mutual care and concern are possible among the related monasteries.[9] Finally, if we look at the *Exordium Parvum*, we find the only kind of love it mentions is that which the first Cistercians had for the harsh demands of the Rule.[10] All these factors point towards the same conclusions, that the earliest Cistercians, with Stephen in the lead, were too concerned about building up a monastic organization in strict harmony with the Rule of Saint Benedict and with clear juridical links among the monasteries to have had much time or energy left over for the language and practice of affectionate love and friendship. Only with the coming of Bernard and his family and friends does this sweet love definitively enter into the cistercian consciousness. Once Bernard is there, the language of love and friendship become so much a part of the cistercian mode of expression that it becomes almost unthinkable that it ever was any different. But from what we can see of Stephen Harding in the very earliest sources, love is the legal bond that results from good relations among monasteries and not the affectionate bond that grows up among individual monks within monasteries. Such love Stephen may well have felt and cultivated, but it is only in Bernard that friendship and affection become a part of the literary fabric of cistercian life.

When Bernard wrote to Archbishop Eskil of Lund in the early 1150s, he used this language of love. Bernard had almost certainly not yet met Eskil, and yet he could address him as his dearest friend:

> Scripta et salutationes vestras immo affectiones cordis vestri tam libenter suscepi; quam specialiter et diligo vos et diligor a vobis.

> Your letter and greetings, or rather your expressions of affection, were most welcome because of the special love you and I have for each other.[11]

The language Bernard uses had long since become a collection of commonplaces for him in his letters. There is nothing new or unique in the themes he builds on in the course of his letter to Eskil: the sharing of love, the concern for the friend in his need, the desire to see him face to face and to talk to him but the use of the letter as the next-best solution, the hope that his feelings will be conveyed by the emissary bringing the letter back to the friend, and irritation over the requirement that the letter be ended because of the call of secular business. How many similar letters Bernard wrote during his career, and how artificial his language can sound, for we know how many literary artifices he manipulated in order to gain the effect he desired. Eskil must have known this too, for he had the same ability. In a letter written to the danish church from captivity in Germany in 1157, Eskil evidenced a similar command of the language of love and the use of literary figures. Eskil and Bernard were both masters of the epistolary idiom of their time in the service of their ideals.[12]

But Bernard's letter to Eskil is by no means a non-committal letter of friendship to a man he never before had seen. Bernard not only expresses his affection for Eskil. He promises to take care of an important matter about which Eskil had written him. Bernard does not specify the problem, but his concern expressed for Eskil's *molestias et anxietates* points to an affair of great seriousness. Until recently it was thought that it was a question either of Eskil's desire to visit Bernard at Clairvaux or his desire to leave his office and retire there. But now it is seen that Eskil's *secretum* was his fear that the archbishop of Hamburg-Bremen, Hartvig, would succeed in asserting the primacy of his see over Lund and removing the archbishopric from Eskil.[13] This had happened once before in 1133, and because of the pope's need for the support of the german ruler in the 1140s, it was a very great danger. The death of Conrad III in February of 1152, however, removed the central support to the spread of Hamburg-Bremen, and in a letter to the cistercian pope Eugenius III, Bernard indicated that there now was no reason to pursue the matter further.[14] From Bernard's response to Eskil, it is clear that he intended to take the archbishop of Lund's side and to use the cistercian monk William at the papal court to pursue the matter.[15] Bernard shows every sympathy towards Eskil and takes him into the european net of his friendships and political-ecclesiastical alliances.

One question that arises here is why Bernard was being so friendly to this distant archbishop. No one has really considered this matter, for the letter has usualy been taken at face value as a typical declaration of friendship from one prominent twelfth-century churchman to another. It is perhaps not surprising in the light of twelfth-century monastic literary standards that Bernard wrote so passionately to a man he had never before seen. Anselm did the same. But Anselm was writing to prospective candidates to the monastic life. He thus could idealize his correspondents and convert them into beloved friends because he hoped they would soon join his favoured band.[16] Similarly Bernard could write with such affection to Eskil because the archbishop of Lund already had seen to it that three cistercian houses had been founded in Scandinavia in the 1140s: Alvastra, and the settlement that ended up at Nydala, both in Sweden, and Herrisvad in Scania.

Because of our lack of sources from these foundations, we cannot determine the exact nature of Eskil's
contribution, but as archbishop of Lund and metropolitan,
he had to give his consent to these foundations. One
danish historian has gone so far as to speak of cooperation between the Swedish king Sverker and Archbishop
Eskil is starting Alvastra and Nydala.[17] Such an
assertion is based on likelihood rather than on any
contemporary source. We have only a thirteenth-century
narrative which attributes these foundations to the
swedish king and his queen Alvilde.[18] But if we look
at the cistercian foundations made in Denmark later
in the twelfth century, in the 1160s, 1170s and 1180s,
it is clear that almost every time, the diocesan bishop
had a central role; so it would be justified to assume
that the same thing happened in the 1140s.[19] In the
case of Sweden, Lund retained metropolitan rights
until the establishment of an archbishopric at Uppsala
in the 1160s (appropriately with a Cistercian from
Herrisvad, Stephen, as Eskil's choice for the first
archbishop). The swedish monarchy had to turn to
Eskil in order to establish new monasteries. At Herrisvad
Cistercians installed themselves geographically close
to Lund itself, with its well-established monastic houses
and its cathedral chapter, which Eskil in the same
decade was expanding. It is impossible to imagine
that such a potential competitor in lands and donors
would have found a place in the landscape of Scania
without the blessing and cooperation of the archbishop
of Lund.

When Bernard wrote to Eskil, he wrote to the
man ˎwho had helped three new cistercian foundations
on their way in Scandinavia, and so he may have
felt a debt that could be repaid by his offer to help
Eskil with the matter that weighed so heavily on the
archbishop. This explanation of Bernard's behaviour
agrees with that given by Adriaan Bredero in a seminal
article on the personality of Bernard: his behaviour
can usually be explained not in terms of deep psychological motives but through his desire at all times and
in all places to spread the cistercian Order.[20] Wherever
Bernard went, new cistercian houses sprang up. He
never got to Scandinavia, but through men like Eskil,
Bernard could ensure that the Cistercians got there
too. Once they did so, he felt a debt to Eskil that
he expresses in his declaration of friendship, and
in a concrete offer of political help with the cistercian
pope. From Bernard's letter to Eugenius, it is clear
that he did what he promised.

It might be worthwhile at this point to look more

closely at Bernard's letter, for he uses language
that apparently had a strong effect on the archbishop.
Expressing his delight at Eskil's devotion to him,
Bernard asks how he can repay him. This can be
done only through Our Lord, who has repaid Bernard's
debts and who enables Eskil to seek out Bernard in
affection:

> Et si ego retribuere non potero. Non est
> mortuus retributor meus; quia dominus retribuet
> pro me. Dominus inquam in quo et pro quo
> tanta nos devotione complecteris; tanta stringis
> affectione.

> And if I cannot repay you, then he who
> repays for me had not died, for the Lord
> will repay for me. The Lord, I say, in and
> for whom you embrace us with such devotion
> and bind us with so much affection.[21]

Bernard's idea is simple: Eskil seeks Bernard
in the love he has for Christ, and it is Christ who
has provided the initial repayment that makes all
love possible. Through Christ both love and the payment
of debts are possible. Bernard is dealing with the
functioning of the act of redemption in human life
and relationships. His language is based on Psalm
137:8: *Dominus retribuet pro me.* Repayment for Bernard
meant not so much a legal act but a movement of
love and devotion from one human being to another.
When Eskil wrote from captivity in 1157 to the
danish church and described his situation, he said
that he did not want to be ransomed, for Christ already
had bought him, and the whole church, back through
his redemption:

> Ego etenim, semel Christi sanguine redemptus.
> iterum non requiro redimi....Sanguis eius
> redempcio mea. Sanguis eius precium meum.
> Indignum est ut sub precio redigar, cuius
> precium sine precio est.

> I indeed have already been redeemed by
> the blood of Christ, and I do not need to
> be redeemed again...His blood is my redemption.
> His blood is my price. It is unworthy that
> I be given a price, for the price of redemption
> is without price.[22]

This central passage of Eskil's letter has been seen
in recent danish historiography as an expression of
a magnate's fear of being reduced to servile status

through ransom.[23] Although such an interpretation
can cast light on a possibly subconscious appeal by
Eskil to his class origins, I find it of much greater
significance that Eskil here interprets the act of redemption in a way that points to Bernard. In Bernard's
mind, Christ is the only being who can repay our
debts. Through him, all debts are cancelled out and
human and divine love are made possible.[24] Eskil
is saying the same in his letter. His vocabulary is
different, but his meaning alike. Only through Christ
comes redemption. His blood has paid for us, and
so any other form of payment for us is in vain. By
using this argument, Eskil can emphasize his own
inner freedom as well as the freedom of the scandinavian
church from german aggression: *infamis est redempcio,
qua libertas perit ecclesie, qua servitus comparatur*
(That redemption is infamous by which the freedom
of the church perishes and servitude is purchased).

A comparison of the two letters provides no verbal
agreement and thus no proof that Eskil was borrowing
directly from Bernard in developing his idea of liberty
and ransom. But it is nevertheless clear that both
Eskil and Bernard were very much caught up in formulat-
ing how redemption functions. For both of them, the
sufferings and death of Christ make up for all human
weakness and failure. They give us a position of
strength and hope in coping with the demands of life
and death. Eskil and Bernard spoke the same language,
both in emotional and in intellectual terms.

When Eskil finally came to Clairvaux for the
first time in 1152 or early 1153 and met Bernard,
he made a deep impression not just on the abbot but
also on his secretary, Geoffrey of Auxerre. Geoffrey's
letter to Eskil on the death of Bernard is one of the
most famous pieces of cistercian literature, because
it was affixed at the begining of what became the
fifth book of the *Vita Prima*.[25] In writing to Eskil
about the death of Bernard, Geoffrey was addressing
the entire secular church, but it is still significant
that he chose Eskil as his correspondent as a representative of the non-monastic church which would grieve
with the Cistercians on the death of their beloved
Bernard.

Already on his first trip to Clairvaux in 1152
or early 1153, Eskil made sure that the Cistercians
realized how expensive and difficult it was for him
to come down all the way from the North. In Geoffrey's
description of Eskil's stay there, we find the same
boastful, self-centered person who emerges from the
stories told to Herbert in the late 1170s, when Eskil
had come to Clairvaux for good:

Nam de expensis dicere non est magnum,
quamvis eumdem audierimus protestantem,
quod expenderit in itinere ipso argenti marcas
amplius quam sexcentas.

For it is not a central concern to speak
of his expenses, though we heard him claim
that on the journey itself he had expended
more than six-hundred silver marks.[26]

Eskil did not just boast, he also wept with the
monks. He showed respect not just for Bernard but
also for 'the least of those brothers', for Geoffrey
himself. Eskil found at Clairvaux the love, acceptance,
and harmony that he apparently never could realize
at home in Lund, where he constantly was at odds
with the various ruling cliques of Denmark.

Eskil's success at Clairvaux was probably also
due to the fact that he filled a need that Bernard
may have felt after the death of his Irish friend
Malachy, also a heroic figure from a distant land
who had sought out the sanctity and friendship of
Bernard, helped establish cistercian monasteries in
his country, and had to fight against the wiles of
a barbaric, non-latin people. Malachy had been exciting,
exotic, and, most important of all for Bernard, totally
devoted to the Cistercians. After his death in 1148
Bernard wrote his biography, a clear indication of
the importance he attached to Malachy's work for
the church and for the Cistercians.[27] In some ways
Eskil could have been a second Malachy for Bernard.[28]
There was not time to establish so close a friendship,
but after Bernard's death, Geoffrey could inherit Eskil
as Bernard's friend, write to him, and cultivate him
as a great and powerful churchman who furthered
the cause of the Cistercians in the North. So began
the Clairvaux tradition that emphasized the link between
Eskil and Bernard and which culminates in the stories
about Eskil included in the *Exordium Magnum Cisterciense*.[29] These are nothing more than a medley of
the tales told by Geoffrey and by Herbert of Clairvaux,
but they emphasize the fact that the Cistercians of
Clairvaux took Eskil seriously, respected him for his
friendship with Bernard, and felt that in commemorating
him they were securing one of the foundations of their
Order.

Cistercian Spiritual Power and Scandinavian Magnates

With this broader understanding of the significance
of the contact between Eskil and Bernard, we can
return to our original question: why did the Cistercians

come to Scandinavia, and how were they able to remain
in such a hostile climate, where Benedictines already
abounded? The answer is clear. The monks came and
stayed because the establishment wanted and felt a
need for them. In the case of Alvastra we find that
King Sverker gave the monks land right next to one
of his residences. He would be sure to have them
at hand for all his needs.[30] It has been said that
the Cistercians were invited to Scandinavia because
they were the church's fashionable monastic order
in the early twelfth century, and this is certainly
true. Also it has been pointed out that the french
monks were wanted as a necessary counterweight to
german influence and hegemony in Scandinavia.[31]
But these two explanations make use of relatively
superficial cultural phenomena without going into
the depths of human emotions and social needs. In
the case of Eskil and Bernard we can see two complex
personalities at work, influencing and complementing
each other. We have no similar sources to reveal the
minds and mentalities of danish kings and magnates
in the same period, but it is still clear that these
people were willing to offer money and land to the
Cistercians because they found in them a locus of
spiritual power that they felt they needed for themselves,
their families, their country. The Cistercians were
attractive not just as French and modern in the twelfth
century. They were necessary participants and helpers
for any christian magnate concerned with the salvation
of his own soul and those of his family members.
The Cistercians alone could manifest the confidence
that all their members, if they lived according to
the Rule, would gain eternal salvation.[32] They were
communities of heaven-bound men on earth, and no
scandinavian magnate could afford to be without them.

An indication of the spiritual power manifested
by the Cistercians is provided by a story told by
Geoffrey of Auxerre, which he says he obtained from
the men who accompanied Eskil on a visit to Clairvaux
in 1155.[33] Geoffrey included the story because it manifested the spiritual power of Bernard's relics, but for
any of the danish magnates who lived near Esrum,
where the events probably took place, the miracle
could have provided a guarantee that the new community
was in possession of a source of unlimited power.
The story is that one of Eskil's relatives, probably
Niels Grevsun (also called Count Niels), who is known
from a donation to Esrum, decided to reform his ways
and entered this cistercian house.[34] Once there, he
apparently became a good brother and died in the
bosom of the community. At this juncture the devil

is said to have become angry at the loss of a soul
he had long thought would be his, and so he invaded
the body of another brother *(ex ejusdem...liberatione
animae, quam ex multis diebus irrepabiliter sese occu-
passe credebat, iram magnam concipiens...)*. His seizure
appears to have manifested itself as we today might
experience an epileptic fit: involuntary bodily movements,
ravings, and total loss of motor control:

> He no longer spoke the language which he
> before had known but a new one which none
> of those standing around him knew. And
> when they understood nothing which he said,
> they realized that he was freely and without
> hindrance speaking out words that made
> sense, so that there was no doubt for them
> that he was using another language. After
> some hours, when the brothers in violent
> confusion were thinking anxiously about what
> to do, one of them through divine inspiration
> thought of a salvific counsel, and ordered
> the sacred relics which had been brought
> there the same year by the archbishop himself,
> the hair and beard, as well as a tooth of
> our blessed father Bernard. These were to
> be put on the man's chest. When this was
> done, the evil spirit began in the German
> language through the man's mouth to cry
> out:
>   'Take it away, take it away, remove
> Bernard!' And he said, 'Alas, how heavy
> you have become, Bernard, how weighty,
> that you are unbearable for me? When the
> brother had said this and similar things
> for a while in crying out, he became silent
> for a moment and then he opened his eyes
> as if he were waking from a deep sleep,
> was amazed at the fact that the brothers
> were standing around him and that he was
> bound by chains, and asked why they were
> treating him in such a shameful manner or
> what had happened. From that hour he got
> back his original health of mind and body
> through the merits of the Holy Father, and
> remembering nothing at all about how he
> had been in such a serious condition or
> what he had said.[35]

I have given a complete translation of the passage
because it provides such a clear description of the
interaction between the relics of Bernard, the fear

of the community, and the violent sufferings of the brother. The miracle is Geoffrey's main interest, but ours is the explanation of the devil's attack by the belief that he was furious at the loss of the soul of a danish aristocrat whose evil life prior to his entrance to a cistercian house had more or less determined that he belonged to the devil. The devil's rage and its dire consequences for the brother and the community could be overcome only by the relics of Saint Bernard. It was the community itself and its way of life that initially provoked the devil to such behaviour. However much we have to concede that this is a typically cistercian story with an international flavour, far removed in its telling from the wilds of Denmark, we must also admit that we get here a glimpse of the power that could be exercised through cistercian piety and bernardine relics.

In the stories told by Eskil to Geoffrey and to Herbert, the devil is very much present. In the minds of the Clairvaux monks, the devil was used to carrying off the souls of scandinavian magnates, whose lives were bloody and whose Christianity was superficial. This attitude is also reflected in a remarkable story told in the thirteenth century by the cistercian chronicler Alberic of Trois Fontaines. He told how the cries of the souls of dead magnates killed at the danish battle at Fotevig in 1134 were heard by shepherds on Iceland.[36] Alberic claims that the story was told at the General Chapter, and even though this is unlikely, because there were no scandinavian Cistercian monasteries at the time, the story underlines the cistercian belief that men whose lives are based on violence and self-will end up being taken away by the devil or his helpers. Only the almost unlimited spiritual power of cistercian prayer and bernardine relics could put a stop to the devil's incursions.

Once again we can turn to Eskil for an indication of the mental world that characterized danish magnates in the early twelfth century. As a young man at school in Hildesheim in Germany, he became ill and nearly died.[37] In the midst of his fever, he dreamed that he was burning in hell. A door appeared, and through it he entered a room where he met an angry woman who told him that he was going to burn forever because he had not given her sufficient attention and devotion. Eskil, already aware of his social position, offered to buy his freedom from hellfire by giving her all the gold his family owned. The woman, however, had no desire for gold: she demanded that he found monasteries for her. Once again we have a story which in being written down was fully integrated into a cistercian context. Herbert of Clairvaux, and after him Conrad of Eberbach, used the story to explain Eskil's foundations of cistercian houses in Scandinavia. But if we assume that Eskil really did have a traumatic dream in his teenage years, one that he remembered decades later when he was an old man at Clairvaux, it becomes clear that when he was sick and thought to be dying, one of his main fears reached out of his subconscious and into a dream that remained with him for the rest of his life. The young Eskil was afraid of going to hell. For him the christian religion and even Mary herself were primarily reminders of the danger of eternal damnation. Only by placating them could Eskil hope to avoid this awful fire.

Eskil tried to ransom himself with gold when he was a boy. As an adult and archbishop of Lund, he refused any offer of gold in order to ransom himself. By then he had come to accept Bernard's tenet that our ransom comes only through Christ. In Eskil's language, Christ has already paid the price that no one else could pay. Bernard helped Eskil emerge from his old, punitive interpretation of Christianity, where the main object is to avoid hell, and to experience a newer, more affectionate variety of Christianity in which the love of God is made manifest through our redemption in Christ.[38] It is my contention that Eskil's boyhood dream, much more than his adult letter from captivity, puts us into contact with the minds and hearts of his fellow scandinavian magnates. Eskil did not want to burn in hell, so he would promise Mary anything. She did not want money. She preferred monasteries in her honour. What better could Eskil and his fellow magnates do than to found cistercian houses to the glory of God and the honour of the Blessed Virgin Mary? The devils that threatened, lay in wait, grew furious if they did not catch the souls of the magnates; these awful creatures could no longer cast them into the volcanic fires of Iceland once Mary extended her protection and ensured the effects of her Son's redemption for them.

It is perhaps a statement of the obvious that aristocrats founded monasteries because they were afraid of burning in hell. But truisms need to be asserted when they tend to be forgotten or ignored. Recent scandinavian historiography has emphasized materialistic motives to such a point that basic human impulses of fear and hope have been forgotten or ignored.[39] Perhaps some historians have also felt that we simply do not know enough about such motives in history. But however limited the scandinavian sources may be, they still indirectly tell us something about

the men responsible for the first cistercian houses.
If we allow Eskil to act as a representative of the
scandinavian–magnate mentality, then it is clear from
the stories he told Herbert in the 1170s that the retired
archbishop was still very much caught up in the punitive
interpretation of Christianity. He was obsessed with
pointing out how men who opposed him came to bad
ends. A case in point is the bishop of Ribe, Elias,
who favoured the german candidate for the papacy
during the schism of the 1160s. Eskil delighted in
describing the man's horrible death. Or he could
tell about an adulterer whom he had warned to take
back his rightful wife. When the man refused, he
was found, together with his mistress and their two
children, dead in their beds. Eskil claimed that once
he had issued his excommunication, the devil had
been able to take control of their bodies and to suffocate
the unfortunate.[40]

The Eskil who emerges from these tales, even
if we subtract Herbert's enjoyment of lurid detail,
is not a very lovable person. He is a man of strong
opinions who was used to fighting for them. He exulted
in Old Testament fashion over the defeat of his enemies
and saw in their downfall an expression of divine
will. Here Eskil is still an exponent of old–style punitive
Christianity. But as R. W. Southern has so aptly
shown, the Cistercians would be just as strict and
unyielding when it came to matters of law as they
were sweet and loving to each other.[41] Eskil could
identify with such behaviour, for it suited well an
insecure existence where friends were essential and
enemies had to be fought with all available weapons.

Eskil is but a single individual in the Scandinavia
of the twelfth century, however important the role
he played in church and society. But through the
stories he told we can at least approach a sense of
what it was like to be a magnate, whether lay or
religious, in this world. There was always the danger
of fire and pain, the constant reminder that a way
of life based on the use of physical force where the
constant likelihood of killing or being killed easily
could result in eternal damnation. This attitude is
expressed in Eskil's story of his two uncles, who
went on a pilgrimage to Jerusalem and sought for,
and received, a swift death in the East. One of the
brothers, a notorious magnate, had repented of his
sins and asked for death because he could not face
the prospect of returning home and being confronted
by all the temptations of his everyday life.[42] Similarly,
Eskil could have a vision of one of his brothers who
died of a sword wound before he could receive communion.

One day as Eskil prayed alone in the church at Clairvaux, he saw his brother. Only his head and shoulders
were visible, but they were enough to show his suffering.
Eskil could recount his vision in good cistercian style
to the assembled brothers in chapter and ask for
their prayers for an unhappy soul.

For Eskil Clairvaux could be a house of prayer
for the souls of his family, just as his successor
as archbishop of Lund, Absalon, could cultivate the
cistercian house at Soro as a house of prayer and
burial for his entire family, the rich and influential
Whites. Both Absalon and Eskil looked to cistercian
spirituality for solid guarantees that they and those
they loved would not end up in hell. There is no
need to seek further motivation for the founding of
cistercian houses in Denmark and Sweden. In the twelfth
century only the Cistercians could provide assurances
of the limitless spiritual power that the northern bishops
and lay magnates needed for themselves and their
families. Whether it was a matter of Bernard's tooth,
of the prayers for the dead at Clairvaux, or a burial
place in the church at Soro, the Cistercians could
offer the scandinavian establishment the hope that
the strict tenets of the still relatively new christian
religion did not exclude them from entrance to heaven.

Here other cistercian literature could be included
to show that laymen really were afraid of hell. It
is in the mid-twelfth century, for example, that the
story of the purgatory of Saint Patrick in Ireland
arises from the meeting of a knight with a cistercian
milieu.43 At about the same time, a child who later
became a Knight Templar in Germany had a nightmare
about how the devil came to take him because he
had stolen a small sum of money. Decades later he
told Caesarius of Heisterbach about the experience.44
Such stories are taken from other parts of Europe
than the southern Scandinavia on which we have been
concentrating. Here it is essential to realize that
there must have been magnates in the North who looked
upon Christianity almost as a foreign element. They
had their own saga traditions and pagan heroes,
and even if Christianity had come to stay, it still
was the religion of the south. The question was how
to come to terms with the demands it made, and the
best way to do this was to incorporate into daily
life the most immediate and convincing manifestations
of christian power. If the countryside was full of
devils, then what better way to deal with them than
by populating it with cistercian houses? The Cistercians
were preferred not just because they were fashionable
but because, in the twelfth-century spiritual sense,

they were virile.
      Eskil's dreams and visions, his tales about his
experiences as archbishop, all are translated into
cistercian language and yet still bring us into contact
with the scandinavian reception of Christianity and
especially of monasticism in the twelfth century. It
is probably no accident that Anselm of Canterbury's
central childhood dream, as told by Eadmer, concerned
his admission into the court of heaven, while Eskil
dreamed about his entrance into hell. For Anselm
heaven was a place where he went to complain about
negligent labourers, but the Alps were just outside
Aosta and he still felt as a southern european, that
heaven was close-by. For Eskil hell was much more
immediate, and only a life involved with the foundation
of monastic houses could push the nightmare into the
background.
      The Cistercians led Eskil to Bernard, and there
he found a man for whom the idea of heaven was
as convincing and vivid as that of hell. When Geoffrey
of Auxerre wrote to Eskil about Bernard's death, he
could develop this belief in heaven and express a
limitless hope and trust in Bernard's salvation. Through
Bernard the entire Cistercian world could find its
way to heaven. He nullified the devil's power and
became their path first to Mary and through her to
Jesus. We can only guess at Eskil's personal excitement
at this perception, but the language of his letter
from captivity shows that Bernard's world of redemption
and freedom through Christ had become his own. In
Eskil Bernard found a northern hero who could help
spread his Cistercians. In Bernard Eskil found a
southern saint who could help him and his countrymen
to find their way to heaven.
            *   *   *   *   *
*A New Chronology for Eskil's Involvement
with the Cistercians*

      In writing about the coming of the Cistercians
to Denmark, I have long been bedevilled by the problem
of when the first Cistercians came from Clairvaux
and arrived at Esrum on Zealand. In an article on
Esrum and in my book on the Cistercians in Denmark,
I accepted the assertion of Professor Niels Skyum-Nielsen
that Esrum never had been a benedictine community
prior to its becoming cistercian, as once was thought
to be the case.[45] This view had been the result of
a passage in a papal confirmation of Esrum properties
in 1228, where villages are said to have belonged
to Esrum before the cistercian foundation there.[46]
According to Skyum-Nielsen, this phrase was inserted

by the papal chancellery to excuse the fact that a cistercian house right from the start had owned villages, something that was forbidden in the earliest cistercian statutes of 1134. Therefore the phrase about an earlier house was a fiction, and Esrum was Cistercian from its start.

The problem with this explanation is that several earlier papal bulls for Esrum mention the presence of villages owned by the abbey without explaining them away in similar terms.[47] Also, if we compare developments at Esrum with what was happening elsewhere in the Order, it is clear that by the 1150s, it was generally accepted that cistercian houses could own villages. The most famous case is discussed by Louis Lekai. The cistercian pope Eugenius III defended to the General Chapter the fact that his own roman abbey of Tre Fontane owned villages, and the Chapter gave in to his arguments.[48] After this time, there is no official removal of the prohibition from 1134 against abbeys' owning whole villages, but there is plentiful evidence that this was a common practice. Thus there would have been no reason at so late a date as the 1220s, when the impulses of cistercian asceticism and renewal had long since diminished, to hide the fact that Esrum as a cistercian house only owned villages because they had been acquired while it still was benedictine. In mentioning an earlier, non-cistercian foundation at Esrum, the papal chancellery and the Esrum monks had nothing to gain except the assertion of an historical fact that otherwise cannot be confirmed. For we have no early chronicle of Esrum's twelfth-century history.

We do know, however, that during the reign of Erik Lam (1137–46), Eskil bought property from the king in Northern Zealand and handed it over to a monastic foundation there. We have no contemporary charter, but the event is mentioned in a charter from King Svend Grathe for Esrum.[49] The language of this charter is usually interpreted as showing that Eskil simply had bought the land in preparation for the later foundation of a cistercian house at Esrum. His purchase would have taken place at some time between 1137 and 1146, but Esrum's foundation is normally placed at about 1150, and at the latest by 27 December 1151, when our friend the cistercian William obtained from Eugenius III a papal bull of foundation for Esrum with himself as abbot.[50]

In Svend Grathe's charter, dated between 1151 and 1157, Eskil's purchase of property is said to have taken place at the same time as there was a community of monks at Esrum:

Quippe beate memorie Eskildus sancte Lundensis
ecclesie archiepiscopus. villam prefatam ab
antecessore meo Herico rege, precariando
acquisivit, et usui immo necessitati *fratrum
ibidem Deo servientium* substituit.

For Eskil, the fondly remembered archbishop
of the holy church of Lund, acquired the
said village from my predecessor Eric as
precarial property and handed it over to
the use, or more correctly, the needs, of
the brothers who serve God there.

Most experts have been concerned with the phrase
beate memorie, which later would indicate that the
person mentioned was dead, but as the editors of
the *Diplomatarium Danicum* point out, the expression
in the mid-twelfth century can be merely a term of
respect for a living person. What is problematical
here is the translation of the phrase I have italicized.
Did the man who drafted the charter in Latin lack
a proper sense of nuance, and should he have added
an essential adverb like *iam* to distinguish between
past events and what now existed at Esrum? Taken
at face value the charter points to the presence of
'brothers serving God there' at Esrum in the early
1140s when the land was purchased.

On the basis of the language of Svend Grathe's
charter and that of the 1228 papal privilege for Esrum,
I think it is time to return to the assertion that Eskil
was involved with a benedictine house at Esrum before
it became Cistercian. This would help explain why
he, as archbishop of Lund, shortly after 1150 supported
the Cistercians' move to Esrum. The monastery was
in the territory of the bishop of Roskilde, and Eskil
really had little say there. But since by the early
1140s, or perhaps even in 1137 or 1138 when he still
was himself bishop of Roskilde, he was already involved
with Esrum, it was natural for him to sponsor the
conversion of Esrum to a cistercian community. Eskil
had interests at Esrum, but it now appears that his
initial involvement there was with a traditional benedictine community, as the one whose establishment he
supported at Naestved in 1135.[51] After the early 1140s,
Eskil became ever more involved with the Cistercians,
and it was natural for him to support the conversion
of the original benedictine house to a cistercian one.
This helps explain why the Lund Necrology mentions
a certain Folmer as the first abbot at Esrum.[52] Folmer
does not sound like the name of any french Cistercian.
He was probably a solid danish Benedictine who in

the 1140s directed Esrum and after whose death Esrum became cistercian under Eskil's and Bernard's friend, William.

None of this is to claim that Eskil actually founded Esrum. In the great charter he had drawn up for the monastery and which is dated to 1158, he never uses the word *fundare* for his work there.[53] But as bishop of Roskilde, Eskil may well have helped Esrum get started. He certainly donated land to the monastery sometime between 1137 and 1146, and probably in the late 1140s he began making arrangements for Cistercians to come from Clairvaux to Esrum. It is clear from Eskil's own charter for Esrum that he brought Cistercians with him from Clairvaux in 1153 after his first visit there, and this perhaps explains why 1153 is given as the traditional date for the cistercian foundation of Esrum.[54] But there may already have been a cistercian community there.

With this new interpretation of the 1228 reference to an earlier foundation at Esrum, and in the light of well-established international cistercian acceptance of villages as legitimate properties for their houses, we can provide the following revised chronology for Eskil's cistercian involvement:

1. In 1135 as bishop of Roskilde he confirmed the foundation of a traditional benedictine house at Naestved on Zealand.

2. In 1137/38, as bishop of Roskilde, or after 1138 and before 1146, as archbishop of Lund, Eskil bought the village of Esrum from King Erik Lam and handed it over to a benedictine community already in existence there and whose exact origins we cannot determine.

3. In 1138 Eskil became archbishop of Lund. As the result of his constant attempt to maintain his archbishopric, he became ever more involved in negotiations and diplomacy with the international church. Already in 1139 he was visited at Lund by a papal legate, the cardinal Theodewin, who is one of the witnesses to a typical document of Eskil's involvement with monastic foundations, a reorganization of the benedictine cathedral priory at Odense.[55]

4. In the early 1140s, Eskil cooperated with the swedish king and queen in bringing the Cistercians from Clairvaux to Alvastra and what became Nydala. At the same time Eskil managed to ahve a community sent from Cîteaux to found Herrisvad in his own

diocese. His exact material contribution to this house is not clear, but his moral and legal support were necessary.

5. In the later 1140s, Eskil had to fight in order to maintain his archbishopric against Hartwig of Bremen–Hamburg. As part of this offensive, he made contact with Bernard of Clairvaux through the Cistercian monk William. Bernard wrote the famous letter to Eskil where he promised his help and sent William off to the papal curia.

6. In December of 1151, William, now abbot of Esrum, obtained a letter from Pope Eugenius to support a cistercian foundation there. Soon afterwards, the death of Conrad III diminished the threat to Lund's position. William probably returned to Denmark in the spring of 1152—or else he went back to Clairvaux and met Eskil there.

7. During the summer of 1152 (but also possibly in the beginning of 1153), Eskil made his first and most memorable visit to Clairvaux, where Bernard was still alive. He brought back with him a group of Cistercians, possibly the first to be at Esrum, more probably a supplement to a contingent that has been there since the start of the 1150s. In any case, the cistercian presence at Esrum was greatly strengthened by this addition, and there were sufficient numbers to start a daughter house at Sorø in 1161.

8. During the rest of the 1150s Eskil showed some generosity towards Esrum, culminating in his great charter of 1158. He defended the monks' properties against hostile claims. Because of the papal schism during the 1160s, he was often outside of Denmark, and from about 1160 his main involvement with the Cistercians was not with those in Denmark but with those at Clairvaux and Cîteaux. This helps explain his relatively limited material contribution to the new cistercian houses that sprang up during these decades.

9. Finally, in 1177 Eskil gave up his archbishopric to Absalon and returned to what had become his spiritual home, Clairvaux, where he spent his last years edifying and thrilling the brothers with tales from the North and where he was buried in a place of honour near his friend Bernard.

This reinterpretation of events still does not allow us to establish an exact date when monks first settled in Esrum or when the Cistercians arrived there. But we can now say that there most probably was a benedictine community at Esrum in the 1140s which was replaced by a cistercian group in the 1150s. This development would be parallel with what happened elsewhere in Denmark: at Sorø on Zealand, and at Veng, Seem, and Guldholm on Jutland. Here, established benedictine communities had to make way for the Cistercians. Such an understanding of events at Esrum enables us to see Eskil as a gradual convert to cistercian monasticism. In the 1130s he identified monasticism with benedictine houses, but after 1140 became aware of the international monastic reform movement led by the Cistercians. Eskil and the Cistercians found each other slowly over a ten-year period from about 1142-52. We can touch on no decisive moment, only a steady increase in contacts. By the time Bernard first met Eskil at Clairvaux in 1152 or early 1153, the two already had become friends by letter and through intermediaries. Bernard felt a debt of gratitude to Eskil for his help in spreading the Order, while Eskil must have looked to Bernard as the one man who could help him when his archbishopric and the freedom of the scandinavian church were in danger. Spiritually and politically the two supported each other. The result was a friendship that cemented the cistercian establishment in Denmark and secured continuing links between Clairvaux and the North.

Friendship, Spiritual Power and the Christianization of the North

The Cistercians came to Scandinavia because they were invited by the magnates, both lay and clerical. It is unthinkable that the monks would have come all the way from France solely on their own initiative, without any preparation or incentives. Later sources, such as the Øm Abbey Chronicle, make it quite clear that some members of the establishment, especially women, often had other plans and did their best to oppose new cistercian houses.[56] The cistercian advance in the North must thus be seen as a conscious choice by the scandinavian establishment, and especially its male sector, to get these monks to come to their lands and to support them materially.

The Cistercians stayed in Scandinavia, despite the hostile climate, benedictine resistance, and the lack of any missionary role, because of the support provided by churchmen like Eskil who themselves were inspired by friendships with Cistercians. Bernard is not the only friend involved here. When Abbot Henry of Varnhem fled his monastery with his monks in the late 1150s and stopped at Roskilde on his way south to seek papal aid, Eskil met him there and convinced Henry to allow his house to be refounded in Jutland. Eskil arranged the negotiations that led to the royal donation of a farm at Vitskol.[57] Eskil gave nothing of his own property in this instance, but his moral and political backing of a new cistercian foundation was all-important. Eskil could go to the newly-established king, Valdemar I, and point out to him that in founding a cistercian house, he was linking his infant monarchy to a source of limitless spiritual power. Eskil could have told Valdemar about the wonders of Clairvaux, the fervours of its monks, and especially the miracles of Bernard. The Cistercians thereby became linked with the propaganda of a new royal house, thanks to Eskil's own propaganda on their behalf.

The Cistercians managed to find favour within all elements of the danish ruling class. The old view of them as taking Eskil's side during the papal schism of the 1160s has been replaced by an awareness of how flexible they were in sizing up political problems in terms of local as well as international exigencies. Thus the cistercian success was not due to political factors alone (the usefulness of having Cistercians as guarantors of political legitimacy for a new monarchy) but also to the christianization of the danish upper class. The Cistercians remained and did well in Scandinavia not only because Eskil befriended them but also because they lived up to the expectations of clerical and lay magnates that they would provide loci of spiritual power. In Eskil's childhood dream and ,in his archepiscopal reforming marriage practices, we meet the consciousness of a society where christian myths were just beginning to penetrate the minds and mores of the strong men of society. For them the Cistercians could deal with the devil at a time when pagan memories of trolls and christian ideas about the devil were still much confused in popular consciousness.[58] For such people, like Eskil's relative Count Niels, the best way to assure salvation lay in joining the Cistercians. Only then could the devil's intentions be frustrated. It was not just a question of being fashionable or of forging valuable french links but of maintaining a slim hope that despite a violent way of life and the devil's onslaughts, the magnates could find in the Cistercians the pure power of christian asceticism.[59]

The cistercian success in the North can thus be seen as the result of many factors which interacted in ways that we can only glimpse: Bernard's ability to make friends and win over people to his cause; his intense language of love; the fear of hell felt by Eskil and other members of the magnate class, as well as their hope for heaven. All these elements, much more than any clearly definable political motives, help explain not just why the Cistercians came, but also how they were able to stay and flourish in lands that were just taking their place as part of western European christian society.

Skamstrup/The Medieval Centre
Copenhagen University

NOTES

1. In southern Scandinavia I include all of what is Denmark today (the peninsula of Jutland, the islands of Fyn or Fünen, Sjaelland or Zealand, together with Lolland and Falster and a number of smaller islands), plus southern Sweden, making up the provinces of Scania, Halland and Blekinge, which until the seventeenth century belonged to Denmark.
2. There is no satisfactory recent treatment of the benedictine houses. For general information, see H. N. Garner, *Atlas over danske klostre* (Copenhagen, 1968), as well as Niels Skyum-Nielsen, *Kvinde og slave* (Copenhagen, 1971). See also the helpful bibliography in Tore Nyberg, 'Lists of monasteries in some thirteenth-century wills. Monastic history and historical method: a contribution', *Mediaeval Scandinavia* 5 (1972) 49–74.
3. For the claims made in these sources, see my *The Cistercians in Denmark: Attitudes, Roles and Functions in Medieval Society*, CS 35 (Kalamazoo, 1982). A full bibliography can be found there for a number of statements made in this article. I would emphasize, however, that the book was written during the 1970s, and since then I have revised some of my conclusions, which appear in this article for the first time.
4. In the sense used by Orderic Vitalis in the deathbed speech of William the Conqueror: 'Deinde ducatus mei tempore decem et septem monachorum atque sanctimonialium sex cenobia constructa sunt. ubi magnum servitium et plures elemosinae pro summi

regis amore cotidie fiunt. Huiusmodi castris munita est Normannia, et in his discunt terrigenae preliari contra demones et carnis vitia'. Book VII, in Marjorie Chibnall, *The Ecclesiastical History of Orderic Vitalis*, Volume IV (Oxford Medieval Texts, 1973) p. 92. It is likely that danish eleventh and twelfth-century rulers looked upon monasteries in a similar manner.

5. For the course of the entire debate in danish historiography, see the comprehensive and sober analysis by Svend E. Green-Pedersen, 'De danske cistercienserklostres grundlaeggelse og den politiske magtkamp i det 12. arhundrede', *Middelalder, metode og medier:* Festskrift til Niels Skyum-Nielsen pa 60-arsdagen den 17. oktober 1981 (copenhagen; Museum Tusculanum, 1981) 41–65.

6. For Saxo, the most enlightened recent treatment is that of Kurt Johannesson, *Saxo Grammaticus: Composition och Världsbild i Gesta Danorum* (Stockholm, 1978).

7. 'Notes towards the Exegesis of a Letter by Saint Stephen Harding', *Noble Piety and Reformed Monasticism*, CS 65 (Kalamazoo, 1981) 10–39.

8. Father Waddell admits in his exegesis (pp. 16–17) that Stephen Harding's formula about the purpose of letters to express charity could be translated in a more or less 'intense' manner. But if we compare Stephen's language to Bernard's in his letters, it is clear that the former is being more polite than intense.

9. As is pointed out in Jean de la Croix Bouton and Jean Baptiste Van Damme's introduction to *Les Plus Anciens Textes de Cîteaux, Cîteaux— Commentarii Cistercienses: Studia et Documenta*, II (Achel, 1974) p. 14: 'Cependant le concept de charité qui caractérise la Charte et lui donne son nom, sans perdre son sens évangélique, présente avant tout une portée canonique'.

10. *Les Plus Anciens Textes de Cîteaux*, p. 82: 'Quorum exemplo senes, juvenes, diversaeque aetatis homines in diversis mundi partibus animati, videntes scilicet in istis possibile fore, quod antea impossibile in custodienda regula formidabant, postea illuc currere, superba colla jugo Christi suavi subdere, *dura et aspera regula praecepta ardenter amare*, ecclesiamque illam mirabiliter laetificare et corroborare coeperunt'.

11. Epistola 390; latin text in *Sancti Bernardi Opera*, volume 8 (abbreviated *SBOp*) ed. Jean Leclercq and Henri Rochais (Rome, 1977) p. 358. Translation by Bruno Scott James, *The Letters of Saint Bernard*

of *Clairvaux* (London, 1953) p. 493 (Listed as Letter 424).

12. Printed in *Diplomatarium Danicum* (abbreviated as DD), edd. Lauritz Weibull and Niels Skyum-Nielsen (Det danske sprog- og litteraturselskab, 1963), I. Raekke, 2. Bind, nr. 119.

13. As pointed out in Stella Maria Szacherska, 'The political role of the Danish monasteries in Pomerania 1171–1223', *Mediaeval Scandinavia* 10 (1976) 134–35. The only problem with this interpretation is that Bernard's letter to Eskil has traditionally been dated to the summer of 1152, by which time german supremacy no longer threatened. This dating, however, is used merely because Bernard's letter to Eskil has been associated with a letter he wrote to Eugenius III in the summer of 1152, where he also mentioned Eskil's problem (DD:I,2, nr.113). But in this letter, he indicates that the problem no longer exists. Thus some months could have gone by from the writing of the letter to Eskil to the time of Bernard's letter to the pope. It is thus likely that the letter to Eskil belongs to the autumn of 1151, not the summer of 1152. This would make a more logical itinerary for Eskil's emissary, the Cistercian monk William: in the late summer of 1151 he would have left Eskil in Lund with the now lost letter for Bernard; in the fall he would have obtained Bernard's reply, and then he would have continued to Rome where, on 29 December, 1151, he obtained from Eugenius III a foundation bull for Esrum Abbey (DD I,2, nr.106).

14. *Ep.* 280; *SBOp* 8:194: 'De negotio domini Lundensis redicimus vobis ad memoriam. Causa dilationis sublata de medio, non est nisi ut fiat quod faciendum erat'. I am grateful to Stella Maria Szacherska for her ingenious and convincing solution to the dilemma of Eskil's *secretum*, which sheds new light on his relationship with Bernard.

15. *Ep.* 390 (note 11 above): 'Nuntium tuum cum magna exsultatione vidimus, et negotium tuum, quantumcumque potuimus, munivimus ad dominum Papam. De secreto autem verbo illo quod tam ardenter ascendit in cor tuum, respondebit tibi ex parte nostra Guillelmus tuus...'. Notice the distinction between *negotium* and *secretum*. It may well be that the first refers to the task of founding a cistercian house at Esrum, for which Bernard has provided and for which he sends William on to the papal court to get a bull of foundation,

while the much more sensitive *secretum* concerns the preservation of the archbishopric of Lund.

16. R. W. Southern, *Saint Anselm and his Biographer* (Cambridge, 1966) p. 72. The letter is *Ep.* 120 in Schmitt's *Opera Omnia Anselmi.*

17. Aksel E. Christensen, *Danmarks historie* 1 (Copenhagen: Gyldendal, 1977) p. 316. Professor Christensen was also aware that Bernard supported Eskil's attempt to maintain his archbishopric, but his chronology is not clear (p. 294).

18. The *Narratiuncula de Fundatione Monasterii Vitaescholae in Cimbri* starts: 'Swercho, rex Swecie, et Wluildis regina, duos conventus monachorum temporibus beati Bernhardi ex Claravalle, eiusdem patris monasterio, assumentes, duas ex eis abbatias in regno Sweecie et patrimonio fundaverunt...'. *Scriptores Minores Historiae Danicae Medii Aevi,* ed. M. Cl. Gertz II (photographic reprint, Copenhagen 1970) p. 138.

19. Cases in point are Øm, dependent on the bishop of Arhus; and Løgum, indebted to the bishop of Ribe; and Guldholm-Ryd, beholden to the bishop of Slesvig. If we knew more about the early history of Holme on Fyn, we would probably be able here to point to the influence of the bishop of Odense. See my *Cistercians in Denmark.*

20. 'St Bernard and the Historians', in M. Basil Pennington, ed., *Saint Bernard of Clairvaux: Studies Commemorating the Eighth Centenary of his Canonization,* CS 28 (Kalamazoo, 1977) 27–62, especially pp. 57–58: '...the political activity of St Bernard in his day, insofar as he was not motivated by papal request, can be attributed to his continual striving for the promotion and expansion of the Cistercian Order. Even when the initiative for his mingling in politics originated elsewhere, he never let a chance escape for founding or acquiring new monasteries...'.

21. *Ep.* 390 (note 11 above). The English translation is my own. It is closer to the Latin text than that of Bruno Scott James.

22. DD I,2, nr.119 (note 12 above). Translation my own.

23. *Kvinde og slave* (note 2 above) p. 166.

24. For Bernard's teaching on the redemption, see his *Tractatus contra quaedam capitula errorum Abaelardi;* PL 182:1053–72.

25. Latin text in DD I,2, nr.114. Denis Farkasfalvy, 'The Authenticity of St Bernard's Letter from His Deathbed', *Analecta Cisterciensia* 36 (1980) p. 264, deals with the contact between Geoffrey

and Eskil after Bernard's death.
26. *S. Bernardi Vita Prima*, PL 185:335. Translation
     my own. I wonder if *magnum* is a misreading
     for *dignum*. We sorely need a critical edition
     of the *Vita Prima*, as well as of Herbert's Liber
     miraculorum.
27. *Vita sancti Malachiae*, SBOp 3 (Rome, 1963) translat-
     ed by Robert T. Meyer. *The Life and Death of
     Saint Malachy the Irishman*, CF 10 (1978).
28. In Bernard's description of Malachy's church
     reforms in Ireland, one can see the activities
     that also would have captured his attention when
     Eskil would have spoken of his work in the scandina-
     vian church: 'Cessit duritia, quievit barbaries,
     et domus exasperans paulatim leniri coepit, paulatim
     correptionem admittere, recipere disciplinam. Fiunt
     de medio barbaricae leges, Romanae introducuntur;
     recipiuntur ubique ecclesiasticae consuetudines,
     contrariae reiciuntur; reaedificantur basilicae,
     ordinatur clerus in illis. Sacramentorum rite sollem-
     nia celebrantur, confessiones fiunt, ad ecclesiam
     conveniunt plebes, concubinatus honestat celebritas
     nuptiarum, postremo sic mutata in melius omnia...'.
     Vita Sancti Malachiae, SBOp 17; SBOp 3:326. See
     Thomas J. Renna, 'St Bernard and Abelard as
     Hagiographers', *Cîteaux: Commentarii Cistercienses*
     29 (1978) 41–59.
29. Dist. III, 27–28; ed. Bruno Griesser, Series Scrip-
     torum S. Ordinis Cisterciensis, II (Rome, 1961),
     pp. 210–17. See my 'Structure and Consciousness
     in the *Exordium magnum cisterciense:* The Clairvaux
     Cistercians after Bernard', *Cahiers de l'Institut
     du Moyen Age grec et latin* 30 (1979) 33–90.
30. Hilding Johannsson, *Ritus Cisterciensis: Studier
     i de svenska cisterciensklostrens liturgi*, Bibliotheca
     Theologiae Practicae, 18 (Lund, 1964) p. 64.
31. In Svend E. Green-Pedersen (note 5 above). See
     also my 'Clairvaux og Nordens cisterciensere
     i 1100-tallet', *Logumkloster studier* 1 (1978) 11–
     29, English summary pp. 158–59.
32. As promised by Bernard and remembered in the
     Exordium Magnum, Dist. II, ch. 5 (note 28 above),
     p. 101: 'In veritate dico vobis, quia, si filius
     ille perditionis Judas, qui vendidit et tradidit
     Dominum in hac schola Christi sederet et huic
     ordini incorporatus esset, per paenitentiam veniam
     consequeretur'.
     This record of a sermon by Bernard to the brothers
     at Clairvaux cannot be supported by earlier Clair-
     vaux literature, but the idea conforms with the
     confidence shown by the historical Bernard that

33. the way to Clairvaux was the sure path to salvation.
     PL 185:335–6.
34. DD I,2, nr.127, dated to 8 August 1158.
35. PL 185:336: 'Nec illa quam prius nosset lingua,
     sed nova quadam, quam nec astantium quisquam
     noverat, loquebatur. Et cum nihil quod diceret
     intelligerent, tam libere tamen et sine offendiculo
     non inconcinnas eum audiebant edere voces, ut
     indubitanter crederent quod lingua aliqua loqueretur.
     Post aliquantas igitur horas, cum vehementer
     confusi fratres quid agere possent anxie cogitarent,
     et studiose conquirerent; unus ex eis salubre
     consilium Domino inspirante concipiens, sacra
     pignora ab ipso archiepiscopo eodem anno istic
     deposita, videlicet de capillis et barba, et dentem
     unum beati patris nostri Bernardi afferri monet,
     et ejus pectori superponi. Quod ut factum est,
     Germanica lingua per os ejus coepit horrendis
     vocibus nequam spiritus exclamare: 'Tollite, tollite,
     amovete Bernardus'. Et dicebat, 'Heu, quam pondero-
     sus factus es, Bernarde! quam gravis, quam intolera-
     bilis factus es mihi!' Cumque haec et similia
     aliquamdiu clamitans loqueretur, factum est breve
     silentium, et subito frater idem Domino miserante
     purgatus, aperuit oculos, ac velut de gravi somno
     evigilans, circumstantes fratres et sua plurimum
     vincula mirabatur, verecunde satis quidnam sibi
     vellent haec, vel quid accidisset, interrogans.
     Ex ea igitur hora pristinam sanitatem mentis
     et corporis per beati Patris merita sancta recepit,
     nil penitus quod in illo tam gravi casu fecerit
     aut locutus fuerit, recordatus'.
          Notice that the brother cried out in German,
     perhaps a good indication of french–danish dislike
     for german power and politics!
36. Contained in Pertz, *Monumenta Germaniae Historica.*
     Scriptores, 23 (Hannover) p. 829: 'De hac autem
     congressione et morte Magni filii regis Nicolay
     et quinque episcoporum et relique multitudinis
     dicitur a quodam abbate ordinis Cisterciensis
     de Suecia, quod ipsa die, qua mutuo se interfece-
     runt, vise sunt a pastoribus in Hysselandia anime
     eorum avolantes in similitudine nigrorum corvorum
     et aliarum avium diversi generis et clamantes:
     'Ve, ve, nobis, quid est quod fecimus? ve ve
     nobis, quid nobis contigit?' Et alie immanissime
     aves quasi griphes istas inpellebant, et ipsis
     pastoribus videntibus omnes in infernum Hysselandie
     ceciderunt; et unus ex illis qui vidit fuit postea
     monachus Cisterciensis ordinis, qui omnia que
     vidit per ordinem sepissime referebat. Sed et

abbates de Dacia in generali capitulo apud Cistercium per omnia vera esse protestati sunt'.
The This is followed by a story about the volcanoes on Iceland, taken from Herbert of Clairvaux, while the story about the black crows after Fotevig is not to be found in Herbert and must be based on a cistercian oral tradition.

37. The story is contained in Herbert's *Liber miraculorum*, but not in the version printed in PL 185. Conrad of Eberbach used the story in the *Exordium Magnum Cisterciense* (III.27), but Herbert's original version was published by Lauritz Weibull, 'En samtida berättelse från Clairvaux om ärkebiskop Eskil av Lund', *Scandia* IV (1931) 270–90, esp. 276–9.

38. As expressed in R. W. Southern's masterful chapter 'From Epic to Romance' in *The Making of the Middle Ages* (London, 1953). See also my 'God-Man and the Devil in Medieval Theology and Culture', *Cahiers de l'Institut du Moyen-Age grec et latin* 18 (1976) 18–82.

39. As Aksel E. Christensen pointed out in his *Danmarks historie* (note 17 above), it is difficult to be specific about motives beyond those of abstract piety: 'Is it then possible to find more concrete notives aside from piety than the desire that well-disposed churchmen and monks provided a measure of moral support for royal power?' (p. 318, my translation from the Danish).

40. Lauritz Weibull (note 36 above) pp. 280–82. The most grisly stories, as these two, were either trimmed down or completely omitted from Conrad's reuse of materials on Eskil from Herbert in the *Exordium Magnum*.

41. *Western Society and the Church*, Pelican History of the Church 2 (Harmondsworth, 1970) p. 257: The first Cistercians spoke equally confidently with two voices. The first was the voice of the military aristocracy from which they sprang, and this voice is most clearly heard in their legislation. The second voice was the one which they used in the cloister—it was the voice of mutual friendship, of introspection and spiritual sweetness.

42. Weibull (note 36 above) pp. 288–89. Also in *Exordium Magnum* (note 28 above) III.28; p. 216 (the repentant sinner prays for an instant death instead of a return to temptations): 'Et nunc, Domine Deus, suspecta est mihi valde fragilitas mea et dudum inolita peccandi consuetudo multumque timeo mihi a memetipso, ne forte reversus ad patria blandiente

rerum prosperitate, peccati quoque materia illiciente ad pristinas meas pravitates relabi compellar'. Notice the word *compellar*, as if the magnate felt helpless in coping with future temptations.

43. See PL 180:975–1004. Caesarius of Heisterbach (c. 1180–1240) has a version of this story in his *Dialogus miraculorum* (ed. J. Strange: Cologne, 1851, reprinted New Jersey, 1966) Dist. XII, ch. 38, another indication of the popularity of this narration in the cistercian milieu.

44. *Dialogus miraculorum* (see note 42 above) XII.57; Strange Vol. 2:360–61: 'Quae de illo dicturus sum, ipse mihi ore suo non semel sed saepius recitavit'. See my 'Friends and Tales in the Cloister: Oral Sources in Caesarius of Heisterbach's *Dialogus Miraculorum*' *Analecta Cisterciensia* 36 (1980) 167–247.

45. *Kvinde og slave* (note 2 above) p. 120, and my 'Property and Politics at Esrum Abbey: 1151–1251', *Mediaeval Scandinavia* 6 (1973) p. 125.

46. '...villas cum omnibus pertinentiis earundem, quas dictum monasterium, antequam Cisterciensium fratrum instituta susciperet, possidebat...'. *Codex Esromensis. Esrom Klosters Brevbog*, ed. O. Nielsen (Copenhagen: Selskabet for Udgivelse af Kilder til Dansk Historie, 1880–81; photographic reprint, 1973) 18.

47. As the privilege of Celestine III from 1193, *Codex Esrom.*, p. 14: '...cum villis, pratis, silvis et reliquis appendiciis suis...'. Same phrase in privilege of Clement III from 1189, p. 10, and in that of Lucius III from 1184, the word *villam* is used four times.

48. Louis J. Lekai, *The Cistercians: Ideals and Reality* (Kent State, Ohio; 1977) p. 94.

49. DD I,2, nr. 107. Also in *Codex Esrom.*, p. 135.

50. DD I,2, nr.106. *Codex Esrom*, p. 3.

51. DD I,2, nr.64.

52. *Necrologium Lundense*, ed. Lauritz Weibull (Lund: Monumenta Scaniae historica; 1923) p. 66.

53. As pointed out by Green–Pedersen and before him by Kai Hørby, (note 5 above), pp. 45–46. Eskil's charter is in DD I,2, nr.126 and in *Codex Esrom*, pp. 86–88.

54. DD I,2, nr.126: 'Quamobrem de diversis ordinibus fideles collectos per predicte regionis partes. passim ordinavimus. ac ne Cisterciensis ordinis fratres nobis deessent. ad beatissimum Clarevallensis cenobii patrem dominum Bernardum quamvis multo labore et sumptu pervenimus. de cuius filiis semen unde seges postera fidelium animarum pululare

[posset] nobiscum in terram nostram adduximus'.
55. DD I,2, 77, dated 8 August 1139.
56. As at Veng, as described in the Øm Abbey Chronicle. See my *Conflict and Continuity at Øm Abbey. A Cistercian Experience in Medieval Denmark* (Copenhagen: Museum Tusculanum, 1976) 35–38. An expert on medieval womens' history, Nanna Damsholt of Copenhagen, has interpreted this and similar passages as evidence of cistercian anti–feminism. I would reply that the Cistercians were anti–anyone who disturbed their plans, whether man or woman.
57. DD I,2, 120. This charter has long been looked at—and rightly so—as a piece of royal propaganda in which Valdemar justifies his rule. But Valdemar's foundation without Eskil's confirmation is unthinkable: 'praesente venerabili archiepiscopo, apostolicae sedis legato Eschillo atque id ipsum confirmante...'.
58. For a story of the devil at Vitskøl Abbey, who lived like one of the brothers, see Ellen Jørgensen, *Danske Studier* 1912, p. 16. Jørgensen linked this story to pagan mythology and its remnants in Scandinavia in the Middle Ages.
59. For fascinating analyses of the role of holiness and holy men in christian culture, see the work of Peter Brown, especially his 'The Rise and Function of the Holy Man in Late Antiquity', *Journal of Roman Studies* 61 (1971) 80–101.

Table of Abbreviations

General Abbreviations

CC	Corpus Christianorum series. Turnhout, Belgium, 1953–.
CCCM	Corpus Christianorum, Continuatio Medievalis. Turnhout, 1953–.
CF	Cistercian Fathers series. Spencer, Washington, Kalamazoo, 1969–.
Coll.	*Collectanea OCR/Collectania cisterciensia.* Rome, Scourmont, 1934–.
CS	Cistercian Studies series. Spencer, Washington, Kalamazoo, 1969–.
DSp	*Dictionnaire de Spiritualité.* Paris, 1932–.
DThC	*Dictionnaire de théologie catholique.* Paris, (1899) 1903–50.
ETL	*Ephemerides theologicae Lovaniensis.* Louvain, 1960–.
PL	J.-P. Migne, *Patrologia …latina.* Paris, 1844–64.
RB	*Regula Benedicti/Rule of St Benedict.*
Rech. SR	*Recherches de science religieuse.* Paris, 1910–.
SAn	Studia Anselmiana. Rome, 1933–.
SBOp	Jean Leclercq–H.M. Rochais, edd., *Sancti Bernardi Opera*, Rome, 1957–.
SCh	Sources chrétiennes. Paris, 1941–.

The Works of Bernard of Clairvaux

Adv	Sermo in adventu domini
Apo	Apologia ad Guillelmum abbatem
Asc	Sermo in ascensione domini
Asspt	Sermo in assumptione BVM
Ben	Sermo in natali sancti Benedicti
Csi	De consideratione libri v
Ded	Sermo in dedicatione ecclesiae
Dil	Liber de diligendo deo
Div	Sermones de diversis
Ep(p)	Epistola(e)
Gra	Liber de gratia et libero arbitrio
Hum	De gradibus humilitatis et superbiae
JB	Sermo in nativitate sancti Ioannis Baptistae
Miss	Homilia super *missus est* in laudibus Virginis Matris
Mor	De moribus et officiis episcoporum
1 Nov	Sermo in dominica I novembris
O Asspt	Sermo infra octavam assumptionis
O Pasc	Sermo in octava paschae
Palm	Sermo in ramis palmarum
Par	Parabolae

Pent	Sermo in die sancto pentecostes
Pur	Sermo in purificatione BVM
QH	Sermo super psalmum *Qui habitat*
Quad	Sermo in quadragesima
Rog	Sermo in rogationibus
SC	Sermones super cantica canticorum
Sent	Sententiae
Sept	Sermo in septuagesima
V Nat	Sermo in vigilia nativitatis domini

The Works of Aelred of Rievaulx

Inst incl	De institutione inclusarum
Jesu	De Iesu puero duodenni
Spec car	Speculum caritatis
Spir amic	De spirituali amicitia

The Works of William of St Thierry

Ep aur	Epistola aurea ad fratres de Monte Dei

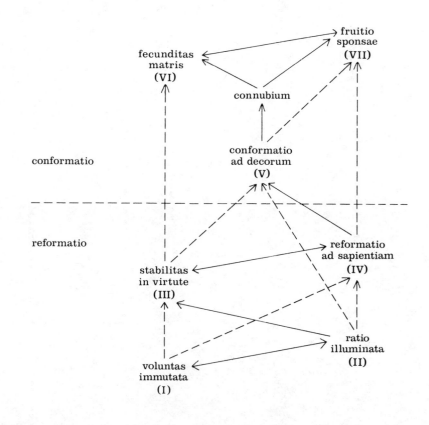

Sabersky, Fig. 1   The   Compositional   Structure   of   the
Seven Steps in SC 85.

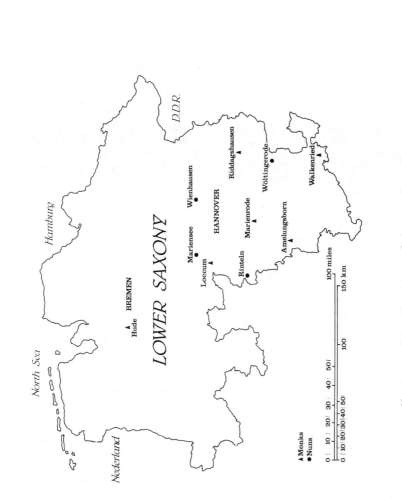

Heutger, Fig. 1   Map of Lower Saxony.

Heutger, Fig. 2   Walkenried, 1654.

Heutger, Fig. 3   Walkenried today; seal of the Historic
Society of Walkenried.

Heutger, Fig. 4   Amelungsborn: nave   ca.   1150,   choir
ca. 1350.

Heutger, Fig. 5 Amelungsborn: gothic window.

Heutger, Fig. 6   Marienrode near Hildesheim.

Heutger, Fig. 7 Loccum; founded in 1163. Today a Lutheran Abbey.

292

Heutger, Fig. 8   Monastery   Loccum.   Main   building
(18th   century)   with   the   rooms   of
the Lutheran Abbot.

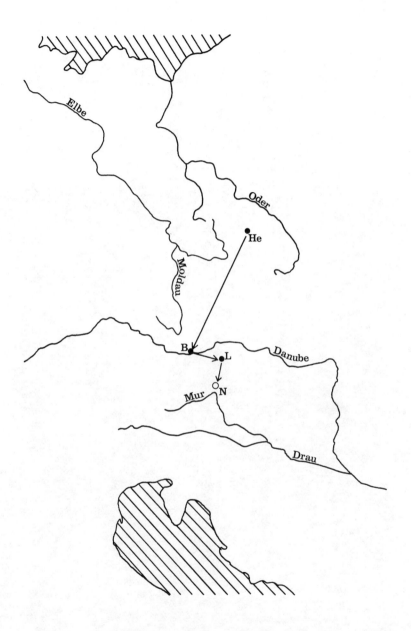

Jaritz, Fig. 1 The example of the migrating monk
Augustin of Heinrichau (1439)

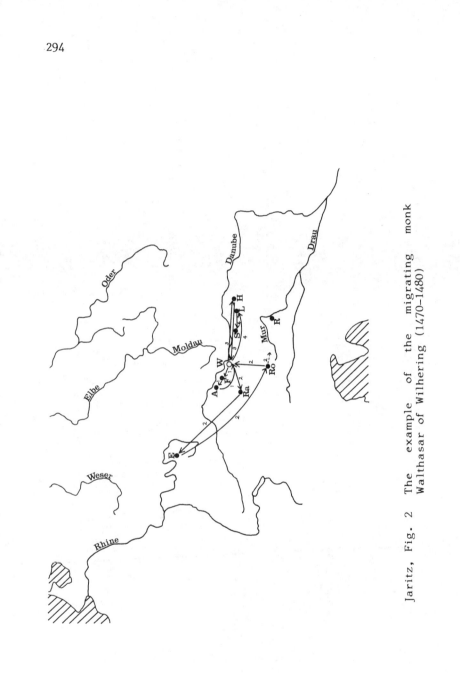

Jaritz, Fig. 2 The example of the migrating monk Walthasar of Wilhering (1470–1480)

Jaritz, Fig. 3   Monks   migrating   to   Neuberg   (mainly
          in the first half of the fifteenth century)

296

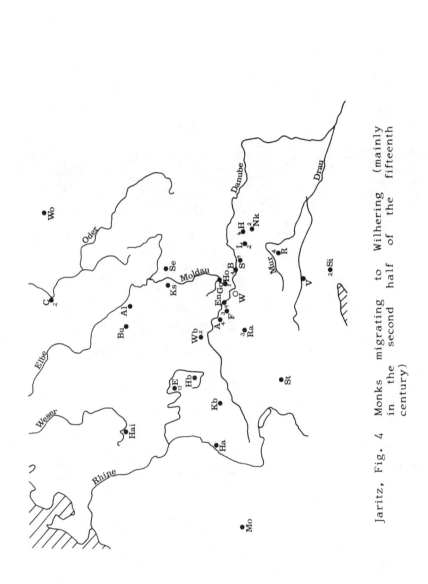

Jaritz, Fig. 4 Monks migrating to Wilhering (mainly in the second half of the fifteenth century)

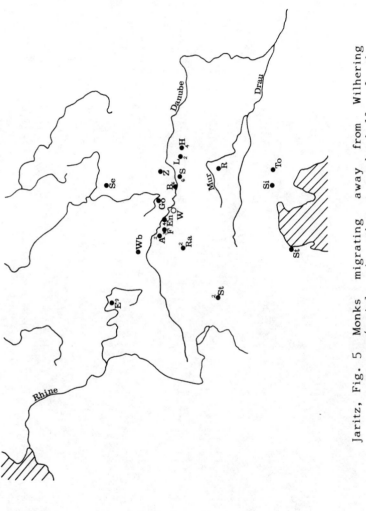

Jaritz, Fig. 5 Monks migrating away from Wilhering (mainly in the second half of the fifteenth century)

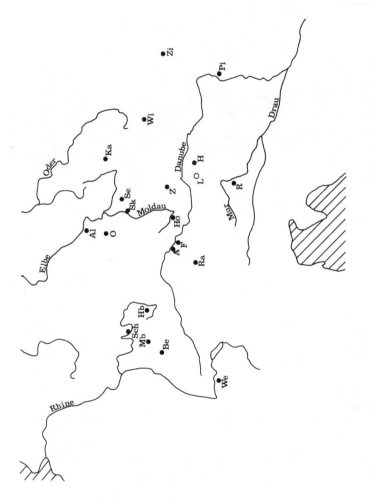

Jaritz, Fig. 6   Monks migrating to Lilienfeld (fourteenth/
fifteenth century)

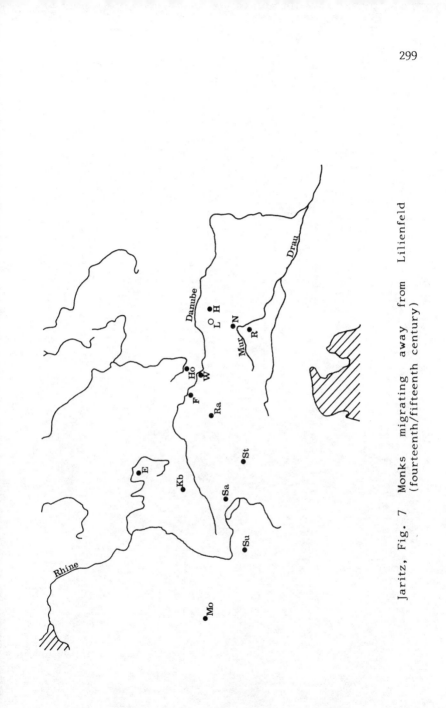

Jaritz, Fig. 7 Monks migrating away from Lilienfeld (fourteenth/fifteenth century)

Temporarily out of print   † *Forthcoming*

CISTERCIAN PUBLICATIONS INC.
Kalamazoo, Michigan

Texts and Studies in the Monastic Tradition

TITLES LISTING

THE CISTERCIAN FATHERS SERIES

* *Temporarily out of print*   † *Forthcoming*